A Precarious Life

CLARENDON STUDIES IN CRIMINOLOGY

Published under the auspices of the Institute of Criminology,
University of Cambridge; the Mannheim Centre, London School of
Economics; and the Centre for Criminology, University of Oxford.

General Editors:
Mary Bosworth and Carolyn Hoyle
(*University of Oxford*)

Editors:
Alison Liebling, Paolo Campana, Loraine Gelsthorpe, and Kyle Treiber
(*University of Cambridge*)

Tim Newburn, Jill Peay, Coretta Phillips, Peter Ramsay, and Robert Reiner
(*London School of Economics*)

Ian Loader and Lucia Zedner
(*University of Oxford*)

Recent titles in this Series:
Penality in the Underground:
The IRA's Pursuit of Informers
Ron Dudai

Assessing the Harms of Crime:
A New Framework for Criminal Policy
Greenfield and Paoli

Armed Robbers:
Identity and Cultural Mythscapes in the Lucky Country
Taylor

Crime, Justice, and Social Order:
Essays in Honour of A. E. Bottoms
Liebling, Shapland, Sparks, and Tankebe

Policing Human Rights
Martin

Normalizing Extreme Imprisonment:
The Case of Life Without Parole in California
Vannier

Respect and Criminal Justice
Watson

Neighbourhood Policing:
The Rise and Fall of a Policing Model
Innes, Roberts, Lowe, Innes

Respectable Citizens—Shady Practices:
The Economic Morality of the Middle Classes
Farrall and Karstedt

Advocates of Humanity:
Human Rights NGOs in International Criminal Justice
Lohne

A Precarious Life

Community and Conflict in a Deindustrialized Town

Roxana Willis

Great Clarendon Street, Oxford, OX2 6DP,
United Kingdom

Oxford University Press is a department of the University of Oxford.
It furthers the University's objective of excellence in research, scholarship,
and education by publishing worldwide. Oxford is a registered trade mark of
Oxford University Press in the UK and in certain other countries

© Roxana Willis 2023

The moral rights of the author have been asserted

First Edition published in 2023

All rights reserved. No part of this publication may be reproduced, stored in
a retrieval system, or transmitted, in any form or by any means, without the
prior permission in writing of Oxford University Press, or as expressly permitted
by law, by licence or under terms agreed with the appropriate reprographics
rights organization. Enquiries concerning reproduction outside the scope of the
above should be sent to the Rights Department, Oxford University Press, at the
address above

You must not circulate this work in any other form
and you must impose this same condition on any acquirer

Public sector information reproduced under Open Government Licence v3.0
(http://www.nationalarchives.gov.uk/doc/open-government-licence/open-government-licence.htm)

Published in the United States of America by Oxford University Press
198 Madison Avenue, New York, NY 10016, United States of America

British Library Cataloguing in Publication Data

Data available

Library of Congress Control Number: 2023932537

ISBN 978–0–19–885514–9

DOI: 10.1093/oso/9780198855149.001.0001

Printed and bound in the UK by
TJ Books Limited

Links to third party websites are provided by Oxford in good faith and
for information only. Oxford disclaims any responsibility for the materials
contained in any third party website referenced in this work.

*In loving memory of Paul Raymond Willis
and for his grandchild Otto Ray, whom he passed too soon to meet*

General Editors Introduction

The *Clarendon Studies in Criminology series* aims to provide a forum for outstanding theoretical and empirical work in all aspects of criminology and criminal justice, broadly understood. The Editors welcome submissions from established scholars, as well as manuscripts based on excellent PhD dissertations. The Series was inaugurated in 1994, with Roger Hood as its first General Editor, following discussions between Oxford University Press and Oxford's then Centre for Criminological Research. It is edited under the auspices of three centres: The Centre for Criminology at the University of Oxford, the Institute of Criminology at the University of Cambridge, and the Mannheim Centre for Criminology at the London School of Economics. Each supplies members of the Editorial Board and, in turn, the Series General Editor or Editors.

In *A Precarious Life: Community and Conflict in a Deindustrialized Town*, Roxana Willis provides a socio-legal, ethnographic account of violence that is in some respects, autobiographical. Unusually, Willis directs her empirical attention to the council housing estate she grew up on, the Lincoln estate in Corby, in the East Midlands of England. In particular, she focuses on the life (and death, during her research) of her father who ran a mobile grocery shop on that estate, becoming a source of support and counsel for residents in one of the most socio-economically deprived housing estates in the UK.

Willis explores what happens when those in her father's community fall into conflict with one another, and how conflicts are managed, particularly when the criminal justice system is involved. She critiques liberal legal scholarship by drawing on the experiences of those socio-economically disadvantaged and racialized communities most affected by the justice system. She develops two frameworks (loosely conceived) to illuminate the moral normative order within which this 'precariat' community lives; one that speaks to their autonomy, which draws on a Bourdieusian (hegemonic) concept of legitimacy; the other to mutuality, a sense of people being interconnected and co-dependent in a network of caring relationships that can provide a counterbalance to the power of the state.

viii General Editors Introduction

Having grown up there, the Lincoln estate was already familiar to Willis, but she spent over a year conducting her fieldwork, accompanying her father on his mobile grocery round, participating in various local initiatives and drawing on her father's Facebook social network for further empirical data. In 2013 and 2014, this was a highly unusual approach. While the Covid-19 pandemic turned many of us into digital researchers, using social media to gain access to data or as a data source in itself, eight years ago this was not the case and Willis presents her data and the ethical issues raised by her research, with care and sensitivity.

While this highly original monograph adopts an unusual empirical method, which brings with it a truly authentic authorial voice, it is at the same time sophisticated in its theoretical approach. In a strongly normative project, Willis concludes that in the absence of structural change to the British class system, something that seems less likely today than over the past decade or so, the criminal law ought to recognize and accommodate a framework of mutuality by which the least advantaged orient themselves in order to survive.

This rich, thick account of one housing estate illustrates the significance of relational harm and explains why those who live there, and in similarly situated places, use violence and other informal measures to resolve disputes. By situating violence and conflict within the framework of mutuality, the reader sees why certain forms of harm become pervasive and why these are not yet addressed adequately by the legal system. In so doing, Willis does not romanticize her estate, nor does she excuse those who commit violence towards each other. Rather, she makes these conflicts intelligible and shows why a justice response that looks only at the individual actors involved can never be sufficient.

It is an engaging book, rich in narratives, legal analysis, and sociological theory. We are pleased to include it in the Clarendon Studies in Criminology.

Carolyn Hoyle and Mary Bosworth
General Editors
Centre for Criminology, University of Oxford
May 2022

Acknowledgements

Many contributors to this collective piece of work are unknown and must remain unnamed. With thanks to the efforts of historians, such as E. P. Thompson, I have been able to access wisdom gained through generations of class struggle, which ultimately made it possible to write this book. And through the continued efforts of contemporary anthropologists and sociologists, whose work is cited throughout, I have been afforded access to the insights of those who continue to experience the hardships of class inequality in Britain. This knowledge is enhanced by the many people who form the research community included in the study, some of whom I anonymously quote herein, and more whom I do not quote but who guided me to the findings. So much value contained in these pages must be credited to these unnamed contributors.

Financial support during the doctorate and post-doctorate made the project a reality, and I am grateful to the panellists and peer reviewers who helped me to access these awards. During the doctoral period, I benefited from The Leverhulme Trade Charities Trust, which offers assistance for grocers, travelling salespersons, chemists, and their families to engage in further education. I was also supported by the St Edmund Hall William R. Miller Award and educational grants from The Ruby and George Will Trust, The Rowlett Trust, and Soroptimist International. Bodies such as these are essential for diversifying participation in academia. I was subsequently granted a British Academy Postdoctoral Fellowship and a Junior Research Fellowship in Law at University College, Oxford. The University College funding I received stems from a donation by Simon Bennet, whose family invested in the East India and Virginia Companies. Bennet directly donated an area of Northamptonshire woodland to University College, which generated revenue from the sale of timber and the collection of rents from farmland. In this way, the input of English labourers fed into the efforts of colonized and enslaved persons, which created an endowment that

x Acknowledgements

made it possible for me to produce this work centuries later. I completed the final part of the book during a Marie Skłodowska-Curie Fellowship sponsored by the European Union and hosted by the Freiburg Institute for Advanced Studies, University of Freiburg.

Academic supporters of the work include my doctoral supervisors, Carolyn Hoyle and Alpa Parmar, who provided crucial guidance, feedback, and direction during the first four years of the study. If not for Carolyn opening her door and heart when I was lost in the Oxford system, this study would not exist. And if not for Alpa, I would have missed the importance of race for the study of social class in Britain. I would like to further acknowledge my first-stage examiners, Rachel Condry and David Mills, who delivered much needed direction at a difficult time. And I will always remember the day Shadd Maruna and Ben Bradford awarded me the doctorate—I especially appreciate Shadd and Ben advising me to focus on the ethnographic parts of the study for a manuscript and for giving me an opportunity to do this as a postdoctoral researcher. During the postdoctorate, I benefited from the mentorship of Ian Loader, which is when the work blossomed. As a first reader of the book, Ian gifted ample encouragement which aided the completion of this project. Early anonymous reviewers of the book provided additional guidance which markedly shaped the work—I later discovered that one of the reviewers was Insa Koch, whose suggestions and earlier work has been enormously influential on my own. I am also grateful to the academic support of Nicola Lacey, Mavis Maclean, Jonathan Herring, Peter Muchlinski, Nick Foster, John Fitzpatrick, Lucy Newlyn, Nic Cheeseman, Linda Mulcahy, Ruth Chang, Judy Laing, Seena Fazel, Daniel Freeman, Mike Savage, David Soskice, and Timothy Endicott who gifted time and built up my confidence to pursue an academic career.

Love and support from family, friends, and colleagues over the years has been essential. Many thanks to family, including Paul, Nikki, Kit, Jenai, Tamara, Ashley, Paul-Nicholas, and Tabatha, as well as wider family and friends from home who made this work possible, including Rena, Carol, Gordon, Snoddy, Nathan, Lisa, Alex, Lee, Dan, Darren, Gary, Mandy, and many more. Other invaluable supportive relationships include Caroline Mbinkar, Radha Ramaswamy, Mia Harris, Marie Tidball, Insa Koch, Arushi Garg, Bronwyn Hayward, Lucia Sarmiento, Max Harris, Marek Sullivan, Tom Rochester, Dhruti Babariya, Leila Ullrich, Patsilí Toledo, Sophie Smith, Elizabeth Adams, Dan Hicks, Paulina Mascianica, Barry Potter, Andrew Gregory, and many more. My apologies to those I have not named.

A final word of thanks to the most significant contributor to this decade-long piece of work, James Angove. From lengthy philosophical discussions during the undergraduate degree, through to the Charles Taylor reading group, and from invaluable input on bottomless drafts, to help with the final proofing—I couldn't have completed this without you.

Contents

Introduction: Back to the Rough Ground	1
Revisiting the Liberal Foundations of Criminal Law	3
Philosophical Context: Frameworks	7
Framework of autonomy	11
Framework of mutuality	20
The Contours of the Study	24
An overview of the argument and chapters	28
The Mobile Grocer	31
1. From Schoolyards to Factory Floors	33
Schooling the Precariat	38
The collective struggle for scholastic success	41
An alternative game	44
Dreams of success	46
From Steelwork to Precarious Work	48
The winter of precarity	49
Finding work: The lucky ones	51
Fired for farting: The unlucky ones	56
Conclusion	60
A Helping Hand	62
2. The Necessity of Community	64
'Estate of Fear'	71
Sharing Practices: An Informal Web of Support	76
Sharing advice, skills, and assistance	80
Love and emotional support	84
Good personhood and moneylending	88
Co-dependence on the Imagined Community	90
Conclusion	92
Remember, Remember	94

xiv Contents

3. Violence — 97
Normative Uses of Force — 102
The Fair Fight and the Bully — 110
Strategies to Displace Violence — 119
Conclusion — 123

Amnesty — 125

4. Thin Blue Line — 128
Wrongs of a Different Flavour — 131
Protecting the Social Order — 135
Calling on the Police — 141
'Personalizing the State' — 148
Conclusion — 151

The Refuge — 153

5. Foreigners — 155
Resisting Difference and Change — 160
Fairness and Belonging — 165
Becoming an Insider — 168
'We're All the Same' — 171
'Stranger Danger' — 175
Conclusion — 181

The Boating Lake — 184

6. A Violence Continuum — 186
Enduring Loss of Life and Limb — 190
Demolished but Not Forgotten — 195
The Immorality of Poverty — 199
The Reality of Unemployment — 206
Conclusion — 210

An Ending Looms — 213

7. Moral Dilemmas — 216
The Markers of a Tramp — 221
Ethical Deliberations — 228
    The trampy mum dilemma — 228
    The pyjama dilemma — 231
    The smoking dilemma — 234
Conclusion — 238

Contents **xv**

'Only love can kill a demon' 240

8. Questions of Moral Motivation 242
The Morally Inferior 249
Neutralizing Distinction 254
Equality Rights in a Sea of Class Disadvantage 259
Personalizing Equality Rights 263
The Ignorant, Arrogant, and Out of Touch 266
Conclusion 269

Hard Goodbye 271

Conclusion: Life after Loss 272

References 281
Index 307

Introduction: Back to the Rough Ground

On a summer morning in 2018, paramedics were called to a house at the top of my street. By the time the ambulance arrived, Adam had already passed away (pseudonyms used herein). According to local news reports, Adam had sustained thirty-five blunt trauma injuries to his body, broken ribs, a fractured skull, a lacerated liver, and two collapsed lungs. Most injuries were inflicted by a young man on the estate, Martin. Adam owed Martin a £20 drug debt and, unable to pay it back immediately, Martin planned to hold Adam for a couple of days until the money came through. During this time, Martin reportedly beat Adam, doubled the debt, walked Adam to different houses on the estate, and made him repeatedly say 'I'm a bad person'. The fatal attack occurred during the first night of confinement. Adam had been resting when he was woken with kicks and blows that drained the life from him in the hours that followed. Martin eventually pleaded guilty to manslaughter and is currently serving time. Adam leaves behind two young children, a wider family, and close friends.

Adam's death was not the first distressing killing on my estate—nor was it the last, nor the most shocking. While the criminal justice system responds to the individual elements of the homicide, identifying a victim who was unlawfully killed by a culpable offender, conditions that recurrently foster violence remain unchanged. If a crime happens once, perhaps placing sole blame on an individual is warranted. But when a particular kind of crime repeatedly keeps happening, in the same space, at some point the discussion must move beyond individual responsibility. Individualized explanations, which have dominated legal scholarship for the best part of half a century, certainly capture an aspect of wrongdoing. However, to make full sense of the recurrent and complex forms of violence socio-economically disadvantaged communities endure, we cannot only focus on individual action. For an improved account, we require thicker analysis.

A Precarious Life. Roxana Willis, Oxford University Press. © Roxana Willis 2023.
DOI: 10.1093/oso/9780198855149.003.0001

2 Introduction: Back to the Rough Ground

In this book, I offer a socio-legal, ethnographic account of violence told through the life and death of my father. When his local steelworks closed down, unemployment engulfed my home community. Certain council estates, such as mine, then became areas of concentrated disadvantage, generations of which were neglected by the state and largely left to fend for themselves. Although my father was among the thousands forced into unemployment, he managed to escape insecure labour by running a mobile grocery shop. The shop became a lifeline on our abandoned estate, where few residents had cars and access to basic amenities. Yet my father was more than a 'van man': he became a go-to person for assistance and advice in times of need. In this role, he was a pillar of support for some of the most disadvantaged families in Britain. This study explores daily life within my father's community, including what happened when community participants fell into disagreement, and the difficulties they experienced when taking conflicts into the criminal justice system.

I present the ethnography in the form of a traditional piece of scholarship. The decision to do so was driven by my intended audience, which is academic rather than the precariously positioned persons included in the study who already have a sense of the social reality I reveal herein. This is not to suggest that such an awareness is fully articulated among my home community, nor that I provide a wholly agreeable account of precariat experience. On the one hand, I incorporate a range of perspectives through fieldwork and by drawing on studies with comparable communities; on the other, as the researcher I have the power to develop ideas and emphasize certain points over others. Still, I suspect that many of the insights contained in this work will seem obvious to those included in the study, since these understandings stem from shared experiences which have been dismissed or sidelined in scholarly debates.[1] As I see it, mainstream academics and criminal lawyers have the most to gain from an improved understanding of socio-economic disadvantage; otherwise, we are left labouring with inappropriate theoretical tools to determine how the state ought to respond to norm violations. My aim, then, is to translate, as it were, precariat experiences and collective wisdom into an academic form for greater scholarly attention.

---

[1] This suspicion is partly derived from experience guest lecturing on the Learning Together Programme at HM Prison Grendon (2018–2019). Some students on the programme who were serving time noted that certain insights I also present herein are 'stating the obvious'. I am in the process of communicating the findings to a broader audience, to encourage wider discussion and critique.

In the first part of this introduction, I overview the legal scholarship I am responding to, and the alternative scholarship I build on and contribute to. I then detail the theoretical framework developed during the ethnographic project, which is primarily influenced by the philosophy of Charles Taylor. Alongside my exposition of the philosophical context, I provide a historical account of the emergence of class inequality in Britain which has relevance to the research community. Finally, I outline the contours of the study, which includes a note about the research community, clarification of the concepts 'community' and 'precariat', and an overview of the coming chapters.

Revisiting the Liberal Foundations of Criminal Law

The criminal law understands violence in a way which diverges from lived experience. When the criminal justice system handles a violent incident, it abstracts aspects of the real-world event into legal concepts, and judicial experts then determine the outcome of the case by applying pre-formulated principles. Accordingly, the criminal justice system treats certain features of an incident as of limited relevance, sidelining or disregarding them, while centring other components. For example, ongoing relational differences, stresses of poverty, or struggles with addiction, which may have been fundamental to an event, are mostly insignificant for a determination of guilt. Conversely, the identification of a criminal act, and a defendant's state of mind at the time of committing the act, are the basis of assigning criminal responsibility. By highlighting the defendant's act, questions about *what* ought to be a crime are brought to the fore, and by focusing on the defendant's mental state, questions about *whom* we ought to label criminal become significant (see Farmer, 2016).

Present concern with a defendant's act and mental state derives from liberal influences that dominate contemporary criminal law thinking—as Alan Norrie (2014: 13) notes, '[c]riminal law is, at heart, a practical application of liberal philosophy'. This philosophical backdrop characterizes several notable features. For one, the individual is treated as the primary unit of analysis, detached from relational ties and collective connections (see Loughnan, 2019). By concentrating on the individual, criminal lawyers tend to maintain that only those with capacity who intend or foresee the harmful consequences of their actions ought to be held criminally responsible (Duff

4 Introduction: Back to the Rough Ground

and Von Hirsch, 1997; Hart, 1968; cf. Norrie, 1996). Relatedly, lawyers emphasize the rights of individuals who are tried under the criminal law, with a view to limiting arbitrary reaches of the state (Ashworth, 1993; Von Hirsch, 1992; Dworkin, 2013; cf. Farmer, 2010).

Important gains have been made by these liberal pursuits, which includes making the law less discretionary, more predictable, and in many ways fairer (see Wiener, 1994). Nonetheless, there are shortcomings. For instance, in contrast to the over-criminalization of individuals from socio-economically disadvantaged populations, corporate entities are markedly under-criminalized in liberal democracies, even though corporate crime injures larger numbers of people, more frequently, and to a greater degree than interpersonal crime (Box, 1983, 1987; Hillyard et al., 2004; Sutherland, 1983; Wells, 2001). Similarly, criminal responsibility of state institutions is underdeveloped, and the individualistic focus has left us with an impoverished conception of the social good (for discussion see Lacey, 1988: ch 7).

Sustained philosophical critique of the liberal philosophical tradition, by scholars such as Michael Walzer (1983), Charles Taylor (1985b), Michael Sandel (1982), Allister Macintyre (1981), Alison Jaggar (1985), and Nicola Lacey (1988), among others, reveals the liberal fiction of a pre-social human being to be implausible, instead showing a particular kind of socialization as prerequisite for the autonomous individual to form. Subsequently, there has been growing academic recognition that we require numerous conditions for individuals to become autonomous (see Nussbaum, 2009; Raz, 1986; Sen, 1999). Yet mainstream criminal law scholarship has not meaningfully engaged with these theoretical developments, and the discipline continues to work under the (often implicit) presupposition that autonomy is naturally attained by the age of ten (barring limited exceptions), and that failure by the state to recognize a person as autonomous is to undermine their dignity (see Gardner, 2003; Hart, 1968). Notwithstanding the appeal of such liberal sentiments, if the fiction of the autonomous individual by nature is implausible, and if society is not shaped for all to realize autonomy, then criminal law principles based on the concept of the autonomous individual will inevitably be defective to some degree.

Mainstream criminal law under the influence of the liberal philosophical tradition treats its guiding liberal principles (e.g. the rule of law, the harm principle, fair labelling, proportionality, just deserts, and so on) as though they were self-contained doctrines, governed by an internal logic which leads to just results, without regard to the historical conditions that fostered the emergence of these concepts or the socio-economic conditions

Revisiting the Liberal Foundations of Criminal Law **5**

that constrain legal subjects (cf. Farmer, 2016; Loughnan, 2019: ch 1). These acontextual and ahistorical principles are then applied in legal debates to justify certain criminal reforms: for instance, the moral language of freedom and autonomy is invoked to make a case for what ought to be criminalized, and theories on rights are used to limit the amount of state intervention in the delivery of punishment (Ashworth, 1986; Hart, 1968; Gardner, 2003; Duff, 2007; Von Hirsch, 1992). As a result, contemporary criminal law has developed on its own terms without sustained reflection on itself as prioritizing a particular vision of the good—one that privileges individuals and contested conceptions of autonomy and reason—or whether that vision is apt for the subjects who are brought under the jurisdiction of the criminal law.

The dominance of liberal thought in the modern criminal law has not passed without theoretical challenge. Prominent critical accounts can be found in the works of Nicola Lacey (1988, 2016; Frazer and Lacey, 1993) and Alan Norrie (1996, 2000, 2014), among others (including Hillyard et al., 2004; Hudson, 1994; Box, 1983; Nelken, 1987; Grigg-Spall and Ireland, 1992; Tamanaha, 2001; Lacey et al., 2003; Loughnan, 2012, 2019), who draw our attention to the liberal underpinnings of the criminal law and put forward proposals for more socially responsive developments. Similarly, Martha Nussbaum (2000, 2004, 2009) engages in rigorous evaluation of liberal legal theory and its applicability to law but arrives at an explicitly liberal normative position, albeit one with important adjustments. For instance, Nussbaum is clear that many liberal ideals require the prior attainment of minimal social conditions; she challenges the exclusion of women, persons living with disability, non-citizens, and animals from legal protection; and takes a considered view of the role of emotions in the development of theory. These critical scholars have laid an important, partly overlapping theoretical groundwork, on which I have the benefit of building. Therefore, I can re-examine the moral underpinnings of the criminal law without extensively revisiting the foundational liberal-communitarian debate, which is now comprehensively attended to (see Bell, 1993; Mulhall and Swift, 1996; Christman, 2009). Rather than returning to this debate in depth, I hope to continue applying, as others have begun to do, these philosophical insights to criminal law.

Alongside theoretical challenges, important advancements have been made to situate the modern English criminal law in its recent historical context (e.g. Farmer, 2010, 2016; Loughnan, 2012, 2019; Zedner, 1991, 2004). Once again, Lacey (2009, 2016) has been a key driver, prompting us to reflect

6 Introduction: Back to the Rough Ground

on how the contemporary emphasis on criminal responsibility is a particularly modern concern. By considering the works of leading legal thinkers from William Blackstone in the eighteenth century to James Fitzjames Stephen in the nineteenth century and Glanville Williams in the twentieth century, Lacey reveals earlier scholarship as having no pronounced emphasis on criminal responsibility, where responsibility concerns are at most marginal considerations and of a different sort. It is not until the twentieth century that criminal responsibility becomes a growing concern to lawyers, and a particular version of criminal responsibility understood as capacity, which centres the individual and the subjective mindset, comes to the forefront. Despite the dominance of criminal responsibility based on human capacity, Lacey recalls alternative forms of responsibility applying to different degrees, at different points in time. In so doing, Lacey reminds us of the fluidity of the concept of criminal responsibility and the heterogeneity of normative principles contained within the criminal law (see also Loughnan, 2019 on 'relations of responsibility').

Lindsay Farmer (2010) has made another significant inroad to the contemporary nature of the criminal law, situating it within the context of the last few centuries. Farmer (2010: 5) notes that the modern criminal law, as a separate, self-contained, and unified body of rules, embedded within the apparatus of the nation state, 'did not exist in any meaningful sense before the end of the eighteenth or the beginning of the nineteenth centuries'. Hence, coinciding with the growth of the modern nation state (see Anderson, 1991; Newman, 1986), a commitment to civil order emerges, which is rooted in the sensibilities of a rising bourgeois class and the drive towards civilizing society. On Farmer's account, past elites were primarily concerned with maintaining social order, while from the eighteenth century onwards, the criminal law emerges as a distinct means of securing civil order.

Combined, these accounts challenge the dominant view of the criminal law as a pure set of self-contained and ahistorical rules. Instead, we can see in operation a variety of competing principles and that theoretical concerns have shifted across time. In terms of criminal responsibility and the individualized legal subject, this scholarship illuminates the emergence and increasing dominance of legal concepts over the course of several centuries, not existing prior to the law. By recognizing the contingent, social formation of these ideas, we can position ourselves beyond the internal liberal view, exposing its problems and exploring solutions for the criminal law.

I wish to contribute to this body of scholarship by developing a thicker account of criminal justice. For enhanced understanding, it is imperative to examine the criminal law's operation from the perspectives of those most affected by its remit, which includes socio-economically disadvantaged communities and persons who are racialized (Alexander, 2010; Fassin, 2013; Maguire, 2020; Reiman, 1979; Wacquant, 2009). In an ethnographic study of the penal turn in liberal democracies, Insa Koch (2018b) moves us in this direction. In so doing, Koch demonstrates the value of developing emic theory, which incorporates the knowledge and wisdom of those who receive the brunt of the law's application. Building on Koch's legal anthropology, in this work I re-theorize the modern criminal law from the experience of socio-economic disadvantage. I aim to reorient legal discussion to the view of those disempowered by the operation of the law, in contrast to prevalent theories which offer a view from the position of privilege. As E. P. Thompson observed in 1980, 'descriptions of the social order ... as seen from above, are far more common than are attempts to reconstruct the view from below' (Thompson, 1993a: 22).

Philosophical Context: Frameworks

To make visible the disjuncture between mainstream criminal law's conception of the individual, on the one hand, and those subjects who most typically fall under its jurisdiction on the other, I suggest we consider what Charles Taylor simply calls 'frameworks'. For this task, I borrow from Taylor's *Sources of The Self* (1989), where he argues that human beings live inescapably within a background normative order as a fundamental feature of being human. Taylor terms these background orders 'frameworks', which are 'crucial set(s)' of qualitative distinctions, by which we regard some goods as 'incomparably higher' than others—such distinctions therefore act as standards against which we measure our own desires and inclinations (Taylor, 1989: 19–20). For example, Taylor describes one historical framework as applicable to an older 'warrior society', where a person 'might ask whether his tale of courageous deeds lives up to the promise of his lineage or the demands of his station' (Taylor, 1989: 16; cf. Abbey, 2000: 33–4; Elshtain, 2004: 128, 133). Later, he describes a series of historical changes leading to the 'affirmation of ordinary life', a framework within which the values of production (work) and reproduction (family) assert themselves over previous goods such as fame in war or theoretical

8 Introduction: Back to the Rough Ground

contemplation (see Taylor, 1989: 13–14, 23 for introductory discussion on these ideas). In a contemporary setting, Taylor argues, we often find ourselves enmeshed within several frameworks, which we variously draw on to make sense of our lives in (sometimes) creative ways. Moreover, Taylor shows how the frameworks within which we presently live each have a particular historical trajectory, which explains their persistence and continuing meaning. Importantly, although we might live within several frameworks (being oriented to the especially valued goods within them), Taylor does not suggest that we simply choose a good by which to live our lives, since our moral orientations are intricately connected with the societal conditions in which we are born and raised (for an illuminating example, see Taylor, 1989: 39–40).

This notion of a framework is, I think, especially useful for analysing interpersonal conflicts such as those handled by the criminal justice system, because people inevitably do make appeal—explicitly or implicitly—to the things that matter to them. They do this in explaining their behaviour to themselves and others, in arguing for what is right and wrong, and in attempting to resolve disagreements. Notably, we also make appeal to values within *different* frameworks (or even debate the nature and priority of values within one framework) in trying to make intelligible our lives (something Taylor (1989: 23–4) identifies as peculiarly modern), and because of this tendency, we are especially prone to encountering moral conflicts.

Considering Taylor's outlines of particular frameworks, we might ask ourselves how identifiable they are, whether we should speak of them as distinct sets of norms that structure relations among people from certain eras and places. I think it would be wrong to picture how we encounter frameworks in such a very direct or clear way. We do indeed live our lives guided by ideals, normally strongly valuing some over others, but at the ground level there is some creativity in articulating those ideals (cf. Taylor, 1989: 22 on frameworks and invention). Similarly, I think the researcher may draw out and emphasize the norms that make the best sense of social phenomena, while being informed by those engaging in the moral deliberations of interest. It might be possible to try analysing the discussions of this book using some variants of the 'warrior' ethic and the 'affirmation of ordinary life', but for the above sort of reasons, it seems to me that this would fail to do justice to the particular norms, values, and way of life we are looking at. For example, the values of family and autonomy are somewhat bound together in Taylor's notion of ordinary life, whereas the normative orientations I outline here, the frameworks, are in tension just because

Philosophical Context: Frameworks 9

those within them place strong evaluations on family and autonomy at the expense of each other.

I articulate two prominent frameworks which I think best describe the moral normative order within which the precariat community under study lives. I refer to the first framework as that of 'autonomy', the historical trajectory of which traverses Enlightenment thinking and gradually expands with the development of the modern nation state (cf. Farmer, 2016; Schneewind, 1998). In accordance with autonomy, the foremost explanation for social phenomena is individual agency, where the individual is conceived as free in principle from relational ties and capable of a particular form of rationality and self-governance.

I explain autonomy as the *legitimate* framework because, in my view, it has the most influence in contemporary British society. It is embedded in institutions of the modern state and provides the normative backdrop for mainstream criminal legal theory as outlined above. I employ a Bourdieusian concept of legitimacy here, referring to how certain norms and practices become authoritative—reaffirmed and reproduced through channels such as news media, public policy, and other influential outlets (see also Hall et al., 2013). In developing this concept, Bourdieu (1984: 241–54, 1990, 1990: 139, 1996) argues it is the prerogative of powerful groups to determine what holds legitimacy, since these groups control state and economic institutions and dominant channels of communication. But even though the legitimate framework ultimately reflects powerful interests, an important feature of legitimacy is that wider society recognizes these moral standards as valid, even those disadvantaged by them. Whereas, in the past, the legitimate framework may have been of a religious flavour, the framework of autonomy, which is entwined with religious ideas, has ascended as the legitimate moral order and is dominant in the present. Accordingly, in this book I often employ the term 'legitimate' to refer to this Bourdieusian hegemonic sense of legitimacy—that is, when I am talking about topics concerned with the framework of autonomy, conveying its dominant status.

I refer to the second prominent framework as that of 'mutuality' (nodding to Graeber, 2011), the logic of which I think bears a strong resemblance to E. P. Thompson's notion of a moral economy in his historical account of custom and culture in eighteenth-century England (Thompson, 1993b; see also Dennis et al., 1956; Goldthorpe, 1968; Hoggart, 1957; Thompson, 1963). Like the autonomy framework in the present, at an earlier point in time, some framework of mutuality would, I think, have been the legitimate framework in English society, gradually becoming displaced. Although the

10 Introduction: Back to the Rough Ground

framework of mutuality is embedded in an era prior to that of autonomy, it has not remained static. We might say that mutuality norms have altered in degree and presentation, yet the substance and underlying logic of the normative order has endured. In contrast to autonomy, I suggest that mutuality is more attuned to the ontological nature of human beings as interconnected and innately co-dependent: it gives normative significance to protecting caring relationships and safeguarding against imbalances of power. In accordance with mutuality, while there is space for individual action, virtue is less a matter of self-advancement and individual gain, and more about the subsistence of the collective of which the individual is part. In discussing the framework of mutuality, I occasionally refer to norms and values as 'legitimate', but here this is notably different to the above usage indicating hegemonic status. Rather, when I describe the legitimacy of a given norm, say, I am depicting its internally accepted place in the framework of mutuality.

Although I acknowledge and examine at least two co-existing frameworks in the course of this work, I do not suggest we are thereby saddled with a cultural relativism. Instead of treating each framework as ethically equivalent, distinguished only by power differentials, careful investigation of the roles played by frameworks and how they relate to the self and its nature puts us in a position to gauge how well they 'fit' our modern human condition. As Taylor (1985a, 1989: 69–75) argues, we are able to offer a 'best account'—to determine what aspects of frameworks make our moral lives most intelligible to us. I hope that the ethnographic analysis presented herein contributes to a best (or at least better) account of frameworks of autonomy and mutuality, so that by the end of the study we are better equipped to make ethical assessments about the goods that ought to be prioritized. This is a task I touch on in the conclusion, but ultimately leave open for further discussion.

I will, henceforth, sometimes refer to autonomy *as* a framework (e.g. 'according to autonomy'), or 'the framework of autonomy', which is really shorthand for saying 'that framework within which we centre on/orient toward autonomy'. Likewise, I will sometimes refer to mutuality *as* a framework (e.g. 'according to mutuality'), or 'the framework of mutuality', which is really shorthand for saying 'that framework within which we centre on/orient toward mutuality'.

I now turn to the task of detailing the substance of the frameworks, with an emphasis on historical formation. Since my work offers a view from below, I focus on features of socio-economic inequality. The following

Philosophical Context: Frameworks   **11**

discussion can be treated as a map of sorts, where signposts mark moments in the criminalization of the least well-off in English society, which a reader may wish to explore in greater depth.

Framework of autonomy

Moral sources have transformed throughout human history. *Morality* here means something broader than a given set of specific moral obligations (Taylor, 1989: 14, 63–4): we are talking about a source of what defines our 'moral' life—the goods that we orient towards and which define us, ideas of the good life, of what gives life meaning for us, or even which allow us to ask about the meaning of life. Given shifting moral sources, societies in former periods inevitably conceived of the world differently to how contemporaries do, which can be difficult to grasp fully from our present place. For example, in the present, it is quite normal for us to speak of the 'self' and to comprehend notions of independence and autonomy, and in turn for the criminal law to treat individuals as culpable for their acts. But for ancient societies, some of these aspects are alien. Starting with the different frameworks plausibly part of the ancient moral world, Taylor (1989) traces how the concept of the self gradually emerged in western thought. He portrays some background frameworks within which the ancients worked as involving a belief in and esteem of the cosmos: in contrast to contemporary thought, human beings were conceived as holistically interconnected with the universe and nature. By some ancient frameworks, then, explanations for actions and misdeeds were partly sought in the cosmos.

Moving beyond the ancients, Taylor charts the shift of moral sources with the ascendence of major religions. For instance, in accordance with Christianity, the moral source is found upwards in God instead of outwards in the cosmos. Yet Taylor also discusses the source of morality as beginning to alter within Christianity itself: while initially religious institutions and elites mediated the route to God, the Protestant Reformation in the sixteenth century reconfigured this pathway, so that God could now theoretically be reached through individual action and thought, without religious intermediaries. Taylor refers to this as an 'inward turn', which he suggests has its roots in Plato's idea of self-mastery, passing through to the 'radical reflexivity' of Augustine, eventually channelling through Descartes, and into Locke's conception of (in Taylor's terms) the 'punctual self' (see esp. Taylor, 1989: 115–76). Far from being a linear path, Taylor takes time to

12 Introduction: Back to the Rough Ground

show digressions in the development of these ideas, which proceed along different forks in the road, and feed into a range of competing positions that subsist in the present. For our purposes, let us focus on how features of this inward turn bear on the emergence of social class in England.

The inward turn on Taylor's account was vital for human progress, since notions of individual agency and independent thought contributed to the growth of modern science and disrupted older hierarchies. Scholars such as Galileo Galilei and Francis Bacon advanced inductive methods of reason, laying the foundation for modern sciences and empirical methods. The growth of scientific thought and subsequent technological advances (made possible with mass wealth generated by enslaved and coerced labourers (see Williams, 1994; James, 2001)), led to substantial social and economic developments and enabled a new European bourgeois class to grow in power and influence. Combined, these developments had a marked levelling force in traditional hierarchical societies, since power contained in the hands of the landed classes diffused into a new professional bourgeoisie. Notable European scholars such as Locke, Kant, Hume, and Mill, among others, can be seen as part of this new influential bourgeoisie, who in turn nurtured further developments of ideas about autonomy.

The moral ideal of this emergent framework of autonomy is the independent individual who has the capacity to act rationally, exercise self-control, and make good choices in life. In the early stages of the growth of these ideas, the autonomous ideal was restricted to men, conceived as white, able-bodied, and in possession of property (Hall, 1992). However, as contemporary scholars have compellingly shown, the moral ideal of the autonomous man was not brought into being through a process of self-identification, instead forming through the classification of less powerful groups as dependant, deficient, uncivilized, and irrational (Bhabha, 1984; Fanon, 1968; Hall, 2007; Mbembe, 2017; McClintock, 1995; Said, 2003; Savage, 2000; Skeggs, 2011; Stoler, 1995). Hence, through the development of the immoral 'other', the ideal of the autonomous man was born.

In English society, groups designated as dependent were already positioned in relative disadvantage, meaning that ideas about immorality under the emergent framework of autonomy were able to build on pre-existing beliefs about natural hierarchy and the innate inferiority of certain groups. For instance, in the Middle Ages, idleness among the poor was seen as an affliction caused by the devil, which later fed into modern ideas of the impoverished being personally responsible for their poverty and failure to secure stable employment (Golding and Middleton, 1982). Likewise,

Philosophical Context: Frameworks 13

traditional patriarchal English society positioned women in relative subordination (Dubber, 2005), providing fertile soil for growth of ideas concerning the innate dependency of women among some bourgeois circles (Hall, 1992; McClintock, 1995; Wiener, 2004). Echoing these transformations, whiteness, which was formerly a descriptive notion associated with divinity, and thus a symbol of the natural God-ordained superiority of the aristocracy, converted into a broader moral status through the invention of race (Bonnett, 2000: 32; Allen, 2012). Accordingly, older beliefs and meanings had fed into contemporary moral understandings, within which subjugated groups, once deemed to be of lower status due to their God-given position in the social order, begin to deserve their status; their alleged personal vices now prevented subordinates from attaining the moral status of autonomy.

On the one hand, the emergence of bourgeois thought was a means of empowering the masses in Britain, affording them agency as moral actors, and encouraging them to better themselves though work and private religious devotion—as contrasted with earlier conceptions of a natural order which encouraged them to accept social position through birth. On the other hand, emerging ideas about autonomy also made people responsible and blameworthy for their misfortunes, which has disproportionately weighed on the most socio-economically disadvantaged in the social order ever since.

Peter Golding and Sue Middleton's (1982) account of the emergence of welfare policy in England effectively makes apparent the impact of the inward turn and framework of autonomy on the least advantaged. They note that pre-Elizabethan canon law stresses the innocence of poverty— captured by the Latin dictum, '*Paupertas non est de numero malorum*' (1982: 7).[2] While this moral order associates idleness with vice, for the most part it treats almsgiving as a virtue and poverty not as something one could deter through punishment. Indeed, according to Golding and Middleton (1982: ch 2), it is the need to control the movement of labour for the benefit of the landed classes which motivates fourteenth-century laws on vagrancy and deterrence against charitable giving in England, without heavy moralizing tones. But in the centuries that follow, this approach markedly changes.

---

[2] Brian Tierney (1959: 13) offers the following translation: 'Poverty is not among the number of things evil', i.e. 'things criminal or morally reprehensible.'

14 Introduction: Back to the Rough Ground

By the early sixteenth century, as Golding and Middleton (1982: ch 2) tell us, the rationale for controlling the poor transforms: instead of an explicit interest in labour, concern turns to the immorality of worklessness and destitution. Consequently, certain forms of pauperism became reconceptualized as chosen lifestyles, beginning to be treated as markers of criminality. In contrast to the genuinely 'impotent'—such as the sick, orphans, and the elderly—the thriftless rioters, vagabonds, and the idle required punishment to deter their immoral behaviour. Under the Elizabethan Act of 1576, penalties for failure to work included the house of correction and other spectacular punishments, such as whipping, branding, pillorying, and executions (Golding and Middleton, 1982: 10).

Several studies on welfare and poverty in Britain document how the development of successive Poor Laws further moralizes pauperism, increasingly blurring the line between poverty and criminality (Golding and Middleton, 1982; Howe, 1990; Koch, 2018b; Morris, 2002). The Poor Law Act of 1601 is what first consolidates control over the behaviour of the least advantaged: it limited welfare provisions to those unable to work, targeted the unemployed able-bodied, and assigned correction for those deemed wilfully idle. Legislation became increasingly severe, and in 1834 the notorious Poor Law Amendment Act introduced the principle of 'less eligibility'. This sought to make the provisions of poor relief as unappealing and humiliating as possible, enforced through a regime of discipline with the aim of deterring dependency as a lifestyle choice.

Thus, in tandem with legislative changes, the emerging normative social backdrop that is the framework of autonomy comes to embrace at its heart the value 'hard work', which casts as immoral those deemed to fall short of its standard. Initially, not only paupers were treated as immoral: the new bourgeoisie also critiqued the aristocracy for their perceived failure to endure hard work and their tendency towards excess. However, as Catherine Hall (1992: 78–82) explains, nineteenth-century attention shifts from the immorality of those higher up in the social order and concentrates on the risks posed by the subjugated masses at home, as well as in the colonies abroad. Successive proletariat revolutions and uprisings towards the end of the eighteenth century—from the Gordon Riots in London (1780) to the overthrow of European elites during the French Revolution (1779–1789)—motivated this shift; the subsequent defeat of slave owners during the Haitian Revolution (1791–1804) further fuelled fears about the dangers of the uncontrolled masses (James, 2001; see also Wiener, 1994: 35–7; Beier, 1985: 65).

By the turn of the nineteenth century, the commercial interests of the traditional elite had become entwined with the bourgeois global economic project (Thompson, 1993a; Savage et al., 1995; Linebaugh and Rediker, 2012). The revolutionary potential of the masses now threatened the interests of traditional elites and the new professional bourgeois class alike, both of which were invested in fixing the new world order. Accordingly, concern about elite excess—its lack of hard work—dissipated, and state policy turned toward the task of civilizing the lower orders into dispositions of self-constraint (Hall, 1992, 2007).

It is in this context that we begin to see what I am calling the framework of autonomy really begin to mature. As Farmer discusses (2016), concerning the nineteenth-century civilizing ambitions of the criminal law, controlling the lower orders involved a parallel process of indoctrinating the working class into the bourgeois ethos of respectability, while heavily moralizing those who failed to adapt (see Booth, 1890; Dickens, 2003 [1853]; Mayhew, 1985 [1862]). The core tenets of respectability exemplify the strongly held values of the autonomy framework, including such virtues as work, self-control, and taking responsibility for personal circumstances, behaviour, and health (Hall, 1992; McClintock, 1995). A range of institutions then ingrained these ideas into the national psyche, including welfare services, educational facilities, and churches; these ideas were also widely disseminated through new popular forms of entertainment, such as novels, travel biographies, newspapers, songs in music halls, theatre performances, lantern shows, exhibitions, and so on (Finn et al., 1978; Hall, 2007; Heathorn, 2000; Skeggs, 1997; Thompson, 1988; Virdee, 2014). Consequently, instead of encouraging solidarity and sympathy for those excluded from the fruits of capitalist economic development, the stable working class were co-opted to align with the interests of the middle classes. Gareth Stedman Jones (2013: 303) describes this process as 'wooing the respectable working class' to protect the newly established civil order against the threat of the least advantaged. By the end of the nineteenth century, the implementation of respectability had been markedly successful, now widely accepted as the legitimate moral order (Wiener, 1994: 185).

Martin Wiener (1994: 11) suggests that, as part of the civilization drive, the English legislature began to treat members of the public as more rational and responsible than before, aiming to foster 'disciplined behaviour and a broad ethos of respectability'. Thus, in contrast to the contemporary view of the legal subject as already autonomous and responsible, this nineteenth-century view of legal subjects had regarded them as not yet fully

16   Introduction: Back to the Rough Ground

self-governing and responsible, but as having the potential to become so through a pedagogical process of being held responsible for their actions. From this viewpoint, the criminal law is a source of moral education to build the character of the population. Wiener's historical account (1994: 49) details the criminal law's expansion under this moralization drive, charting the marked rise in the number of laws targeting the 'unrespectable poor'.

On the back of this civilization drive, which among other things cements a normative framework of autonomy as the moral reference point by which individuals begin to judge themselves and others, the poor begin to be morally typecast as criminal. Nineteenth-century bourgeois writers commonly and explicitly conflated the most disadvantaged segments of the working class—those unable to adapt to the requirements of respectability—and criminality. This is pronounced in Henry Mayhew's writings (2011 [1862]), in which he speaks of the most socio-economically disadvantaged in England as 'criminal tribes'. A range of professionals repeated this language of a 'criminal class', including magistrates, politicians, artists, researchers, and policymakers (Beier, 2005: 499). Karl Marx and Friedrich Engels's notorious concept of *lumpenproletariat* captures a similar sentiment, defined as '[t]he "dangerous class," the social scum, that passively rotting mass thrown off by the lowest layers of the old society' (2004 [1848]). As the nineteenth century progressed, conviction grew that this *lumpen* segment of society was unable to adapt to the conditions of the new political economy and would continue to behave in immoral ways reflective of the older order.

Indeed, concern about the very least advantaged in the social order continued to pervade British politics throughout the twentieth century. In a study of the 'underclass', John Welshman (2014) reveals the persistent moralization of poverty from the seventeenth-century Poor Laws up to the present. According to Welshman (2014: ch 2), in the late nineteenth century, the Trojan Horse concept of the 'unemployable' gained ground in the UK, which saw policymakers and researchers searching for a group of persons believed to be inherently unable or unwilling to labour. However, when full employment became available during the First World War, this lumpen group could not be found (see also Jones, 2013). Nevertheless, as Welshman (2014: ch 3) discusses, twentieth-century concerns about the unemployable resurrect in a new search for the 'social problem group', again failing to be found. In the mid-twentieth century, the quest morphed into finding the 'problem family', also ultimately elusive (Welshman, 2014: ch 4).

Following the Second World War, from around 1950 to 1973, British policy fleetingly changes direction during a period of social democracy.

Philosophical Context: Frameworks 17

Ian Loader and Aogán Mulcahy (2003: ch 1) describe this as a moment of economic growth, where the masses acquired greater purchasing power, benefited from technological developments in accessible household devices such as televisions and washing machines, and experienced general improvements in the standard of living—developments aptly captured by John Goldthorpe's (1968) research into the new 'affluent worker'. In tandem with the greater economic prosperity of this period, the social democratic governments of the time instituted and maintained national insurance and the welfare state. But notably, even this 'heyday' of welfare reform and social progress was not experienced equally. The so-called undeserving poor continued to be excluded from the provisions of the expanding welfare state (see Koch, 2018b). Similarly, the racialized segment of the British working classes from commonwealth countries experienced a whole host of hardships and exclusions (see Loader and Mulcahy, 2003: ch 5; Virdee, 2014: ch 6). In spite of the social and economic benefits ushered in by the social democratic phase, the early 1970s saw a period of economic decline, marked by the oil crisis in 1973 and subsequent growing unemployment, and political unrest including the miners' strikes and increased racial tensions. This confluence of factors brought in a wind of change, departing from social democratic ambitions and spinning back towards conservative politics, now led by Margaret Thatcher and her free-market, privatization agenda—a political and economic direction which has largely remained since (see Hall, 2021). Alongside this change of the political order, too, was a renewed normative focus on the autonomous individual and the immorality of its opposite.

In recent decades, historically rooted myths about the immorality of the most impoverished fed into the social exclusion policy of the Tony Blair Labour government. What is more, the 'problem family' concept re-emerged towards the end of the Blair period, and went on to form the basis of the 'Troubled Families' programme of the Conservative-led coalition (Welshman, 2014: chs 9, 10) as part of austerity politics pursued in the wake of the 2008 financial crisis. Much as with 'unemployable', 'social problem group', and 'problem family', research discredits this classification of 'troubled families', which illustrates how poverty is consistently mythologized in British politics (Crossley, 2018; see also MacDonald et al., 2014; Shildrick et al., 2012). By tracing the evolution of these policies, we can see how ideas about the immorality of poverty continue to pervade contemporary beliefs and drive the concerns of the modern state, despite counter-evidence. The notion of a deficient segment of society which the state must control has

18 Introduction: Back to the Rough Ground

been part of British history for so long, it has come to form the bedrock of a national common sense, irrespective of the empirical reality on which these beliefs are based. Moreover, belief in these folk devils—figures of immorality (marked by characteristics of class, race, gender, sexuality, and so on) who threaten the social order—prompts particular kinds of reaction and is used to justify extensions of the criminal law (see Hall et al., 2013; Jensen, 2018; Shildrick et al., 2012). Therefore, these historically anchored myths have very real effects on those whom the intrusive forces of the state periodically target.

The modern criminal law in England and Wales continues to play an instrumental role in attempts to control the least advantaged. Punitivism infuses the modern criminal law, extending into policies on welfare, education, immigration, and beyond (Garland, 2001; Simon, 2012; Wacquant, 2009; Zedner, 2010). It is common in the literature to discuss this so-called 'punitive turn' as part of a wider neoliberal politics, which involves excessive deregulation of sectors categorized as 'private', while the punitive reach of the state extends ever further into areas categorized as 'public', such as crime and welfare, disproportionately undermining the freedoms of underprivileged actors. There is a wealth of critical research about the punitive turn in criminal policy (reviews include Campbell, 2015; Koch, 2017a; Loader, 2006), from the notorious anti-social behaviour orders implemented under Blair to increased criminalization of immigration and withdrawal of citizenship rights. Common to these policies is the tendency to centre the individual and hold them wholly responsible for wrongdoing, affording limited consideration to historical and structural conditions that contribute to such outcomes. Thus, contemporary political and legal formations in Britain come to reflect well the normative evaluations definitive of what I am calling a framework of autonomy, centring responsibility, respectability, and the autonomous ideal of the self-made individual.

Indeed, mainstream criminal law's present focus, as detailed above, on capacity and subjective responsibility of defendants complements neoliberal politics, since it presupposes the legal subject as a disengaged autonomous actor who is fully responsible for their actions, irrespective of historical and structural factors. Thus, in contrast to James Fitzjames Stephen's nineteenth-century framing of criminal law as moralizing its subjects (see Farmer, 2016), contemporary criminal lawyers treat this process as already having occurred: by virtue of being born in the present, for the most part an individual is considered legally culpable (excepting those

Philosophical Context: Frameworks   19

considered not to have capacity in law). Rather than questioning whether all persons in society have had sufficient opportunity to acquire the moral status of the autonomous actor, which concerned legal scholars in the past, the modern criminal law treats structural considerations as outside its remit. Among other aims, in this book, I seek to bring relevant structural factors back onto the agenda by offering a socio-legal account of the moral terrain which the criminal law traverses. The criminal law's subjects live, I argue, within a plurality of moral frameworks—a condition I call framework pluralism—which shapes and makes sense of their conflicts and journeys into the legal system.

Unlike former, overt inculcations of moral standards of autonomy, the modern state and legal institutions circulates and reinforces its legitimate standards in concealed forms, which are misrecognized as neutral. It is as though these standards are, as in Ludwig Wittgenstein's words (1953: §103) (in discussing a different notion), 'like a pair of glasses on our nose through which we see whatever we look at. It never occurs to us to take them off.' Bourdieu (1977, 1984) captures this phenomenon with the concept of the *doxa*, which refers to our presumptions about the social world as natural and our beliefs as rooted in 'common sense'. In my terms, we can say that contemporary British society has largely come to accept the standards of autonomy, and in so doing deems the individual as responsible for their successes and failures. Moreover, this social acceptance tends to be relatively unreflective. That is, we are nurtured to accept the *doxa* without affording sustained attention to any inequalities and injustices that may structure it.

There is, then, a long history of ideas in which the ideal of autonomy plays a dominant role and around which a legitimate normative framework forms. In some of its earlier formations, the value of autonomy may have been explicit and even sought after by state structures and institutions. In later, more modern society, we find the value of autonomy is ubiquitous in our moral lives—the assumed common sense, the doxa, that we accept as natural and refer to in making sense of our own and others' decisions, inclinations, and actions. This orienting background normative order, which places special value on autonomy, I have referred to here as the framework of autonomy. This framework is, I think, of critical importance to understanding the nature and logic of the English criminal law, and also its misjudgement of those most falling under its remit. For, as I argue in this book, the decisions and deliberations of my research community are most intelligible as responsive to a different normative order: the framework of mutuality.

20 Introduction: Back to the Rough Ground

Framework of mutuality

As discussed above, from the nineteenth century onwards, studies of the English poor have described a segment of society—amounting to approximately 10 percent of the population—purportedly unable or unwilling to adapt to conditions of modernity (see Morris, 2002). Notions such as 'residuum' (Marshall, 1890), 'criminal class' (Mayhew, 1985), '*lumpenproletariat*' (Marx and Engels, 2004 [1848]), and 'underclass' (Murray, 1984) aim to capture this group, which is often targeted in government campaigns against the allegedly 'unemployable', 'the social problem group', 'the troubled family', and so on (see Welshman, 2014). In the present, it is the section of society which the criminal law continues to disproportionately affect, as well as those overly exposed to the punitive reaches of the state in policy areas such as welfare, immigration, state education, and so on. It is also the section of society that my research community is part of—the most socio-economically disadvantaged 10 percent.

Rather than socio-economic disadvantage being explained by individualized factors of deficiency or choice (Herrnstein and Murray, 1994; Lewis, 1963; Moynihan, 1965; Murray, 1984), it is that the most disadvantaged in British society have never been fully included in the provisions of the modern state. Unlike advantaged groups, who can lean on the state and other formal institutions in ways that are largely taken for granted and presumed to be part of the natural order, the most disadvantaged must use alternative forms of assistance to survive. A background structure which facilitates the pursuit of other life goals and cushions against bad luck and hardship is what empowers those with access to property rights, the services of the police, financial institutions, certain forms of education, decent healthcare, and so on. It is only within (and against) a framework of such extensive background support that the autonomous ideal can emerge. Yet, despite the assistive role of the state in the lives of the most advantaged, the moral ideal of autonomy depicts the self-made individual as personally responsible for the successes and failures that they experience in life. Accordingly, the copious assistance and luck which privileged individuals benefit from are hidden from view.

Contrary to this framing of the autonomy ideal, human beings are, by their very nature, co-dependent, which is something the modern state partially conceals by enabling access to impersonal provisions required for survival. For example, instead of depending entirely on personal relations for support, contractual relationships widen the range of those whom we can rely upon and consume the services of. Crucially, rather than viewing this as a relationship of dependency, we attach significance to the element of choice an economic actor has when entering a contractual relationship, which centres individual agency and dislodges other relevant factors. Concealed from view is the fact that individual choice relies on the background structure of the modern liberal state and legal mechanisms, which make these impersonal dependencies both possible and viable. Since not everyone in a class society is structurally positioned to enjoy the impersonal services of others, they must rely on different forms of support and structures of dependency.

Theoretically, most if not all could be supported by the modern state; that is, the social structure could enable more persons to have greater choices in various aspects of their lives. However, the modern liberal state does not prioritize inclusivity and is founded on the inverse principle of exclusion—the moral ideal of autonomy was not formed through the identification of itself, but via recognizing groups categorized as immoral and other (Bhabha, 1984; Fanon, 1968; Mbembe, 2017; Said, 2003). That is, to show oneself as making the right choices, there needs to be a group categorized as making bad choices, and hence demonstrations of morality under the framework of autonomy are predicated on the existence of hierarchy and the moral condemnation of those relegated to the role of moral subordinates.

The most socio-economically disadvantaged 10 percent, largely unable to depend on the full benefits of the modern state, who serve the role of immoral scapegoats against whom the moral ideal is reflected, continue to make use of an alternative support structure to meet basic subsistence needs. In respect of my research community, I show how this structure forms through an assortment of sharing practices, which entail personally knowing and regularly assisting others in ways not captured by the economic logic of self-interest (see also Degnen, 2005; Edwards, 2000; Koch, 2018b; Skeggs, 2011; Smith, 2017b; K. Tyler, 2015). I suggest that Thompson's notion of moral economy (1993b, 1993c) resembles this normative order, which the most disadvantaged 10 percent has remained (at least partially) reliant on due to class exclusion. This moral outlook has undertones of religious virtues such as good neighbourliness, sacrifice, and altruism, and prioritizes equitable access to essential resources for all, over and above the virtues of self-advancement and profit.

I do not provide a full account of mutuality here since this is the task of the substantive chapters (see Chapter 2). Indeed, I think that because the normative order itself is lived far more than it is articulated, the researcher's

22 Introduction: Back to the Rough Ground

best approach in outlining the framework is not to offer some rigid criteria. To do so would formalize what is itself negotiable, formulated through active moral deliberation, and reinforced through action rather than words. As Taylor argues, some frameworks may have their theoretical contemplation 'written in' to them, which he associates with a certain Platonist ethic—in others, articulating the normative structure may be at odds with the framework (such as the framework for 'warrior' societies), or at least not required (Taylor, 1989: 20–1). It seems to me that my research community do clearly live within an identifiable normative structure, placing strong value on particular norms that I summarize with the label 'mutuality': sharing practices, a notion of fairness, resisting power imbalances, and more. These I try to show in the moral deliberations and reflections of my research community, rather than to completely circumscribe what is open-ended.

Because the framework of mutuality has been overlooked in much mainstream academia, in the body of this work I show that this normative order operates at the level of experience and bears on the concerns of criminal lawyers. Importantly, I am not suggesting the research community rejects the value of autonomy. On the contrary, as the legitimate framework, we will see how there is considerable commitment to it. However, conditions of material hardship mean that the framework's particular autonomous ideal is often out of reach for precariously situated persons: because the least advantaged must direct time and resources to sustaining an informal support structure, fewer resources and time are available to pursue the dominant ideal. Crucially, however, when the moral standards of autonomy are unattainable, disadvantaged persons do not operate in a morally empty space. Rather, people so positioned draw on the framework of mutuality, which is prior to autonomy and vital for survival (see also Skeggs, 2011; Koch, 2018).

We require caveats when discussing alternative frameworks, since historically studies in sociology and criminology have tended to leave open the reading that the least advantaged in liberal states are committed to alternative value systems or subcultures as chosen lifestyles (e.g. Anderson, 1999; Cohen, 1955; Miller, 1964; Shaw and McKay, 1942; Wolfgang and Ferracuti, 1967). Indeed, some have featured such ideas in arguing for a so-called cycle of poverty, perpetuating itself regardless of state intervention and redistributive welfare policy (e.g. Lewis, 1963; Moynihan, 1965). Cultural accounts such as these have been particularly pronounced in the US context, where class disadvantage intersects with race in a caste-like manner (cf. Alexander, 2010). In turn, policymakers have tactically cited these studies to justify cuts in welfare budgets and ultimately worsen the

Philosophical Context: Frameworks   23

position of the least well off (e.g. Murray, 1984; Herrnstein and Murray, 1994). The harmful potential of these accounts has exposed them to extensive academic critique for 'blaming the victim' and for failing to sufficiently account for the role of structural and historical inequalities (Kornhauser, 1978; Ryan, 1971; Wacquant, 2002).

A more recent trend, particularly in criminology, has been the use of Bourdieusian theory to explain the experiences of those who are criminalized by the modern liberal state (Sandberg, 2008; Sandberg and Fleetwood, 2017; Sandberg and Pedersen, 2011; Shammas and Sandberg, 2016; Fraser, 2013; Winlow and Hall, 2006). Although I find Bourdieu's theory useful for illuminating the autonomy framework and the struggles that socio-economically disadvantaged persons may experience when encountering formal institutions of the state, it is difficult to see how Bourdieu's work could adequately explain the mutuality framework. For one, as Beverly Skeggs (2011) points out, Bourdieu presupposes the individualized self which I show is not available to or prioritized by all in society. By starting with this presupposition, Bourdieu's work and direct applications of it tend to characterize the least advantaged in terms of deficiency and lack (e.g. Balazs, 1999; Charlesworth, 2000; Christin, 1999; Pialoux, 1999), which contrast with emic accounts that explain socio-economically disadvantaged groups on their own terms (e.g. Edwards, 2000; Koch, 2018b; Smith, 2012; Tyler, 2012; cf. Ndjio, 2005 in the context of Cameroon). Moreover, as Michèle Lamont (1992) and Boaventura de Sousa Santos (2015) observe, applications of Bourdieu's work can be overly ahistorical, failing to capture how class is experienced in different national contexts across history, thus leading to an insufficient picture of how precarity is differentially lived in the present. Attentive to the limits of Bourdieu's work, Andrew Sayer (2005) makes a crucial adjustment; he reveals the significance of the moral dimension of class and appeals for active engagement with these moral features. Given the potential limitations to a purely Bourdieusian approach, for my own work—for the task of creating a more faithful account of precariat experience—I have also found it necessary to cast a different theoretical net: chiefly, by using Taylor's notion of frameworks to interpret the moral landscape of a precariat community, supplementing this analysis with what can be gleaned from a range of anthropological studies.

My analysis suggests that those born into precarity learn the norms of mutuality and how to nurture this normative order because they face the possibility of enduring periods of material hardship and exclusion from state provisions, thus relying on overt support of others at some point in

24   Introduction: Back to the Rough Ground

their lifetime. Due to the failure of the modern state to recognize and enforce mutuality norms, those who depend on this framework must uphold the normative order themselves, which exposes them to the greater moral (bad) luck of being criminalized. While a minority of those born into the most disadvantaged sector will be fortunate and leave this condition, others will find themselves falling on hard times and need to live by the norms of mutuality. Therefore, the framework of mutuality is not contained in people or families, or a chosen way of life, but exists in practices of sharing and support, which are passed on from generation to generation and enforced by those who have internalized the importance of these norms for the greater good and subsistence of the collective.

The Contours of the Study

Now that the theoretical context is set, I provide an overview of the empirical study. The community included in this research is part of a town called Corby in the East Midlands of England. In the early twentieth century, labourers from afar were encouraged to relocate to Corby for jobs in the steel industry. Migration from Scotland had the most significant impact on the town, alongside lighter resettlements from other parts of the UK, Europe, and the commonwealth. Following the closure of the steelworks at the turn of 1980, many former steelworkers left the town in search of alternative employment; those who stayed endured decades of material hardship and accompanying stigmatization. Regeneration efforts, particularly post millennium, have created an increased industrial presence on the outskirts of the town and rates of employment have realigned with the national average. Following the membership of Accession-8 states to the European Union in 2004, Corby become a leading destination for Polish workers who were drawn to the area for employment opportunities. As a result of layers of industrialization and migration, Corby is a diverse and heterogeneous place.

There are affluent areas of Corby, whose boundaries include surrounding villages and housing estates on the outskirts of the town, some of which are in the vicinity of one of the highest performing state schools in the Northamptonshire County. However, a significant section of the town has consistently been recorded as among the most socio-economically disadvantaged 10 percent in England, having sustained a range of social and economic hardships. The particular community included in this study is among the most disadvantaged nationally and within Corby itself. Specifically, the research community consists of a network of friends, companions, and acquaintances of my late father, Paul, many of whom were resident on the Lincoln estate and neighbouring areas at some point in their lifetime.

My main ethnographic observations were conducted between 2013 and 2014, when I spent a full year living back home on the Lincoln estate in Corby, though my observations continued in subsequent years during fortnightly visits home. In the fieldwork period, I accompanied my father on his mobile grocery rounds, spent time on the estate and the areas where my father visited, and participated in various local programmes and initiatives. An unexpected source of observation I drew on was my father's Facebook social network. Each Facebook user has a unique 'News Feed', which displays updates of those within a particular network. My father's Facebook network comprised 3,307 'friends', largely consisting of people from the estate and other areas he ran the mobile shop in, as well as people who used to live on the estate, but had since moved to other parts of the town or, occasionally, further afield. Consequently, my research involved recording both online and offline observations within my father's relational community. When I include textual conversations in the study, these are non-verbatim extracts from my father's News Feed, unless specified otherwise.

A range of ethical issues surfaced during the research (see Willis, 2017). Limited space prohibits a full account of the extensive moral deliberations and methodological decisions made throughout this work, yet developments in anthropology and related disciplines highlight the need for researchers to reflect on their positionality and engage in a constant process of reflexivity. This thought builds on the realization that we do not observe the social world 'from nowhere', for we are always situated within background normative orders, which ultimately affect our place within a given research community and how we come to understand and alter the social practices we record and analyse (see Jones, 1970; Clifford and Marcus, 1986; Harrison, 2008). There is some debate about how much of the reflective work undertaken by a researcher must be made explicit and a related concern that, depending on the nature of the study, too much manifest reflexivity might detract from the research itself (for discussion see Skeggs, 2004). Much of the reflective activity undertaken during this project rests in the background and will be explored in accompanying methods papers. On the question of positionality, instead of outlining features of my identity by listing characteristics, such as my class, ethnicity, gender, sexuality, disabilities, religion, nationality, and so on, I offer a relational understanding of my place in the research by sharing a range of ethnographic vignettes

26 Introduction: Back to the Rough Ground

between chapters. The narratives I share are necessarily partial, selective, and creative retellings, yet I hope they provide a sense of my position within the research community, which brings into view emotional aspect of class and features of the constitutive relationships that inspired and informed this work (see Gilroy, 1993; Hall, 1996 on the complexity and thickness of identity).

I have opted to use the term 'precariat' to refer to the most socio-economically disadvantaged 10 percent included in this study, which is influenced by the work of Mike Savage et al. (2013). The term is borrowed from Guy Standing (2011), who writes about inequality from a global perspective. In a Bourdieusian inspired research project about class in Britain, Savage et al. use the term 'precariat' to delineate a section of the UK population with the least amounts of economic capital, social capital, and cultural capital. Large parts of Corby, including my estate, fall into this precariat classification (BBC, 2013).

Comparable studies use the term 'working-class' to refer to a similarly positioned group. On the one hand, 'working-class' is a useful descriptor because it overcomes the risk of stigmatizing socio-economically disadvantaged people, in contrast to terms such as the 'underclass' (cf. Wilson, 1987, 1996). However, on the other hand, because so many people in Britain self-identify as working-class (see Reay, 2017), the term may conceal severe forms of structural disadvantage experienced by the most underprivileged. Although widespread affinity to working-class identity in Britain is valid, since the masses were part of the historic working-class struggle, sometimes the 'working-class' identifier acts as a form of distinction which implies an individual in the present has succeeded despite perceived (or avowed) humble beginnings. But, since we are conditioned to ignore substantial privileges that facilitate our individual successes, the term may also conceal structural advantages experienced by the relatively privileged. Accordingly, I opt for this alternative class marker of the precariat. While there is always the potential for a term describing disempowered groups to be appropriated and misused by dominant actors, by structurally and historically situating the 'precariat' concept throughout this work I hope to lessen this risk.

In addition to referring to the research group as precariat, I refer to the collective of people included in the study as forming part of a community. 'Community' is another contested concept with a thorny past, and one that carries an exclusionary risk (Abel, 1995; Ahmed, 2000; Crawford, 2002; Delgado, 2000; Frazer and Lacey, 1993; Friedman, 1989; Pavlich, 2001; Weisberg, 2003). Without going into the extensive literature on the concept

The Contours of the Study 27

of community, when I speak of my father's community, I am referring to those with whom my father had a relational connection; that is, people who were known to my father, Paul, and/or who knew him. For the most part, Paul's relational community was geographically formed, although it did not include everyone on the Lincoln estate and surrounding areas but a subsection of residents. Moreover, it also includes many people who had moved away from the estate, often to different parts of the town though sometimes further away due to demolition and housing transfers. Throughout this study, I denote Paul's relational community with phrases such as 'Paul's community', 'Paul's friends', 'Paul's peers', and 'Paul's neighbours'.[3] By these phrases, I do not mean to imply that Paul's relational community exhausts the relevant communities sharing similar normative structures. Rather, Paul's is a particular window into a constellation of many such relational communities, who in their overlapping connections partially constitute a more or less determinate precariat group. 'Paul's community', then, serves as a shorthand for multiple relational groupings within the relational vicinity of Paul, the majority of whose members are in fact connected to Paul locally, and many of whom further via Facebook. Beyond the relational community, at points in the study I also refer to the 'town community' or the 'Corby community', which incorporates Benedict Anderson's (1991) notion of an imagined community, by which persons who are otherwise unknown to one another can gain a sense of connection through a shared history and collective memory (for further discussion, see Chapter 2).

Despite the concept's contested status and history, I have opted to stick with the term 'community' rather than, e.g. 'network'. One reason is that 'network' may connote the idea of voluntary, sometimes casual, groups of acquaintances, whereas I want to indicate a phenomenon less transitory and contingent. Indeed, both community forms discussed above can be understood as *constitutive* communities (following Bell, 1993), meaning that rather than simply being chosen, the relational and imagined community have a deeper place in the lives of those included, for they partly constitute a person's identity and feelings of belonging. These constitutive communities

---

[3] I am not completely satisfied with this framing. I wish to describe something less rigid than what 'community' may connote, and relationships more distant, often, than what 'friends' implies. I use the term 'peers' and 'neighbours' in a broader sense, where 'peers' includes a subset of people across generations and 'neighbours' refers to relational connections not necessarily confined within a geographical space. In spite of my misgivings, I still need descriptors for analytical purposes, so I invite the reader to understand the terminology I have settled on with the present caveats in mind.

28 Introduction: Back to the Rough Ground

are collective formations of which Paul was intricately part, and from which he could not easily detach himself without experiencing some form of psychic damage to his personhood and sense of self (cf. Bell, 1993; Walkerdine and Jimenez, 2012). This is not to make a normative claim about the good of community, nor to present an idealized account; indeed, scholars have long shown how the notion of community is infused with issues of power imbalance and exclusion. Still, I find the concept of community a helpful means of referring to collective experiences.

An overview of the argument and chapters

In the chapters that follow, I illustrate how my father, Paul, and his precariously situated peers navigate the world within a plurality of moral frameworks. Structural inequality guarantees that most within the precariat cannot attain the legitimate standards of autonomy, being denied access to resources requisite for the autonomous figure to surface. Therefore, despite being oriented to the framework of autonomy, efforts by Paul and his neighbours to act in accordance with it are frequently thwarted. This means that a prior framework of mutuality has maintained an important place in the lives of the least advantaged, for its continuation ensures the collective can subsist from one generation to the next. Due to its vital role for survival, I suggest that mutuality is the primary framework that influences the practices and actions of Paul and his peers. At times, this leaves the precariat exposed to the forces of (bad) moral luck and criminalization.

The criminal law often conceals the reality of framework pluralism I present herein by failing to recognize precariat experiences in full. Instead of acknowledging how a particular action might have been influenced by the norms of mutuality, the criminal law translates all action through the framework of autonomy. At times, this results in socio-economically disadvantaged groups being labelled as immoral in accordance with autonomy and subjected to forms of criminalization that other social classes are not. In the interest of social justice, I argue that if the criminal law expects all persons in Britain to meet the standards of autonomy, then the structural conditions for this realization must be fostered. Alternatively, especially if structural change is not forthcoming and British society maintains its class system, then the criminal law ought to recognize and accommodate the framework of mutuality by which the least advantaged orient themselves

The Contours of the Study   29

in order to survive. At the very least, criminal lawyers should engage with these issues which class inequality raises.

I open the study in Chapter 1 by examining how the class system prevents disadvantaged children from attaining autonomy in England. I begin by scrutinizing structural barriers at school, which ensure that the most socio-economically disadvantaged children are the most likely to enter precarious and coercive forms of labour, irrespective of individual potential and merit. Having provided a flavour of the barriers that inhibit universal autonomy (a condition which the criminal law presupposes), I move on to explain how the framework of mutuality operates in the lives of those who are denied autonomy.

I introduce the logic of mutuality more fully in Chapter 2. Instead of prioritizing the individual and self-interest, a relational understanding of the self is apparent in Paul's community. In a context of material hardship, the community actively engages in a range of sharing practices, and prioritizes virtues such as empathy, solidarity, friendship, charity, support, and care over profit-making, self-advancement, and one-upmanship. During this discussion, I show how a relational understanding of the human being markedly affects the application of certain mainstream theories which presuppose the individualized self.

Extending this latter insight, and drawing on historical analysis, in Chapter 3, I contend that a framework of mutuality provides a better explanation for some instances of violence in Paul's community than a framework of autonomy does. This finding is notable since criminal lawyers and criminologists tend to explain violence only through the lens of autonomy. Not only does this fail to capture violence in full, but it can also distort and misrepresent it.

Chapter 4 complements the discussion on violence by showing how the criminal justice system primarily enforces the norms of autonomy to the exclusion of those of mutuality. Therefore, the state often fails to respond to the needs of precariat communities, which in turn necessitates informal community responses. However, the precariat is not passive in the face of an indifferent state—they employ a range of strategies to urge state responses to local needs.

In Chapter 5, I address racial tensions in the research community in the context of the Brexit referendum. For the time being, I explain these tensions by exploring the framework of mutuality, as with Chapter 3's discussion of violence. However, I later return to the issue of race in Chapter 8 and assess how to understand the moral motivations behind these tensions,

30 Introduction: Back to the Rough Ground

which are challenging questions lawyers must grapple with in conditions of framework pluralism.

Chapters 6 and 7 focus on the how the framework of autonomy surfaces within the research community. In Chapter 6, I explore the framework in relation to violence, and how the least advantaged are exposed to structural and symbolic violence, which are less overt forms that nevertheless have devastating consequences. Though less obvious, I argue these forms of violence operate to a similar effect and ought to be included in legal debates about violence.

In Chapter 7, I examine how Paul's peers are at times unable to act in accordance with the moral standards of autonomy, and in such moments engage in public moral deliberations. This might involve setting autonomy aside in preference for mutuality, but it does not involve the complete rejection of moral reasoning and wider social approval. It would be fruitful for lawyers to be attuned to ethical conversations that regularly occur among some of the least advantaged: it shines a light on the moral complexities raised by conditions of precarity and suggests how the criminal law might also engage with the reality of framework pluralism.

As anticipated, in Chapter 8, I return to the issue of racial tensions and questions of moral motivation. In conditions of framework pluralism, it is not always clear whether someone is motivated by the pursuit of autonomy or mutuality, or even bigotry. I suggest that those within Paul's community are primarily, though not exclusively, motivated by mutuality, which can affect the meaning of a practice such as the use of a derogatory insult. Not only might this affect whether an act properly constitutes a hate crime, but it raises complexities for equality law more broadly.

In the conclusion, I sum up significant findings, reflect on the moral framework(s) the criminal law ought to recognize, and suggest ways these discussions might be taken forward.

The Mobile Grocer

Children from the estate gathered on a patch of grass. Three sides of the patch were framed by houses, some with immaculate front lawns, others with chalk writings on walls. Tatty furniture lay discarded by a run-down end house, spilling onto the road that led to garages. Despite the onset of night, a summer sun hovered on the skyline.

In the centre of the grass, two scooters rested at children's feet, beside a 'no ball games' sign. A teenage boy attempted to grab the purple scooter, but a girl a fraction of his size kicked him away, warning 'if you touch ma scooter again, I'll batter ya.' Among the commotion, a toddler weaved around on a miniature pushbike, wearing a black, oversized motorbike helmet that inevitably made his head flop to one side.

'How long?' asked little Connor, squeezing his fists and fidgeting his feet to help him bear the wait.

'Soon,' Meghan said, her thirteen years making her a source of wisdom for the younger children.

Hoot-hoot, hoot-hoot-hoot.

The distant, high-pitched sound was like a flash of energy. A small boy started spinning in circles, until dizziness toppled him over. Other children jumped and squealed in delight. The older children formed a queue, bumping each other out of the way, and insisting, 'The line starts *here*'.

'I'm first!' a girl with striking orange hair shouted, prepared to stand her ground against anyone who tried to take her place at the edge of the path.

Hoot-hoot, hoot-hoot-hoot, hoot-hoot.

The horn sounded again, growing louder and more frequent.

Older people began to appear. A woman in her late twenties, wearing grey sweatpants and a loose-fitted top stood to the side of the queue, puffing at the end of a cigarette. 'Calm it,' she wearily warned the children. The woman's stern face melted when she spotted her friend heading over from the opposite side of the square with a newborn baby in her arms. A middle-aged man, supported by a cane, joined the line.

A Precarious Life. Roxana Willis, Oxford University Press. © Roxana Willis 2023.
DOI: 10.1093/oso/9780198855149.003.0002

32 The Mobile Grocer

A final sequence of hoots, and an engine roar, marked the arrival of the giant red van with a white-painted roof. The old white van had writing on the side—*Our Mobile Shop*—but, after decades in service, the red one needed no introduction. The square face of the van approached the growing crowd, and the driver returned children's waves as he passed. The giant motor turned at the garages, and eventually pulled up alongside the path where the queue began.

There was one last hustle to the front of the line as the vehicle drew to a standstill. Children immediately piled onto the steel steps, disappearing through a side door. Amid the chaos, the driver slipped into the back and placed a counter down to prevent entry beyond the initial opening.

An irresistible scent filled the nostrils of the lucky ones who made it to the front—a mixture of cherry, strawberry, sherbet, and cream. The view behind the counter added to the children's delight: on each wall, layers of shelves packed with shiny multi-coloured sweets, chocolates, and fizzy pop. Paul-on-the-van had arrived.

'Hello Shannon!' Paul said to the redheaded girl who managed to keep her front-place position, 'What can I get for you today?'

1
From Schoolyards to Factory Floors

We can understand the autonomous individual as a moral ideal in advanced liberal societies. Following Enlightenment developments, ideas about rational agency and beliefs in the disengaged subject as distinct from the collective body grew in force in European political thought. Influential philosophers, including Grotius, Locke, and Hobbes, had taken as their primary unit of analysis the disengaged subject—i.e. an individual disconnected from other human beings and background normative frameworks. A presupposed vision of the social world often complemented this picture of the individual: society could form, in principle, from a set of lone individuals agreeing to cooperate. Social contract theories often assume that the disengaged subject would sacrifice a degree of personal autonomy by entering into social agreements to enhance security and develop collective enterprises. This view implies that individuals enter society already oriented to a certain moral view of the world and in possession of personal property (or some proto-property), which must be respected by the collective body if individuals are to co-operate. In these theories, individuals are deemed to be rational actors, self-interested by nature.

Notwithstanding the historical significance of these philosophical arguments, or the social gains facilitated by conceptualizing the individual as disengaged, in the last fifty or so years, much philosophy has interrogated the underlying metaphysics—in turn, liberal theory itself has made significant revisions. At the ontological level, political philosophers have compellingly shown the implausibility of the disengaged subject as capable of existing in principle prior to society, since the language, dispositions, values, and ways of being which very much (as the argument goes) constitute us are essentially communal too (MacIntyre, 1981; Sandel, 1982; Walzer, 1983; Taylor, 1985a; Jaggar, 1985; Lacey, 1988). In response to these penetrating critiques, the revised liberal position generally no longer commits itself to an atomized metaphysical view of the individual. Instead, contemporary liberal theory tends to pitch itself at the normative level— i.e. concerned not simply with 'what is' but with 'what ought to be'—being

A Precarious Life. Roxana Willis, Oxford University Press. © Roxana Willis 2023.
DOI: 10.1093/oso/9780198855149.003.0003

34 From Schoolyards to Factory Floors

more self-aware as theory which pushes a particular conception of the good life, albeit one that prioritizes individual autonomy (Raz, 1986; Nussbaum, 2009; Mills, 2014; Friedman, 1989).

In recognition of the ontological missteps of earlier liberal theories, then, some contemporary scholars have accepted normative positions about the value of nurturing individual liberty; although it is accepted that human beings are not fully autonomous subjects by their nature, some legal thinkers of the liberal tradition argue that autonomy should nevertheless be pursued as a moral good. Joseph Raz (1986) is a proponent of this position, advancing a normative jurisprudential thesis for an autonomy-oriented conception of individual freedom. Raz outlines the moral ideal of autonomy:

> The ruling idea behind the ideal of personal autonomy is that people should make their own lives. The autonomous person is a (part) author of his own life. The ideal of personal autonomy is the vision of people controlling, to some degree, their own destiny, fashioning it through successive decisions throughout their lives (Raz, 1986: 369).

Raz appreciates that individual autonomy is not a given; that, therefore, we must actively realize conditions for autonomy; and that social conditions can be more or less ripe for an individual to make choices. Raz suggests three conditions for autonomy (1986: 327): (1) the development of mental abilities, so that individuals have an awareness of available options and can appreciate their meaning; (2) the need for an adequate range of options, which requires that a variety of qualitative goods are available; and (3) the independence for individuals to make their choices. Amartya Sen (1999) and Martha Nussbaum (2000) offer further takes on the types of capabilities that ought to be nurtured to realize individual liberty.

Such liberal theories acknowledge that to secure conditions for autonomy, we must engage in an active process, and cannot simply treat autonomy as a natural feature of the human condition. In a similar way, Charles Taylor (1985b) advises that, if autonomy is a fundamental good in liberal societies, then the conditions which make autonomy possible must not be taken for granted but nurtured and maintained. Likewise, Nicola Lacey (1988: 176–81) encourages us to acknowledge how our ability to exercise autonomy depends to some degree on background social factors, and that, having recognized the social nature of the self, our conception of autonomy must connect (rather than conflict) with the social good. These more recent works—from both the liberal and so-called communitarian

From Schoolyards to Factory Floors **35**

tradition—recognize explicitly that autonomy is a normative ideal; they stress that societies which value autonomy must structure themselves to make possible the realization of this ideal.

The foundational philosophical debate about the nature of the self, and the bearings it has on the need for structural conditions to conduce to the autonomous ideal, had occurred during a period of political change which runs counter to these insights (and continues to do so). From the late 1970s onwards, popular political discourse in the UK, the US, and elsewhere has undergone what some call a 'penal turn': a hyper-emphasis on the individual, limited state intervention for welfare provisions, and unprecedented state involvement in the punishment of individuals deemed responsible for norm violations in various social spheres, including criminal justice, school, work, welfare, and immigration (critical accounts include Aliverti, 2012; Brown, 2019; Ericson, 2007; Garland, 1985; Harvey, 2007; Simon, 2007; I. Tyler, 2015; Wacquant, 2009; Zedner, 2010). Instead of recognizing that to attain the moral ideal of the autonomous individual we first require conditions conducive to developing autonomy, recent crime policy takes the fully formed autonomous individual largely as a given; it is this which provides a justificatory basis for punishing those who fail to act in accordance with certain standards. Consequently, irrespective of structural barriers preventing socio-economically disadvantaged persons from attaining an autonomous status, those unable to live up to the dominant social norms are held to be responsible for their failings.

In tandem with the political discourse, contemporary criminal law theory in Britain for the most part also takes the autonomous individual as the starting point for legal analysis, as Barbara Hudson (1994: 302) aptly captures:

> That individuals have choices is a basic legal assumption: that circumstances constrain choices is not. Legal reasoning seems unable to appreciate that the existential view of the world as an arena for acting out free choices is a perspective of the privileged, and that potential for self-actualization is far from apparent to those whose lives are constricted by material or ideological handicaps.

In accordance with mainstream legal scholarship, the notion of subjective fault is pursued as a principal ideal of the English and Welsh criminal law, according to which a defendant's state of mind has become increasingly important to determining culpability and corresponding punishment

36 From Schoolyards to Factory Floors

(Ashworth, 1989; Ashworth and Zedner, 2014; Duff, 2007; Gardner, 2003). On this view, the more a defendant wills a criminal act, the more responsible they ought to be held for the consequences that occur. While there is a degree of recognition by mainstream criminal law theorists that socio-economic inequality is relevant to legal inquiry—if certain persons are denied the means to develop into autonomous selves, then it is arguably unfair to treat those persons as fully responsible in the eyes of the law (see Ashworth and Horder, 2013)—for the most part, these questions are sidelined, regarded as outside the scope of mainstream legal scholarship.

If society is structured so that only persons of certain categories can acquire an autonomous status, then liberal criminal law doctrine advanced by mainstream theory is best seen as aspirational for justice, at which society might aim but is yet to achieve. Without the caveat that personal autonomy itself is aspirational, we may fail to nurture conditions required for the autonomous ideal, in the process holding those denied the opportunity to acquire this status, unfairly, to out-of-reach standards of behaviour. In this respect, I follow Marina Oshana (2014, 2016) in her development of a substantive socio-relational concept of autonomy, which recognizes that a person lacks autonomy in oppressive and coercive conditions. Importantly, however, as Oshana (2014: 6–7) notes, to say a person is denied the conditions to attain autonomy is not to deny that the person ought to be entitled to autonomy. Instead, Oshana's account pushes us to assess what is presently lacking in the lives of those without autonomy, and to actively redress this lack. Indeed, without due recognition of the social reality of coercive conditions, liberal theory is left resting on an unstable foundation that undermines principles of justice.

In the Introduction, I sketched out the notion of what I am calling the framework of autonomy, within which people live and by which they orient themselves, especially in their moral deliberations. In later chapters, we will see just what such normative activity amounts to. However, featuring within this framework is the moral ideal of autonomy itself. In this chapter, I examine that moral ideal in advanced liberal society, assessing the degree to which it is feasible for persons born into socio-economically disadvantaged positions in England to attain it.

I begin this task by reflecting on a common trajectory that those born into disadvantaged class positions in Britain follow, from school into insecure forms of employment. A rich body of work has developed which plausibly explains why disadvantaged children have consistently entered the most precarious forms of labour, by bringing to the fore a range of structural limitations that disadvantaged children confront in the present day (Ball, 2003; Evans, 2006, 2006; Lareau, 2011; Lawler, 2005; Reay, 1998; Reay et al., 2007; Rollock et al., 2014; Skeggs, 1997; Walkerdine et al., 2001; Willis, 1977). The studies I draw on incorporate theoretical concepts influenced by the work of Pierre Bourdieu, illuminating the complex ways in which the development of the autonomous self is stifled for socio-economically disadvantaged persons in a classed society. Beginning with childhood helps us trace limits on the attainment of autonomy, since infancy is one of the few recognized exceptions to criminal liability (see Loughnan, 2012). The period of youth provides us with a point in time when a person moves from a social status of dependency to autonomy for the purposes of criminal capacity (drawn sharply at the age of ten in England and Wales).

I adopt an ethnographic portrait method to illustrate how the theory plays out at the level of practice, which involves sharing aspects of my father's biography, interwoven with the experiences of his peers across the generations. By examining society as a lived phenomenon, we may bring into view some of the structural barriers that prevent the emergence of the autonomous ideal. Countering the tendency of popular discourse to over-emphasize exceptional cases—the stories of those born into class disadvantage who defy the odds and achieve a degree of social mobility—I focus on how my father moved from school into precarious work, which demonstrates the norm in a socially immobile Britain. My father's life presents us with a challenge to make sense of: he was born into the most disadvantaged of circumstances and presented the most remarkable of talents, yet instead of society's being structured in such a way that his talents were nurtured, formal state institutions had a disabling effect. Hence, the liberal ideal of equal opportunity did not manifest. Crucially, we will see how these barriers are not faced by lone individuals but are in fact the shared reality of class disadvantage.

The first part of the chapter examines how my father, Paul, and other participants in his community experienced education. After exploring some of the challenges in the social sphere of school, we look at the conditions of precarious work which early school-leavers are likely to enter. Here we examine precarious wage labour in Britain to find that, instead of helping to flourish the moral ideal of the autonomous individual, such labour subjects workers to intrusive methods of employer surveillance and coercive control, and curtails their individual choice and self-governance—so much so, that individuals who attain autonomy are unlikely to flourish in such workspaces. By the end of the chapter, we will have a feel for the difficulties that

38 From Schoolyards to Factory Floors

community participants face when they encounter formal state systems, which sets the scene for an alternative form of life I explain further in the following chapters.

Schooling the Precariat

Like many Corby residents, Paul's family migrated to the town for employment in the late 1940s. Paul's family had an industrial background. On the paternal side, Paul's grandfather was a cobbler, and his father worked in the tarmac and steel industries until ill health forced him into periods of unemployment. On the maternal side, Paul's mother left school at fourteen to work in a clothing factory, and her close ancestors had worked as servants at Althorp Palace, as chimney cleaners, foundry workers, and caregivers, among other vocations. Both sides of the family were actively involved in the national war efforts: Paul's mother worked in the Land Army during the Second World War; his father was in the Royal Air Forces; and his maternal grandfather returned from the First World War with suspected 'shellshock', which in turn haunted the childhood of Paul's mother.

Paul was born in 1947, and his sister, Carol, two years later. Paul did not talk much about his childhood. He had good memories of working in the allotment with his grandfather, shared stories about well-executed pranks in school, and when he reminisced about the single school trip he went on to London, it made him smile. Carol struggled to think of a happy memory from their shared childhood. Carol remembers being embarrassed of her dirty uniform, the pain of a frozen house in winter, ice forming on the insides of the windows, and sleeping under coats. Occasionally, Carol remembers, she and Paul would sneak downstairs in the middle of the night to turn the oven on with the door open for a moment of warmth. Carol recalls Christmas as particularly bleak; however, one year, their Aunt Nelly brought them each a book, the boys' and girls' handbook. Carol and Paul cherished the books, and each night they tested each other on the names of capital cities, national flags, and other facts that the handbooks revealed. Paul never got an answer wrong—he had a phenomenal memory.

Despite the absence of academic pursuits in the family, Paul managed to secure a place at the Grammar School in Corby, joined a couple of years later by his younger sister. One of Paul's fondest memories was being taught Latin by Colin Dexter, who later went on to write the popular British detective series *Inspector Morse*. Notwithstanding his love of chemistry, Paul

Schooling the Precariat   **39**

described himself as years behind other children by the time he entered school, a starting point from which he struggled to catch up. Apart from the sciences, Paul received mostly low grades and school reports paint a picture of a mischievous child. Paul recalls his best performances were in examinations that other students had difficultly preparing for; it was in these moments Paul was able to excel beyond his more privileged peers. Even though Paul stood out for his intellectual abilities—an IQ in the top few percentiles, a photographic memory, and notable problem-solving capabilities[1]—Paul did not excel, mirroring the qualities of many highly able children from socio-economically disadvantaged backgrounds who entered the grammar school system in the late 1950s (cf. Reay, 2017; Todd, 2014: ch 10).

For much of my life, I have tried to make sense of the discrepancy between my father's evident intellectual abilities and his low achievements in school, which seemed to be something of an enigma. The liberal values that cloak the English education system would have us believe that if someone is intelligent and tries hard, then they have sufficient opportunity to do well in school, and if someone lacks intelligence or fails to apply themselves then they do less well in school, and in this way casts school outcomes and the social distribution of privileges that result as in some sense fair. But this fiction could never account for my father, and indeed others I grew up with, who were highly capable thinkers and extremely hardworking, and yet did not attain the markers of scholastic success. The further I progressed in higher education, the more apparent the discrepancy between qualifications and intellectual ability became.

In some ways, Paul's lack of social mobility is consonant with the historical role of education in English society. Schooling in England, as in other places in Europe, has always functioned on a tiered basis, where those lower down in the social order are channelled into disadvantaged forms of schooling, which primarily ensures civil obedience rather than equal learning opportunities (Müller et al., 1989; Gorard and Siddiqui, 2018). When compulsory education was introduced in England in the late-nineteenth century, it was overtly classed, implemented to instil middle-class values and sensibilities in the disadvantaged, while maintaining social distance between working-class children and the rest (cf. Davidoff and Hall, 2013; Hopkins, 1994; Tomlinson, 2019). Like other modern state

---

[1] For an important discussion on the largely socialized aspect of intelligence and the IQ test, in particular, see Stephen Gould (1996). On the significance of nurture over nature, see also Dalton Conley et al. (2015), and Danny Dorling and Sally Tomlinson (2019: ch 3).

40   From Schoolyards to Factory Floors

institutions, the hope was that education could shape socio-economically disadvantaged persons into respectable individuals who embodied a Puritan work ethic and a self-controlled way of being in the world (Finn et al., 1978; Skeggs, 1997). Hence, early educational provisions for the English poor did not serve as apparatuses for individual flourishing but as an institutional means of nurturing, within the underprivileged, an acceptance of their place in the civil order—a place lower than the middle classes, but above the racialized subjects at home and in the colonies abroad (Heathorn, 2000; Virdee, 2014). Although English schooling no longer has the explicit aim of instilling in children an acceptance of their position at birth, given its having been structured in that manner and the absence of significant structural change, the schooling system continues to produce largely the same effect.

Bourdieu (1977, 1984, 1998) offers us a way to develop a thicker description of contemporary educational inequalities. Instead of reading school achievement from its surface appearance, as a form of fair competition in which the most academically bright simply do better in examinations, Bourdieu recognizes a whole host of concealed social resources that individuals acquire in the course of their lifetimes, enhancing their performance in school and other social arenas. Bourdieu (1986) explains resources in terms of capital: economic capital (e.g. our financial and material assets), social capital (e.g. the networks we can rely on for assistance), and cultural capital (e.g. what we come to know and like). Whereas some social resources benefitting individuals are more obvious, such as economic resources, cultural capital can be less apparent, for it can become embodied by the capital holder. When an individual embodies cultural capital, Bourdieu suggests that it forms part of their 'habitus', and hence it affects their dispositions and learned ways of being in the world—it becomes a feature of who they are. The more well suited a child's capital and habitus are to a given activity or arena, the more likely they will flourish in that social space.

Sociologists have effectively applied Bourdieu's work to explain the persistence of class-based inequality in school. For instance, observations of middle-class parenting in Britain and the US show how parents strategically direct their social resources to access more advantageous forms of schooling and adopt styles of parenting that enhance their children's skills and abilities, in turn helping children to excel in school (Ball, 2003; Lareau, 2007; Reay, 1998; Rollock et al., 2014). Annette Lareau (2011: 16) terms this middle-class style of parenting 'concerted cultivation', which develops a 'sense of entitlement' in children that advantages them in the educational

Schooling the Precariat   **41**

field. In contrast, Lareau shows that socio-economically disadvantaged parents have fewer social resources on which to draw, and so must apply the limited resources that they do have on daily subsistence and survival. Accordingly, Lareau (2011: 16) describes this parenting style as facilitating 'the accomplishment of natural growth', which nurtures in children the skills needed for survival in precarious conditions, rather than the skills that facilitate success in school.

As Beverly Skeggs (1997) and Gillian Evans (2006) note, due to stark environmental differences, socio-economically disadvantaged pupils tend to be drawn to more practical styles of learning which have real-world application, rather than abstract and detached forms of thought that are nurtured in school and are used to determine scholastic success and the distribution of resources. Unlike their advantaged peers, disadvantaged children must learn about necessity, which in turn further handicaps them in the competitive struggle for scholastic achievement. Crucially, this body of work provides an explanation for the collective experience of educational failure among the least advantaged in the social order.

The collective struggle for scholastic success

A structural account, which moves beyond the individual level of explanation, equips us with a means to make intelligible the shared reality of school failure among Paul's multigenerational peers. Young people in the community, who were pupils at the time of my fieldwork, also encounter school as a site of disappointment, several decades after Paul attended school. Many adolescent youths whom I spent time with on the estate had been subjected to periods of exclusion from school, both temporary and permanent, or spent time in 'isolation' for bad behaviour—a punitive measure that requires a student to work alone in a supervised room. Even after leaving school, painful memories endured for some, such as for a teenage boy in Paul's community who commented that 'even though I don't go school any more the staff still piss me off'. Conversely, other young adults regretted leaving school at the earliest opportunity instead of going to college or (in their words) trying harder. Internalizing educational failure in this way is indicative of what Bourdieu refers to as symbolic violence, a concept I return to later in the study (see Chapter 6).

The community showed signs of collective knowledge about the rigged conditions at play. For those exposed to structural barriers, who then

42   From Schoolyards to Factory Floors

observe their own struggles repeated in the lives of their children, the unfairness of the educational system is more apparent—such as in this discussion between mothers in Paul's community about UK educational policy:

> DONNA: Switched off the news. Total bollocks the government saying children with learning difficulties can be expelled for being problem kids. If these children had support they wouldn't be made to feel like outcasts
> CINDY: The gov need to put more money into helping children with special needs. What they gonna do, expel them all?
> NICOLA: I've worked with kids with special needs, it takes time and patience but they can be the most loving souls when you gain their trust.

Instead of accepting the assignment of blame and punishment to children with learning disabilities, the women in this example make visible structural and political factors that results in school inequalities (cf. Lareau, 2007; Reay, 1998). By focusing on learning disabilities, which are sources of educational disadvantage that have gained a degree of official recognition, the mothers publicly affirm the unfairness of the educational system. And rather than accepting that responsibility for schooling difficulties ought to lie with children or their parents, they deem the government accountable for inadequately funding educational provisions.

Whereas some mothers in Paul's community wanted an educational system more receptive to the needs of their children, other parents proposed more radical solutions to the problem, such as removing children from the harmful system altogether:

> JENNY: Anyone know anyone that home schools in this area?
> GEORGE: My sister does if that helps
> SUE: I have a friend looking into it, she has 5 kids so could point you in the right direction
> PIPPA: Can I ask why hun?
> JENNY: A few big reasons ... but mainly because the whole education system sucks. I want my girls to keep their imagination and creativity, and for them to be safe and to have free will to learn what they're interested in. I'm so excited to show them the world that school shuts out.

This discussion brings out the distinction between education as a process of learning, which parents in Paul's community greatly valued, and the

Schooling the Precariat   **43**

institutionalized system of school, which for many was an unpleasant experience that failed to nurture and support intellectual growth (see Carlen, 1992). Although the full opportunities provided by school were not always immediately apparent, Paul's neighbours nevertheless widely valued and encouraged education, as other studies among working-class communities have found (Evans, 2006; Rogaly and Taylor, 2016: ch 5; Vincent, 1981). Women in Paul's community often self-described as a 'proud mummy' when their younger child performed well in school, was awarded student of the week, had the best homework, or received a good report on parent-teacher evenings. Other parents referred to their older children doing well in exams, and on three occasions I observed parents praising their children for obtaining an A or B as their end-of-school subject grades. Although it was mothers who primarily took on the role of praising children for school achievements, they praised boys doing well in school in a comparable way to girls.

Despite parents imparting the value of education to the youth, teenagers in Paul's community ultimately shared scepticism about the fairness of school as well. Take the next extract, for example, in which a teenage boy attempts to challenge the educational system in which they are obliged to participate.

DECLAN: Imagine if we didn't have to go to school. That would be ace
SARAH-JANE: You would end up a bum
DECLAN: Yeah, but so would everyone else.

The discussion shows an awareness of the defining nature of school achievement and how a pupil's performance interconnects with those of others. Declan fantasizes about a state of play where there is no schooling. In doing so, he brings to attention what Bourdieu (1977) terms the *doxa*—the presumed natural order of the social world—and imagines what life would be like if the current structure did not exist. In Declan's thought experiment, if no one went to school, then everyone would 'end up a bum'; and if everyone were to 'end up a bum', then the distinctions created by the educational system would cease to have effect: we would (according to the thought experiment) achieve a form of equality. This resembles Bourdieu's (1984) thesis that it is precisely because of the exclusionary nature of capital (in its different forms) that some can generate advantage over others. Indeed, for Bourdieu, school is a prime site for the reproduction of advantage, to the severe detriment of those lacking the required social resources.

44 From Schoolyards to Factory Floors

An alternative game

In response to the classed environment of the school, Paul found another role for himself, one to which he was far better suited: creating new and innovative ways to make other students laugh. Like the 'lads' in Paul Willis's (1977) ethnography,[2] Paul relished classroom pranks which lightened the school day (cf. Woods, 1976; Nayak and Kehily, 2001). One of his favourite activities was using his chemistry skills to make an explosive substance, which he and two friends would use to line the inside lids of fellow pupils' desks. When the lids were closed, they made a bang, giving the teacher and other students a surprise. Carol remembers Paul once snuck out of class to play a perfected rendition of Tchaikovsky's 'Nutcracker' on the school corridor piano, which bellowed through the classrooms—'Caroline,' asked the teacher, instantly knowing who the naughty culprit would be, 'is Paul in today?' Paul managed to memorize the song by watching his father perform. Paul's father had played the piano during his wartime service, and his ability to sight-read music earned him free drinks in local pubs—something of a lifeline for a heavy drinker during lengthy periods of unemployment.

Even the types of jokes Paul participated in reflected his class background. Paul enjoyed practical jokes, which combined his creativity with hands-on skills, rather than jokes of an abstract, and possibly less disruptive, nature, such as puns, which involve a linguistic mastery more commonly cultivated among the advantaged (cf. Lareau, 2011; Nayak and Kehily, 2001). From a pedagogical perspective, the classroom prankster might be an unwelcome nuisance, seemingly only acting in defiance of the school rules. Yet research in working-class communities recurringly finds humour to be an important means of coping with the stresses of poverty, serving as a vital levelling force (Rogaly and Taylor, 2016: 79–80). For example, Gillian Evans (2006: 35–6) observes how humour can be an effective challenge to inequality, for a shared joke brings people to the same level, teasing away pretensions, and creates a sense of similarity among those who share in the enjoyment of the laugh. The extent to which the humour is a levelling force depends on the status of the prankster and the target of the joke: humour that targets a more powerful subject might act to level out social differences, whereas a joke that targets a less powerful subject could become a form of domination, an issue I return to in Chapter 8. By making

---

[2] Here, I refer to Paul Willis the sociologist and not Paul Willis my father—there is no relation.

authority figures the target of the joke, school afforded Paul an opportunity to cultivate alternative social skills, which may have involved encouraging his peers to acknowledge their shared subordination and humanity, rather than 'putting his head down' to pursue self-advancement, which would afford him a higher social status, as per legitimate standards. While the formal terms of school did not value these skills, they became useful when Paul began his working life.

Paul left school with nine low-grade O-Levels. He later retook his science A-Levels in a technical college and was offered a place to read chemistry at degree level at Warwick University. In the months between sitting his A-Levels and waiting for university to begin, Paul searched for a full-time job to tide him over. A friend who worked at the Golden Wonder crisp factory helped him find work there as a nightshift cleaner. Though the hours were long, the job paid well, and Paul was able to earn more than his father and grandfather had done. It was the first time he tasted economic independence. From the moment Paul opened his first pay packet, he never wanted to return to being poor again: university was no longer an option. Paul surrendered his place at Warwick University and decided to work in industry instead, just as his mother, father, and grandparents before him had done.

Turning down university was an important moment in Paul's trajectory, and it was a decision that his family struggled to understand: why would such a capable young man seemingly throw away such a life-changing opportunity? Following his rejection of university, Paul's father and sister perceived him as a failure who had simply chosen not to continue education. However, individualizing Paul's decision seems erroneous when we consider the fact that many individuals in comparable socio-economic positions have taken the same path, even in present times when university attendance is more common. Ben Rogaly and Becky Taylor (2016: 157), for example, found that participants in their English study, some of whom had significant academic potential, opted to stay in their working-class locality rather than pursue education elsewhere. Valerie Walkerdine and Luis Jimenez (2012: 66–9) similarly observe how former steelworkers in a Welsh post-industrial town have great difficulty moving away. In keeping with these qualitative studies, census data indicates that pursuing higher university education is still the exception rather than the rule in Corby: the town was recorded as having the second-lowest rates of young people entering higher education in England and Wales (Office for National Statistics, 2014: 30),

46 From Schoolyards to Factory Floors

and as having among the lowest rates of school social mobility in the UK (Social Mobility Commission, 2017).

These collective patterns suggest that Paul's decision to turn down university is not best explained only in individualistic terms, for we still need to make sense of why so many young men in Paul's class position make this same 'choice'. According to John Goldthorpe's (1998) rational actor perspective, economic considerations are noteworthy, since the ability to earn immediate wages over prospective future earnings is arguably a rational one for a working-class man in Paul's position to make. Indeed, Paul and his mother both cited economic factors as the main reason why he turned down university. Yet a lifetime of conversations with my father, and so a deep familiarity with the values he imparted, leads me to believe that there is a deeper explanation for the vocational path he pursued.

As we saw, Paul's position in the educational field was not a comfortable one: school was not a place where he naturally excelled. Instead, school was a site of failure, where Paul's personality and humour were constantly reprimanded. Rather than being treated as a morally good person, at school Paul was viewed as naughty and unruly. Consequently, the emotions school invoked for Paul were unpleasant ones, such as frustration, shame, and embarrassment (cf. Sennett and Cobb, 1972; Sayer, 2005). By contrast, when Paul entered the factory floor, he fitted in, like a fish in water, and it felt good. This setting was where Paul gained a sense of belonging and found value in the relationships he fostered. For Paul, to detach himself from the collective body that he was part of, which generations of his forefathers had helped develop and relied on for survival, invoked a sense of fear and dread. Walkerdine and Jimenez (2012) encourage us to recognize this sort of phenomenon as collective trauma born from the experiences of precarity which invoke survival responses in inheritors of such conditions. Instead of explaining Paul's trajectory in terms of rational choice, I propose that Paul's entry into industry formed part of an intergenerational process in which he was deeply entwined, which necessitated a different kind of rationality and an alternative logic.

Dreams of success

Some of Paul's friends explicitly referred to themselves as having done well despite struggling in school. One young woman described herself as 'proving everyone wrong' by bucking the trend and managing to secure a place at university, notwithstanding school difficulties. Another man in his thirties reflected on how a teacher told him he would 'get nowhere in life with his attitude', and yet he had worked his way up to a high-salaried city job and owned various properties and flashy cars. In response, many of his friends congratulated him on his success. Similarly, a woman in her late twenties described herself as 'born and bred on the Lincoln estate' (one of the most disadvantaged and stigmatized council estates in Corby, on which Paul also lived), and yet she had been promoted to a management role. Those sharing stories of 'riffraff done well' emphasized the notion that 'if you never give up, you can do it too.' In this way, Paul's peers heavily individualize narratives of success; they present achievement as the result of hard work, individual effort, and fortitude—as possible for anyone who tried hard enough (cf. Gillies, 2005; Hey, 2003; Lamont, 2009; Silva, 2013).

Some of the most disadvantaged young people in Paul's community expressed the belief that determination is all it takes to overcome structural marginalization, even in the absence of educational qualifications. Some youths ferociously kicked back against a perception that because of their disengagement in school and involvement in alternative lifestyles, they would never achieve material desires. Martin, for example, a teenager who carried the weight of being a carer for a terminally ill single parent, railed against that expectation:

> I've had enough of people telling me I aint gonna do anything with ma life. Yeah I drink and smoke weed every day with ma mates, but I know one day I'm gunna be living in ma own house with a sound car.

Despite doing things contrary to perceived societal expectations—the daily drinking and smoking of cannabis in the period of youth—Martin's hope for his future is to be part of wider society and achieve legitimate forms of success. In essence, Martin dreams of an autonomous existence. Material ambitions to become a homeowner and have a nice car are recurringly found in studies that examine the perspective of working-class men (cf. Rogaly and Taylor, 2016: 97; Winlow and Hall, 2006: 36–7). Coupled with a belief in individual agency, work is especially important, for it is one of the only avenues which allows the working class to legitimately realize material aspirations.

48   From Schoolyards to Factory Floors

From Steelwork to Precarious Work

Paul had ambitions to excel in his working life. It did not take long working as a nightshift cleaner at the Golden Wonder factory before his strengths were noticed. First, he was promoted to a chemist role, and eventually given his own office where he was responsible for solving technical issues within the company when they surfaced. For instance, if a machine malfunctioned or an issue in production arose, managers called on Paul to find a solution and report on how it could be resolved again in the future. Although he was an asset to the company, Paul felt frustrated when university graduates joined the factory in comparable roles while being paid grossly higher salaries. Dissatisfied with the disparity, Paul insisted on a fair pay rise. When his employer offered only a nominal wage increase, Paul resigned from the job and found alternative employment at the steelworks.

Paul joined the Corby Steel Works as an electrician's mate, and soon picked up the trade. The work was initially based in the coke ovens of the works, which Paul described as 'a terrifying and unfriendly place'. Paul had difficulty breathing near the ovens and recalled having to step outside for fresh air. At times, he would cough up a thick black mucus mixed with blood, which troubled him. Paul was fortunate that others recognized his methodical way of thinking and chemistry skills, and encouraged him to apply for the position of Metallurgical Technician. In his promoted role, Paul tested the quality of the steel being produced. While the conditions at the steelworks were hard, even brutal at times, Paul's intelligence was fostered, and he found the job rewarding.

Paul looked back on the steelworks years as some of the best of his life. He especially enjoyed the company of his workmates, who shared the same sense of humour and appreciation of a good prank. Just as Paul's chemistry education enhanced his pranking abilities as a schoolboy, so too did his electrician's skills as a young adult—potentially a deadly combination. One of Paul's best executed jokes involved rigging a foghorn to the inside of a work friend's locker, so when his friend arrived to start an early shift, on opening his locker he was greeted with an ear-shattering alarm call. Another prank involved rewiring a clothing iron a workmate had brought in for repair, so when it was plugged in, instead of heating up, it sparked and exploded. Unlike in school, where such humour was chastised and punished, in the steelworks, Paul recalls the workforce cheering on innovative pranks. Practical jokes generated moments of collective enjoyment, which added variety to otherwise monotonous shifts.

From Steelwork to Precarious Work   **49**

Like many industrial towns in England, Corby suffered a devastating blow in 1979 when the imminent closure of the steelworks was finally announced (Rusbridger, 1979). Into the 1980s and onwards, a significant part of Britain's industrial base was dismantled, which marked a historical shift from a producer economy to a neoliberal service- and finance-based one. Around 20,000 people, more than 30 percent of Corby's population, either directly or indirectly lost their jobs, giving Corby the second-highest rate of unemployment in the UK (Corby District Council, 1989). Unable to find alternative employment, large numbers of residents left the town (Addis and Mercer, 2000). Those who remained lived through the loss of industry, social deprivation, and a period of economic and social neglect.

Although Paul was among the thousands of people forced into unemployment, unlike many others, he was able to secure alternative work by becoming a full-time, self-employed mobile grocer. Paul purchased his first mobile shop van from a neighbour in 1978 who allowed Paul to pay off the debt in weekly instalments from profits made. At the start, it looked like this debt would take quite some time to settle—on his first day as a 'van man', Paul had one customer, who bought a single packet of painkillers. During the early years, Paul ran the mobile shop part-time, alongside shift work at the steelworks. However, when the steelworks closed down, Paul kept the van going full time. To generate a sustainable income to support his family, Paul had to work long hours, deep into the night, seven days a week, taking only two weeks off over Christmas. Paul continued to run the mobile shop in this way for thirty-five years, renovating two replacement vans along the way. Paul eventually retired on 31 August 2015 at the age of sixty eight. As an indication of Paul's earnings, in the last ten years of his work—working lengthy hours, seven days a week, fifty weeks of the year—his annual net profits ranged from £9,000 to £12,000; the average national income at that time was £22,800 in 2005 and £27,600 in 2015.

The winter of precarity

In a contemporary study of ex-steelworkers in a post-industrial town in Wales, Walkerdine and Jimenez (2012: ch 2) reflect on how precarity has been a long-running feature of the steel industry (cf. Edwards, 2000; Moody, 2019). They note that steelwork, being intricately tied to the global economy, continuously fluctuates, requiring industrial communities to adapt to the periods of high demand and corresponding work and periods

50   From Schoolyards to Factory Floors

of low demand with little to no work. Mindful of these patterns of fluctuation, they observe how the complete closure of the steel industry, and the accompanying demolition of the steelworks plants, created new forms of insecurity and disrupted strategies of survival that steel-working families had fostered through the generations. This analysis might help us grasp the intensity of the struggles that Paul and his community likewise faced following the closure of the Corby steelworks.

The employment scene in Corby following the closure of the steelworks was bleak, and it soon required external intervention. In 1979, Corby was granted 'Development Area Status', and received funds from the European Economic Community (since incorporated into the European Union) to become a designated 'Enterprise Zone' (Read, 1982). Accordingly, businesses were incentivized to relocate to Corby, and a more varied factory and industrial presence gradually grew on the outskirts of the town. Even though the 2001 census indicated that unemployment in Corby was beginning to return closer to the national average (Office for National Statistics, 2001), areas of unemployment became concentrated, particularly on the Lincoln estate, where Paul lived and where his van route was based.[3] In the 2001 census, 6,594 people (approximately 16 percent of the town population) fell into category E, which includes those on state benefit, unemployed, or lowest-grade workers, and a further 11,326 people (approximately 28 percent) were recorded as being semi-skilled and unskilled manual workers (Office for National Statistics, 2001). Comparably, the 2011 census records the major employment in Corby to be in manufacturing, accounting for 38 percent of employment, with only 2 percent of residents in the town recorded as being engaged in 'professional, scientific, and technical activities' (UK Census Data, 2011).

Mike Savage et al. (2013), who conducted a contemporary study of class in Britain, report on a similar employment landscape: they found large parts of Corby to be home to the most socio-economically disadvantaged. Influenced by Bourdieu, Savage et al. devised a survey to record levels of economic, social, and cultural capital of British individuals, which led them to propose a seven-tiered class system. The most advantaged class

---

[3] The 2001 Census recorded unemployment in Corby at 4.2 percent, compared with the national average of this time, which was 3.4 percent. And in 2001, the rate of unemployment in the Kingswood area was 6.6 percent, compared to the national average of 3.4 percent. Figures in 2007 again recorded the Lincoln estate to have a higher level of unemployment compared to the rest of the town, and almost double the national average (Corby Borough Council, 2007: 19).

From Steelwork to Precarious Work **51**

in the stratification is termed 'elite', which consists of individuals with the highest, concentrated levels of economic, social, and cultural capital; the least advantaged class is classified as the 'precariat', which comprises individuals with the lowest levels of economic, social, and cultural capital (BBC, 2013b). Savage et al.'s classifications would place most of Corby, including the Lincoln estate and surrounding areas where Paul's community is formed, in the 'precariat' category (BBC, 2013a). On the outskirts of Corby, Savage et al. identify a cluster of 'new affluent workers', which includes trade workers such as plumbers and electricians, who have been able to acquire substantial economic capital. Common occupations within the precariat include cleaners, van drivers, care workers, carpenters and joiners, caretakers, security guards, shopkeepers, retail cashiers, and warehouse and factory labourers, among others (Savage et al., 2013: 232–3).

The description by Savage et al. of a precariat landscape reflects my qualitative observations. Many of Paul's neighbours worked in insecure waged-industrial and service-sector employment or were experiencing unemployment. Community posts online recurrently reference shift- and waged-work. Specific types of employment mentioned included factory and warehouse work; labouring, such as building, forklift driving, plastering, carpet-fitting, and landscaping; retail work in supermarkets; care work; and services such as hairdressing, bartending, lorry-driving, bookkeeping, and working for a taxi company. The only mentions of public-sector or salaried work were from a handful of people who worked as nurses, army personnel, or at the local council. A woman in her thirties summed up the common work trajectory in Paul's community in the following way: 'they were all riff-raff back in the day but I'm sure they're all decent blue collar hard working men now'.

Finding work: The lucky ones

Job scarcity and insecurity are a common part of daily life in Paul's community (cf. Beck and Camiller, 2000; MacDonald, 1999; Sennett, 2011). A question often asked was 'anyone know of anywhere taking on?'—to which others would respond with suggestions, or occasionally share some grim news: 'I've been looking for weeks now mate, nobody's taking on.' One young man recounted having submitted more than fifty applications to no avail. For some, the struggle to find work had become a source of severe distress; as one man announced in a status update, 'I am going to break down

52 From Schoolyards to Factory Floors

if work doesn't come through soon', and a middle-aged woman posted, 'I can't go on anymore. What more can a woman do to get a job round here? All I've done is applications, how much longer?' Another man announced, 'I'm gonna go loco soon and just get arrested and go back to jail, fuckin had enough man', which reveals the extent of choices perceived to be available (cf. Maguire, 2020). Such sentiments have been recorded in other English ethnographies among the precariat, such as by Lisa McKenzie (2015: 93–4), who documents feelings of 'hopelessness' experienced by some men from her council estate in their futile search for work.

The desperate struggle to access employment left many in the community reliant on the town's several private employment agencies, which offered to match workers to low-skilled employment in return for a cut of their earned income. Consequently, workers employed through agencies would earn substantially less than if they were able to work for the company directly, with the agency providing few, if any, work-related benefits, and little to no job security. One of Paul's friends expressed understandable frustration at 'working for £6.50 an hour while other non-agency staff get over £11', and another asked if anyone knew of any jobs going, since he 'had enough of working ridiculous hours for the agency and getting paid fuck all'. Indeed, agency work was portrayed as on par with selling drugs—a desperate last-choice line of work if nothing else came through. Some community participants claimed to work through an agency for years without ever being offered a permanent in-house job by the factory. Companies noted by community participants for recruiting workers on a long-term basis through agencies included RS Components, Solway Foods, and Oxford University Press.

Agency workers found they may end up at the very bottom of a labour hierarchy. For instance, one woman said she was laughed at by full-time staff in a factory because she was made to mop the floor but received less money for the job than the cleaners earned. Similarly, Michèle Lamont (2009: 136–8) found in her study that white labourers in the US scorned part-time workers slightly more precariously positioned than themselves. Notably, Paul's precariat community, rather than ridiculing those at the bottom of the formal labour market, frequently shared empathy, more in line with the attitudes of the French white workers and US black workers in Lamont's study. Many individuals in Paul's community had worked through agencies and, therefore, instead of ridiculing agency workers, they directed anger at the agencies and companies who opted to employ through such exploitative means. The following conversation is infused with some of these

From Steelwork to Precarious Work **53**

frustrations and is illustrative of a general feeling among Paul's community about such labour practices.

EMMA: Any luck on the job front pal?

DEAN: Nothing mate, can you believe it? I'm proper pissed with these agency arseholes promising work to get you signed up, only to tell you it's quiet for the next few weeks and to ring back. I am signed up to 16 agencies, and not one can offer me anything.

EMMA: Agencies, they're the biggest con. They killed the work industry. I heard there might be something coming up our end. Is your CPC [professional driving certificate] class 1 or 2?

DEAN: Bollocks. It expired with the new CPC Act. The government sure know how to fuck people over. It's killing me being out of work

EMMA: That's unlucky. Those agencies are a waste of time, they pay you in pennies and treat you like shit. I swear there would be full-time jobs if they didn't exist.

Emma and Dean are critical of both employment agencies and the government. Emma suggests that the very existence of agencies has had a negative impact on working conditions. Indeed, Emma's observations chime with recent studies on agency and other forms of low-waged and precarious employment in Britain, which shine a light on how law and policy structures unequal and exploitative labour relationships (see Hayes, 2017; Shildrick et al., 2012). Dean further points to the fact that government policy—which in this instance rendered a qualification Dean obtained meaningless—may worsen already tough circumstances, rather than alleviating the hardship. Moreover, his experience demonstrates that even low-paid and exploitative agency work is not guaranteed. Flexible work, which responds to the needs of businesses, entails that workers like Dean face unpredictable periods of no work, but then must periodically work long hours when business picks up, which can have a devastating impact on claims for welfare support (see Shildrick, 2018).

Some in the community also blame the difficult employment environment on the competing presence of migrant workers. Corby received among the highest rates of Polish migrants in the country (The Economist, 2013), many of whom worked in similar low-skilled industries, which led to various tensions that become evident in the course of this study. Participants in Paul's community recurrently voiced belief that Polish workers were prioritized by employers, making it in their view even harder

54 From Schoolyards to Factory Floors

to find work. For example, a man in his thirties was frustrated with a factory he approached for work: according to Paul's friend, the manager agreed to contact him when a position became available, only for him to bump into '8 foreign guys' on the bus a few weeks later asking for directions to the very same factory to start work. One of the main reasons why community participants believed that employers prioritize migrant workers over longer-term local workers was because of a stronger work ethic, explained by a man in his twenties: 'That awkward moment when you ask for a pay rise and the gaffer says "the new polish bloke is doing your job better and faster than you!" (And for less money)'. In these instances, community participants view apparent migrant competition as an additional barrier to accessing work and fair pay.

Those in Paul's community employed outside of agencies also spoke of battling temporary contracts and reduced working hours, especially women. A woman in her early twenties posted: 'I'm not impressed, my hours have been cut from 60 to 30 with no warning, bang out of order.' Similarly, a woman in her fifties announced, 'it looks like I'll have to start from nothing again—the arseholes have cut my hours. I give up I really do. Talk about a massive hit to the confidence.' This experience echoes the feelings of a care worker interviewed by Lydia Hayes (2017: 38) who described herself as 'mentally bruised' from losing work. Like flexible hours, reduced hours can have contradictory effects on government benefits, as a mother during her search for a part-time job explained: 'all our hours have just been cut to 10 a week, but if I don't do 16 I'll lose my tax credits. I'll then be working for £25 a week and will need to go back on benefits.'

In such a temperamental employment environment, the community frequently hoped for good luck to see a job come through. Some of Paul's friends willed for their 'luck to change', others kept their 'fingers crossed', and others still did all they could not to 'tempt fate'. The central place of luck and superstition among disadvantaged communities has long been documented (e.g. Charlesworth, 2000; Hoggart, 1957; Jones, 2012; Miller, 1964); gambling machines, bookies, and bingo halls are often not far away in socioeconomically disadvantaged spaces. Current employment conditions in the UK expose disadvantaged individuals to fewer choices and more bad luck than other groups: the odds are stacked against them. By willing for their luck to change and invoking superstitions, community participants sought to gain a sense of control over the unavoidable precariousness of their lives.

The celebratory news of those fortunate to secure a job invoked collective, positive feelings. Extreme declarations were made when work came through, such as that by a woman who felt that being offered a job was 'the best news in the world', and a lady who claimed 'nothing's taking the smile from my face', having signed a contract to make her role permanent. Such posts received high numbers of 'likes' and congratulatory messages from friends. Emotions of appreciation and all-round hope for the future infused such positive news; participants were relieved 'not to be on the dole anymore', taking whatever hours they could and adopting phrases such as 'another day, another dollar'. Accordingly, we can see that, contrary to accusations in popular discourse that socio-economically disadvantaged persons in England are work-shy, the value and reality of work was central to the lives of Paul and his neighbours (cf. MacDonald et al., 2014; Wacquant, 2002).

Paul's employed friends often suffered long and unsociable hours of work. On several occasions, participants referred to feeling 'shattered' having just finished a lengthy shift, or shared daily declarations of tiredness, such as that by a woman who said she wanted to 'sleep for a week'. Outside of the working day, bed was often seen as the ultimate destination; one man explained it as 'the moment I have been waiting for all night'. Sometimes people note extreme tiredness; a woman described pain in her eyes, limbs, head, and brain, to indicate that 'this is exhaustion'. Nightshifts seemed to hit workers hardest. In a globalized economy, there is no time for many companies to close; therefore, despite well-documented detrimental mental and physical health effects of shift work (cf. Shildrick et al., 2012), the labour must go on. A man in his early twenties, having finished a nightshift rotation, described it as having 'well and truly fucked up my game'. A conversation between three middle-aged women in Paul's community illuminates this feeling of being thrown off from reality and the hardship of nightshift:

SHANNON: Nightshift catches up with you. All I've done since I finished work is sleep. I shouldn't feel this tired! Thank God I've four nights off.
LINDA: I know what you mean, I was a total nightmare on nightshifts. Even when you get free time, you waste it sleeping.
DEBS: It knocks you for six. I've just finished three weeks of it and I don't know whether I'm coming or going.

56 From Schoolyards to Factory Floors

Such workers associated nightshifts with various sleep difficulties. Several wrote their frustrations at being unable to sleep through daytime noises, such as neighbours' decorating activities and children playing on the streets. Even workers on other shift patterns were sometimes affected by late-night noise that penetrated the walls of inadequately insulated homes (see Koch, 2016). More generally, stress appears to be a common cause for sleep disturbance. While some workers were able to sleep as soon as their head hit the pillow, many others posted irritably, at various times of night, about being unable to sleep and having work the next day. One of Paul's friends wrote of being exhausted all day, but finding when they got into bed, all their worries suddenly came to the fore, snatching sleep away. Another woman 'had a dream [she] got sacked', illustrative of a looming sense of dread that hung over some of the precariously employed in Paul's community—the stress of losing work never far away.

Fired for farting: The unlucky ones

A fate worse than reduced hours, some lost their jobs altogether, either by being made redundant or due to closure of the firm. A number of companies liquidated during the research period (Davies, 2016). One of the most notable closures in 2014 was that of Solways Food factory, which led to the loss of 900 jobs (BBC News, 2014). On learning about the likely closure of a high-street shop, a middle-aged woman shared her anxiety: 're-dundancy for me I think... hard times ahead'. This theme of workplace dismissal accords with Tracy Shildrick et al.'s research (2012: 134–6) into insecure work in Britain. The authors found that, although some workers reported dismissal due to behavioural infringements, they were often involuntarily dismissed.

While some workers in Paul's community lost their job when a company went bust, others were put through disciplinary procedures for misbehaving, eventually being told by their employers that they had lost their job due to their own doing. As one man reported, 'have disciplinary tomorrow (second one) with the big cheese, me and santa will both be getting the sack for xmas'. A mother in her early twenties, already dismissed from work for not turning up to a shift, explained why: 'Just so everyone knows, yeah I did get sacked but the real reason I couldn't turn up to my shift was 'cus I had important family things to take care of. Of course my family is worth more than my job!' The post received wide community approval and close to a hundred 'likes', which illustrates how the value of family is treated as a higher good than waged-labour, especially for mothers. On another occasion, a man employed through an agency reported being 'sacked' for attending a job interview. Appalled, his friend advised him to go to the Citizens Advice Bureau because 'they can't do that, you're allowed to go to interviews'. However, the dismissed worker had already sought such help and was informed 'if you're on a zero-hour agency contract then they can do what they want'.

A further recently unemployed community participant, a man in his twenties, claimed he 'got fired for taking a shit'. Comparably, another claimed that workers in his factory 'can't even go for a piss without an explanation'. Paul's friends often expressed fear of being penalized for 'shitting' or 'farting', something so necessary. I observed several metaphors related to the prohibition of defecation, often made in explicit terms by men to describe the surveillance of factory managers. The usage of crude language such as 'shitting', 'farting', and 'pissing' can be seen as a rejection of standards of respectability and bourgeois manners, which speaks to how undignified the conditions of precarious work in contemporary Britain have become (cf. Ndjio, 2005).

In an undercover investigation of insecure employment inside an Amazon warehouse, James Bloodworth (2016) vividly details the barriers in place that prevented workers from accessing the toilets, which included installing limited facilities, often at a great distance from workstations, and requiring employees to pass through security gates to reach them. In this context, Bloodworth came across a bottle of urine on the warehouse floor, suggestive of the alternative solutions workers had found to ease their bladders during the working day. Likewise, in an inquiry on the conditions of agency workers in the meat and poultry processing sector, the Equality and Human Rights Commission (2010: 11) reported that some workers were denied toilet breaks and documented 'the lasting impact of the humiliation of workers urinating and bleeding on themselves while working at the production line'. Repeat findings that the state and employers have intruded into the most necessary human behaviour, such as toilet usage, casts doubt on just how free, autonomous, and dignified precarious work in Britain is. The liberal aspiration of autonomy is completely undermined when the state permits employers to take proxy control (by fear of reprisal) even of workers' bladder and bowel movements.

58 From Schoolyards to Factory Floors

Alongside encroachment into rest breaks, increased levels of employer surveillance have also restricted other historic forms of defiance by workers, including limiting the pace of labour output and finding ways to share laughs during the working day (cf. McClintock, 1995: 253). The following representative conversation between a group of Paul's friends who worked at the same factory provides a window into the extent of employer surveillance on the factory floor.

ANDY: It's gonna be an interesting year – I've only been back six shifts and I've already received two formals and an interview for so-called bullying. Then wake up this morning to be handed a formal letter
JIM: What happened son?
ANDY: First shift back after the bank holiday and my lift fell through. Now I'm getting done for being late. I had to sign for that shit and all
JIM: You're kidding me. It's becoming a miserable place to work. Did you hear about the motion detectors they're bringing in? It calls when you're not moving
ANDY: Motion detectors?! Aren't the cameras enough? You'd get more freedom in prison these days. I'm honestly scared to fart without a good excuse
JIM: It will only get worse from here on in.

In addition to cameras, Jim and Andy speak of their unease of further intrusive measures rumoured to come, when 'motion detectors' will mean that the movement of their bodies will no longer be fully their own. Not only does the tight surveillance point to the lack of autonomy and trust afforded to precariously positioned workers, for community participants, these conditions are comparable to imprisonment. By once again describing the fear of farting, Andy draws attention to how difficult it has become for workers to know how to behave; for the modern-day precariat worker, their biological human form is grounds for failure.

Absent further information, Andy's reference to 'so-called bullying' in the last extract could be interpreted many ways. One possibility is that it relates to workplace banter. In an ethnography of a working-class community in the north of England, Katharine Smith (2012) pays attention to the practice of banter and the importance it has in everyday conversations in working-class spaces. According to Smith (2012: ch 4), 'having a banter' involves the exchange of quick-witted insults which might be controversial at times, often arising between people who consider themselves companions.

From Steelwork to Precarious Work **59**

Rather than being a tool to offend, Smith analyses the practice of banter as creating a sense of equality between those who engage in it, like the use of humour and practical jokes in school: making fun of difference may bring inequalities to the surface and level them out. However, Smith (2012: 115) notes that if banter is not taken in the spirit intended, then it can be misrecognized as a form of bullying. Nonetheless, it remains possible for humour, even if delivered in the form of banter, to be used as a means of asserting power over a less advantaged work colleague—an issue I return to in Chapter 8.

Plausibly, employer fears about worker motivation feed the need to surveil and control workers. Indeed, the presumption that the most disadvantaged in the social hierarchy will refuse to work and must be coerced into productive activity has been a long-running feature of global capitalism and is arguably built into the structure of modern-day labour relations. W.E.B. Du Bois (1917) suggests the violent enslavement of persons from the African continent established the foundations for current economic relationships: 'Modern world commerce, modern imperialism, the modern factory system and the modern labor problem began with the African slave trade.' In keeping with this view, Howard Winant (2001) and Lisa Lowe (2015), among others, reject clear-cut distinctions when characterizing the transition from chattel slavery to other forms of labour in the modern capitalist economy, as older methods of coercion infused into later labour forms. Reflecting on the English context, Douglas Hay and Paul Craven (2004) detail how various legislative changes from the fourteenth century onwards were designed to coerce the least advantaged to labour for the benefit of the landed classes, which included a whole host of legal measures from the dispossession of land to the introduction of laws on vagrancy, and statutes that regulated the relationships between masters and servants. Therefore, while the trans-Atlantic slave trade exhibited the most violent and overtly coercive forms of labour exploitation, we can place modern labour relations on a continuum of exploitative and imbalanced relations.

In the present, employment legislation in England and Wales continues to reinforce and structure the inequalities of the labour market. Hayes's (2017) ethnographic study of female care workers in England reveals deep disparities in employment law and the devastating effects which such minimal protections have on those consigned to the most precarious forms of work. Hayes's legal analysis of precarious work in the care sector shows that the legislative framework leans heavily on the employer's side. Like those in Paul's community who suffered extensive punishment at work, the

60 From Schoolyards to Factory Floors

accounts of Hayes's interviewees are infused with anxiety about the fear of losing work for any small act: as one of the participants explained, '[i]f you do just one thing wrong, they get rid of you' (2017: 75). Hayes (2017: ch 2) demonstrates that temporary contracts, which supposedly provide more autonomy, choice, and flexibility for workers as well as employers, have rendered low-paid workers in Britain less powerful and more disposable. Hayes (2017: 90–91) argues that the law, by treating precarious employment as a contractual rather than a public policy issue, favours the power of the employer to create the terms of contractual obligations, leaving workers unprotected and easily exploited. The legal framework here threatens the possibility of autonomous existence for the least advantaged (notwithstanding that such deregulation and worker flexibility may be presented as supporting the individual freedom of the employee).

Conclusion

I opened the chapter by detailing a presupposition of mainstream criminal law theory: that of a legal subject who is autonomous and fully responsible for the consequences of their chosen actions. In contrast to older liberal theories, I noted how a revised liberal position tends to recognize that we require minimal conditions to manifest the ideal of the autonomous individual. On Raz's terms, this includes access to an adequate range of options and a variety of qualitative goods, having an awareness of available options, and having independence to make choices. However, by examining the collective experiences of persons among the most socio-economically disadvantaged in English society, we have begun to see that autonomy-conducive conditions are far from available to all. The English education system continues to operate by original design, as an institution to control socio-economically disadvantaged children and encourage them to accept their place in the social order, rather than providing an equal opportunity to flourish. Likewise, the coercive and exploitative labour relations that formed the basis of the modern capitalist system continue to vibrate into the present, albeit now in transmuted and less overt forms.

In a society structured to make use of coercive, exploitative, and un-regulated forms of labour, regardless of how much potential an individual has and how deeply they aspire to autonomy, the most marginalized in the social order will inevitably be consigned to such labour roles. Although a lucky individual might escape this fate, these instances appear to be the exceptions—the anomalies—and not the rule. For the most underprivileged in the collective, the odds are heavily stacked against them, which makes enduring a life of limited autonomy likely. The liberal ideal of the autonomous individual struggles to materialize, except as aspirational, in these conditions, where the imbalance of power has left the most disadvantaged describing their experiences at work as though they are 'scared to fart without a good excuse'. Survival in conditions where even bowel and bladder movements are under an employer's command requires developing resilience to gruelling and humiliating working conditions.

It is in this context that an alternative normative orientation becomes visible. Individuals in the English precariat experience the world differently to how advantaged individuals do. From the perspective of those in Paul's community, it is easier to grasp that autonomy is not a given, a shared reality, but only something aspired to in the distance. While participants in Paul's community pursue autonomy, in conditions where it is out of reach, they require and access the support of others. Instead of acting exclusively on the logic of self-advancement, they live by other norms, such as by prioritizing family and kin. Criminal lawyers and criminologists must gain a better appreciation of this different normative orientation to grasp the conflicts that surface among those most directly affected by criminal justice processes. It is to this task I now turn. In the next chapters, we will illuminate a moral framework operative in Paul's community, rooted not in autonomy, but an alternative logic of mutuality.

A Helping Hand

I waited in the kitchen for my father to return home from work. It had gone 23:20, he was running late.

The floodlight marked his arrival. I ran into the garden to open the gates so the van could be parked up and unloaded. Cigarette trays and a tub full of coins were taken inside, empty crates were refilled with two-litre bottles of *Irn Bru*.

'Sandwiches?'

'I fancy fish and chips tonight,' my father said, turning the oven on. I took a box of fish and bag of chips from the freezer and laid out the food on a tray. He set the alarm, and as the oven heated, he attached a can opener to a *Happy Shopper* 39p tin of mushy peas and wound it round. 'Are you coming to walk the dog?'

We walked the dog together most evenings; it was an unspoken understanding that my presence in the kitchen when my father finished work was a precursor to our night-time walks. He rarely asked if I was joining him, unless he had something he needed to talk about.

'That'll be nice,' I said, picking up an additional coat from the hallway, feeling a mix of interest and apprehension about what we might discuss.

My father dropped a heavy rubber ball, the size of a cricket ball, in the garden. A signal we were leaving. Its repeated thump against the concrete ground sent our large black dog, Twister, into frenzy. Twister snapped the ball up, spiralling around in chaotic rings, in accordance with his name. My father managed to attach a metal chain to the spiked dog collar.

We didn't go straight out of the gate as usual. My father first went into the garden shed and opened the spare freezer. From it he took several microwavable meals—roast dinners, curries, pizzas, and fish—piling them into a white freezer bag.

We then left the garden without explanation.

Instead of our normal route, down an alleyway to the sports field across the road, we headed through a maze of passages at the front of the house.

A Precarious Life. Roxana Willis, Oxford University Press. © Roxana Willis 2023.
DOI: 10.1093/oso/9780198855149.003.0004

A Helping Hand   **63**

This part of the estate remained reminiscent of the old Lincoln project, before the council demolished its unruly core.

'I need to drop something off,' my father said. 'Justin, a lad I've known since he was a kid, is in a difficult situation.'

I nodded, as he continued.

'He popped on the van earlier and asked me to tick him a packet of crisps. I gave him a few bags, and said it was good to see him, it'd been a while. Turns out he was recently let out of St Michael's, and hasn't got a penny to his name. Too paranoid to ask for help.'

'Does he have family?' I asked.

'His mum and sisters washed their hands of him—had enough of him robbing them. He got hooked on heroin in his teens, and the addiction followed him since.'

We weaved through alleys and walkways, my father expertly navigating the warren.

'The last few years he's been in and out of hospital for a tirade of physical and mental health problems. It's a real shame; he's a lovely lad with terrific potential. If he'd grown up in better circumstances, it'd be a very different story.'

We stopped at a row of attached houses about five minutes from ours. My father softly tapped a letterbox on a faded blue door, flakes of paint peeling from the edge.

A figure appeared behind the frosted glass. Its shadow hung motionless in the frame.

'Justin, it's Paul—Paul-on-the-van—I'm walking the dog with my daughter. Here's a bit of food to tide you over.'

The shadow paused behind the glass a moment more. Then the door opened to a young, bony face; eerily handsome, beneath the greying skin of a life robbed too fast.

'Alright Paul,' Justin croaked. 'Nice to see ya bud.'

2
The Necessity of Community

Using Pierre Bourdieu's theory to comprehend the experiences of socio-economically disadvantaged groups presents certain limits. Although Bourdieusian analysis is apt for exploring the struggles that disadvantaged individuals experience in formal social fields like the school and other state institutions, building on the insights of Beverly Skeggs (2004, 2011), I find Bourdieu's analysis does not provide a comprehensive account of the alternative form of life operative in Paul's precariat community. Bourdieusian theory does help elucidate the individualistic starting point which state institutions in Britain tend to presuppose; that is, Bourdieu's work effectively demonstrates how an individual can amass greater or fewer social resources throughout their lifetime, affecting how well they perform in a given social space. Yet, as we saw in Chapter 1, not all individuals in English society are born into conditions that are conducive for the development of autonomous selves. It seems to me that Bourdieu's work does not elucidate well the experiences of those living in circumstances which constrain the pursuit of autonomy. We require an alternative theory to appreciate a different way of being in the world.

As noted in the Introduction, for an individual to be independent, they must have their basic needs met, such as access to food, water, shelter, security, and so on, which requires some form of social support (see Nussbaum and Sen, 1993; Sen, 1999; Nussbaum, 2000; King, 2012). For many British citizens, the state facilitates access to a comprehensive social support system, either directly through the delivery of services or indirectly by providing a legal framework that regulates socio-economic activity. Worries about meeting daily needs can be kept at a distance when the state recognizes property rights, and protects capital accumulation, financial transactions, inheritance, and so on, which allows advantaged individuals to amass wealth and purchase the basics (and more). Individuals in these circumstances are free to invest their time and resources (social, cultural, and economic) in the pursuit of other ends, such as abstract learning in school. Under such conditions, it is easy to take the role of the

A Precarious Life. Roxana Willis, Oxford University Press. © Roxana Willis 2023.
DOI: 10.1093/oso/9780198855149.003.0005

state for granted and overlook how advantaged individuals are deeply dependant on state-maintained social structures. If we think about property, for example, these bundles of rights have come to be accepted as the natural, unquestioned order of things (the *doxa*); yet achieving this established order has involved centuries of exclusion and discrimination, the infliction of state violence, and continuing state action to protect private interests (cf. Bhandar, 2018; Hay, 1975; Savage et al., 1995; Thompson, 1975). Private property has only become normative and appears natural in a history of state-enforced practices. Thus, if we ignore the role of the state here, if privileges are concealed and relegated to the background, then individuals—now not obviously resting on any supports—appear to have achieved success fully or mostly on their own. We may thereby abstract them as complete and as capable of independent survival. However, without extensive social contributions, the ideal of autonomy instantiated by such figures cannot be realized.

When the state is truly absent or unsupportive, an individual's co-dependency on others becomes apparent. This is particularly evident in a classed society, where the state does not represent the interests of all equally and fails to afford security to those most precariously positioned in the social order. In England and Wales, for example, the state fosters conditions for precarious employment by implementing weak employment protection laws that favour the power of employers to define the terms of the contract and so forth (see Hayes, 2017). Moreover, the English and Welsh legislator further aids advantaged classes when it reduces security of tenure for residential lettings, permits the market and landlords to control rent prices, and erodes tenant eviction protections (see the Housing Act 1985 and subsequent legislation). In such a legislative landscape, the state does not support the material interests of socio-economically disadvantaged individuals to the extent it supports those of privileged individuals. Consequently, disadvantaged persons must pursue alternative means, outside of the formal system, to 'get by' in times of need; they cannot rely on state institutions.

The social conditions for individuals thus differ depending on how they are situated in relation to the state, which creates different orientations to the world. Those who have a certain degree of financial security do not need to exclusively direct personal resources toward ensuring daily survival; instead, they can be invested in the aid of personal advancement. This is where Bourdieu's conceptions of capital most readily apply; social resources human beings acquire and embody during their lifetimes enable them to

66 The Necessity of Community

generate further advantage. However, for those who face a greater degree of economic uncertainty, rather than being oriented to self-advancement, individuals must focus on securing their basic needs and directing social resources towards these ends. Such different conditions inevitably produce an alternative orientation that is less about advancement in the future, and more about subsisting in the moment. As Skeggs (2011: 506) explains:

> living with precarity produces different orientations towards others: 'you never know when it will happen to you', clichés that condense the recognition that future problems may be shared. 'Keeping an eye out for those less well off' has sound economic reasons when insecurity is on the horizon, pre-disposing them to different forms of sociality than individualisation.

Accordingly, a key thesis of this chapter is that different orientations affect how people relate to others, and to make those differences salient, to render those relationships intelligible, we need to shift our theoretical approach to consider the normative frameworks people live within.

Scholars often use Bourdieusian social capital theory to analyse relational forms. This theory explores the ways in which individuals can draw from relational networks, which form an important source of personal advantage (Bourdieu, 1986; Coleman, 1990; Portes, 1998). This literature distinguishes between 'strong ties' and 'weak ties' (Putnam, 2000): strong ties are pictured as the types of relationships commonly fostered in disadvantaged spaces, which involve close, tightknit networks of family and friends (Coleman, 1988, 1990; Hagan, 1993; Horvat et al., 2003); weak ties, by contrast, are conceived as more frequently cultivated among advantaged groups, which, being looser, bind together more distant relationships, such as between acquaintances (Horvat et al., 2003; Newman and Massengill, 2006). Theorists such as Robert Putman (2000) and Amitai Etzioni (1996) have suggested that in order for liberal societies to overcome the apparent crises of social fragmentation and social ills, governments ought to foster the growth of relational networks and thus restore community. These ideas have been heavily influential in criminology (e.g. Kubrin and Weitzer, 2003; Morenoff et al., 2001; Pattillo, 1998; Rose and Clear, 1998; Sampson et al., 1997), and fed into the so-called communitarian policies of the British New Labour government, which from 1997 to 2010 encouraged forms of volunteering throughout the criminal justice system as a way to rebuild communities (Fyfe and Milligan, 2003; Miliband, 1994; Morison, 2000).

The Necessity of Community **67**

While social capital theory might be apt for theorizing the networks of relatively advantaged individuals, and especially those poised to become socially mobile, I propose that it fails to capture in full the relational logic of disadvantaged spaces. Since social capital theory does not engage with the differential role of the state in the lives of disadvantaged individuals, it builds on the mistaken presupposition that all individuals start from a position of autonomy and self-interest. For advantaged individuals, who benefit from the social structure upheld by the state, attaining autonomy is more feasible, and under such conditions, relationships can function as resources which generate further advantage; the logic of social capital here makes sense. However, disadvantaged individuals, not supported by the state structure in the same way, must direct relational resources towards maintaining an informal support system: i.e. they must use social resources to create what advantaged individuals already have. When people need relational networks to subsist, they cannot simply redirect them towards personal advancement. While my focus here is on social capital theory, in my view much mainstream theory begins from similar presuppositions about the nature of the self; if so, it will therefore often be inappropriate to rely on such theory to comprehend the experiences of the least advantaged.

Rather than conceiving of relational connections thinly—as a series of individual desires and agreements to connect with one another for the purpose of self-advancement—I build on the work of Insa Koch (2018b) to offer a deeper view of relationships in Paul's community, which constitute the substance of a complex informal support structure. Cathrine Degnen's (2005, 2013) work may help us comprehend this structure. In an ethnographic study of an English village, Degnen observes villagers regularly engaging in sharing practices: residents frequently shared information, stories, and memories about people present and past, often interwoven with the physical space, which Degnen suggests formed intricate webs of connectivity and meaning (cf. Geertz, 1973). Notably, as well as villagers sharing information about people in their own networks, Degnen also found that they shared information about other people's networks, expanding the assortment of people known to each other to varying degrees. Connections therefore included intergenerational links to the past and expansive links across the present. In an earlier study in a northern English town, Jeanette Edwards (2000: 139) offers further insight on types of sharing practices, which includes the sharing of a cup of tea, kind words, a joint (cannabis), collective anecdotes, and jokes. As I show in this chapter, we can imagine similar practices of remembering and sharing in Paul's

68 The Necessity of Community

community as multiple and intricate overlapping threads which form the tapestry of an informal sphere of social support that shapes what I call the framework of mutuality.

For us to understand the logic of this informal order, rather than relying on theory that begins with the autonomous individual as the unit of analysis, we need theory that is suited to the kind of relationships that form in precariat conditions. 'Mutuality' is an anthropologically informed theory suggested by David Graeber (2011) to explain a relational logic that is found in most societies, at different moments in time: instead of goods being *exchanged* in order to personally benefit, sometimes goods are *shared* to ensure each person has enough. The spirit of mutuality reflects, I think, the internal logic of what E. P. Thompson (1993a, 1993b) refers to as a moral economy, prevalent in eighteenth-century England prior to the growth of a new political economy which valorized free-market principles. It is with Graeber and Thompson's work in mind that I advance the notion of a normative framework of mutuality.

To bring the good of mutuality into view, we may have to shift theoretical underpinnings by putting aside the contractarian view of society, in which (in principle or practice) lone individuals voluntarily enter relationships which advantage them. Instead of this disengaged view of the subject, we acknowledge that human beings are partially constituted by social relations. And indeed for those without privilege—those less supported by the state—it is easier to recognize that the self and the community's welfare are not deeply in tension, because the self is more plainly experienced as partly constituted by the community: the concerns and interests of self and other overlap in so many ways. Accordingly, to understand social interactions among the precariat, I suggest we begin from a different ontological assumption than that of the free-floating, initially self-serving individual (following Skeggs, 2004, 2011).

Once we appreciate our co-dependency, the conviction that human beings are inherently self-interested by nature also requires scrutiny. Influential theories often start with the presumption of individuals as concerned with advancing their own interests over and above the welfare of others (e.g. Smith, 1976; Rawls, 1971; Hobbes, 1968; Durkheim, 2012). Although liberal society has increasingly become structured in such a way that self-interested behaviour yields reward in various spheres of life, this structure does not thereby confer such a nature on humans (see MacIntyre, 1981; Sandel, 1982; Walzer, 1983; Taylor, 1985a). In fact, it is quite plausible that human beings are, first and foremost, co-operative, which is precisely

The Necessity of Community   **69**

what enabled humankind to advance (cf. Bregman, 2020; Graeber, 2011; Graeber and Wengrow, 2021; Taylor, 2018). In keeping with these findings, anthropological and sociological studies among socio-economically disadvantaged groups have recurringly identified the existence of caring and collaborative forms of relationships which defy dominant self-interested value systems (Degnen, 2005; Edwards, 2000; Evans, 2006; Gillies, 2007; Koch, 2018b; McKenzie, 2015; Skeggs, 1997; Smith, 2012; Strathern, 1981; K. Tyler, 2015; Dalmiya, 2016 among others). Taken together, this scholarship presents a compelling challenge to the presumption of the self-interested actor by nature. Instead, it seems more accurate to cast the individualized self as a moral ideal advanced in liberal societies, which certain subjects may begin to realize by virtue of their position in the social order. For those who are structurally prevented from achieving the ideal, caring and co-operative relations continue to form the substance of social life and thus hold moral weight: they live within and are primarily oriented by a framework of mutuality.

As an alternative to the individualized self, Graeber (2011: 94) suggests a communist way of thinking, in which certain human relationships operate on the principle of 'from each according to their abilities, to each according to their needs.' Graeber (2011: 95–6) contends that we often follow this communist rule; for example, when we collaborate on a common project or experience emergency situations, those with the ability to help the collective often navigate towards supporting those in need. G. A. Cohen's (2009) example of a camping trip aptly illustrates Graeber's point: when a group goes on a camping trip, resources are shared, and different tasks are often assigned (e.g. hunting, fishing, cooking, cleaning, etc.) based on the strengths of those in the group, with all partaking in the outcomes. Cohen notes that while economic exchange principles could be applied on the trip, not only would these be time-consuming and tedious, it would also undermine the nature of the whole collective endeavour. I deem it quite plausible that the closer a community finds itself to conditions of real-world necessity, the more noticeable are the collective principles which apply among the group.

We could view such collective principles in terms of reciprocity. Yet Graeber (2011: 103) urges us to think in terms of mutuality instead, pointing to a mentality of sharing rather than self-gain. Reciprocity is often understood along the lines of, *I do something for you, and in return you do something for me as and when is required or appropriate*. This relational form is taken as a given in both Bourdieu's (1977) and Marcel Mauss's

70 The Necessity of Community

(2002) analyses of gift exchange. Yet something can be given without the expectation of return. Indeed, Graeber (2011: 103) notes that the practice of giving might serve a deeper and 'eternal' purpose (i.e. stretching beyond the lifespan of any single individual, or even generational group) of maintaining a normative social order which ensures that those in need will be helped by the wider collective, so that if a community member *were* to experience hardship, they could feel assured that the collective *would* act as a source of support. By making this move, Graeber's account of giving begins to align with how Georgina Stewart (2017: 8) recommends we understand particular Māori practices, such as gift giving, as 'taking account of the kinship relationships between humans, gods and non-human aspects of the natural world'. This mutuality outlook departs from the dominant liberal view of individuals tacitly agreeing to help one another in return for future reward, and is more attuned to African philosophical thought as captured by the Bantu concept of Ubuntu, which recognizes an ontology of co-being.[1] Ndjodi Ndeunyema (2019: 342) describes Ubuntu as a multi-generational and multi-dimensional concept that embraces 'interconnectedness, common humanity, collective sharing, obedience, humility, solidarity, communalism, dignity and responsibility to each other'.[2] On this view, rather than using the words 'mutual exchange' or 'mutual responsibility', 'mutuality' better captures the logic of certain sharing practices (Graeber, 2011; cf. Bauman, 1991).

In this chapter, I sketch a picture of mutuality as a normative framework that makes fuller sense of relationships in Paul's community than does individualistic theory, rooted in the presumption of the self-interested actor. I accordingly focus on moments of mutuality in a comparable way to how a scholar might zoom in on moments of conflict. This is not to suggest that the community simply directs itself towards mutual ends in a simple and unproblematic way, nor to allude to some idealistic form of community

---

[1] This also resembles the Swahili notion of Ujamaa, as developed in Julius Nyerere (1967, 1968), which centres an idea of how we become human through our relationships with others. For further discussion, see de Sousa Santos (2018).

[2] Since these alternative bodies of thought have helped me to see beyond the liberal framework, I nod to them here. However, we cannot simply apply the philosophy of Ubuntu to the English context without some distortion, because African thought and experience are core to these ideas (see Broodryk 2002; Ramose 2001). Comparably, in reference to Māori concepts, Stewart (2017: 7) reminds us that such notions 'straddle multiple dimensions simultaneously'. Accordingly, to apply Māori concepts appropriately, we must comprehend the historically embedded philosophical context, which requires deeper engagement than space permits here.

where each person is supportive and cooperative. On the contrary, as is acutely apparent in the chapters that follow, these relationships are fraught with tensions and divisions. However, because these features of precariat life have been unobserved, misunderstood, and misrepresented in a great deal of mainstream scholarship, this chapter brings the framework of mutuality into clearer view, so that these features of precariat life are more readily recognized moving forwards.

I begin the analysis by setting the scene. For us to comprehend the nature of informal support among Paul and his neighbours, we must first acknowledge the material insecurity that precariously positioned individuals face. Just as school and work pose structural challenges, so too does day-to-day life on the estate. Accordingly, I open the chapter with an introduction to the Lincoln estate, which is where Paul's relational community and van route formed. A socio-historical overview of the deterioration of the estate reveals the limits of state provisions for this disadvantaged section of English society, and a corresponding need for reliance on others. Next, we examine how community participants managed to subsist without the full assistance of the state, and how a variety of sharing practices, which operate on the logic of a mutuality framework, constitute a matrix of support. In the final section, we see how support extended beyond Paul's relational community: the imagined, town-wide community of Corby provided a further layer of survival.

'Estate of Fear'

The state funded a housing development in the west of Corby under the New Towns Act 1965 to accommodate industrial growth and the expansion of the steelworks. The Kingswood development, inspired by the 'Radburn Concept' of the American architects Stein & Wright, comprised four council estates, one of which was the Lincoln, where Paul's relational community developed (cf. Ravetz, 2001; McKenzie, 2015: 35). Paul and his first wife moved onto the Lincoln when it was initially built, accessing a council home when they conceived a child in their teenage years. The young couple found themselves in a life of seeming independence, with most of the trimmings of adulthood—waged employment, an affordable garden home, an infant. In early years, when work was available and the experience of being 'grown-up' novel, it was an exciting and hopeful time. However, the heydays were not to last. The Lincoln estate became one of

72 The Necessity of Community

the most socio-economically deprived places in Britain and has been subjected to two waves of state demolition in a purported attempt to tackle the difficulties.

The implementation of the Radburn Concept in Corby had structural problems from the outset (cf. Koch, 2018a). One fundamental aspect of the design emphasizes privacy by turning the main living areas inwards to face private gardens, rather than looking outwards into wider residential communities. However, instead of giving residents sufficient space for privacy, the solitude built into the Lincoln estate was rather illusory. The original architectural design called for low-density housing, but British council housing consisted of rows and terraces rather than detached or semi-detached plots (Corby Development and Corby District Council, 1977). Consequently, much of the Corby Kingswood development was built to accommodate high-density housing, for a neighbourhood of over 2,000 homes (Hamilton, 1976). The Lincoln estate had the highest density housing, comprising 587 dwellings, mostly located along the 'spine' in the form of flats and maisonettes (Grundy, 1966): '115 persons per acre was an approximate average figure [on the spine] compared with approximately 65 persons per acre for the whole of the Lincoln estate and 70 per acre for the whole of the Kingswood Neighbourhood' (Corby Development and Corby District Council, 1977: 21). The spine provided the backbone of the Lincoln estate, hosting most of the social facilities. Paul rented two homes consecutively from the council, both connected to the Lincoln spine.

Within a decade of being built, problems on the Lincoln estate surfaced. The Corby Development Corporation (1976), the authority responsible for building and managing the Lincoln estate at the time, recorded problems including 'noise, disturbance, concentrated pedestrian flow, vandalism, break-ins etc.' The architects received awards for such a successful design, and yet residents on the Lincoln estate made frequent complaints. A sociological survey explored this disjuncture, finding that while people mostly favoured the design, their problems included small cupboards, no upstairs heating, expensive underfloor heating, insufficient space, noise, and living too near a public house (Journal of Corby Consumer Group, 1969). Notably, several of these early problems related to the dense nature of the build—squeezing families into small spaces made for tensions (see Hanley, 2017; Koch, 2018a; Willis, 2009).

Documents in the local archive indicate that the local authority received numerous complaints about life on the Lincoln spine. Security proved especially inadequate, which residents at the time claimed was 'instanced by

'Estate of Fear' **73**

the number of break-ins and muggings' (Kingswood Working Party, 1977). A resident in one of the Lincoln flats described the living conditions in a letter of complaint sent to the council in 1974:

> The Kingswood estates are becoming difficult places in which to live peacefully. For example, in the space of approximately eighteen months my flat has been burgled twice, entry attempted on another occasion, and our wastepaper chute set alight filling the stairwell and the apartments with dense acrid smoke.[3]

The Radburn design appeared to worsen these problems because the chain of alleyways that interlinked the entire Kingswood project made the area difficult for outsiders to navigate (Corby Development Corporation, 1965; Housing Committee, 1977). A doctor, for example, wrote a complaint to the local council in 1972 because he struggled to find a heart-attack patient in the confusing maze of the estate.[4] However, certain residents familiar with the area found the mystifying layout an advantage; for example, those wishing to avoid the police could use the roofs of higher flats to look out for police cars as they entered the estate, and then expertly escape through the labyrinth of passages only accessible by foot. By increasing the density of the Radburn design, the government had inadvertently created the perfect conditions for the game of 'cops and robbers' (similarly, see Fraser, 2013; Hanley, 2017).

Tenants sent the Corby Development Corporation (1976; 1977) multiple requests to transfer from the Lincoln estate. In 1977, residents living on the Lincoln spine had sent eighty-six out of 240 requests for transfers in the whole Kingswood area. Ninety-four of all those requesting to transfer from the estate gave the reason that they disliked the area. Indeed, the Lincoln estate was gaining a reputation as an undesirable place to live. Properties on the spine were especially difficult to let and many became vacant (Housing Committee, 1976). In 1977, properties on the spine constituted almost 70 percent of empty Kingswood properties (Corby Development and Corby District Council, 1977: 26).

---

[3] Letter sent by Graham Plant, 60 Culross Walk, to Brigadier Hamilton, General Manager of Corby Development Corporation, dated 7th October 1974, received 9th October 1974 (available from the Northamptonshire Record Office).

[4] Letter sent by Dr Hollingworth to Mr. Perez at the Corby Development Corporation, dated 10th August 1972 regarding inadequate signposting (available from the Northamptonshire Record Office).

74   The Necessity of Community

Only the most socio-economically vulnerable—those with limited choice—accepted a council house on the Lincoln. This led tenants who belonged to a neighbourhood working group to claim that the estate was being 'used as "dumping grounds" for low standard tenants' (Kingswood Working Party, 1977). Another member of the neighbourhood association asserted that '[t]here seems to be a twin policy of sending "problem" families to estates that have a fair share of problems and of only allowing the "best" tenants to move to better estates' (Corby Development and Corby District Council, 1977: 65; cf. Power, 1987: 98). Here, we see residents using language which has a long history, further discussed in Chapter 6, about the deserving and underserving poor, and notions of 'problem families' advanced by welfare policy in Britain, to explain the challenges they faced (see Welshman, 2014).

Housing transfers in the 1970s set in motion a process that increased socio-economic disadvantage on the Lincoln estate. Further exacerbating inequality, the Thatcher government then implemented national policy which aimed to transform Britain into a nation of homeowners as part of a shift towards a deregulated, free-market economy (Glyn, 2006; Hall, 2021; Mullins and Murie, 2006). This economic ideology committed itself to de-industrialization, which led to the closure of the Corby steelworks and widespread unemployment. Accordingly, the British state at once inflicted economic insecurity on a large part of the Corby population and urged people to purchase council houses. Policies encouraging residents to purchase their homes included cuts to social housing expenditure, increased council rents, and subsidized mortgages (Cole and Furbey, 1994: 79–195). However, exercising the Right to Buy ultimately required purchasing power, and therefore not all had the choice to become a homeowner—those thrown into unemployment even less so (cf. Wacquant, 2007: 75–80).

Paul managed to stay self-employed after losing his job at the steelworks by running a mobile grocery van full time. Consequently, in being able to purchase a council house, Paul was in the minority of residents on the Lincoln estate. Paul and his first wife bought their three-bedroomed terraced house on the Lincoln spine from Corby Borough Council in 1980 for the discounted sum of £4,418, which Paul later re-mortgaged to cover his business costs. Paul cherished becoming a homeowner because it meant he and his family were no longer subjected to the interference of housing officers (see also Edwards, 2000: 127; Hyatt, 2003; Rogaly and Taylor, 2016: 61; K. Tyler, 2015: 1174). A desire for greater autonomy may have underlain his aspiration to become a homeowner and pursue self-employment; however,

'Estate of Fear' **75**

Paul spoke of a yearning to be free from state and employer coercion, rather than a longing to retreat from the collective. By owning his home and running his own business, Paul secured his place on the estate.

Most properties on the Lincoln estate remained council-owned, and especially the properties on and around the spine. Instead of purchasing property on the Lincoln, those with a degree of economic power tended to purchase property elsewhere. Therefore, mirroring the pattern of council housing transfers pre-1980, the Right to Buy empowered residents of relative socio-economic advantage to leave the estate, while residents with low (or no) incomes necessarily stayed put (cf. Page, 2000)—not everyone was structurally situated to have a choice, and some had fewer choices than others. The local council eventually sold off hard-to-sell properties on the Lincoln spine at significantly reduced rates, primarily to buy-to-let landlords, some of whom then rented them back to the council to fill a growing social housing need (cf. Balchin, 1985). Even after reducing prices, by 2005 almost 50 percent of Lincoln estate properties remained on Corby Borough Council's rent account (Corby Borough Council, 2007); in contrast, 71 percent of British housing was owner occupied (Morgan, 2007).

This policy landscape reveals the state as sometimes providing greater assistance to certain class sectors of society than others. The introduction of the Right to Buy did not support the interests of all (see Jones and Murie, 2008). Prior to its implementation, relatively privileged tenants possessed the most desirable council houses, and the least privileged possessed the least desirable properties. The state's privatization of housing cemented these pre-existing inequalities, since advantaged beneficiaries could acquire property that accrued greater economic value than property purchased in less favourable areas (Forrest and Murie, 1991: 101). Homeowners who did not benefit from the direct purchase of a council house indirectly benefited from rapidly rising property values, produced by increased demand for housing in the wake of mass privatization. Thus, while certain actors were afforded greater economic power and choice over where to live, options for the least advantaged were severely curtailed: a reduced pool of social housing remained available, predominantly in areas that others deemed undesirable to live in.

In addition to widening economic inequality, privatization heightened the tendency to stigmatize and blame the least advantaged. As noted in the Introduction, the autonomous moral ideal begins to form only as disadvantaged groups are classified as immoral and 'other'. Privatization from the 1980s onwards has shaped the present-day immoral figure, as government

76   The Necessity of Community

policy and media discourse then blames the most disadvantaged for having failed to exercise prudent economic choice, hence treating them as personally responsible for living in areas such as the Lincoln estate. Not only were residents on certain council estates stigmatized for living in these areas, they were also held responsible for making the areas bad (see Crump, 2002; McKenzie, 2015; Skeggs, 2004; I. Tyler, 2015; Wacquant, 2007; Watt, 2006). As Imogen Tyler (2015: 162) explains, '[t]he council estate became metonymic shorthand for the "new class of problem people", and the poverty associated with these places was imagined as a self-induced pathological condition'. In this way, the state could offload accountability for the effects of its policy—unemployment, poor quality housing, exposure to drugs and violence—onto the most disadvantaged in society.

In the shadow of these policies, the Lincoln estate became a place of concentrated disadvantage, housing the most unfortunate persons, who had limited access to resources or state assistance to address their complex social hardships. Under the weight of shame and stigma, addiction took hold of the Lincoln estate; heroin provided the most devastating effects. Government policy, combined with local news reporting, produced moral panic about the estate (cf. Hall et al., 2013; I. Tyler, 2015: 160): from the 1990s into the new millennium, newspaper headlines were rife with stories about violent crime, and the Lincoln was labelled an 'Estate of Fear' (see Ortenberg, 2008: 150). Residents who lived through the decades of state-induced decline have endured an inconceivable amount of loss. And in the absence of full state support, other ways to subsist and manage local problems have developed. For Paul and his multigenerational peers, survival has depended on the support, care, and solidarity of each other—here, a framework of mutuality shapes the social world.

Sharing Practices: An Informal Web of Support

Paul ran his mobile shop late into the night on an estate with a reputation for addiction, violence, disorder, and danger. This meant taking the van out every evening, like clockwork, alone, into isolated areas, with thousands of pounds' worth of goods. Not once was Paul robbed or violently harmed. Neither was his van or house ever broken into, which were located on the most deprived part of the estate, with a garage to its side filled with stock, including hundreds of packets of expensive cigarettes. As I see it, Paul and

Sharing Practices: An Informal Web of Support   77

his family were secure, possibly more so than they might have been elsewhere, because he was deeply embedded within relational webs which produced a collective striving for subsistence and the avoidance of harm.

Paul's van offers us a window into how an alternative orientation to the world operates for those in the precariat trying to survive on the periphery of mainstream society (cf. McKenzie, 2015). Rather than running the van to maximize profit, Paul's business worked on a different logic: he operated on the traditional model of giving people goods 'on tick' till payday (cf. Rogaly and Taylor, 2016: 100); accepted payment in pennies—many times customers entered the van in a desperate state, with a piggy bank in hand; sold single cigarettes and single nappies at a relative price no higher than their worth in multipack form; sourced decent quality, affordable products as alternatives to the more expensive brands so that people could access what they needed; sourced particular goods on request; would stock an item even if only one regular needed it; and always made sure consumables were considerably within their sell-by dates. Consequently, several residents I spoke with on the estate, while waiting for the van to arrive, described their preference for the van over other kinds of food suppliers in terms of trust. As a mother on the estate saw it, 'it's the community van'.

Over and above the exchange of goods and money, one of the most crucial things the van offered was time (cf. Skeggs, 2011: 509; Koch, 2018b: 175). When its horn sounded, community participants came out onto the street and spent time catching up with each other while in the queue. On several stops, especially on sunny days, residents congregated much earlier than Paul's arrival in order to spend longer together, often while children played. Importantly, the van provided only enough space so that just one person or small group could be served in the small entrance at a time, and queues outside did not rush those on the van; community participants described it as 'getting your turn' with Paul. The giving of time was crucial to what Paul did, and children could spend ten minutes or longer at the counter trying to decide how to spend their 50p pocket money while telling Paul about their day. Paul patiently listened and talked with the children to help build their confidence, and offered advice on problems they were experiencing, as he did with adults.

Commonly, a person would wait at the back of the queue, letting others go in front, so that they could have the last spot with Paul, who allotted the longest time to this place. A person usually took that spot when needing to talk with Paul about something more serious, either a problem with which they needed help or advice or longer-term support. For example, a

78 The Necessity of Community

woman I spoke with in her late twenties, who had experienced an extremely painful life, described Paul as her counsellor and said that she would have committed suicide had it not been for his emotional support on the van. Another woman described Paul as the only person to whom some of the elderly residents on the estate could talk, and they waited all day for the van's arrival. Others shared stories of how Paul helped them to understand the biology behind their opioid addiction and supported them through recovery; Paul once managed to convince a close friend not to retaliate against a drug dealer for giving her 'shit' heroin during a period of recovery, by explaining how methadone prevents heroin taking effect.

In addition to having an aptitude for problem solving, Paul never forgot a name—not only an individual's name, but their parents' names, and those of their parents before them. Some people I spoke with described being amazed, after having left the estate years before, that when they returned Paul still remembered them and their family, and the things they had talked about. Through such memory-sharing, Paul supported the maintenance of relational connections to the past as well as present (cf. Degnen, 2005, 2013). Moreover, by using his talents in this way, Paul reinforced the humanity of estate residents, countering the negative valuations imposed on children at school, adults at work, and through other interactions with the state and wider society (cf. Koch, 2018b; Smith, 2012). Rather than employing these talents in a more formalized setting where he could have advanced himself, Paul shared his talents with the collective, and in so doing he helped to reinforce a counter narrative: people on our estate matter.

Several English ethnographies have identified the importance of being known (see also Degnen, 2013; Hanley, 2017: ch 4; Koch, 2018b: ch 2; Rogaly and Taylor, 2016: ch 2; Smith, 2017b). For example, Edwards (2000: 8) interprets belonging in her research community as connected with knowing; more than simply coming from a place, Edwards explains that the notion of being 'born and bred' means also having an extensive knowledge of the locality, which includes the people, anecdotes, and the locality of events, past and present. In a more recent context, Lisa McKenzie (2015: 154–8) discusses the importance of 'being known' on a socio-economically deprived English council estate as a strategy for avoiding harm. While outsiders might view certain estates as dangerous and unsafe, for residents who are 'known' on the estate (in the right way), they can be among the most harmless places in the world, safe havens from stigma and judgement—places of love and support. Hence, Paul and participants in his community embrace a

Sharing Practices: An Informal Web of Support   79

different form of knowledge to that valorized by formal educational institutions (cf. Gillies, 2007; Lareau, 2011; Skeggs, 1997).

Some children on the estate who were later in life charged with serious criminal offences grew up knowing Paul as someone to whom they could talk in difficult moments. During the fieldwork, some young men on the estate who had been convicted for drug dealing sent Paul a humorous 'I miss you' card from prison, with the message 'have a drink on us' inside, and an unused teabag enclosed. At another point in the fieldwork, a mother from the estate facing a prison sentence asked Paul to become a foster parent to her toddler. One woman I interviewed described Paul as 'more of a dad than the arseholes my mum brought home', a man in his twenties described Paul as 'a father to us all', a young single mum called him the 'granddad of Corby', and a timid young boy I met on the street pronounced him as 'my best friend'. Paul upheld community norms and looked out for others, especially those who were most vulnerable and exposed to violence. By being embedded in the life and norms of the community, Paul contributed to making the estate a safer place for himself and others alike.

The above discussion illustrates some community norms, mediated through the social role of Paul's van. Within the community, the social practice and its meaning was a given, but an outsider might misconstrue it. Paul shared one such example, which demonstrates the protective nature of the community in turn. On this occasion, a police officer happened to drive past as Paul sounded his horn one night to let people at the back of the estate know he had arrived. According to Paul, the 'bolshie young policeman' came onto the van and demanded to know what Paul was doing making such noise after hours and attracting a crowd, looking to mark Paul's behaviour as 'antisocial'. Before Paul had a chance to respond, residents who had gathered around the van turned on the policeman, telling him to 'get tae fuck' and to 'go and catch some real criminals instead of bothering Paul who's just doing his job.' Paul laughed when he recounted the story, describing the police officer as turning and leaving the situation at a very fast pace, never returning to trouble the van again.[5]

Throughout this discussion, we have seen how the practices enveloping Paul's van operated outside of the logic of profit and exchange. Although Paul ran a business, which he relied on to support his family, profit was not

---

[5] Anecdotes such as this are reminiscent of the historic tendency of working-class communities to resist the impositions of the state and police authority in nineteenth-century England (see Wood, 2004: 134).

80   The Necessity of Community

his primary motivation; there were far more profitable ways Paul could have run the shop or used his skills and talents. For Paul, sociality and support took priority. Take, for instance, another fieldwork observation. At one of Paul's afternoon stops, an impatient man stood in the queue, seemingly unfamiliar with the norms of the van. Growing increasingly agitated by the line's glacial pace, the man tried to rush Paul and the mother and child he was serving. Several times, the man shouted toward the van, 'hurry up!'. When Paul heard the command, he came off the van, furious, and told the man to 'fuck off' because he was 'getting fuck all' by acting like that. Unsupported by the crowd, the man left. This offers an empirical example of what Skeggs (2011: 509) describes as a value model based on relationality—'time and energy with and for others'—over the economic logic of profit-making. Connectivity characterized the social practice of the van; it incorporated a deeper, more fundamental purpose for its participants than self-advancement—the self *was* advanced, but through time spent with others rather than through, say, one-upmanship or consumption.

Paul's centrality to the practices discussed in this section should not lead us to conclude that without him, such practices would not develop. Consider also the main gatekeeper in Koch's work, Tracy, who tirelessly supports other locals in need; an assortment of people in socio-economically disadvantaged areas perform these roles. Rather than stemming from individual action, practices of sociability are part of a wider normative order, a framework of mutuality, within which community participants are collectively embedded. As an illustration of this wider phenomenon, in the next sections I examine several forms of sharing between Paul's neighbours, beyond the activities on the van.

Sharing advice, skills, and assistance

The instrumental support that advantaged individuals receive from the state is relegated to the background of daily practices. That is why we can easily overlook what enables the attainment of autonomy, such as property rights, investments, inheritance, and qualifications. Conversely, the informal normative order that Paul and his peers rely on lacks state recognition and formalization. Perhaps this is why, as I show, those within the community consistently and overtly affirm the availability of informal support, such as is conducted through day-to-day sharing practices.

Paul's neighbours regularly shared advice with one another about the job centre and benefits claims, local bus services, food takeaways, builders, painters and decorators, and suggestions on where to purchase specific items (cf. Mollona, 2009: ch 3). Additionally—and very often—mothers shared parenting tips, for example to help out newer mothers seeking help (cf. Jensen, 2018). Moreover, Paul's neighbours frequently lent items to one another, e.g. household electrical equipment, computer equipment, and tools for renovation and decorating. At least three community participants borrowed large items such as cars so that they could travel to places further afield for family days out and to visit relatives. I observed a general enthusiasm to assist others, or otherwise regretful expressions of being unable to help.

On rarer occasions, I observed a handful of Paul's friends attempt to trade goods on the logic of exchange. For example, in response to a teenage boy who asked to borrow a phone charger, another teenage boy offered to sell his old one. In another instance, a man proposed to sell someone his old computer. This indicates that some in the community gave precedence to income through sale of goods. Notably, no-one visibly responded to the offers of sale, perhaps suggesting that the practice of selling an item when someone requests to borrow it is not widely accepted or acted upon.

We saw in the last chapter that participants in Paul's community often asked friends for advice about job openings, and shared information when companies were 'taking on' (cf. Mollona, 2009: 29–30; Rogaly and Taylor, 2016: 82). At times, participants sought more specific advice. For example, a woman asked, 'my nurse friends, how do you deal with panic when things go wrong with the patient? And how do you not feel responsible when someone dies? I'm worried I might not be able to handle these things.' In response, friends gave advice, and several offered to speak further over coffee or nominated another friend to help.

Paul's peers also helped each other apply for jobs. In the following conversation, Natalie offers to help her friend prepare a curriculum vitae (cf. Koch, 2018b: 58–9).

GEMMA: Can anyone help me sort out my CV and show me how to send it out for jobs? I'm desperate!

NATALIE: Of course hen email it over and I'll sort it out for you

GEMMA: I can't even do stuff like that. I'm a complete dummy when it comes to computers, that's why I work in factories! But I'm a hard worker

82 The Necessity of Community

NATALIE: I'll drop round after work. Once we get your CV up to date, I'll show you how to work your emails. You're not stupid, it's a piece of piss once someone shows you how.

Several of Paul's younger peers struggled with computer literacy, which is a skill that might be taken for granted in other class sectors among the same age demographics. Even a teenager I spent time with on the estate had great difficulty using a computer and could only access the internet by borrowing his mother's phone. Illiteracy further heightened his difficulty; he relied on broken phonetic text speech to communicate when he eventually got online. In response to Gemma's self-deprecating comment in the above extract, where she describes herself as a 'complete dummy' for lacking computer skills, Natalie astutely comments that 'it's a piece of piss once someone shows you how.' Indeed, like all skills, when we have an opportunity to learn, practise, and master them, it is as though they come naturally (see Bourdieu, 2000).

Rather than treating Gemma as a socio-economic competitor, Natalie supports her friend in the search for employment. My wider observations indicate that providing support with job applications, skills development, and examinations was common in Paul's community. Again, Paul provides a helpful further example. Two chance meetings during the fieldwork revealed that Paul had tutored others on the estate, including a man I met at a funeral, and the child of a woman whom I spoke with on the estate. On both occasions, Paul had given maths tuition to help them pass exams. Paul also taught a couple of other residents on the estate how to build their own computer.

In Bourdieu's terms, we could view Natalie and Paul (and others who provide this kind of assistance) as sources of social capital, since they provide support with skills development within the network, which aids the personal advancement of other individuals. However, I find that this application of Bourdieusian theory fails to capture the practice in full; moreover, it can only process these events as a deficient form of the social capital ideal. For, in contrast to socio-economically advantaged individuals, who might have powerful connections that generate lucrative employment opportunities for those in their network (Ball, 2003; Granovetter, 1973, 1974), opportunities shared among disadvantaged groups such as Paul's are of limited reproductive power (Bourdieu, 1984). For instance, instead of sharing information about (say) an internship at the BBC, community participants share information about local factories looking for workers. Similarly,

Sharing Practices: An Informal Web of Support   83

when Paul and his neighbours offer each other support with examinations or job applications, the help encompasses only the skills embodied by those within the network. Overall, then, the value of social capital in Paul's community is of minimal generative effect; it does not aid the accumulation of resources in the same way that access to advantaged networks might. Thus, theorized in terms of social capital, we can only understand these events as somehow defective—as behaviour that mimics the social capital practices of the privileged, but without conferring generative advantages (cf. Skeggs and Loveday, 2012: 475–6; Skeggs and Wood, 2012: 7).

Indeed, the unequal effect of social capital in a classed society is core to Bourdieu's development of the concept. Unlike accounts that treat social capital as an ultimate good (Coleman, 1988; Etzioni, 1993; Putnam, 2000), Bourdieu's analysis reveals that the very operation of social capital requires some individuals and groups to have advantage over others, and hence its overall effect is unequal (see also DeFilippis, 2001; Gillies and Edwards, 2006). Bourdieu (1986) points out that in order for these social networks to generate advantage for the capital holder, value must lie precisely in their being exclusive and out of reach to those external to them—social capital operates as a source of distinction and works through exclusion. Hence, Bourdieu's analysis might lead us to view social capital activity in Paul's community as mimicking the role it plays for advantaged groups, just to a lesser effect (cf. Comaroff and Comaroff, 2006 b). As I see it, this fails to capture the true nature of the practice and its inherent value.

What is more, social capital theory does not account for those instances of wider information-sharing about job openings and other forms of support in Paul's community, since, in those cases, such information is not kept exclusive to maximize exchange value. Instead of explaining support in Paul's community through an individualistic frame in the mould of social capital theory, we can take an emic perspective of the practice and reveal something deeper and more significant—something we only grasp when we read a thicker description of relationships. In my view, rather than being motivated by competition and gaining advantage, support in Paul's community is better explained in terms of mutuality and care. Regular and wide-scope forms of sharing within the community operate to weave, as it were, a web of support upon which participants can rely, if and when they need to (Degnen, 2005; Edwards, 2000). This process appears not much concerned with reciprocity, since more advantaged community participants might contribute comparably more resources than others to the sharing pool and be fortunate to rarely need assistance themselves. Instead,

84 The Necessity of Community

community participants redistributed resources to those in need, with the effect that the collective as a whole can subsist in unpredictable times of hardship (cf. Walkerdine and Jimenez, 2012).

Given the alternative interpretation I am offering, the above examples of intra-community support, such as helping each other to access qualifications and sharing employment opportunities, are far more significant than we would deem them to be if we saw them only as ineffective attempts to mimic the practices of the privileged. By frequently asking for assistance and visibly helping others, community participants carry out an informal system of support, the value of which stretches beyond the logic of exchange. Supportive parties treat beneficiaries as valuable members of a community, affirming that others are there for them and they are not alone. In the process, those providing assistance manifest a commitment to the norms of a framework of mutuality and show themselves to be a good person by the standards of the community (following Koch, 2018b; Smith, 2017b; see below). And those who participate in and observe these sharing practices gain a sense of assurance that a system of informal support exists, on which anyone might need to rely at some point in their lifetime.

Love and emotional support

Caring relationships are the substance of support among Paul's neighbours. Mothers demonstrated extensive care for their children, and the position of being a mother and grandmother mattered greatly (see Evans, 2006; Gillies, 2006, 2007; Koch, 2018b; Skeggs and Loveday, 2012). The depth of such sentiment speaks for itself in the following announcement by a soon-to-be grandmother:

> I carried my kids, wore the stretch marks, bore the pains of labour, nursed them when they were sick, sat with them when they couldn't sleep, put clothes on their back, and gave them unconditional love. They left this home as exceptional adults – not perfect, but no one is. And that's why I'm a proud mummy and soon to be granny!

Likewise, fatherhood mattered greatly and multiple men publicly declared their commitment to fatherhood. For example, a teenage boy proclaimed that 'being a father is the most important role I'll ever take on, if I do this right then nothing else really matters in life'. A man in his twenties echoed

Sharing Practices: An Informal Web of Support 85

the sentiment: 'any boy can be a dad but it takes a man to be a father, recognise your mistakes, rectify them, and be the person your child deserves'. And a man in his thirties succinctly announced, 'my life is my kids'.

Parents often expressed love for children in the context of economic hardship. For instance, some, especially around Christmas, expressed disappointment that they did not have enough money to celebrate the event 'properly' by providing lots of gifts. One mother said, 'it makes [her] feel inferior' knowing how much other children will receive; however, she planned to reconcile this by giving her children 'plenty of cuddles and love'. Mothers at Easter spoke of similar challenges, e.g. at the trend to give children gifts in addition to Easter eggs. In response, several mothers in Paul's community insisted that love was enough. As one explained, 'mine got a few Easter eggs and that's it. All your kids need is a warm bed and clean clothes, a full tummy and plenty of love. Quality not quantity'.

Friendships are also important in Paul's community, and good friends are akin to family (see also Koch, 2018b; Stacey, 1990; Stack, 1974). Hence, people often spoke openly about love and loyalty for friends. A woman in her thirties expressed a widely shared sentiment: 'a friend is one of the nicest things you can be and one of the best things you can have'. Another woman offers related advice: 'Some people have their priorities all wrong, instead of thinking about yourself and what you want, sort your home life out and get back what's really important! Family and friendship. If you've got that you can conquer anything'.

Contrary to the ideal of the autonomous, self-interested subject, an alternative virtue is encouraged here, which emphasizes the importance of others. From this perspective, those who succeed in cultivating and sustaining close relationships are better equipped to overcome challenges. Men were as expressive about the virtue of good friends as women. One man gratefully acknowledged a friend who dropped off a spliff following a hard day at work, and another in his thirties commented, 'you know true mates when they are there, respect boys, love ya'.

Being there for friends involves emotional support. Paul's friends regularly offered positive words to others feeling down, condolences when bad things happened, and invitations for a cup of tea and a talk when needed. Sometimes a person might express vulnerability; in which case, they were often met with assurances of care and support.

SHANE: apologies to all of yous, felt under pressure in recent months, but no excuse for my outbursts

86   The Necessity of Community

TOM: best to share it with those that care about you bud and not keep it bottled up

WILLY: don't worry we all go through bad patches

JANET: hope you're ok, life can be rough

JIMMY: for a person to never have worries or emotions, positive or negative, they wouldn't be human at all. We're living in troubled times which test the patience of a saint, so we can all be forgiven for those moments when we're frustrated and stressed out by the bullshit of society. We're all feeing similar pains bro

FRANK: no worries mate, ur ma friend and one of the most genuine amongst us. We're lucky we have an accepting bunch here in Corby with very little bullshit

STACY: we love you.

Shane's friends prioritize empathy, acceptance, and care. They encourage him to share his struggles, reinforcing that he is a good person whom they love. Rather than seeing emotional restraint as a virtue, Jimmy recognizes the validity of emotions as a fundamental feature of being human. Thus, instead of shaming Shane for expressing his feelings and treating this as a defect of character, others emotively reciprocate. Indeed, as Frank puts it, a person like Shane, who opens up, is a 'genuine' person, and accordingly exhibits the virtue of authenticity.

Paul also supported friends and relied on their emotional support in difficult times. For example, during a family mental health crisis, one of Paul's closest friends, whom he had mentored through heroin addiction and recovery, comforted Paul through his worries about his son and helped the family access mental health services. And when Paul passed away, an adolescent boy on the estate—categorized by the state as part of a 'troubled family'—gave Paul's widow the warmest hug when he saw her in the street, an act beyond words. For those living in precarity, hard times are frequent and emotional connection with others is vital to make it through.

There are many cases where participants in Paul's community experienced the hardship that fell on a person as a shared struggle. As we saw in Chapter 1, job losses were often made public and jointly mourned, and the search for a new job was a communal process. Similarly, when something good happened in the community, for example when someone excelled in business or the creative arts, a collective triumph often followed; while the community acknowledged individual achievement, the success ultimately rippled through the community as a shared accomplishment. A notable example concerns a local young man who had struggled in school, who, despite obtaining minimal educational qualifications, managed to set up a successful clothing label, *Saint Pierre*. In response to news of his success, community participants spoke of pride and delight, and some purchased the brand, proudly wearing the NN18 label, which refers to the postcode that includes the Lincoln estate.

While Paul's community collectively offered emotional support as a necessary strategy for coping, it was not always sufficient. I observed multiple instances of Paul's neighbours claiming that there was no-one there for them when they needed help. Several women described the feeling of being invisible, to which friends offered comforting messages and offers to talk, assuring the friend that they had not realized she was feeling low. Others described being 'let down by so-called mates'; in reply to one such assertion, a woman in her twenties tried explaining to her friend that she was unable to rearrange her plans for a last-minute visit but that she would try to see her friend soon.

In some cases, people shared the grievance that, despite being a supportive person for others, in their own time of need, they encountered a lack of support themselves. For example, a teenage boy uploaded the following status update:

> (feeling drunk) everyone can go fuck themselves, not getting treated like a mug no more! Pisses me off the fact that I'm always there to help them out and yet when I'm stuck no fucker wants to know! Get bent! All of yous.

Such appeals highlight the fragility of informal social support networks, since there might be times when support is not forthcoming. To have been there when others are not in turn is to be 'taken for a mug'. This might be thought to indicate a trend towards individualism (cf. Charlesworth, 2000; Goffman, 2015; Silva, 2013; Winlow and Hall, 2006). However, plausibly such calls point towards a normative expectation for others to be there in times of need. Not having support is significant, worthy of public comment, and the very appeal to the violation of the norm might be a way to spark action.

88 The Necessity of Community

Good personhood and moneylending

In an ethnography on an English council estate, Koch (2018b: ch 2) distinguishes between 'good citizenship' and 'good personhood': good citizenship embodies values endorsed by the state, which includes the prioritization of individual autonomy, whereas good personhood involves connectedness with others, and prioritizing relational values such as loyalty, care, and love. The concept 'good personhood' may help us explore virtues within the framework of mutuality. Other aspects of good personhood in Paul's community include generosity, honesty, and authenticity. Paul's peers across the generations deem forthrightness and forwardness virtuous, since they allow others to know where they stand (cf. Charlesworth, 2000: 229). A young man in Paul's community expresses it thus, 'people should speak their minds, regardless of whether it hurts'. Those who failed to speak openly and honestly, and those who betrayed trust, were described with the term 'snake', invoking a sense of cunning, deceit, and danger. Once branded a snake, a person is no longer deemed to have good personhood and could accordingly be excluded from an inner circle of friends.

Paul's community lent money to each other as an important informal means of assistance, which was also a way to perform good personhood (following Smith, 2017b). (Notably, and in contrast to the other assistive acts discussed above, people do expect the return of money loaned, which indicates a degree of material equality within the relationship (cf. Graeber, 2011).) I observed several incidents where a friend offered to loan money to someone if their wages did not come through, or if they came up short that week. Likewise, in a comparable English ethnography, Ben Rogaly and Becky Taylor (2016: 90) identify the practice of borrowing money from a family member or friend in order to survive the week, which they suggest is a crucial coping strategy to counter insecure labour. Comparable to an interest-free loan, Paul provided essential goods 'on tick' until the loanee's wages came through, with a rough limit of £20 per person, which increased for longer-term friends in need. In addition to helping friends access material goods, informal lending of money also contributed to relationships of trust.

While we could analyse moneylending as a form of market exchange, I find more apt a relational understanding of the practice, such as Katherine Smith (2017b) offers. Smith analyses how people in a community like Paul's in the north of England negotiated the terms of moneylending. She sets the scene by showing that work did not always create enough income

Sharing Practices: An Informal Web of Support   89

for participants in her study to be freed of money worries, and those on government benefits often struggled, especially when meeting unexpected costs (cf. Koch, 2018b; Shildrick, 2018). Consequently, the ability to borrow money was vital. But rather than borrowing being a judgemental or shameful process, Smith presents informal moneylending as an opportunity to demonstrate good personhood: loaners may exhibit compassion and fairness; recipients may demonstrate reliability, honesty, and trustworthiness by repaying a loan as promised (cf. Mollona, 2009: 56–9).

A core feature of moneylending Smith identified is the sharing of personal information as part of the loaning process. Smith (2012: 130) emphasizes the importance of the negotiation: 'as people borrow and lend money with each other more often, they express themselves, their situations and their anxieties for the future as they "negotiate" and agree on the terms of the loan'. And so the process of moneylending provides another means of connection and forming solidarities. Such moments of need create an opportunity for people to be vulnerable with one another, to share the stresses of poverty, and to talk with someone about lived difficulties. Both the lender and debtor give time to this process.

On the limited occasions of moneylending I observed in Paul's community, the loans appeared to be interest-free, and hence not made to profit. Nor, seemingly, were loans given with the assumption that the lender could request a loan in return from the borrower at a future point. Instead, moneylending worked on the premise that those who were able to help others would do so. In this way, community participants who experienced relative advantage, such as Paul, tended to provide a greater amount of material support than community participants who struggled to subsist. For those in dire need, participants in Paul's community gave support with no expectation of return, a principle which also redistributed resources more evenly. Empathy is central here—'putting yourself in someone else's shoes' (Smith, 2017b; Skeggs, 2011)—which involves recognizing that money difficulties are often not the fault of an individual and could happen to anyone who is precariously situated.

At one point in the fieldwork, I was surprised by how upset my father became when a new neighbour in the square took £20 worth of goods on tick from the van and then refused to pay it back. At the time, I thought that the level of distress my father expressed was disproportionate to the amount owed. On reflection, I came to realize that my father's frustration was less about the amount of money and more about the violation of the sharing norm. The neighbour's norm violation risked damaging the social support

90   The Necessity of Community

structure, which operated outside the coercive enforcement of the state and relied on good faith. In failing to repay as promised, the man marked himself as an outsider, not only in Paul's eyes, but in the eyes of other participants in the community who came to learn of his transgression. Although the neighbour may have gained £20, by showing the community he was not to be trusted, he may have lost in other incalculable ways.

How a person is perceived by others is especially significant within a community such as Paul's because they are less likely to formalize personal achievement with qualifications, honours, and other symbolic provisions. Instead, an individual's social status might be dependent on their character as known by others. Indeed, without mainstream markers of success, reputation is one of the few remaining channels of achieving social recognition. Rather than gaining recognition through demonstrations of autonomy and self-advancement, personhood is secured on a different logic in Paul's community—being known as an honest, trustworthy, and reliable participant of the community matters.

Co-dependence on the Imagined Community

The 'imagined community' of Corby provided a way for people to assist others they might not personally know, which constituted an additional safety net in times of need. Benedict Anderson (1991) developed the concept of imagined community to explain how nation states are able to connect large numbers of individuals, including strangers who may never meet face-to-face, through a shared sense of togetherness and collective history and identity. In a comparable way, I suggest the town of Corby forms an imagined community, with a distinctive shared history of the steelworks, migration (especially from Scotland), and collective memories of mutual hardship and endurance, which create a local identity that connects strangers. Therefore, when an unknown person or family in Corby needed assistance, residents of the town were forthcoming with support.

A prominent historical example of this, which forms part of the town's collective memory, occurred in the late 1990s. Despite many residents facing severe financial hardship and social deprivation, Corby's residents raised hundreds of thousands of pounds to help a young girl in Corby access surgery in America, which was unavailable in Britain (Northamptonshire Telegraph, 2017). Similarly, during my fieldwork, Corby residents jointly raised thousands of pounds to support the local cancer hospice and homeless shelter, and there were several instances of collection boxes being placed in local shops to raise money for flowers to honour a resident who had passed away or to provide material support for families who had suffered from a house fire. At Christmas, a family on the Lincoln estate turned their garden into a 'Winter Wonderland', with an array of decorations, lights, and activities, which was open to the public and raised funds for a cancer charity. Accordingly, these examples show that the Corby community can provide an additional web of support for families when in need.

The local press reported another illustrative instance. Towards the end of summer 2019, a landlord of a struggling local pub appealed for help on Facebook: 'I need your help, that's something that doesn't come out of my mouth very often, maybe because of pride or stubbornness or a bit of both but I'm at the point where I'm going to have to put those both aside and finally ask for help.' The landlord then explained the difficulties the pub was facing, admitting his mistakes, as well as noting the 'love and effort' he had put into the place. Finally, he asked for the 'amazing local community' to use the pub before it was forced to shut down.

Corby residents shared the landlord's appeal widely, and responded by filling the pub on consecutive nights. In response, the landlord commented in the local press (Northamptonshire Telegraph, 2019):

> Overnight it's turned the business around ... I know in my heart of hearts if I'd have been in any other part of the country I wouldn't have had nearly half the response I've been given by the fantastic people of Corby and surrounding area. I'm not originally from the area but I know there's nowhere else I'd rather be. You ask for help in Corby and they give it.

By sharing his personal story, and by articulating the experience in terms of love and care, the landlord showed himself to be down-to-earth, which resonated with local norms of mutuality (cf. Smith, 2017b). It did not matter that the landlord was originally from outside of the area (not 'born and bred'), because he was willing to act in accordance with local values (see K. Tyler, 2015). And by being vulnerable and asking for help, he created an opportunity for the community to affirm that the wider safety net was operative.

Support given to unknown individuals occurred on a one-to-one, as well as collective, basis. During the fieldwork period, at least four times participants in Paul's community spoke of having helped an unknown elderly

92   The Necessity of Community

person: on three occasions, women posted about having helped elderly residents who appeared to be suffering a form of dementia find their home, families, or the police, and on another occasion a man noted that he helped an 'old boy' who had consumed too much alcohol and fallen into the road. Similarly, a woman in Paul's community announced her gratitude about an anonymous stranger who came to her aid after she fell in the supermarket. Two women also mentioned spotting children wandering lost in the street, whom they helped to find their parents. A particularly moving post detailed an incident where a lady overheard a mother in a shop explaining to her three children that only one of them could have new shoes at the start of the school year due to financial difficulties. In response, the lady who overheard the conversation offered to cover the cost of two additional pairs of shoes, explaining that she had also struggled as a lone parent and was happy to help now she could.

This last story was shared by the mother who received support; however, at times the giver of support shared information about their own kind act. Sharing information about one's own virtuous behaviour might be interpreted as immodest or disingenuous when looking through an individualistic lens. Yet, with a framework of mutuality in mind, publicizing kind acts and sharing practices makes sense insofar as it reinforces the existence of generosity norms. Bringing these features of life into view weaves further threads into the tapestry of informal support and presents an opportunity to affirm the collective standards of good moral personhood. This is not to suggest a conscious and purposeful aim. Broadcasting acts of generosity sends out a message, intentionally or otherwise, that there is a normative expectation in the community to help those in need when one can.

Conclusion

Rather than presupposing the autonomous self as a starting point, in this chapter we positioned the interactions of Paul's community within what I have called a framework of mutuality. By doing so, I think, we have been able to develop an account of precariat experience thicker than it otherwise might be. For example, thinking about sharing practices in Paul's community as guided by norms concerned with strengthening the collective and distributing wealth reveals them as far more than mere low-value exchanges in anticipation of later return. Instead, we can view sharing as an activity that is more enduring than the act itself, which connects people to the past via traditions as well as the present via the net effect of strengthening communal bonds. For, by engaging in these practices, community participants became unified in intricate ways, as though spinning imaginary threads between various people and places, growing in density and strength. And by visibly doing so, the community reinforces the value of this supportive net, making its maintenance a matter of concern to all.

It has been helpful, also, to position not only the various sharing practices within a framework of mutuality, but the community's supportive interpersonal interactions. Public displays of vulnerability and affection might easily be misconstrued as somewhat disposable, insincere, or performative, especially if we have in mind at the outside the idea of an individual as a self-interested actor pursuing advantages in a competitive space. But situating these supportive displays within a framework of mutuality—where people place special value on virtues of generosity, honesty, openness, and friendship—allows a different significance to show. Moreover, doing so allows us to see how tightly social recognition is tied to a social reputation gained through (or lost via) these supportive interactions and displays. That is, good personhood becomes an important social marker and aspiration in a community guided by a framework of mutuality, especially since the markers of success that characterize the lives of those with greater autonomy (educational qualifications and other symbolic provisions) lay out of reach. And this means, among other things, that moneylending practices are better seen not as profitmaking exercises, but as opportunities for supporting the welfare of others and for demonstrating good personhood.

In this chapter, I have focussed in part on social capital theory to show how theory which incorporates the presupposition of the individual as autonomous and self-interested, either explicitly or implicitly, might be inappropriate for understanding the experiences of precarity, for it risks distorting and misrecognizing local practices. This concern extends to theory beyond that of social capital. Indeed, as we see in Chapter 3, by analysing violence in Paul's precariat community with the framework of mutuality in mind, we can make better sense of what violent acts mean and why they occur than were we to begin by assuming a moral framework of autonomy for the community in question.

Remember, Remember

Paul's favourite period was bonfire night, its oversized blazes and its booming spectacles of colour in the evening sky.

In childhood, Paul gathered wood year-round for the local celebrations. And as November approached, he and a few friends collected neighbourhood donations for the firework display. Paul's contribution came from saving up wages from his newspaper round, transforming dull pennies into puffs of gunpowder. An old friend remembers Paul's bonfires as the biggest around, drawing people in from off the estate.

Unlike other festivities, bonfire night was free from the church and stretched beyond the family—likeminded folk sharing good humour and occasion.

* * *

In later years, bonfire celebrations moved to the Boating Lake. The annual event was held by the local council on a weekend close to the 5th. Unlike other events, the Corby show was free of charge, so all could attend.

Paul drove the van home earlier on this evening and the family wrapped up in several layers ahead of the walk to the nearby common. First, a ritual of sparklers and toffee apples in the square outside the front of the house, the rapid spinning of wrists spraying sparkles into the crisp night, conjuring fleeting letters that made up names.

The walk took off from there, passing by neighbours' houses, zigzagging through alleyways, crossing flats, and onward to Gainsborough Road. A thickening crowd signalled the nearing lake, the chill of night fading into the rhythm of the march. Bricks replaced by woodland, firm paths turning into squishy trails, a peaty scent growing more distinct, hellos, hugs, and handshakes more regular.

As the effigy of Guy Fawkes blackened to embers, the firework display took over. Each explosion more impressive than the last, building up to a grand finale of awe-inducing eruptions. Seconds of silence lingering into

A Precarious Life. Roxana Willis, Oxford University Press. © Roxana Willis 2023.
DOI: 10.1093/oso/9780198855149.003.0006

a smoky mist. Then the thunderous applause—whistles and cheers resurrecting the night.

* * *

Towards the end of summer, Paul dismantled the old garden shed, which left a mass of wood for disposal. He kept the waste dry until autumn—seeds of a plot budding.

Demolition of the estate had started some years before. The spine of the Lincoln was turned to rubble, leaving residents with a gaping area of wasteland in the middle of houses, which took the council years longer to fill. The hollowed-out core of the estate, where social life once thrived, was an ideal spot for a collective blaze.

November 5th happened to fall mid-week that year, sparking the possibility for celebrations on the estate as well as by the lake. In preparation, Paul purchased an assortment of fireworks from the local 'Cash and Carry', opting for the high-end variety to ensure a good show.

On the night of the festivities, worn-out timber made up a triangular heap where the flats of friends once stood. Local kids and older youths who had heard about the plan through the van gathered first, intrigued by the structure of the pre-lit mound. Word of mouth of passers-by spread the news further. Older residents trickled in.

Like the infamous bonfires Paul crafted as a youngster, the Lincoln fire was colossal. Once the fuelled-up base was alight, the flames progressively extended into the sky, auburn shards rising far above the surviving houses.

Before lighting the fireworks, Paul shared sweets from the van—hoping to create an experience the estate's youth could hold onto, like his own memories of bonfire night. The display started with simple rockets, whizzing upwards and fizzling out, giving way to larger fireworks. Each box contained an array of multicoloured explosions marking distinct patterns into the star-dotted sky.

The boldness of the festivities ultimately brought unwelcome guests. Elongated sirens penetrated the crowd. When the intermittent blue lights of the fire engine appeared, some bunched closer into an indistinguishable mass. Others, including Paul's wife, instinctively put their hoods up and ran.

Paul went over to greet the fire workers.

'Who started this?' An officer asked, looking toward the bonfire, which, although no longer in its prime, flickered on defiantly.

'Some of the kids wanted to celebrate bonfire night,' Paul explained, 'but they've just run off.' He pointed in the direction of his wife, whose tiny figure

96 Remember, Remember

and hooded back pelting towards an alleyway in the distance appeared to corroborate the story.

Paul offered to keep watch of the fire and make sure it was out before leaving. The attending officers agreed and thanked him, swiftly departing the estate. Residents were left to be together once again.

3
Violence

Studies on violence tend to identify the phenomenon as prevalent among socio-economically disadvantaged groups, which criminological scholarship has sought to explain (for overviews see Alvarez and Bachman, 2008; Heitmeyer and Hagan, 2003; Riedel and Welsh, 2008). However, associating violence with poverty is relatively recent, the connection forming in the seventeenth century and developing into a dominant belief from the nineteenth century onwards. Accordingly, for us to appreciate violence in the present, it will be useful to examine historical practices and reflect on features of continuity. For this task, I build on J. Carter Wood's (2004) account of the changing meanings of violence in nineteenth-century England. Wood explains that, prior to the seventeenth century, what we would today deem to be violent behaviour was often socially accepted as a valid form of expression in English society, and the use of physical force was widespread throughout the social order. Therefore, according to Wood, rather than deemed a moral transgression, prior to the nineteenth century, violence was seen as a legitimate means to attain social standing and, if used correctly, effective public displays of aggression enabled an aggressor to assert their authority over others.

Wood (2004) suggests that violence was formerly used in at least two socially acceptable ways: first, by a person in authority to signal inappropriate behaviour of a subordinate, and second, between persons of equal social standing to acquire social status. We can see the first use of violence, by authority figures, as part of an earlier patriarchal order in England—as influenced by Christian beliefs which justified social hierarchy and the dominance of certain men over women and children (cf. Dubber, 2005). This normative order permitted husbands, as the patriarchal head of house, to enact their will using physical force as part of a repertoire of rule over subordinates; in turn, it authorized wives to use force when required to control the behaviour of children and servants. In this way, violence constituted a valid form of discipline to maintain good order and norms constrained its

A Precarious Life. Roxana Willis, Oxford University Press. © Roxana Willis 2023.
DOI: 10.1093/oso/9780198855149.003.0007

98 Violence

use. Abuses of violence happened despite such constraints, as detailed in historical court records about fatal uses of force (Amussen, 1995; Wood, 2004). Indeed, the normative term 'violence' in these records plausibly referred to force deemed illegitimate when the patriarch's power was used in excess. The fact that authorities in eighteenth-century England handled incidents of excessive force, and found patriarchs guilty of offences, indicates that social norms prohibited fatal levels of violence and required a degree of proportionality (Amussen, 1995: 14–17). The second use of force which Wood outlines is that between persons of equal standing. In contrast to the hierarchical imposition of force by a patriarch, when persons settled grievances with those of relatively equivalent status, the practice took on ritualized forms, such as in duelling and prize-fighting, which were governed by codes of honour (Wiener, 2004; Wood, 2004).

Alongside developments in European thought about the self (see Schneewind, 1998; Taylor, 1989), attitudes towards violence and its social meanings began to change. Instead of holding certain displays of aggression in moral regard, Enlightenment scholars conceptualized physical force in terms of animalistic, impulsive, and primitive tendencies of man, and a core tenet of civility was to move away from violent temperaments (Wood, 2004: ch 2). The normative departure from violence is apparent in the work of Thomas Hobbes (1968), who describes the state of nature in heathenistic terms and provides an alternative moral ideal of civil order, which society ought to strive towards to overcome the innate evils of human nature. Similarly, Voltaire (1763) condemns war and violence fuelled by religion in preference for religious pluralism and toleration. These ideas progress into the eighteenth century, and feed into the discourse on civility, which gradually spread among the higher orders (Hall, 2007). Then, in the nineteenth century, the bourgeoisie diffused ideals of civility to the masses through pedagogical processes facilitated by the growth of the modern state, as detailed in the Introduction (Skeggs, 1997; Virdee, 2014). Consequently, English society progressively discouraged overt forms of violence over time, inscribing them afresh with meanings of brutality, savageness, and backwardness.

European thinkers brought the moral ideal of autonomy into being by identifying and condemning its moral antithesis (Fanon, 1968; Mbembe, 2017; McClintock, 1995; Said, 2003), a point I return to at different points in the study. That is, society had recast physical and forceful forms of expression—normative practices which previously all sectors of society engaged in—as primitive and located within the lower orders, thereby

Violence **99**

contrasting them with the civility and refinement of the new bourgeoisie (Wood, 2004: 32). Not only did this process apply such moral ideals to the least advantaged in the English order, but it cast entire societies on these terms, eventually forming the justificatory basis for colonization, under the guise of saving weaker groups around the globe (Stoler, 1995; Mbembe, 2001: ch 1; Hall, 2007). Likewise, this moral shift reimagines women as frail and especially vulnerable to violent victimization and thus most in need of protection from the aggressions of uncivilized men (see Lacey, 2008; cf. Zedner, 1991). Accordingly, violence became associated with overt displays of male aggression among the lower and racialized orders and social commentary increasingly focuses on this contemporary social problem (Wiener, 2004; Wood, 2004).

The bourgeois departure from violence developed in a context of contradiction. Alongside growing concern with the violent impulses of the lower orders at home, the most spectacular forms of violence were employed by the bourgeoisie overseas in a drive to civilize allegedly aggressive populations the world over (James, 2001; Scheper-Hughes and Bourgois, 2004; Thomas, 2011; Winant, 2001). Achille Mbembe (2017: 67) discusses the gulf between moral standards propagated by the European bourgeoisie and violence inflicted in practice by showcasing how thinkers such as Jacques Rousseau and Voltaire recognized the violence and repugnance of slavery, while showing 'wilful ignorance' to the trade in enslaved persons underway at the time they wrote. There is much to be said about this, beyond this present study's scope, but it is important to recognize the stark contradiction in the historical moral standards of bourgeois violence. Not least because we might fail to recognize how bourgeois violence then transmuted and cloaked itself into more modern economic forms.

Indeed, a related discussion in Chapter 6 is worth prefacing here. Legal and trading mechanisms facilitated by the modern state have gradually replaced overt uses of violence by propertied actors, providing them with alternative means to impose their will on and assert power over others, without need for direct force. For example, instead of using overt force to make people labour, a combination of property rights, imbalanced labour contracts, high costs of living, the stigmatization of welfare, and so on, performs this coercive function indirectly instead. Indeed, as Adam Smith (1976) famously contended in his economic argument for the abolition of slavery, the fear of hunger and the threat of homelessness are powerful incentives for labour, without the need for chains and whips—in fact, on Smith's analysis, reliance on indirect pressures has the potential to extract

100   Violence

even greater profits from the worker. In the present, then, a complex matrix of law and bureaucracy, which requires the services of professionals to navigate, replaces the need for the most socio-economically advantaged to engage in direct forms of violence.

Accompanying the growth of the modern state and legal institutions in the nineteenth century was the expansion of centralized police forces in England, which further enforced the will of advantaged classes over subordinates (Wiener, 2004: 19). Instead of inflicting violence by their own hands, the state increasingly encouraged the propertied to rely on its monopoly of legitimate force to secure personal interests. Initially, both the bourgeoisie and the working classes resist the expanding police force in England, but as the nineteenth century progressed, most of society moved away from overt displays of aggression and came to accept the police as an alternative way to enact individual will (Wood, 2004). However, as Chapter 4 shows, the lower orders have never been able to rely on the police in the same way as advantaged individuals. Consequently, although less prevalent in contemporary times, physical force continues to operate as a means of conflict resolution among the most disadvantaged in English society.

Against the backdrop of this historical context, the threat and presence of direct and physical violence was real for Paul and his neighbours. During the fieldwork period, official figures recorded Corby as having higher rates of violent and sexual offences than comparable areas (O'Neill, 2013; Police, UK, 2022; UK Crimestats, 2016), and several serious violent offences and homicides occurred on the Lincoln estate during the research, which add to an expansive collective trauma endured by residents over the decades. My fieldwork observations reflect official crime reports: Paul and his neighbours regularly shared details about violent incidents and crimes, sometimes later affirmed by local newspaper reports. Specifically, I observed first-hand accounts of homicides, sexual violence, fist-fights, stabbings, domestic violence, aggravated thefts, and arson. Even more commonly, I saw threats of violence in response to norm transgressions and active attempts to settle conflict within the community.

Extending Chapter 2's discussion of mutuality, in this chapter I argue that the precariat must continue to rely on physical force to maintain social order because, unlike privileged individuals who depend on the state to enforce their will, socio-economically disadvantaged communities lack full state support and instead use informal mechanisms. I have shown how participants in Paul's community, in the absence of full state support, continue to rely on overt and active forms of social support. Relationships in

Violence **101**

this context are formed within the framework of mutuality. I now show how overt uses of force in Paul's community are likewise best understood as reflecting this framework, which orients individuals towards ensuring the subsistence and survival of the collective. On this view, violence is a means of enforcing the normative ideals of mutuality, whose practical instantiations community participants depend on and yet cannot rely on the state to protect. Therefore, moving our theoretical gaze to this framework of mutuality allows us to make out a rationale for precariat violence which makes it predictable and coherent, instead of simply arbitrary and disorderly (see also Auyero et al., 2015; Comaroff and Comaroff, 2006a).

I find E. P. Thompson's (1993a, 1993b) development of the 'moral economy' concept a crucial starting point to comprehend patterns of violence among the precariat in contemporary times. Thompson offers insight into the English peasant resistance against the imposition of a new 'political economy' in the eighteenth century, which often threatened the subsistence of the collective, and hence clashed with a moral economy of customary norms and expectations. Thus, Thompson brings into view particular customs which guided action and local understandings of right and wrong. Although significant normative shifts have occurred since the eighteenth century, the moral economy concept is helpful for understanding the moral source of the mutuality framework, as well as what happens when Paul and his multigenerational peers use force to protect the normative order. Accordingly, in the course of this chapter I draw on and contribute to the work of scholars who have applied Thompson's insights to aspects of criminalization in the modern day, and those who have developed the apt notion of a 'moral economy of violence' in particular (e.g. Chabal and Daloz, 1999; Fassin, 2011; Karandinos et al., 2015; Rodgers, 2015; Roitman, 2006).

In the following analysis, I continue the task of historically situating present day uses of force in Paul's community and offer an interpretation which places the violence within a mutuality framework, and hence recognizes the relational embeddedness of actors. In the first section, I focus on the normative use of force, which I suggest echoes older customary forms of ritual fighting. Mirroring my discussion on social capital theory in the previous chapter, I suggest that we give ourselves a better account of precariat experience by deploying the 'moral economy of violence' concept because it departs from the presupposition of inherently self-interested actors. As I see it, this is where the strength of Thompson's concept lies, since it provides us with a different lens through which to examine the person. In the second section, I extend the contextualized analysis by reflecting on the notion of a

102 Violence

fair fight, and how Paul's peers interpret the use of force beyond these limits as illegitimate and in relation to bullying. In the final section, I explore two widespread strategies in Paul's community to displace violence, which are again reminiscent of customary practices: namely, 'name and shame' and reliance on karma. I extend this discussion in Chapter 4 when the role of the state comes into sharper focus.

Normative Uses of Force

Prior to the seventeenth century, physical force was a socially accepted form of expression throughout English society. However, this did not permit the unrestrained use of violence—it was limited by customary norms and practices, such as duelling and fist-fights, which were governed by a set of rules that determined acceptable and unacceptable forms of combat. As discussed by Wood (2004), ritual fighting gradually diminished among the middle classes, who were increasingly included in the discourse of civility and manners, while ritual fighting remained a common and acceptable form of expression among the working classes well into the nineteenth century. As the respectability discourse spread further, fighting became less common among the English working classes, especially those included within the remit of respectability. And in the present, fist-fighting is markedly less prevalent among all class sectors in England. Yet, as criminologists document, fighting among certain socio-economically disadvantaged groups reportedly continues (Hobbs et al., 2003; Nayak, 2006; Winlow and Hall, 2006).

In Paul's community, those most likely to engage in fights were teenagers, and girls were just as likely to fight as boys. Though these fights occurred in a variety of youth spaces, including on the estate, outside of school, and in local parks, a local annual funfair in Corby was a notable site of violence. Fairs and public houses have historically been prime places of ritual fighting (Amussen, 1995: 24; Wood, 2004), which criminologists similarly identify in the present (Nayak, 2006; Winlow and Hall, 2006). In the year of my fieldwork, several fights broke out during a single fair. A group of teenagers described the fighting at the fair that year in the following way:

KYLIE: The fair was mental tonight!
JOE: What happened?
BILLY: Ha ha, it was rough! I got hit so many times!

Normative Uses of Force 103

KYLIE: Everyone was getting hit or shoved, it was madness down there.

One teenager frustratedly announced that his friends had not supported him with their presence, which led to his being targeted by a group of youths and given a severe 'kicking'. Another boy delighted in how good the fighting at the fair that year had been. A father threatened in advance to batter (inflict violence on) anyone who might have touched his daughter there. And an older girl announced that she was heading to the fair to find out who had hit her younger sister, the implication being that she would retaliate on her sister's behalf.

Criminological literature has analysed this kind of fighting as an alternative way for disadvantaged individuals to secure respect, in circumstances where mainstream markers of success, such as work and material possessions, are out of reach (Anderson, 1999; Bourgois, 1995; Winlow and Hall, 2006). While this offers one level of explanation, the motivations attributed here do not fully capture the normative background that makes fighting intelligible. I think we can go deeper by appreciating how the framework of mutuality likely shapes this practice, infusing it with a relational and collective significance (see Karandinos et al., 2015). For one thing, while it is plausible that violence confers status on individuals which is not formalizable as a symbolic reward (as, say, educational attainments are), nonetheless gaining such recognition relies on the collective body acknowledging and approving the fight. Thus, recognition for fighting is dependent on community approval, itself on a normative basis: as we see in the next section, Paul's community is very much concerned with the shared criteria for a 'fair fight'. And so analysing ritual fighting among socio-economically disadvantaged communities only as a search for respect absent formalized markers of success, may be another case where framing the matter as defectively mimicking the practices of the privileged obscures an underlying thickness of meaning (see Chapter 2).

The most violent forms of conflict I observed in Paul's community were those prompted by financial debts. In these instances, men commit particularly brutal violence against other men. For example, threats circulated along the lines of 'time to kick fuck out of some tramp bodies', and I heard about various estate beatings due to money owed. In one case, a debtor was allegedly tied up and kidnapped in the boot of a car. I also observed two videos of attacks uploaded to social media by Paul's friends: one of a person struck with a hammer; the other involved a man being attacked in his home by a group wearing knuckledusters and balaclavas. People encouraged others to share this footage widely, as a warning.

104 Violence

One understanding of why these retaliative acts were so open, and why the perpetrators encouraged circulation of them, is that the process is self-serving: the attackers demonstrate their physical power, which they use to advance their own economic interests. However, what appears to be of even greater significance is public affirmation that a mutuality norm had been breached and such violations have consequences. This is informed by the discussion in Chapter 2, where we saw that reliance on others is crucial; when someone fails to pay back a loan as promised, they demonstrate themselves to be a bad and dishonest person, which risks upsetting an informal order dependant on trust (see Koch, 2018b; Smith, 2012). In keeping with this, when a boy in his late teens shared that a friend had been avoiding him because he owed £20, an older man advised the boy that the appropriate response was violence, 'out of principle'. The principle here stretches beyond act of disrespect against the individual: failure to repay a debt undermines the wider informal moral order which necessitates redress for the collective benefit.

This is how I propose we extend Karandinos et al.'s analysis of the 'moral economy of violence' in a Puerto Rican section of Philadelphia, USA. Karandinos et al. creatively combine several theories in their development of the moral economy of violence, which includes Marcel Mauss's (2002) analysis of the gift and Bourdieu's (1984) discussion on capital forms and habitus, alongside Thompson's (1993a) moral economy thesis. In fact, increasingly scholars apply Bourdieu's work to understand the phenomenon of violence in marginalized sectors of society (Sandberg, 2008; Sandberg and Fleetwood, 2017; Sandberg and Pedersen, 2011; Winlow and Hall, 2006). However, as I noted in Chapter 2, Bourdieu begins with the unexamined presupposition of the individual as inherently self-interested by nature, and in pursuit of social resources for self-advancement. Correspondingly, there are several points in Karandinos et al.'s (2015) analysis where they ascribe motivations of self-interest and reciprocity (on the rationale: *I do something for you and in return you do something for me*) to explain violence. Although self-interest, reciprocity, and the pursuit of individualized goals might prove motivating factors for violence in particular circumstances, I urge us to remain open to the possibility that we are warranted to read a thicker description of violence.

The thesis I developed in Chapter 2 is that sometimes the best account of human action is not one rooted in motivations of self-interest. Since the individual often thrives when a constitutive community also thrives, it is plausible that an individual might be motivated by something deeper and more eternal than individualistic goals of self-advancement and reciprocity (cf. Graeber, 2011). For those who have matured while being aware of their co-dependence on others, of being intricately connected to an informal normative order that operates beyond the state, a different orientation to the world can manifest (cf. Skeggs, 2011)—one that I am outlining as a framework of mutuality. Thompson (1993a) makes some such move with his own moral economy concept, which recognizes an alternative way of being in the world that contrasted to the Smithian conception of the self-interested economic actor. To me, this is a significant strength of Thompson's work; we ought thus to retain it in subsequent developments of the moral economy concept.

An example from Karandinos et al.'s (2015: 50–5) work illustrates how our analysis might become inapt unless we do retain Thompson's commitment to portraying alternative moral frameworks. Karandinos et al. introduce a local 'big shot' drug dealer, Benito, who ran a drug dealing enterprise in the neighbourhood they studied, which residents tolerated but withdrew their support of after a shoot-out happened. According to the authors' account, the reckless shoot-out marked a tipping point in the neighbourhood, and criticism began to circulate about Benito's greed and failure to give back. Karandinos et al. note how this lack of generosity undermined moral economy norms, which require the sharing of resources—something I suggest is a central tenet of the framework of mutuality. When residents who previously tolerated the drug trade withdrew their support, Benito stopped his business. However, after some months, Karandinos et al. were surprised to see Benito resume his drug dealing trade, which they suggest happened after Benito rebuilt neighbourly relationships by offering financial and emotional support to those in need.

In this example, we can see how Karandinos et al. capture vital aspects of mutuality in their analysis by bringing relational motivations into view. However, they also extend their analysis with an individualistic and instrumental interpretation. Benito, they suggest, 'resuscitated his self-serving commitment to a local moral economy just-in-time, and managed to cement the legitimacy of his monopoly of drug-dealing rights' (Karandinos et al., 2015: 55). Self-interest might indeed be the primary factor that motivates the drug economy, which operates on the logic of market forces, yet there is another layer of understanding available, if we reflect further on the framework of mutuality. What is notable in Karandinos et al.'s analysis is Benito's co-dependency on the collective body for survival: Benito attempts to widen his share of the drug market, as one might do in the capitalist

106 Violence

economy; however, unlike a formal business which can accumulate wealth without limit, the collective body of which Benito is part interprets such behaviour as greedy. When the community withdraws support, perhaps they remind Benito of his co-dependency—that, among other things, he can only advance himself if the collective is advanced. If so, beyond self-interest and reciprocity, Benito must engage in an altogether different way of thinking, which centres being with and for others to ensure collective subsistence and survival (see Skeggs, 2011). This explanation might not be readily available to those engaging in these practices, but it might be available for us to discover when thinking about the norms that structure their world.

This is not to say that violence evades a more individualist analysis rooted, say, in Bourdieu's notion of kinds of capital. It is possible that the dominant moral figure of the individualized self has 'meshed' (to borrow from Karandinos et al. (2015)) with customary norms that delimit the use of violence, which may be particularly acute in the US (extending Wacquant, 2009). When people lend money informally, or accumulate as part of the illicit economy, such as through drug sales, they cannot resort to formal policing measures to rectify the wrong of a debtor's failed payment, and therefore likely need alternative forms of coercion (cf. Anderson, 1999). In such circumstances, plausibly physical strength and aggression may form cultural capital that allows violent perpetrators to secure an advantage (Hobbs et al., 2003; Karandinos et al., 2015; Sandberg and Pedersen, 2011). Nevertheless, we should remain mindful that an alternative framework may structure the normative world of these communities; for instance, Michèle Lamont (2009) finds that (what I call mutuality) norms of solidarity and empathy are operative among black workers in the US, as they are among white workers in France. If we only view violence as a means of self-advancement, even when recognizing that this might be relationally rooted, we might miss a crucial aspect of the practice.

Returning to Paul's community, even when Paul's friends develop a reputation as successful fighters who can forcefully impose their will, the use of force must remain within the bounds of community acceptance. Take, for instance, a conversation instigated by one of Paul's friends, who was known for selling drugs and ability to use violence:

RAY: am I a good guy or a bad guy
COURTNEY: good guy cus you don't take shit from no one
BRIAN: good mate
FELICITY: You're a good guy. You just don't take no one's shit!

Normative Uses of Force 107

Despite a reputation for toughness, Ray still actively and publicly seeks validation that he acts in accordance with the standards of good personhood. It is not enough to have a reputation as someone who can fight and look after themselves; the community must also trust that these skills are used in a just manner. Those who are seen to engage in gratuitous violence, or to start fights out of turn, do not meet the moral standard of good personhood, and the acquired reputation is not one of honour, but of unpredictability and distrust. This is apparent in a discussion between a group of youths commenting on how one of their peers, Justin, 'starts shit with everyone', with examples shared of Justin's inappropriate use of violence against weaker boys. In response, a girl in the peer group commented, 'he's getting a name for himself and it's a bad one'. Another teenager put himself forwards to 'teach [Justin] a lesson' by fighting him on behalf of the group, and hence reiterating the correct fighting norms.

Rather than becoming known for their fighting abilities, perhaps more valuable in Paul's community is being closely connected to someone with a reputation for violence. For instance, community participants often shared warnings such as, 'betta not throw threats ma way pal do you know who ma uncle is?'; in this particular instance the uncle had a reputation for being 'hard' and had served time in prison. That said, carrying the weight of a tough reputation oneself is not easy. As Karandinos et al. (2015: 55) observe, 'the propensity to flare into rage at a moment's notice' can be an advantage for fighting, but being prone to such rage can likewise disadvantage a person in terms of their relationship to the state. The person who behaves as a 'nutter' or who goes 'mental', which is the language used in Paul's community, is the antithesis of the autonomous person. By 'losing it' to defend the self and others, the 'nutter' is liable to have their autonomy severely curtailed, whether through imprisonment or by becoming the target of violence in return. Thus, rather than advancing the self, the 'nutter' plays a protectionist role for others—by acting as a martyr, the fighter is valued locally, which the stigma of prison cannot hamper.

Accordingly, not everyone in the community need gain a reputation as a notorious fighter; solidarity and a willingness to 'jump in' to defend family and friends are sufficient. A person with alternative skills may be less likely to fill the role of the physical protector of the group, for their contribution to the collective can consist in other activities, such as sharing economic wealth or supporting interactions with state entities. Here, we could think of the concept of wealth-in-people as developed by Jane Guyer and Samuel Eno Belinga (1995) in the context of Cameroon. Wealth-in-people refers to

108 Violence

an alternative distribution of power and resources, which consists in people rather than through property. According to this alternative social ordering, different people possess particular skills and abilities, and power lies in the ability to mobilize relevant forms of support when needed. Applying this thesis to Paul's community, people can be seen as being valued for a range of contributions they make to the subsistence of the group, only some of which are in the form of physical protection.

Another strategy to ward off threats adopted by Paul's peers is through the show of collective solidarity. As Jeanette Edwards (2000: 158) observes in an ethnographic study in the north of England, in addition to a reputation for toughness, success in a fight requires the ability to mobilize kin 'in order to portray the kind of solidarity that was needed to overcome more powerful adversaries'. In keeping with Edwards's findings, in Paul's community wider family members would often offer support in a dispute. As the next example shows, insulting a member of the family is serious enough a transgression to justify wholesale retaliation.

TEENAGE BOY: If you've got something to say about me or my family then don't be a keyboard warrior, come say it to ma face and we'll see what happens

GRANDMA: Tut tut, don't give into small minded people my sweetie, you know you're to send them to me instead

MOTHER: Once granny's done with them, send the little fuckers to me

LIAM: I need to let off steam, I'll sort it out for ya pal

GREG: Inbox me their names. I will go to their houses with a baseball bat.

The propensity for entire families to act in defence of one another has led to the escalation of family feuds in Paul's community. One of the severest examples involved a series of retaliatory attacks between two families, eventually accumulating in a spectacular act of violence involving a spiked baseball bat that left a man in a vegetative state for fourteen years until his death in 2016—four other community participants served lengthy prison sentences for the crime (BBC News, 2018). The memory of such feuds acts as an impetus for Paul's neighbours to try first settling disagreements, which includes contacting the police for early intervention, a response we discuss in Chapter 4.

Rather than attaching love to educational and material success (Evans, 2006), and beyond expressing love in words, those in Paul's community can

Normative Uses of Force   **109**

demonstrate love in other ways (cf. Louis, 2019). This includes expressing love through acts of protection (Rodgers, 2015: 29), evident in the following parental attempts to help a teenage daughter.

TINA: I'm raging! You upset ma daughter, you upset me!
WILLY: Who, I'll fucking kill 'em I swear
JODIE: Leave it yous, please. It's gunna make things worse
WILLY: I wont say anything more pet, cus you've asked me to, but just give us a bell if you need us
CORINA: Nothing will be made worse my lovely, let those that care help if you need them to.

Tina's explanation of the injury here reaches to the heart of mutuality: to harm a loved one is to harm the collective body of which the individual is part. While Willy accepts Jodie's request for her parents not to get involved, an older friend of the family, Corina, frames the parent's intervention in terms of care; instead of encouraging Jodie to be independent, Corina highlights the virtue of accepting support from those who love her.

Importantly, a person prone to violence is not the only valuable type of person to know in a conflict situation; a skilful arbitrator is also an asset. This is illustrated in the following dispute between two young adults, which was defused by an older man in the community.

GARY: no matter where u go ur always gunna shit on people who help ya, ur a down and out junkie
SHANE: don't hate cus I didn't give u that £25. U said u was gunna burn my mum's photos, good luck on that mate, cus you would have most of the world after ya. I'm moving cus of people like yous.
GARY: u owe me and Alan 50 each, I told u what would happen if u didn't pay up
SHEILA: no one is daft enough to burn mum's photos
OWEN: if he does, come see me, I've got ur back
DAVID: listen you 2, I'm telling you now, give it a break. No one else is involved, leave them to sort it out. Gary, not nice what you said about the photos, apologise to him, and Shane, you're rude getting other people involved, apologise to him. You Corby boys aren't fighting each other, give it a break and when you're ready to talk to each other, sort it out like adults.

110 Violence

By knowing and articulating the norms being violated by each party, Dave was able to put an end to this online confrontation. Paul was also well-placed on the estate to adopt the arbitration role, and several mothers in the community likewise performed this task, advising youth either to fight one-on-one or to 'grow up' and stop the behaviour altogether. For a community participant to be an effective arbitrator, they must be well-known, respected, and often older—and hence able to provide wisdom that accords with community norms and offer an assessment of the situation from a distanced position. Wise arbitrators were especially vital for reiterating and passing down the norms of a fair fight.

The Fair Fight and the Bully

During the research, I participated in two restorative justice programmes operating in Corby. One case I followed involved a fight between young people from Paul's community and illustrates the widely shared fighting norms. The fight occurred in a local school between two twelve-year-old boys. Following a police referral by the school, the parents agreed to engage in a restorative conference to resolve the conflict. The conference took place at the school and involved three teenage boys: Tyler, the instigator of the fight, joined by his mother; Ethan, the boy who was attacked, joined by his mother; and Richard, who was filmed encouraging the fight, joined by both of his parents. Additional participants included a teacher, two community volunteers, and the co-ordinator of the restorative programme, who was also a retired police officer. During the restorative conference, each participant had an opportunity to discuss the incident in response to scripted questions.

Tyler, who had instigated the fight, was asked why he attacked Ethan. He explained his reasons as follows:

> I heard Ethan had said stuff about my grandad, and so I punched him. Then some year 10s [three years above] told me to punch him again. So I went over and pretended to apologise by going to shake his hand. But then I punched him a few more times instead.

The moral impetus for the fight, according to Tyler, was to defend his grandfather, which is reminiscent of 'the fighting ritual' as rooted in customary practice. Wood (2004: 78) explains how the first stage of ritual fighting in

The Fair Fight and the Bully **111**

the nineteenth century often involved an exchange of insults, which included undermining a man's honour or character, and insulting a family member.

Most fights I observed between teenagers in Paul's community involved alleged insults about a family member, often in the form of rumours, and the norm of fighting to defend family members was frequently reiterated. A representative example of this pretext for fighting is evident in a discussion between two teenage girls:

MARY-ANNE: if someone says something about your dad or stepdad then knock them on the floor, will teach them to mess with ya
LILLY: I second that, if anyone says shit about your family then there's your excuse to go nuts on them.

While violence in excess of what is deemed required is not permissible within the framework of mutuality, perhaps reference to an 'excuse to go nuts' here speaks instead to the emotional pains of precarity, where violent encounters might provide a fleeting moment in which to release anger and frustration (cf. Wacquant, 2007; Winlow and Hall, 2006; Louis, 2017)—a thought I return to in Chapter 6 in an analysis of structural violence.

The expectation to defend loved ones applied as much to women as men in Paul's community, and several other restorative justice conferences I followed involved fights between girls from Paul's estate. Wood (2004) explains that, historically, the customary prize fight was a male endeavour, the patriarch being the one to defend and enforce the authority of the house. Yet, under this customary order, women had greater freedom to use force as a valid form of expression, for example within the home or to resolve an argument over shared resources. It is only with the strict enforcement of gender norms in the nineteenth century and advancement of civility that female violence came to be seen as an apparent perversion of nature (Lacey, 2008; Wiener, 2004; Wood, 2004; Zedner 1991). Growing up in tough circumstances, however, exposes women to just as much, if not more, violence than their male counterparts. Hence, the necessity to defend oneself and one's family is pressing irrespective of gender.

The imperative to defend family applies as irrespective of sexuality as it is so of gender. Consider how this young man responded to an older man threatening to harm his mother:

112 Violence

> I will slap the taste outta his mouth. He's not a big man anymore and nearly got chinned by a poof. I still have blue blood, jock family, brought up in Corby. I may be a poof but I'll still skelp anyone who wanna line up for a scrap today.

This presentation resonates with Vanessa Panfil's research (2014), which explores how men from working-class backgrounds, who might have experienced prejudice because of their sexuality, at times actively resist this through portrayals of 'muscular masculinity' and the ability and willingness to fight back. In the above extract, Paul's friend highlights several markers to show his intersectional identity of being gay and working-class, with class equated to hardness through references to his 'blue blood', 'jock' (Scottish) heritage, and being from Corby.

When the parents in the restorative justice conference had a chance to comment on the boys' fight, they each emphasized different aspects of the event and appeared to use the forum as an opportunity to educate the youths about appropriate fighting norms. Richard's parents had seen a film of the fight and their son egging it on; they were displeased their son was party to breaching the norm of a fair fight, as Richard's father here discusses it:

> I was very angry. It wasn't a fair fight; the lad wasn't fighting them. It was bullying and nasty. It was a cheap shot, tricking the lad into shaking his hand then hurting him. Lads will be lads and fight, but that was bullying. I am disappointed in Richard. I thought we brought him up better than that.

The concept of a fair fight can once again be understood in the context of custom, which continues to inform legitimate uses of violence in precarious communities such as Paul's. Wood (2004: ch 4) traces these norms to the seventeenth-century prize-fighting customs, which gradually developed into generalized guidelines for fighting, from Broughton's Rules in the mid-eighteenth century, to Owen Swift's *Handbook of Boxing* in 1840, and became more formalized from the Queensberry Rules onwards. With respect to the nineteenth-century context, Wood (2004: 72) comments, 'the rituals of prizefighters in boxing rings were virtually identical to those of laborers in streets and fields'. While fighting was a means to acquire status, the fight had to be fought fairly, which was judged and debated by peer observers. Rules of a fair fight identified by Wood (2004: 82–7) include concern for fighters to be of a similar size and ability, and thus have no unfair

The Fair Fight and the Bully **113**

advantage, the avoidance of dirty tactics such as attacking a man while down, fighting one-on-one, and prohibiting the use of weapons. But, Wood (2004: 89) notes, when the civilization drive took hold in the nineteenth century, fighting norms became volatile, with fighting increasingly seen as illegitimate and characteristic of the rougher sectors of society.

Notwithstanding ambiguities about fighting norms, notions of fairness continue to guide the acceptability of fights in Paul's community (cf. Edwards, 2000: 162). In Paul's community, fair fights must involve one-to-one encounters, and the idea of proportionality is evident: a combatant should only inflict the amount of harm necessary for the offence caused; violence beyond that limit is considered unacceptable. The use of weapons is seen as a sign of weakness, especially if pre-emptively carried; although the ability to use makeshift weapons from the surroundings was sometimes viewed as valid, if deemed necessary and if the fighter was at a disadvantage in size. Overall, a fair fight should not involve an older person inflicting harm on a younger person, though parents might breach this norm to defend their children. The community was ambiguous about the legitimacy of men hitting women in a street fight; they seemed just about to accept it, so long as there is sufficient equivalence between the fighters. Consider a threat made by a teenage boy in response to a woman who allegedly 'gave his mum shit'; he warned her he would 'fuck her head off a car door', which he justified by describing the woman in the following masculinized way: 'four-times as wide as me and likely has bigger hairier balls, but I'll have no problem swinging for that fat bitch'. Still, the use of violence by men against women was a grey area, overlapping with a widespread prohibition on domestic violence.

Wood (2004: 126) notes that an important element of nineteenth-century ritual fighting was for the practice to occur between people considered to be social equals, which is a helpful way to comprehend the sense of fairness that guided fighting in Paul's community. For example, teenagers from the estate expressed outrage and disgust when an 'innocent girl', 'who wouldn't harm a fly', was allegedly attacked by a group of 'rough' girls while walking home from school. In response to an 'innocent girl' being targeted, another girl on Paul's estate said she would 'punch them [the perpetrators] in their face'. In this way, a girl who was of a similar social status to those who initiated the first attack stepped forward to redress the power imbalance.

In the fight that led to the restorative justice conference, the norms the parents attempted to instil in their children were notably different to the norms which the school and the retired police officer co-ordinating the

114 Violence

restorative programme sought to promote. Whereas Richard's parents reprimanded their son because he encouraged an unfair fight, the state representatives asserted an alternative norm: no fighting is acceptable, whatsoever. The female teacher first offered the blanket prohibition, advising the pupils that 'all it takes is one kick to kill someone if they fall and hit their head in the wrong place'. The teacher then explained how her friend's daughter had died eighteen years ago that day: 'she was trying to stop a fight and the girls kicked her in the head a few times and killed her'. In response, Richard's parents said at the same time, 'Louise Allen'—a local girl who lost her life at the age of thirteen, an event lodged in the town's collective memory. The retired police officer co-ordinating the restorative conference revealed he was on duty at the time and handled the case, which led him to reiterate the teacher's point: 'it only takes one punch'.

The fatal fight that took Louise's life took place at the annual Corby fair in 1996 and involved youths from the Lincoln estate. *The Independent* broadsheet newspaper reported that Louise had attempted to support her friend who was pulled into a fight, at which point Louise was also attacked; multiple youths then kicked her while down (Wynne-Jones, 1996, 1997). Two girls from the Lincoln estate, aged eleven and twelve at the time, were convicted of manslaughter. Adults in Paul's community repeatedly raised this exceptional case of fatal violence, often as an attempt to teach young people about the dangers of fighting and to stress the importance of a fair fight. In the retelling of the tragedy, adults explain how the norms of a fair fight were violated because a gentle girl was attacked for supporting her friend, she had been outnumbered, was kicked while down, and lethal force was used—the exemplar par excellence of an unfair fight.[1]

It seems to me that the frequency of fights among younger adults, and the public retelling and dissecting of the events, is as much about affirming community norms and socializing the youth as it is about individuals 'campaigning for respect' (cf. Anderson, 1999). By learning how to defend themselves and about the norms of a fight fair, young people can develop skills to survive the tough socio-economic conditions of their birth. Importantly, young people must learn how to limit their use of violence and how to implement self-restraint, even in moments where they 'lose it' and 'go mad'

---

[1] Notably, in an interview with a journalist for *The Independent* broadsheet newspaper, some of the girls reported to be in the 'Canada Square gang' referred to the fight as fair initially, since it was 'one against one', and in their view the fight became unfair when Louise stepped in, which is when they attacked her in response (Wynne-Jones, 1997). This shows how notions of fairness can be slippery. Still, fatal uses of force are rarely justifiable for Paul's community.

The Fair Fight and the Bully   115

when defending themselves and kin. Fighting can thus be seen as a way for youths to learn about the boundaries of violence and how to avoid fatalities. However, such practices are ultimately risky, and there are devastating fatalities. Though rare, illegitimate uses of violence remain alive in the collective memory, revisited and instilled as lessons in the generations to come. Like the sharing practices we examined in Chapter 2, the retelling of violent moments reaffirms that the normative order is present, active, and protected; the norms are continually negotiated and reiterated.

Returning to the restorative justice conference concerning the boys' fight in school, Ethan's mother explained how she was 'fuming' when she heard Ethan had been 'beaten up'. But rather than being angry with Tyler, the mother explained the worst part for her: 'I don't know why he didn't fight back? Why did he just stand there and take it?' In view of the lesson being imparted by the professionals, that all violence should be avoided since it only takes one unlucky blow for an unfortunate fatality, it might be hard to comprehend why Ethan's mother expresses a desire for her son to fight back. Ethan's mother was not alone here—a lesson recurrently taught to children in Paul's community is that 'if someone hits you, hit them back' (see also Lareau, 2011: 163). This lesson naturally extends to cases of child bullying, which Richard's father suggests accurately describes what Tyler did to Ethan. I repeatedly observed relatives and older family friends advising young victims of bullying to fight their tormentors: 'once you hit them, they'll leave you alone'.

What might appear as harsh forms of parenting from an outside perspective can be understood as parental attempts to impart necessary survival skills in children forced to grow up in dangerous environments. Consider how a middle-aged woman who gave advice to a friend's teenage daughter passed down a similar lesson:

> When I was younger, I used to be bullied, got shoved around, pushed, slapped, kicked, punched. But one time, someone started on me on the wrong day, and I lost it. I went mental on them. The moral of the story is no one ever touched me again. You're the sweetest girl, but you need to stand up for yourself. You'll only need to do it once and they'll leave you alone.

Paul's community commonly shared similar pieces of wisdom. Rather than transforming into a violent person, a victim of bullying is advised to 'go mental' just the once. For experience has shown the older generation that

116 Violence

those who fail to stand up for themselves risk a lifetime (or extended period) of victimization. According to the advice, when someone displays an ability to fight back, they are less likely to be targeted in the future—the aggressor must find someone else to direct their anger at.

In contrast to the acceptable use of force in defence, the community widely condemned levels of violence which amounted to bullying. I noted many assertions concerning the hatred of bullies or bullies needing to be put in their place; videos of such events were widely shared. However, at times it was difficult to see where the line between the bully and the bullied lay. A cyclical process can occur. The child ostensibly being bullied should hit back, it is held; but then the parent of the apparent bully, who has now received punishment in turn, may accuse the other child of bullying, advising, again, their own child to hit the 'bully' back next time. Alternatively, sometimes the line would be drawn at whoever had 'thrown the first punch', and so some young persons were advised specifically not to begin a fight. A mother here reinforced that norm in justifying her daughter's hitting another girl:

> I've had enough of little girls messaging my daughter about what happened last night. Nicola hit my Becky, so Becky defended herself. End of. If anyone touches ma daughter, I'll get the police involved.

The mother presents her daughter's act of retaliation as a fair end to the issue, for the imbalance has been restored, so Nicola and Becky are once again equal. However, if anyone were to further retaliate and continue the conflict, then the mother warns that she will invoke the power of the police to put an end to the matter.

Sometimes, however, youths in the community were encouraged to strike first, pre-emptively, to make sure some tormentor left them alone. In these cases, verbal insults were viewed as sufficient wrongs to justify a physical response, which has customary precedence also (see Amussen, 1995: 24; Wood, 2004). A teenage boy's grievance is reminiscent too of that custom:

> I always got told if someone threatens you, you knock the shit out of them. Now school's telling me I'm in the wrong. There's no way I'm gonna let some dick head threaten me!!

Once again, we see how the dominant moral standards of the school, which absolutely prohibit the use of violence, clash with the necessity norms of

The Fair Fight and the Bully   **117**

Paul's peers who must learn to use force in strategic ways. A mother in Paul's community expressed similar frustrations about how her daughter's school reprimanded her child for confronting a bully; the mother proclaimed she was proud of her daughter for standing up for herself and that she would be 'having words' with the school in the morning. While there are no clear-cut lines, and ambivalence is rife, as a rule of thumb, legitimate fights are those that involve parties of equal status or equivalence, and which restore power imbalance, whereas illegitimate uses of force destabilize the balance and involve abuses of power, which is what the notion of bullying depicts.

Lessons about legitimate uses of force imparted during youth have relevance in adult life. It was common for adults in Paul's community to fight back in moments of criminal victimization. For example, a woman in her later teens shared the following incident about being mugged while on her way home from a night out:

SUSIE: Whoever the scumbags were that jumped me outside the pub last night – yous are scum hope yor proud of yourselves. Fully grown men taking my bag and giving me a black eye, you'll get what's coming to you one day!

GEENA: Disgusting scumbags

SUSIE: I sparked one of them, knocked him to the floor, but there were 2 others

LEANNE: Good girl for standing your ground, bet whoever it was is feeling a little gutted getting knocked out by a girl! Report it though, people like that think its okay to do these things

ADAM: Guys that hit girls need putting down.

NINA: Pisses me off reading this. Who the fuck do some men think they are? I've always said if a girl's big enough to give it she can take it, but 3 men robbing a young girl. Someone got stabbed down the Kite as well.

Susie presents herself as having fought back, behaviour which is commended by others. Similarly, when a woman in her early twenties revealed that she was started on by 'crackheads' in the town centre, an older man advised her to 'stay away from them people, and if anything happens, aim for the head or kick them in the balls, just go mad.' I recorded several examples of people fighting back in confrontations with strangers, and others intervening. Consider this anecdote from a man in Paul's community in his early forties:

118 Violence

LIAM: Not often in life now I have a first, but for the first time I had a knife pulled on me while working out of town! He swiftly learnt his lesson, you don't pull a knife on 4 scaffolders who have very short but heavy steel tubes close to hand

NORA: Lucky you weren't in Corby the wee cunts wouldne run

LIAM: This guy didn't run mate, he got taken out (by hand not by tube 'cus that would've been messy).

It is in this wider context of violence that the concern of Ethan's mother about her son's failure to fight back becomes comprehensible. When I first met Ethan, just before the restorative justice conference, his mother said to him, 'do you know whose daughter that is?' When Ethan shook his head, she said, 'it's Paul-on-the-van's kid'. Ethan's face lit up, as did Tyler's, and they both started telling me about different times they had been on the van. Ethan's enthusiasm went further, and he said he wanted to work with Paul, asking if he could help load the van. To me, Ethan came across as innocent, polite, and gentle—more childlike than other youths his age on the estate, though I could imagine him excelling in a protected environment. However, such a childhood was out of reach for Ethan, who must navigate tough conditions for the foreseeable future. This is why Ethan's mother expresses concern for Ethan and the necessity of self-defence for survival on the estate. By contrast, any attempts to foster Ethan's gentle and inquisitive nature would be an injustice to him in the life that the British class system requires him to endure.

Ethan eventually did fight back. I met Ethan and his mother a few months after the conference to discuss how it had gone, and how things had been since then. Ethan was almost unrecognizable. He was wearing fashionable clothing, and his hair was styled. He was now less interested to talk to me, and he chose to walk around the town centre while his mother and I spoke. Ethan's mother was positive about how the school conference had gone, and in her view, restorative justice 'actually works', by putting 'everyone on the same level' and by giving people 'a chance to talk'. In keeping with the philosophical underpinnings of restorative justice and the concept of 'reintegrative shaming' (Braithwaite, 1989), Ethan's mother identified that it was the 'embarrassment' of the boys having to confront the issue in front of their parents that made the difference. Yet what Ethan's mother deemed to be a success is out of accord with how the criminal justice system measures success. Following the conference, Ethan and Tyler became close friends, and, instead of being the victim, Ethan became the aggressor. Ethan's mother explains her relief:

Strategies to Displace Violence **119**

> When I heard what had happened to Ethan, I felt ashamed, or that's not really the right word, but yeah ashamed almost that Ethan hadn't hit the boy back. He just took it. He should have stood up for himself. [...] The teachers were pleased Ethan didn't hit back. [...] His dad was very angry when he heard what had happened and Ethan just took it. He was very angry. You see, he was bullied as a kid and he said you must hit back or people will walk all over you. [...] Now Ethan is standing up for himself, he grabbed a boy in school and got in trouble for it. [...] He's getting excluded, and they're talking about sending him to a school in [a neighbouring town]. [...] But at least now he knows to fight back and not be a walkover.

While not ideal, Ethan's transition from a gentle pupil into a young man who can defend himself and his family means he has a greater chance to survive the hardships that lie ahead.

Strategies to Displace Violence

In this final section, I wish to note strategies Paul's community use to displace violence, which again appear related to customary practice and are suitably explained by the logic of mutuality. It might be that some of the discussions among Paul's peers so far outlined are a means to prevent violence from arising—openly discussing norm-violations, widely sharing information about criminal acts, and warning about different forms of community retaliation if problematic behaviours continue could be forms of deterrence. The power of talking practices is emphasized by Simon Roberts in a review of anthropological observations about violence across societal groupings: 'Through talk, values and norms may be expressly stated, and consequences of departure from them spelled out' (1979: 43).

Likewise, certain aggressive forms of speech might comprise a way to prevent violence, since harsh language warns of the potential for violence and provides opportunity for desistance and retreat. This is evident in violent threats in Paul's community to 'annihilate', 'rip apart', 'go mental', 'knock you the fuck out', and so forth, which seek to mark out the speaker as not an easy target. By presenting oneself as tough through language, as well as bodily posture, threats of violence can, in some instances, be warded off (cf. Charlesworth, 2000: 217). Similarly, volume and tone of voice might serve a protective purpose. For example, some of Paul's friends refer to their 'gobs'

120 Violence

(mouths) as a commanding force in arguments. A mother in Paul's community notes the power of voice when relaying an earlier confrontation with a teacher:

BRYONY: As soon as that teacher broke down in tears in front of everyone, my work was done. Sometimes people need to be taken down a peg or two

AMANDA: I know, mate, I don't give a shit who it is... if it's got to be said then it's got be said

BRYONY: And if they shout, I only shout louder

AMANDA: I'm sure there's few people stupid enough to shout back at ya mate.

In this example, rather than using language to resolve conflict, voice is used to bring an argument to an abrupt end. Conflict resolution through dialogue may advantage those with advanced linguistic skills (Charlesworth, 2000; Lareau, 2011; Willis, 2018). Therefore, in a situation where a teacher perhaps has greater linguistic power, the mother uses vocal volume to eliminate the conditions for (what could be) unfair discussion. Hence, the mother uses the resources she has—the ability to shout, loudly—to fight for her child (see Walkerdine et al., 2001: 126; Blackledge, 2001).

'Naming and shaming' is another non-violent strategy which community participants regularly deployed in conflict situations (see also Roberts, 1979: 61–3). This involved publicly naming a person accused of an offence, such as theft or failure to repay a loan, so that the person would experience shame in the community, functioning also as a warning to others in the community not to trust the named person. The implication of being labelled a thief in this way appeared to matter, and so normally community participants sought to defend against such accusations. On a few occasions, an accused thief would throw an identical insult back at the accuser, or, commonly, deny the offence outright.

Occasionally, parents named and shamed their own children to teach them a lesson. When parents adopted this approach, they were explicit about what they were doing, such as this mother: 'I'm naming and shaming Michael. My own son has stolen from me for the last time. This is the only way he'll learn.'

For those in Paul's community, adolescence is an especially challenging period, when young people had to transition into an adult life of precarity. Rather than naming and shaming to ostracize children from the community, mothers seemingly used this technique to draw on collective support,

Strategies to Displace Violence **121**

to control and discipline pubescent children. On several occasions, naming and shaming was simply threatened and not enacted; norm violators would not be named and shamed *yet*, giving them a chance first of redemption.

It is worth noting again that those within the framework of mutuality place a strong evaluation on good personhood—on being judged a good person in the eyes of the community. Since community participants rely on each other for informal forms of social support, a person who acquires a reputation as untrustworthy may be unable to rely on networks of support in times of need. If someone becomes well known as a repeat norm violator—someone who is regularly named and shamed—then they risk exclusion from mutuality benefits. Indeed, occasionally, the practice of name and shame escalated into vigilante action and community exile, examples we explore further in Chapter 4.

A final non-violent conflict resolution strategy to note here is karma. Recurrently, Paul's community appealed to the work of karma to redress wrongs. The community conceived karma as a spiritual form of justice—encapsulated by 'what goes around comes around'—and as inevitable (cf. Roberts, 1979: 63–5). Therefore, norm violations often led to warnings that a person's karma will 'catch up' with them; Paul's friends often shared reminders that 'karma's a bitch'. Invoking the power of karma seemed a strategy preferred for unknown culprits, since other remedies were unavailable. Public sharing of the fate that awaited an unknown norm violator might prompt the culprit to desist from committing similar wrongs in the future (cf. Roberts, 1979: 62). And when there was a suspected culprit, community participants invoked karma to caution against deception, as by a woman in her late twenties: 'karma, the truth will come out and all those shit stirrers will be found out'.

Though, at times, community participants might state karma as though a simple fact, on others, they sought to conjure it in more elaborate ways. This included linking karma to the forces of evil and invoking it as part of larger vengeful plans. For instance, one middle-aged woman in Paul's community warned, 'haha karma is a bitch and an evil one at that. Let the games begin, hahaha!' And another on a separate occasion wrote ominously, 'Karma is going to creep up on someone and bite them in the arse big time. And when it does, I'll be the one laughing loudest and longest 'cus its gonna get them good!'.

The invocation of karma in these curse-like manners is reflective of former superstitious methods to deter wrongdoing. Susan Amussen (1995) discusses how women's use of curses, which led to witchcraft accusations in

122 Violence

early modern England, often had a disciplinary purpose. Amussen explains that while men might respond to mistreatment through ritual fighting, since it was believed ill-health and misfortune could be invoked through supernatural forces, women could resort to superstition to (aim to) enforce their will or exact revenge. Although this meant women who held grudges risked being accused of witchcraft, Amussen (1995: 30) notes how these 'beliefs gave some power to poor women who otherwise had none', since those fearful of witchcraft might think twice before wronging them for fear of their wrath.

Superstitions continue to circulate in Paul's community. Rather than being throwaway comments, seemingly Paul's peers did believe in the forces of karma. Since the loss of work, economic hardship, and general bad luck are part of precariat life, someone looking for evidence of karma in the lives of others need not wait long to find it. Indeed, on several occasions, I observed Paul's friends make sense of bad things that were happening in their lives as the result of karma from their past misbehaviours. This was evident when a father expressed pain over not being able to see his children on their birthdays, which he explained as the result of karma, since he was 'a knob in the past'. Another man in his early twenties explained the theft of his new bike as his karma for stealing bikes in his youth. And another in his late thirties believed that his wife's terminal illness was his karma for being a troublemaker in his youth. An older man forewarned others, again ominously, that 'karma has no deadline', a sentiment that perhaps sustains belief in karma's ability to catch up with transgressors.

We might also be able to interpret the conviction in karma as part of the framework of mutuality, for it complements a sense of there being a natural equilibrium in the universe which facilitates the redistribution of social resources to create fair balance. Thus, there is a belief that those who act against this sense of fairness will be exposed to natural forces that will remove unfair advantages gained. Such beliefs are important because mutuality does not operate on a reciprocal basis, where individuals always keep track of contributions. Instead, the ethos of mutuality requires those with resources to contribute when they can, and those genuinely in need to access resources. For this system to work, people need to act in good faith—karma is a complementary belief for such a good faith system to be effective.

Despite its prevalence, karma is not always deemed to be a sufficient means of redressing wrongdoing. In a tongue-in-cheek post, which received a good number of 'likes', a man in his thirties challenged the tendency to rely on karma and called for more immediate action instead:

> There's a lot of 'what goes around comes around, karma's a bitch, your day will come' statuses being posted lately. Stop being a shite bag, talk is cheap, get round to their houses and hoof a bastard brick through their window while they're sitting watching telly. You might get jail, but you'll feel good.

This comment makes sense in a context where participants in Paul's community so frequently cite the notion of karma to deal with injustices. In Chapter 4, we examine the types of wrongs that the collective likely deems as warranting an active response, taking them outside the hands of fate, despite the potential to invoke the ire of the state.

Conclusion

This chapter has provided a historically informed analysis of the uses of violence among Paul's community. By adopting Thompson's moral economy concept, we have moved beyond individualistic understandings of violence to see how it might be motivated by a deeper commitment to a relational order of which the individual is intricately part. Therefore, instead of being purely driven by self-interest and the desire to obtain an individualized form of recognition, a community participant might be drawn into moments of violence out of love and care for kin, and what might result is recognition of being someone upon whom others can rely. I have suggested that the norms that legitimize and limit violence are rooted in customary practices, which have ultimately been affected by contemporary conditions. Whereas in the past, the normative order might have had greater cross-class prevalence, in the present there is notable ambiguity over the precise norms that ought to apply, which can become a source of further contention.

Though violence might be deemed acceptable in certain circumstances, this is not to suggest that violence is valorized. In fact, many of the practices we have observed in this chapter can be understood as strategies to limit violence. For instance, not all are expected to be a notorious fighter; instead, certain people take on this role and sacrifice personal autonomy (in the event they become imprisoned) for the protection of loved ones. Others offer arbitration skills and attempt to diffuse violence through negotiation and advice. By teaching young people about the norms of a fair fight, fatal forms of violence might be averted. And, moreover, the injunction to defend oneself allows some young community participants to avoid becoming

124 Violence

the target of bullying, or to inculcate a defensive instinct useful when confronted with violence in adulthood. In addition to talking, naming and shaming and karma are further non-violent strategies of managing conflict.

Nevertheless, being exposed to violence, needing to learn the norms of a fair fight, and learning how to 'go mental' when required presents a volatile terrain to navigate. Those who rely on these methods are exposed to the forces of moral luck, where a fight might inadvertently turn fatal. Consequently, many of Paul's friends have first-hand experience of the criminal process and have spent periods of time in prison. The reason nonetheless that Paul's peers must continue to rely on violent forms of conflict resolution is because the most socio-economically disadvantaged in the English social order have never been fully included in the provisions and protection of the state.

This brings us up to the starting point of the next chapter, where we examine barriers which socio-economically disadvantaged communities face when they try to access state services, and the creative ways excluded persons attempt to move the unresponsive state to action.

Amnesty

Paul settled problems the local way.

In the 1970s, several mobile grocery vans operated in Corby—most run by Bill Baker and Mike Carrey's business, B&G. Paul created his own route on the un-served streets of the Lincoln estate and surrounding areas. But having built a regular customer base, he had to guard against rival drivers who could make decent earnings if they got to Paul's stops before him.

Gordon grew up working on the vans. His grandfather delivered fruit and vegetables by horse and cart in Scotland, and his first job as a boy growing up in Corby was loading the B&G vans, until he purchased his own in his late teens. In search of a van route, Gordon ventured onto the Lincoln estate, unwittingly discovering the one Paul had developed. Gordon remembers hearing Paul's horn sound two streets behind him, but Gordon managed to arrive at the stops just before him.

'It was smashing trade,' Gordon recounts.

But then the sound of Paul's horn faded. Shortly after, Gordon saw a little Bedford Rascal van appear in his wing mirror. The small van drove up on the curb, blocking Gordon in. Paul stepped out, introduced himself, and explained how Gordon was taking his trade. Gordon described Paul as 'completely reasonable', and he agreed to build a new round on a neighbouring estate instead.

After that, Gordon and Paul became close friends, socializing after work, and supporting each other in times of need. Gordon became Uncle Gordon, and his late wife, Aunty Maureen.

Other van rivalries ended less amicably. Gordon recounts a man confronting Paul in the pub during a night out. Paul tried to reason with the man to stop encroaching on his round and create his own. But unlike Gordon, the new rival wouldn't back down. He shouted at Paul and threatened violence. Paul told him to 'wind his neck back down in case he choked on his beer'. Gordon is unsure what happened after that, though the man left the estate and Paul stayed.

A Precarious Life. Roxana Willis, Oxford University Press. © Roxana Willis 2023.
DOI: 10.1093/oso/9780198855149.003.0008

126 Amnesty

Another good friend of Paul's, Snoddy, remembers a subsequent encounter. A budget supermarket opened in the town centre, and a man on a neighbouring estate started buying cheap loaves and selling them on Paul's rounds. Paul asked his pal to have a word with the man. When the rival bread seller refused to talk to Paul, in his heavy Glaswegian accent, Snoddy 'advised' the rival not to park his van too close to the house at night because it could easily catch fire. The warning was understood. The illicit bread seller went to speak with Paul and a solution was found.

* * *

Running the van on the Lincoln also required Paul to resolve day-to-day conflicts on the estate. Over the years, norms established themselves. Violence on the van was prohibited, otherwise people wouldn't be able to get what they needed—a rule collectively enforced.

And so the van became a rare place of amnesty. If someone was being threatened or chased, if they reached the van, Paul helped them make it home safe. Many benefited from this sanctuary; whether it was a child being bullied, a teenager being chased by a group of youths, or an adult caught in a violent attack, the van offered protection for all.

* * *

One incident my father shared occurred during the height of the estate's difficulties. Paul had just finished his Hudson Close stop, at the back of the estate, when a young man, Luke, ran onto the van, his face slashed open, blood pouring out.

Paul grabbed a pack of kitchen towel from a shelf and placed an entire roll over Luke's open wound to stem the bleeding. He told Luke to hold the roll firmly in place and apply as much pressure as possible, or he was going to bleed to death.

Paul then got into the driver's seat and started the van. But as he was driving off, he saw a group of lads running over, one with a bloody samurai sword in hand. Paul rolled down the window and the lad with the sword demanded he hand over Luke, explaining the grievance. Luke had apparently sold his mate's stuff while he was in prison to buy gear (heroin), and his mate was so pissed off, he wanted to kill him.

Paul listened to the furious lad and empathized about Luke taking the piss. But he suggested they'd made their point well enough—*Luke's head has a gaping hole in it. If he doesn't get to hospital, he's going to die.*

Paul assured the lads that he'd not seen anything, and Luke wasn't going to say anything, and that the best thing for everyone was for Luke to get medical care to limit police interference. The wronged lad began to calm down and agreed with Paul's assessment. They shook hands and Paul drove off.

Paul dropped Luke off at a nearby pub where his mum worked. There, they had access to a phone to call an ambulance, and Paul could remain an unseen party. Satisfied Luke was out of danger, Paul cleaned up the van and continued his rounds, slightly behind schedule.

The next day, the headline of the local paper read, 'Pub Landlord Saves Son's Life'.

Paul smiled when he retold the tale.

4
Thin Blue Line

As we saw in the last chapter, the expansion of the modern state has allowed large sections of English society to move away from first-hand use of force, in accordance with the civilization discourse which prioritized self-restraint over physical reaction (Wood, 2004; Wiener, 2004). This move was feasible because the modern state developed alternative avenues for individuals to enforce their will, in instituting the police, courts, and other state services, in addition to privatized forms of policing and security which have proliferated in the modern age (cf. Loader, 1997; Taylor, 1999; Zedner, 2006). However, those excluded from these formalized provisions must deploy strategies themselves to preserve the normative order on which the community, and the interconnected self, relies. Consequently, Paul's neighbours continue to partake in customary forms of fighting and live by norms which both constrain and permit legitimate uses of interpersonal violence.

In this chapter, I further explore the limits of state support from the perspective of those in the precariat. The discussion builds on themes of violence, but I now focus on the disjuncture between the framework of mutuality, which is rooted in customary norms, and the dominant framework of autonomy, which the state advances and upholds (for a theoretical overview of frameworks see the Introduction). More precisely, I examine how these frameworks intersect with notions of justice and injustice, especially when Paul's peers interact with the criminal justice system and state agencies. Since the nation state developed with the growth of the bourgeoisie, the modern legal system has evolved to primarily protect bourgeois interests from the disorder of those below (see Hall, 1992, 2007). The modern criminal law is central to these aims; at its heart is the protection of private property, as defined by the civil law, and the subsequent expansion to protect the individual from particular forms of interpersonal harm (see Wood, 2004; Wiener, 2004; Hay, 1975). In accordance with these developments, the law recognizes a specific vision of the individual, influenced by the Enlightenment ideal of the autonomous actor detached from relational ties and background normative frameworks. However, as I have been

A Precarious Life. Roxana Willis, Oxford University Press. © Roxana Willis 2023.
DOI: 10.1093/oso/9780198855149.003.0009

emphasizing, the moral figure of the autonomous legal subject is in fact an aspiration; the liberal state facilitates the realization of this ideal for some, but not all. And so, for precariously positioned individuals, the ontological reality of co-dependence, rather than autonomy, is greatly pronounced.

Accordingly, those living within what I am calling the moral framework of mutuality place special value on their interconnections, prioritizing trustworthy relationships over and above self-advancement and self-interest, which are highly valued goods in a framework of autonomy. These different normative positions are reflected in how the alternative frameworks characterize justice. The criminal law in England and Wales, itself largely committed to the goods of an autonomy-oriented framework, is infused with the liberal values of procedural justice, where determinations of wrongdoing are largely impersonal affairs; therefore, at least in theory, it does not matter who the victim is and their relationship to the offender. Conversely, relational factors have a significant influence on how Paul and his neighbours, living within a framework of mutuality, perceive the nature of wrongdoing. Building on the insights of Jeanette Edwards (2000), Insa Koch (2018b), and Stuart Hall et al. (2013), among others (Conley and O'Barr, 1990; Merry, 1990; Strathern, 1981), I show that the norms of a mutuality framework grade intra-community harm as a worse offence than harm against an outsider or a corporation, and harm against a vulnerable person as worse than certain crimes against powerful actors.

Relational differences between the frameworks rest on a deeper disjuncture still, concerning power. Those who are chiefly guided by the framework of autonomy place special value on a particular ideal of freedom: becoming autonomous through increasing control over space (i.e. property) and people (i.e. employees for a business, or service-based employees to aid the upkeep of a person's life—such as nannies and cleaners). This ideal of enlarging personal freedom through owning more objects and land, directing others to create more wealth for profit, or employing others to sustain the individual's way of life, does not explicitly endorse power abuse or hierarchy. However, power imbalance (if not abuse) and hierarchy remain necessarily connected to the ideal, even though a person's place within social hierarchies is framed as contingent and moveable. That is, while some in society must work in demeaning jobs with poorer pay, and some in society, by virtue of the present nature of ownership, necessarily do not have free access to what others own (see G. A. Cohen (2017) on lack of freedom for others inherent in the notion of property), according to this framework, anyone

130 Thin Blue Line

in principle is free to move beyond their hierarchical bounds through hard work—they must leverage the basic freedom we all have to succeed.

In contrast, it seems that those oriented towards mutuality have a different relationship to social hierarchy. Rather than tolerating social hierarchies, they actively resist them in preference for social equilibrium. This is apparent when a person asserts power over another—indeed, we will see how Paul's friends tend to resist such impositions, either by framing them as forms of bullying or by actively intervening to balance out unequal relationships. Relevant here are Edwards's (2000) observations in Bacup, a post-industrial town in northern England. Edwards describes her research participants as having a 'propensity to eschew subservience' (2000: 148), and being prone to intervene in circumstances where a person is outnumbered or in a weaker position in some conflict (2000: 160). We will spot a similar sensitivity to power imbalance and aversion to abuses of power in Paul's community.

These foundational differences in the frameworks mean that there are times when the state has no concern to redress, or even recognize, some wrongdoing as conceived on the terms of mutuality, since it rather upholds autonomy norms. In such circumstances, participants in Paul's community find other ways to respond to the wrongdoing, which we explore in the latter part of this chapter as part of a process recognized by Koch (2018b) as 'personalizing the state'. Koch details the strategies that a comparable English community in austerity Britain employs to move the state to act. Rather than framing disadvantaged individuals as powerless and passive objects in the class struggle, Koch shows how disadvantaged residents, excluded from the full remit of state support, resist their mistreatment by creatively co-opting the state to act in their interests. Strategies Koch identifies, which are also present in Paul's community, include vigilantism and enlisting the services of the state in creative ways. I examine how community participants 'personalize the state', alongside local practices of dispute resolution explored in Chapter 3.

This chapter begins by carving out the notion of wrongdoing as it is found in Paul's community, focusing on the offence of theft, and noting how it differs from the sense of wrongdoing enforced by the criminal justice system. I then examine how this local sense of wrongdoing informs the way community participants respond to norm violations. In the third section, I seek to explain the state's unresponsiveness to wrongdoing as perceived by Paul's community. And, in the final section, I explore how Paul's peers 'personalize the state' in Koch's sense. By the end of the chapter, we will begin to see the complex moral terrain Paul and his neighbours must navigate.

Wrongs of a Different Flavour

Sometimes conceptions of wrongdoing in Paul's community differed in important ways from legal conceptions. In my fieldwork, I recorded several examples which illustrate these differences, but here I focus on the offence of theft, which I regard as an example par excellence of the classed application of the legal system (see also Hall et al., 2013; Hay, 1975; Thompson, 1975). Theft is one of the oldest legal prohibitions in England, dating back to at least King Edmund's Code in the tenth century (Whitlock, 2016). From the seventeenth century onwards, the law rapidly expanded to protect new forms of property; most of the laws which formed part of the Bloody Code protected property, infractions of which were punishable by death (see Beattie, 1986; Thompson, 1975). Although historians have noted that juries were reluctant to enforce the death penalty in cases of theft, they would more commonly enforce the punishment of forced emigration and indentured labour in the colonies abroad (see Beattie, 1986; Linebaugh and Rediker, 2012; Whitlock, 2016; Zedner, 1991). In accordance with these legal developments, principally designed to protect the interests of the propertied, the status of the offender and concerns about economic needs are immaterial for the establishment of wrongdoing.

Paul's neighbours tended to accept or overlook certain informal economies and illicit practices, perhaps in appreciating that conditions of precarity necessitate alternative means of subsistence (see also Koch, 2018b; McKenzie, 2015; Rogaly and Taylor, 2016; Smith, 2017a). In this respect, some of Paul's friends tolerated, or on occasion endorsed, theft from a chain store, from the back of a lorry, or, at a stretch, from a richer area. Such attitudes are evident in the following discussion.

STEFF: Gotta love shoplifters, bargains galore!
TANIA: What u get?
STEFF: Loads of make-up and stuff
GRACE: Send them my way
STEFF: They've been and gone, tried to grab them again on my way past but they sold the lot! She's gonna come back tomorrow so inbox me your address and I'll send them your way.

Although handling and purchasing stolen goods constitutes an offence of theft (see Theft Act 1968, section 22), the openness of this discussion, and the absence of moral condemnation, indicates a degree of acceptance

132 Thin Blue Line

(see also McKenzie, 2015: 89). Janet Roitman's (2006: 249) discussion of the 'ethics of illegality' in relation to banditry in the Chad Basin gives us a helpful way of making this moral outlook intelligible: 'Ultimately, while viewed by most as illegal, unregulated economic activities and violent methods of extraction are also described as legitimate.' Thus, Roitman identifies how an illegal activity can be recognized as unlawful and yet still have an internal acceptability among certain groups, especially those who have difficulty participating in the formal economy (see also Edwards, 2000: 163; Hall et al., 2013: 187). I suggest that some in Paul's community apply this same duality of thinking about certain forms of theft; those who are precariously positioned realize that legal routes to access material goods are out of bounds, which validates alternative channels.

However, the normative system of Paul's peers warrants starkly different attitudes towards theft from the powerful versus 'internal' theft: they treated stealing from within the community as an especially grave harm, among the worst transgressions one could commit, and worthy of the most severe moral censure and reprisals. The following discussion demonstrates how differently the wrong of internal theft was perceived and reveals a range of responses.

LUCY: I was at the supermarket with Kayla to pick up bits for the picnic, and these dirty thieving tramps snatched my purse from my handbag! Then the junkies hid it. IN THEIR KID'S PRAM!

BARBARA: Wow! Some people have no shame. In front of their own children

SOPHIE: Oh my God, do you know who it was? Get the police involved

BARBARA: You should have punched the dirty scumbags in the face

LUCY: I went mental, gave them a chance to own up twice and that. Then security came over 'cus of ma shouting. When he said the police were gunna get called they soon handed it over. I would have battered them if I weren't with Kayla... And then I realized their kid's in the same class as Callum at school, so I see them all the time!

SOPHIE: Karma will catch up with them sooner or later

BARBARA: Fuck karma, I'm coming to the school with you tomorrow. We'll batter the tramps when their kids go inside

RACH: Nah, get wee Callum to batter the kid in school, ha ha!

SOPHIE: Who are they? Name and shame

RACH: Poor kids being brought up by junkies like that. I dread to see what type of parents they become

LUCY: I've never seen kids like it, they need disinfecting, teeth cleaned, and hair brushed. It's a real shame.

Wrongs of a Different Flavour   133

In this discussion, stereotypes about the immoral poor are pronounced, which is a topic I address in more detail in Chapter 6. For now, let us focus on how the wrong of theft is perceived. Unlike the toleration (or endorsement) of the shoplifter targeting chain stores, who might redistribute some corporate wealth to struggling locals, in this example, one woman recommends the police as a legitimate response, which plausibly relates to the fact that theft in this instance harms rather than aids others in the locality. Still, for Paul's peers, recourse to the police alone is deemed insufficient to fully redress the wrong of an internal theft. Under the English and Welsh criminal law, the seriousness of a theft largely depends on the degree of financial loss, and, at a stretch, it might consider sentimental and practical value (see CPS, 2019). However, from the perspective of Paul's community, in instances of interpersonal theft, the wrongness transcends the value of the object, since norms of trust have been violated, which jeopardizes the informal social order on which community participants rely. Moreover, the offence of theft is aggravated under the law when an offender further encroaches on the victim's autonomy: for example, when force is used, elevating the offence of theft to robbery; or when theft occurs during illegal entry of a building, amounting to the offence of burglary (see Theft Act 1968, ss 8 and 9). By contrast, what most aggravates an act of theft from the mutuality viewpoint is when relational factors are involved, such as stealing from kin and thus undermining trust.

Stuart Hall et al. (2013: 146–7) suitably capture the multifaceted nature of theft from the perspective of those precariously positioned in the English social order:

> Theft from work and 'fiddles' have an acceptability which they would not be accorded by the law—they are seen as an integral part of redressing the economic imbalance. On the other hand, 'internal' theft within the constitutive circle of friends, relatives and neighbours forms a fundamental breach of the code; it fractures the concrete relations of mutual support.

The legitimacy of some forms of theft in Paul's community accords with the moral framework of mutuality, since the shoplifter redistributes at least some wealth to those with less (cf. Hobsbawm, 1969; Rodgers, 2015; Roitman, 2006). Paul's peers thus regard theft from the richer elements of society as a form of fairness: those with fewer resources take from the (relative) excess resources of the powerful and in so doing marginally improve

134 Thin Blue Line

the position of the least well off. Conversely, stealing from within the community involves imposing force on a comparably positioned person, which becomes an act of domination rather than an act to rebalance the unequal status quo. Worse still, internal theft may damage relationships, which form the substance of informal support, and thereby creates harm beyond the loss of property.

In the last extract, the mothers recommend informal responses in addition to police involvement, seemingly to address the full harm of internal theft. Lucy focuses on the relational aspects of the offence; whereas the criminal justice system makes no distinction about the nature of a victim of theft, here it reaches to the heart of the harm (see Conley and O'Barr, 1990; Goffman, 2015; Koch, 2018b). In this instance, perpetrators targeted a precariously positioned mother while engaged in parental activities. The perpetrators could, we can imagine, attempt to 'neutralize' their act by framing it as a redistributive move, taking from a person with relative privilege (cf. Sykes and Matza, 1957); however, the differences are likely slight when social spaces such as supermarkets and schools are so closely shared. Further aggravating the offence, the alleged offenders commit the act in the presence of their own children and are claimed to have used their child's pram to hide the stolen goods, hence entwining the child with the wrongdoing. It seems that these relational features of the offence worsen the crime in the eyes of Paul's friends and justify responses beyond contacting the police. While the police might deal with the appropriation of property belonging to another as per section 1 of the Theft Act 1968, the relational aspect of the harm would still require redress.

There is particular hostility in Paul's community towards those addicted to alcohol and drugs, and I think this is importantly related to the moral censure of internal theft. Paul's neighbours generally classify individuals living with addiction, even if from within the community, as 'illegitimate' because they see addicts as prone to opportunistic crimes against those within the community, instead of engaging in criminal activity away from the estate; addicts would allegedly 'sell their own granny for a fix'. Out of kilter with good personhood (Koch, 2018b; Smith, 2017b), the repeat offending of those with addiction can easily lead to reputations of bad character. As an example of the community hostility to addicts, some youths in Paul's community shared with me their attempts to eradicate drug use on the estate by engaging in a practice referred to as 'junkie-bashing', which involved chasing and attacking suspected addicts found on the estate. Lisa McKenzie (2015: 61) documents a similar practice on her council estate,

St Anne's in Nottingham, where children would throw bricks and stones at suspected users of crack cocaine. Paul's community also referred to 'alky-bashing', targeting alcoholics specifically.

However, others in Paul's community showed compassion for individuals living with addiction—indeed, several of Paul's closest friends battled with heroin and alcohol addiction. Instead of excluding addicts, some residents on the estate purchased stolen goods from them, which received little moral censure, comparable to the incident of the shoplifter detailed above. On occasions, residents would even purchase stolen goods for which they had no purpose or desire. Paul provides an example of this practice; I recall multiple times a person would come to the front door with obscure items, such as a top-of-the-range protractor set, which Paul would never have any purpose for, but nevertheless purchased. I believe Paul engaged in exchanges such as these to aid those struggling with addiction, many of whom Paul had known since they were children. Paul was once charged with the offence of handling stolen goods, but nevertheless continued to provide this form of support: the virtue of helping others and maintaining caring relationships was more important than the norms of the criminal justice system which prioritize property rights.

In this discussion of theft, we have found that Paul's community characterize and gauge the wrongness of theft in terms of its relational and character-based elements, in contrast to the procedural and rule-based logic of the criminal justice system. Accordingly, to fully address a perceived wrong, community participants cannot employ the criminal justice system—it does not recognize all the norm violations, or place as high a priority on them. Faced with this (in their view) inadequate form of justice, Paul's neighbours rectify norm violations in other ways.

Protecting the Social Order

In an examination of the modern criminal law, Lindsay Farmer (2016) suggests that the legal system developed to uphold the civil order of the modern state, in contrast to *social* order prior to the development of the modern state. We can use this distinction to distinguish between the norms enforced by the state and the framework of mutuality norms Paul's multi-generational peers enforce themselves. For instance, while the state does not always fully redress the relational aspects of a wrong, it does respond to certain aspects of a norm violation, such as the violation of property

136   Thin Blue Line

rights—in so doing, it protects or upholds the civil order. By contrast, the protection of sharing practices and supportive relationships is a means of protecting the social order, as when Paul's friends use force against someone who threatens a family member or who fails to pay back an informal debt (as evident in Chapter 3). In this section, I examine how and when Paul and his neighbours protect the social order.

There are multiple examples, both past and present, of Paul's community taking collective action in response to a perceived wrongdoing. When a wrongdoing purportedly involves child abuse, the community strongly backs responses. From the perspective of Paul's peers, harming children is the most heinous wrong, yet there is a belief that the state fails to adequately address such offences. Some of Paul's friends alleged that state actors colluded with and protected sex offenders by failing to implement harsh sentencing. Consider a discussion about a woman from Corby who was given a prison sentence and banned from a neighbouring town for repeat shoplifting offences, and whose mugshot was shared on social media. Challenging the police narrative about the wrongfulness of the convicted shoplifter, a man in Paul's community contrasted the sentencing outcome with alleged statistics on shorter community sentences given to child sex offenders. Consequently, several of Paul's friends described the government as 'disgusting', 'pathetic', and with 'their heads in their backsides'; one man suggested that there are people in 'authority positions with secret handshakes who get away with this'; and another commented, 'what gets me is every normal person wants these people hung so why don't the government do something about it'. Several of Paul's peers purportedly approved of the death penalty as an appropriate response to sexual offences against children, sometimes specified in the form of the electric chair, hanging, or vividly described forms of torture.

Occasionally, the community's strong moral censure of crimes against children morphed into physical response. Several vigilante groups have formed in Corby in response to rumours of an alleged sex offender living in the town or being released from prison. During my fieldwork, the address of an accused sex offender was shared; it became a target for criminal damage, and the police rehoused the accused. The most violent response to child abuse involved a man in his twenties from Paul's community who was serving time in prison for murdering a young mother on the estate in the presence of her infant (BBC News, 2013). During his imprisonment, the man reportedly murdered a fellow inmate convicted of multiple child sex offences (Cronin, 2014). There was ambivalence in Paul's community about this second homicide. A minority praised the man's actions: he had partially redeemed himself for his prior abhorrent crime by 'getting a nonce'. However, the majority who commented on the incident were of the view that no matter what the offender did, his first crime was unforgivable. I did not encounter any moral censure of the second killing in this case, though I suspect if directly raised, at least some would speak against it too.

Another category of wrongdoing which Paul's community treats as meriting a proactive response concerns harm to animals. One family I met in Corby through the Youth Offender Services shared a past incident, when they were required to leave the town with police assistance because two teenagers in the family were accused of killing a dog in a distressing way. Paul's neighbours often called for perpetrators of animal abuse to receive the same form of injury in turn that they had allegedly inflicted on some animal. For example, several of Paul's friends recommended an apt punishment for a man filmed kicking a cat is 'a kicking'; a woman proposed that a girl filmed throwing a puppy in the river should have 'the same' done to her: 'tie her hands and feet together, glue her mouth shut and throw her in'; upon seeing a picture of a dog with a cut nose, a young man desired a similar fate for the perpetrator: 'pin the owners down and slash them open'; and so on. Calls for retributive, 'eye for an eye' forms of punishment in such cases perhaps indicate that Paul's peers regard humans and animals as equally worthy of moral respect (cf. Nussbaum, 2009); they also demonstrate an aversion to harming those unable to protect themselves.

Indeed, as I see it, it is a sensitivity to power imbalances which most likely motivates these sorts of collective outcries (following Edwards, 2000). While those guided by the framework of autonomy inevitably tolerate, if not endorse, some level of power imbalance and hierarchy, those guided by the framework of mutuality place a special value on the equal moral status of others, and therefore endorse notions of equitable distribution and balanced treatment. Accordingly, when power imbalances—though especially power abuses—manifest in attacks on defenceless human beings and animals, they are experienced by those in Paul's community as deeply unjust; such violence is the antithesis of a fair fight, and abuse towards vulnerable beings undermines the caring relationship. Being on the receiving end of power is a common feature of life for those in precarious social positions— whether in school, at work, in the job centre, or elsewhere, the precariat are liable to feel the relentless downward force of authority—which seems to increase awareness and sympathy for vulnerable others exposed to such forces.

138   Thin Blue Line

When norms of fairness and balance are broken, it seemingly moves those living within the framework of mutuality significantly, prompting them to condemn the norm violations and take steps towards redressing power imbalances, restoring the equilibrium, and, if necessary, eliminating the threat. I think we can see these moral motivations as extensions of the moral economy E. P. Thompson (1993b) describes: rather than rioting for fair access to grain as in Thompson's historical example, the community rallies for fairness in other respects—fair treatment in fights, fair redistribution of wealth in excess through selective (i.e. not internal) theft, and so on. An ethic of subsistence lies at the heart of both (see Scott, 1985).

Calls for community action in response to a series of violent crimes during the research period illustrate well this instinct for the collective to protect weaker community participants:

> I'm a born and bred Corby lad. I grew up here when the town was shit and there were more than a few dangerous folk jumping around. Nowadays, this town is apparently much 'better' yet there are constant rapes, muggings, and even child abductions. Instead of the odd nutter, now we have shady little rapists and robbers hiding in bushes, ambushing young girls and people who can't defend themselves. My warning to them scummy fuckers: Corby doesn't stand for that shit. The last thing you want is a squad of Corby boys finding out where you live! So don't do it. Or fuck off to another town!

In reply, another man agreed:

> On the whole we always had a decent class of criminals in Corby. Wrong side of the law but with morals. These lowlifes who are creeping around in the shadows might soon bump into a few Corby casuals who like to say hello with a spiked bat. These tramps need to be lynched.

We again see moral and immoral criminals distinguished by the status of their (alleged) victims (cf. Hall et al., 2013; Hobsbawm, 1969; Girling et al., 2000: 54–5). The imagined community of Corby is pronounced in these calls for action. The first man describes himself as 'a born and bred Corby lad' (see Edwards, 2000; Smith, 2012), which is a signal that he fully belongs, having been raised with the values of mutuality. Consequently, he feels well placed to step forwards as a protector of the group and can rally others into defensive action. Although the men here tolerate some forms of

Protecting the Social Order   139

criminality—those 'with morals'—they warn those who harm weaker parties to stop the wrongdoing or leave the town. For those who ignore these demands, 'lynching' is permissible.

Continuing the discussion started in Chapter 3, while these threats are overtly violent, we can see warning against unwanted behaviour as a strategy to displace violence. In this respect, we might think back to the eighteenth-century rituals of 'rough music' detailed by Thompson (1993a). 'Rough music' refers to certain customary practices identified in various parts of pre-modern Europe, each with distinct local differences. In the English context, Thompson describes how rough music rituals often involved crowds of locals banging pots and pans and singing humiliating rhymes about some norm transgressor; sometimes the transgressor would be paraded through the village on a pole, sometimes they would be dunked in water, or at other times effigies would be burned. Depending on the norm transgression and level of community disapproval, the ritual would end when the transgressor had been sufficiently shamed, or when the norm violation was rectified, or, in severe cases, when the transgressor moved away. Thus, rather than inflicting the threatened punishment, Thompson suggests that the aim of the practice was to eliminate the behaviour.

Some vigilante action in Paul's community, though quite distinct from the rough music rituals—no verses, drums, or parading the culprits on poles—appears to serve a similar purpose of collectively shaming a wrongdoer until they leave the area. Several historic examples from the Lincoln estate attest to this interpretation, two of which I mention here. In response to the killing of Louise Allen at the fair in 1996 (as detailed in Chapter 3), a widely held belief prevailed among the community that the sentences given to the teenage girls convicted of manslaughter were too lenient and did not capture the harm of this unfair fight. Therefore, in response to the sentencing outcomes, the family home of one offender on the estate became a target of criminal damage until they left the town (the other offender's family had already moved away). Similar methods were used against a couple who partnered with the police to crack down on so-called anti-social behaviour on the Lincoln estate, filmed by the BBC in 2004 and featuring in an unfavourable exposé of the local community. The couple had formed a neighbourhood group who roamed the estate with cameras hidden in torches to catch groups in the act of anti-social behaviour. In response to collusion with the police against locals, the couple's house became a legitimate target, continually being damaged until they sold it and moved.

140   Thin Blue Line

These exclusionary practices did not always seem to be permanent; for example, the family mentioned above, accused of harming a dog, eventually returned to the town. What appears to be most important is eliminating wrongful behaviour and reiterating the normative boundaries, including the norm not to harm vulnerable members of the collective, such as children and animals, who are viewed as relatively defenceless. Moreover, legitimate behaviour requires acting in accordance with unwritten norms upon which the informal social order relies, such as supporting sharing practices and caring relationships, respecting the rules of a fair fight, and not undermining trust by cooperating with the police. Therefore, part of the collective affect (following Walkerdine and Jimenez, 2012), or collective habitus (following Fraser and Clark, 2021), among Paul's peers is an emotional pull, when witnessing or hearing of power imbalances, to defend weaker community participants and the normative order.

Of course, when the community does undertake some vigilante action, it opens a channel for police response, since the state, operating by its norms, must now safeguard any individual whose safety the collective threatens to undermine (see Hornberger, 2013; Koch, 2017b, 2018b). Consequently, vigilante action may prompt the police to remove a norm violator, to protect individual rights, inadvertently satisfying the collective ends. The police's being used in such a manner is an example of what Koch terms 'personalizing the state', which we soon further examine. Comparatively, in the harsher context of mob justice in Cameroon, Rogers Orock (2014: 419) suggests that resort to this form of self-help indicates a desire by citizens 'to contest the state's derogation from its sovereign responsibility': '[w]hat the citizens at the scenes of mob justice express is not the desire for the replacement of state authority; rather they register their discontent with its insufficient performance and their desire to see a stronger and more protective state' (Orock, 2014: 421–2).

A last matter of note in this section concerns something I recorded multiple examples of during the fieldwork year: Corby residents are seemingly moved to protect strangers from harm. Consider a local girl-on-girl fight filmed outside a school. In the clip, a car pulls up during the fight and a man steps out; he pulls the girls apart and reprimands them: 'that's how people get killed, are you that stupid?' Another young woman in the community recalled an event from that day: she witnessed an elderly lady being mugged and depicted herself as intervening to help the elderly woman by tripping the mugger up before he managed to escape with a handbag. Similarly, the local paper reported on a man who intervened in the mugging of a girl in town, and another news article called for an 'anonymous good Samaritan' who stepped in to prevent a violent attack against a woman in a park to come forward. A teenager in Paul's community relayed another incident about a stranger who helped when she and her friend were being chased by a group of men in a car. And, lastly, the local press reported on a woman who, having spotted a group of youths attacking a homeless person in the Corby town centre, placed herself between them and the victim, thereby ending the attack (Northamptonshire Telegraph, 2019). Notably, Edwards (2000: 160) likewise observed locals in her study intervening to support a 'less powerful' fighter, even if the weaker party hailed from outside the town.

Repeated cases of strangers supporting others in dire need may indicate that Paul's peers feel a pull to intervene in violent situations, over and above the instinct for self-preservation. By intervening, individuals remain protected overall, since doing so reinforces the norm to mitigate power imbalance and increases the likelihood that those within the collective will be supported in times of need.

Informal responses to norm violations substitute for the police when the police are unable or unwilling to act. The police might fail to intervene in wrongful conduct for many reasons. For example, they might simply not be present when an offence occurs, or, despite calls from the community for action, the criminal law itself might limit the nature and method of response. However, there are also times when the police can act within the remit of the law but are unwilling to do so, we explore these cases in the next section.

Calling on the Police

Relationships between socio-economically disadvantaged communities and the police can be complex (Fassin, 2013; Hall et al., 2013; Koch, 2018b; Loader, 1996; McKenzie, 2015; Smith, 2017a; Wacquant, 2007). Less advantaged communities are often observed to be sceptical of the police. Stuart Hall et al. (2013: 188) capture a source of such tension: 'In a class society, based on the needs of capital and the protection of private property, the poor and propertyless are *always* in some sense on "the wrong side of the law", whether actually they transgress it or not.' As noted in Chapter 3, police forces developed in England principally to enforce the civil order of the modern state and as a means of urging society away from violent forms of dispute resolution (Wiener, 2004; Wood, 2004). In effect, then, by

142   Thin Blue Line

reinforcing the norms of civility and public order, state policing has from the outset targeted society's lower orders; policing is often something done to poorer communities rather than developed as a service for them. In relation to the present, as Koch (2018b: 14) notes, '[t]hose who are precariously situated with respect to the capitalist market have always been policed in ways not known to their middle-class counterparts'.

Against this backdrop of antagonism between the state and the working class, at least some of Paul's friends overtly disdained the police. For example, they directed several hostile statements towards the police, including 'fucking hate police', 'only good copper is a dead one', and the recurrent use of the acronyms 'FTP' (fuck the police) and 'ACAB' (all cops are bastards). Related to this ill-feeling towards the police, certain community participants spoke out against those who voluntarily engaged with the police, using language such as 'grassing' or 'snitching' (cf. Smith, 2012: 174). On a handful of occasions, participants threatened violence toward suspected police informants, using common threats such as 'snitches get stitches'.

Notwithstanding a degree of hostility towards police informants by some, relationships between the police and community participants were active (see also Bell, 2016; Goffman, 2015; Koch, 2018b; McKenzie, 2015). While there is indeed cynicism towards the police in Paul's community, as well as cynicism towards other state institutions, this is by no means a blanket aversion to the police and state authority. Indeed, Paul's friends do often call for state and police assistance, and they enjoy those benefits of the state which they successfully access. The cynicism that does exist, however, as we discuss in this section, appears to stem from the reluctance of the state in general, and of the police in particular, to respond to perceived wrongdoing. Precariat experience reveals how the state often extends only a limited version of its services to the most disadvantaged.

As noted above, when sharing information about wrongdoing and assessing appropriate responses, Paul's peers commonly threatened to go to the police, or advised their friends likewise. Moreover, on many occasions community participants openly announced that they had gone to the police, without inviting accusations of 'snitching'. They often reported offences against the person, especially against women and children. In relation to protecting children, when a young man reported on Facebook that he could hear a baby crying next door for hours, as though in severe pain, several community participants—men and women of various ages—advised him to 'ring the boys in blue', or alternatively, 'kick the door in'. Police

Calling on the Police   **143**

involvement and direct action both legitimate avenues to ensure the safety of an infant. Likewise, Paul's neighbours have called the police when fearing children to be at risk from suspected predators, or instead taken collective retaliatory action to prompt a police response, as detailed above in the context of vigilantism.

Observably, community participants demanded for police involvement in cases of theft, seemingly because they deem the relevant offenders, such as drug addicts, to be harmful to the community. For instance, a young woman posted on Facebook: 'I'm no grass but I will be now the dirty junkie-scum next door has stolen clothes from my washing line.' In agreement, multiple people were adamant that the police needed to deal with norm violations like this, and that the 'junkies' ought to be moved off the estate by the council.

Police involvement is even more of an imperative for Paul's community when the elements of theft and young victimhood are combined.

SANDY: words can't describe how pissed off I am, went to unpack the rest of the boxes and found Hannah's money box has been emptied, how fucking low do people have to go to steal from a baby?
ANITA: get 'em all round yours and threaten to phone the police, it's horrid stealing off a fucking baby!
GINA: take it to police, say you want fingerprints done
NATASHA: definitely report it hun, disgusting stealing off a baby

A likely intensifier here is not just theft from a baby, but its having occurred within close relations: such a wrong involves a violation of trust. Although Gina's desire for a forensic investigation might seem disproportionate, from the community perspective, such action is warranted to address the deeper and more serious harms of breaching honesty and disrespecting kin. This mirrors Koch's (2018b: 80) finding that when participants in her study had their loyalty and care undermined, calling the authorities became seen as a fair course of action.

Women in Paul's community were most visibly liable to call the police and would often openly do so to ensure the safety of kin. Several comparable studies have observed this trend. For example, Lisa McKenzie (2015: 166) details how a mother reported her son to the police for drug dealing because of the effect it was having on his younger siblings, and Koch (2018b: 153–5) documents a case of a son attempting to enter his mother's flat in the night by banging on the door, and in response his mother called

144 Thin Blue Line

the police and reported him for vandalism. Koch explains how involving the police served to discipline the young man and enabled the mother to maintain good neighbourly relationships. In a cognate vein, I observed a grandmother in Paul's community explain to her granddaughter why she had been asked to leave the front of the grandmother's house: 'you got told to leave 'cus you were at my house with teens, making noise, and it's a neighbourhood watch area, so people called the police. You're always welcome but come without the cronies.' In a US context, Monica Bell (2016) observes similar trends among disadvantaged black mothers.

On other occasions, Paul's friends called the police to protect against violence (see Bell, 2016; Goffman, 2015: ch 4). Several such cases involved bullying; one example involves a mother in Paul's community who reported acts of youth violence to the police, especially when the school failed to respond. Consider the remark of another young mother: 'School is sickening, my daughter gets jumped just outside school, and they say it's not their issue 'cus she left the building. I'll be onto the police tomorrow then.' I also observed women engage the police to prevent their husbands from violently retaliating to another perceived wrongdoing. For example, when a neighbour shouted at a woman and her children, the woman publicly announced through social media that she refused to let her husband 'sort it out' himself in case the neighbour called the police and labelled him the aggressor. Instead, the woman immediately reported the incident herself, and announced that the police would deal with it. By responding in this way, the woman showed her family to be law-abiding citizens who play by the dominant rules, rather than taking matters into their own hands (following Goffman, 2015: 202).

In the next extract, it is the grandmother who contacts the police to protect her teenage grandson from violence.

TIM: It was my nan that called the police not me and it wasn't a fair fight, there were like 9 of yous

FREDDIE: U fucking grass letting ur nan call the police while you cry on her shoulder, gimp

TIM: If you want a 1 v 1 now, on your own, no mates, let's go for it.

Tim seeks to reject the label of being a 'grass' by placing responsibility for the action with his grandmother. Moreover, by appealing to the norm of a fair fight, Tim indicates that Freddie also breached a mutuality norm, which potentially makes his grandmother's involving the police legitimate, in that

Calling on the Police   **145**

it is possibly an attempt to punish a norm violation that matters to those within the framework of mutuality. By offering to engage in a one-to-one fight, which is reflective of the customary ritual fighting form, Tim reaffirms his orientation to the ideal of fairness within this framework.

While women visibly reached out to the police to respond to certain wrongdoing, men intervened in other notable ways, including warning about violent threats and advising friends to take extra care of themselves.

BRAIN: mate it's best u go into hiding, I've just had a phone call, they're coming for u

NICK: he's a snake and never paid me 3 months, lot of money mate. He ran to the police house, so we ran away, he's pure snake and owes a lot of money to a lot of people

BRIAN: just keep ya head down and watch where u go.

The above scenario likely involved an unpaid debt in the unregulated drug economy. By seeking refuge in the police station, it is possible the debtor gave himself time to secure relational support to fight back because now Nick is the one advised to go into hiding. This is perhaps a softer example of what Alice Goffman observes in her US-based ethnography, in which young men with warrants out for their arrest would surrender to the police at strategic moments to avoid imminent violence on the street (Goffman, 2015: ch 4). Notably, in the Corby incident, rather than entering the police station to report the violent threat, it seems that the debtor used the police station as a temporary place of amnesty.

It might be that some of Paul's neighbours actively prefer to respond to wrongdoing in their own manner than to involve the police, which is why they avoid them. However, it is also possible that police protection is not an option for certain groups, which means they must pursue their own solutions to redress a wrong. Indeed, several of Paul's friends evinced the suspicion that, despite trying to obtain police support, the police dismissed them on account of who they or their family are. Consider this example from a teenage girl:

The police tell you that you can't take the law into your own hands but then when you take something to them, they tell you you're lying, your story doesn't add up? It's the first time I've ever gone to the police about something, why the hell would I put myself through that just to make something up?!

146   Thin Blue Line

Gemma, a woman in her twenties, expressed a parallel sentiment when she alleged that the police disregarded her complaint because of who her brother was.

GEMMA: The police act like they want to help and that, but as soon as they hear my brother's name, they don't give a fuck. My brother got attacked with a baseball bat, and the police laugh and lock him up, for getting battered! Police need to take a long hard look at themselves in the mirror— if it was someone in their family they'd soon pull their finger out
LISA: They did the same with John, and then again with Charlene. Police are a waste of space
TOM: Welcome to Corby, the place where police arrest innocent people and the culprits go free. It's happened too many times to me.

The difficulty of going to police is pronounced here: it may require exposing oneself to relationships of power imbalance and the related experience of being dismissed. During the fieldwork period, I received several similar accounts of the police failing to respond. The most severe claim came from a teenage girl who told me that her cousin was stabbed in the local woods, which the police allegedly failed to investigate because of their well-known family name. Irrespective of the full truth of this assertion, the teenager expressed her fears and beliefs about how the police relate to her family and the limits of state protection. Analysing comparable experiences in a working-class community in the north of England, Katherine Smith (2012: 74–6) suggests that the police, and the state more broadly, are placed outside of the local discourse on fairness and belonging and are not necessarily perceived as the primary source of justice. In Paul's community, recurring experiences of unfairness seem to have created a shared understanding that police assistance and protection may be limited and out of reach.

It is not only the police whom Paul and others in his community may experience as unresponsive: their interactions with most state institutions have the potential to be humiliating experiences. Whether it be police officers, teachers, doctors, and so on, for those situated in the precariat, the hostile side of professionals is never far from view. Here, I present a couple of examples of a wider trend. The first relates to a local schoolteacher; tense relationships between teachers and disadvantaged parents are well documented (cf. Dunne and Gazeley, 2008; Gazeley, 2012; Lareau, 1987; Radnor et al., 2007).

Calling on the Police **147**

GILL: Mr. Smith is the biggest twat I've ever met. I don't care where you work and what you get paid, you can't treat people like shit on the bottom of your shoe

SARAH: No one likes a bragger

GILL: No one like someone that thinks he's better than everyone else

BEN: The guy's a prick.

Although nobody here explicitly mentions class, Gill's reference to place of work and salary indicates where she might locate the source of hostility. Notably, the teacher is criticized for acting as though he is superior, which fails to meet the norms of mutuality prescribing care and equilibrium in relationships.

Another state institution seemingly prone to treating the precariously positioned in a hostile manner is the medical sector, and especially general practitioners (cf. Sayer, 2005: 178–9). The following conversation among Paul's friends provides an example of this experience.

HANNAH: I'm devastated, I've never in my life been spoken to so badly and disrespected than by my doctor today. Dr Jones, you're a cock

NICOLE: Down Riverside? I took my mum there last week and a female doctor spoke down to us like we were idiots

HANNAH: It's disgusting they think they have a right to talk to us like that

DAVID: I had Dr Jones as my doctor a few years back. He was abrupt, dismissive and generally rude.

Power imbalances lay in the background of these complaints. While certain teachers and doctors were often praised by Paul's friends, and the National Health Service avidly defended, they openly criticized professionals for behaving badly. These kinds of experience are familiar not only to Paul's community but to many among the most socio-economically disadvantaged in Britain, as studies frequently find (Gillies, 2006; Koch, 2018a; Lareau, 2011; Reay, 1998).[1] As Ben Rogaly and Becky Taylor (2016: 11) aptly comment, these relationships are 'intrinsically classed'. The precariat, then, cannot reliably acquire help from the state through the 'usual channels', such as teachers, GPs, and police officers. Accordingly, they pursue alternative strategies.

---

[1] I had a similar experience during the research period when I was living back on the Lincoln estate and visited the same doctors' surgery as discussed in the last example. During

148 Thin Blue Line

'Personalizing the State'

Socio-economically disadvantaged persons must learn to draw on the services of police and other state actors in strategic ways, which Koch (2017b, 2018b) suggests we can understand as a process of 'personalizing the state'. In similar fashion, Goffman (2015: ch 4) observes a process of 'turning legal troubles into personal resources'. We saw this in action above, when participants in Paul's community take vigilante action in response to perceived wrongdoing, prompting the state to intervene and protect whichever individual the collective then threatens. By such means, the community co-opts the individualistic logic of the state in the pursuit of (what it perceives as) the social good, which to some extent lies outside of the remit of the modern liberal state.

An adversarial form of this co-opting took place within intimate relationships. I observed a trend where some of Paul's neighbours employed the services of the police to gain the upper hand in former familial relationships by making complaints to the police and other authorities, such as social services, the agency for child maintenance payments, solicitors, and so forth. For example, a mother listed a string of accusations which, she claimed, her ex-partner had presented to social services to claim custody of their children. On another occasion, a man in Paul's community advised his friend to call the police if his ex-partner stopped him from seeing their son: 'the law changed bro, you have the same rights as the mother if she holds him from seeing you. Bell the police or just turn up and demand she lets you see them, there's fuck all she can do about it.'

Feuding parties appeared to take formal measures in a tit-for-tat manner. I observed several instances of ex-partners contemplating reporting infringements to state bodies, seemingly to gain power or exact retaliation in a relationship. For example, a middle-aged woman in Paul's community openly discussed whether she should contact her ex-boyfriend's new employer to divulge the reason why he was dismissed from his last job; a friend dissuaded her from doing so, advising her to 'best let this one go.' Similarly, Goffman (2015: 99–106) recounts how women previously loyal to their male partners had invoked the law as a means of acquiring social control in a relationship, sometimes in response to being romantically wronged. Conversely, Koch (2018b: 106) observes how the male ex-partners of

---

the appointment, the doctor asked me what I was currently doing, and when I shared that I was working towards a doctorate, he advised it was time for me to 'get a job'.

'Personalizing the State' **149**

women in her study would threaten to use personal information that could undermine a mother's access to welfare benefits, in order to avoid the responsibilities of fatherhood.

Instances of domestic violence imbue strategic uses of the police with greater complexity, as illustrated in the next discussion initiated by a woman in her early thirties.

ERIKA: him and that scummy mummy have been spreading lies about me. He batters me, threatens me with acid, now this
CHRISTINA: Someone needs to expose them for the scum they are, keep your head high hun
PENNY: What's he gonna do turn up at your house with an axe, oh wait he's already done that. Press charges
MARK: Phone police, play them at their own game
DIANA: Police do fuck all
ERIKA: nah he loves jail, let him rot on the out [outside of prison].

Here, Mark suggests calling the police is like a strategy in a game, which the other side are purportedly already playing. Diana, perhaps from experience, expresses the futility of relying on the police in such circumstances, and Erika notes that her ex-partner is not the kind of person to be phased by such an approach; hence, calling the police does not in her view afford advantage in this situation. Compare this with another case discussed by women in their late forties: in contrast, the ex-partner involved here seemed to be intimidated by the threat of the criminal justice process.

TINA: love it when whores send police to my door! Unlucky cus I'm now getting her done with intimidating a witness
JULIE: you're an idiot for taking him back but been there done that myself
TINA: he knew me taking him back wouldn't be good for my case, but at least I have all the messages and he's admitted it. He came here crying the other week asking me not to go court. He actually had me apologising to him 'cus I went police and its unwritten law that wives don't go police, well maybe if he didn't batter me, I wouldn't have to. I hope the only bed he'll be lying in is a prison cell
JULIE: I wouldn't want him jailed. You're both at fault but he's still in the wrong
TINA: he won't cope with jail, he'll be put on the fragile wing with all the rapists

150 Thin Blue Line

JUSTIN: Rapists get raped. You should've stabbed the fuck out of him in his sleep, you'd get away with it after what he's done.

TINA: I actually feel bad for her even though she rang police and sent social services to me.

MICHA: leave them to it mum, ain't worth it

TINA: I've made this status public to save all the snakes running back telling them.

In this dispute between ex-partners, both sides appear to engage the police. The opening comment reveals the potential importance in a feud of being the first to report an issue to the police. Even though the new partner of Tina's ex has engaged the police against her, Tina can now argue that this is a form of intimidation or harassment. On Tina's account, her ex has invoked counterstrategies to prevent her taking this course of action, such as seemingly resuming the relationship with Tina for a period. Moreover, Tina's ex appears to benefit from her seeming to internalize an informal norm ('wives don't go to the police'), which leads her to feel conflicted and apologize for taking this course of action. Hence, both parties engage in strategies to gain control, some of which involve the police, and others involve emotional persuasion in the relationship.

In contrast to Erika's situation, the threat of prison appears to have force. Unlike the first ex-partner who is described as a 'jail head' and is thus portrayed as having the wrong demeanour to survive prison, here the ex is emasculated and suggested to be an easy target for sexual abuse. The group express mixed feelings about his potentially going to prison. Several people refer to jail as an appropriate punishment for an alleged rape. Conversely, Julie does not think that the man deserves jail and implies that there are complexities to the dispute. It might be that the threat and fear of prison is the chief aim here, and not necessarily a desire for a prison sentence to be handed out.

Perhaps we can read the public taunting of Tina's ex-partner as a modern variant of the customary practice Thompson (1963: ch 12) describes as 'riding the stang', which is a particular form of rough music as introduced above. 'Riding the stang' was used in cases where men had mistreated their wives; it could involve parading a man on a pole or carrying a straw effigy to his door and burning it in front of a 'tooting crowd' (Thompson, 1963: 448). The aim of the practice was to humiliate the man for his failure to abide by the local norms of the time and, in so doing, to alter his behaviour. In like manner, the public taunting of the ex-partner in the last extract may be the chief aim.

Conclusion **151**

Plausibly, Paul's peers involve state authorities in these instances to pursue underlying objectives beyond the substantive legal issues and purported offences. As we have seen, the law has developed to respond to certain forms of wrongdoing and not others. Therefore, to engage the state in areas it is not otherwise geared towards, existing legal provisions must be strategically invoked for other ends. Commenting on similar occurrences in a US context, Goffman (2015: 106) notes that the police and courts can be called on, 'not for the crimes or violations the police are concerned with, but for personal wrongs the police may not know or care about'. Similarly, in the UK context, Koch (2018b: 155) finds that 'people were using the police as personalized tools in the pursuit of their own daily relations; relations that were morally prior to, and more important to them, than, the state's own understanding of "law and order"'. By this discussion, I do not suggest that the issues Paul's peers raise are disingenuous means of using the state; rather, they employ the services of the state in this indirect manner to address matters of real concern to them. Whereas the state responds to violations of official rules, breaches of trust and relational harm might matter more to precariously situated individuals (cf. Conley and O'Barr, 1990). Thereby, the law is remoulded to respond to local needs.

Conclusion

This chapter has shown that those living within a framework of mutuality place special value on some ideals and the norms constitutive of them which are simply out of kilter with the norms enforced by the state. Indeed, the modern liberal state has developed to operate within the framework of autonomy, and in so doing it seeks to safeguard personal liberty and growth, on a particular conception of freedom as control over space and others. Accordingly, it protects the interests of relatively powerful individuals with resources and property rights over the interests and needs of others. Conversely, those living within the framework of mutuality place a special value on collective equality, embracing ideals of resource redistribution and opposing power imbalances.

Thus, the frameworks of autonomy and mutuality at times provide fundamentally different moral orientations, and this has important ramifications for justice. Since the state authorizes the police to uphold values prominent in the framework of autonomy (e.g. the protection of an individual from violent attack), when there is a real conflict of those values with

152   Thin Blue Line

those highly regarded in a framework of mutuality (e.g. an aversion to persons deemed a threat to vulnerable others), the police may not be relied on to rectify (or in some cases recognize) a norm violation. What is more, even when the police can respond, for instance when someone is subjected to a violent attack, due to the classed nature of policing, there may be cases when the police do not help those who are precariously positioned. This means that Paul's neighbours can either take matters into their own hands or find creative ways to induce the state into responding to their needs—or sometimes, as with vigilantism, a combination of both. In moments when Paul's peers thereby 'personalize the state', they may have succeeded in translating, as it were, a norm violation as recognized within the framework of mutuality into one as recognized from within the framework of autonomy.

Notable findings from this chapter include being able to predict when violent and collective action is likely to arise in Paul's community. Specifically, in response to abuses of power, to criminal offences against vulnerable persons, and to violations of trust in relationships. However, settling conflicts by violent or collective action is not without risk, and, as noted in Chapter 3, violence exposes one to the forces of (bad) moral luck.

Finally, we have seen that Paul's multigenerational peers may treat persons living with addiction, persons with paedophilic inclinations, and persons who harm the vulnerable as outsiders and as potential objects of vigilante action. This raises the difficult issue of exclusion, which is the flipside of community inclusion. I pick up on these exclusionary tendencies in Chapter 5 by focusing on the outsider status of being a 'foreigner'.

The Refuge

My mother's journey to Corby strayed from the usual migration routes. Hers took place on a darkened morning, hidden under blankets in the boot of an estate car, with two young children gripping hold of her. She remembers the jerky drive and a pungent smell leaking from a plastic bag the youngest attempted to vomit in. They were being transported to a safe house for battered women in an unknown town, which happened to be on the Lincoln estate.

By this point, the closure of the steelworks had struck, and heroin addiction was spreading through the veins of the estate. The women assigned to the refuge suffered many of the worst effects. Though they shared experiences of bodily violence, a growing reliance on opioids to ameliorate the sorrow was not yet common.

Initially, my mother couldn't leave the refuge—she and her two daughters stayed for weeks in a single room of the shared house. But with support from the women, she built up courage to venture outside and enrolled the children in a local primary school, first changing their names. This was the second time she acquired a new identity. In her younger years, having escaped a forced marriage and feared honour killing, she became Nikki. This time, Nikki fled a voluntary marriage, which ended just as destructively.

Paul met Nikki in a town centre nightclub. The women convinced her to join them on an evening out. Not knowing how to be in such a place, she spent the night sat at the bar awkwardly sipping a Coca Cola as the others danced. Paul knew many of the women from the estate and was intrigued by the new and out-of-place face. Pumped with the boldness of whisky, he asked Nikki on a lunch date at the Littlewoods café in the town centre. She agreed to meet, but never showed up. It was some weeks later before they met again.

The next time Nikki and Paul saw each other was by the playing field near Paul's house. Nikki was walking the girls home from school when the youngest fell over on the concrete pavement, grazing her knee. Paul was walking his dogs and when he heard the cries of a toddler, he went over to

A Precarious Life. Roxana Willis, Oxford University Press. © Roxana Willis 2023.
DOI: 10.1093/oso/9780198855149.003.0010

154   The Refuge

help. He suggested they pop to his home to clean the wound and bandage the cut.

Paul's first marriage had broken down a couple of years earlier and he was just coming out of a second unsuccessful relationship. His sons stayed with their mothers, leaving Paul in the house alone, desperate to be part of a family again.

When Nikki explained the situation she and the girls were in, Paul suggested they move into the spare rooms at his, at least until they sorted themselves out.

From such accidental and ill-fated circumstances, a new jumbled family was formed. In the months and years that followed, my third brother and I came into existence.

5
Foreigners

We have seen how conditions of material hardship erect several barriers for Paul and his neighbours, which stifle their ability to manifest the autonomous ideal. The barriers range from employment regulation imbalances to inadequate and limited access to state services, especially in comparison to those with greater advantage. Without being reliably able to enjoy such services, including state provisions for criminal enforcement, the community engages alternative support mechanisms. I have suggested the normative substance of these mechanisms derives from people's being oriented towards the good of mutuality, on which they place special value. That is, Paul and his peers are guided by norms concerning the fair sharing of goods as needed, the importance of familiarity (i.e. knowing a local web of people), the broadcasting of information about who is virtuous (and who isn't), and the informal means of exacting or pursuing justice against those who damage the normative web.

As I have been suggesting, because participants of the community are situated within a framework of mutuality, they act and treat each other in ways different than those predominantly guided by a framework of autonomy. There is limited opportunity, within Paul's community, for the values of self-interest, personal advancement, and independence from others—goods I portray as given special prominence by those who live within a framework of autonomy—to be realized. Accordingly, we can make sense of how their relationships are structured by keeping in mind these alternative moral orientations: where those within a framework of autonomy might mark themselves out by emphasizing differences, the pursuit of which means accepting various hierarchies, those guided by mutuality norms may emphasize an ethos of balance and equilibrium, which values the levelling of differences and prioritizes conformity to a local way of life (see also Edwards, 2000; Kalb, 2009; Koch, 2018b; Smith, 2012; K Tyler, 2015). And, I have been arguing, since Paul and his peers structure their relationships on such egalitarian norms, they are instinctively averse to power imbalances (and especially power abuses), reacting where possible

A Precarious Life. Roxana Willis, Oxford University Press. © Roxana Willis 2023.
DOI: 10.1093/oso/9780198855149.003.0011

156 Foreigners

to redress them. However, we also briefly alluded to potential deviations from this ideal: those within Paul's community seek to exclude some persons deemed to be harming others or contributing insufficiently to the collective way of life.

In this chapter, we take a closer look at how new arrivals to the town are received, which I discuss with the locally employed term 'foreigner'. When Jeanette Edwards (2000: 85) conducted ethnographic fieldwork in the English town of Bacup in the 1980s, she likewise found that her research participants used the term 'foreigner', in reference to persons who migrated to the town from other parts of England. In Paul's community, 'foreigner' mostly referred to a person of Eastern European heritage as well as racialized foreign nationals. We find this usage in the context of widescale Polish migration to Corby following the expansion of European Union membership in 2002. Notably, in earlier decades, many of Paul's friends were themselves foreigners, who travelled to Corby to labour in the steelworks—a point which longer term residents often raised reflexively. Thus, the term 'foreigner' and its significance have altered with time and context, though broadly being used to mark out newcomers to the pre-existing order.

My aim in this chapter is to develop an emic view of tensions towards 'foreigners' in the community in the lead-up to the Brexit vote, making them intelligible by locating them within a moral framework of mutuality. Thus far I have shown Paul and his multigenerational peers as embedded within relational webs of support and diverse sharing practices (see also Degnen, 2005; Edwards, 2000; Koch, 2016; Smith, 2017b; K Tyler, 2015). Acts of sharing can be metaphorically imagined as spinning intricate and overlapping threads which create a tapestry of informal support on which its contributors can rely (see Chapter 2). The tapestry, and normative practices which keep it spun, are passed on from earlier generations, and to ensure the support is available in the present and future, threads of the tapestry must be constantly renewed. When people join this social space, they could be perceived as an asset and as contributing additional threads which strengthen the tapestry. However, there is also a risk that outsiders fail to recognize and abide by the informal normative order (or be perceived as such) and consequently they could damage or exploit it.

Rather than being clearly articulated, these social practices are represented in the instincts, emotions, and moral sensibilities of those brought up in precariat conditions. Since members of these constitutive communities— consisting of those who are known, connected through relationships, and those who are unknown, connected through the imagined community of

Foreigners **157**

Corby—rely on community for subsistence and survival, they may find terrifying changes which they deem to threaten the support structure. Valerie Walkerdine and Luis Jimenez's (2012) psychological study in a former Welsh steelmaking community depicts well how collective anxieties surface. Noting that communities lack a physical body, Walkerdine and Jimenez describe how nonetheless a 'psychic skin' and sense of containment remain crucial for communities exposed to intergenerational precarity to feel secure. The imagined body and skin which Walkerdine and Jimenez picture have affective relationships at their heart, moving those who inherit memories of collective past traumas to behave in ways that cushion against harms in the present. Yet Walkerdine and Jimenez (2012: 55) also discover a 'cost' to these affective relationships: 'a strict set of rules about conduct, a resistance to outsiders and the inability of people to leave the town.' Hence, reactive tendencies which contribute to the protection of some may exclude others (cf. Ahmed, 2000, 2014).

What we are encountering here, then, is the well-discussed 'dark side' of community, which involves exclusion and the suppression of minority differences in preference for group conformity (see Abel, 1995; Ahmed, 2000; Crawford, 2002; Delgado, 2000; Frazer and Lacey, 1993; Friedman, 1989; Pavlich, 2001; Weisberg, 2003; Young, 1986). Feminist writers and scholars of colour have long raised concerns about the exclusionary tendencies of geographical communities, especially on grounds of race and sexuality (e.g. Young, 1986; Friedman, 1989; Ahmed, 2000). Relatedly, feminist scholars have shown some appeals to community as the narratives of a larger collective drowning out less powerful voices; the development of intersectionality theory, especially by black women, illustrated that even within feminism itself, the concerns of racialized women may be muted (see Crenshaw, 1989; Potter, 2015). Mindful of these concerns, criminologists have assessed and critiqued uses of 'community' in criminal justice initiatives (e.g. Cunneen, 2005; Weisberg, 2003; Crawford and Clear, 2001; Pavlich, 2001; Delgado, 2000). In this chapter, I also revisit these critiques of community in seeking to develop an emic view of tensions towards foreigners.

When I speak of developing an emic view—that is, an internal perspective that explains why some people in the research community express anxiety towards 'foreigners'—in some respects, I am pursuing a similar project to Arlie Hochschild (2016), who sought to understand why white middle-class voters in Louisiana actively supported the presidential election of Donald Trump. Comparatively, I seek to explain from

158 Foreigners

the perspective of Paul's neighbours reasons for anti-immigration sentiment, which, from an internal view, cannot be explained by racism. Like Hochschild, there are moments when I feel the pull to critique certain uses of language or opinions expressed, but I limit this instinct and prioritize explaining the phenomenon as Paul's peers experience it. There is a notable difference in Hochschild's findings and the findings I present herein. A core analogy Hochschild develops to present her findings is the idea of waiting in a line: she describes her research participants as, in their view, having waited in line for the elusive benefits of capitalism, and then feeling as though they had been overtaken and displaced by others whom they deemed less deserving and who should metaphorically wait their turn (primarily on account of race). I find that Hochschild's analysis, which explains the frustration of certain conservative middle-class white Americans, while illuminating of the context in which she writes, does not capture the logic of what is occurring in Paul's precariat community.

Instead of the analogy of a line, Katherine Smith's (2012) work on notions of fairness and belonging in a comparable community to Paul's better captures the internal logic I seek to illuminate here. Smith (2012: 12) describes a 'common sense' among residents in her north English research community, which treats people who have lived in the area all their lives, or those who had family in the area for generations, as legitimately 'belonging' to the locality. This builds on Edwards's (2000) ethnographic findings that the status of being 'born and bred' in Bacup involves knowing people past and present and sharing memories of the area, as well as being born locally. Relatedly, Smith found that whether her research participants deemed something to be 'fair' or 'unfair' often depended on the status of individual involved, with an expectation that certain privileges would be afforded first and foremost to those deemed to 'belong', over and above recent arrivals who were not seen to have contributed to the local way of life to the same degree. Hence, rather than waiting in a metaphorical line, fairness here concerns a sense of there being a deeper cultural heritage and way of life that exists prior to, and existing beyond, the present.

In addition to examining tensions and disconnections between Paul's community peers and those deemed foreign, in this chapter we also examine *interconnections*, building on the work of Katharine Tyler (2012; 2015). Countering a tendency to characterize socio-economically disadvantaged communities as simply racist, Tyler brings into view the ways in which white working-class participants in her Leicestershire study develop relational connections with their British Asian neighbours. In so

Foreigners **159**

doing, Tyler shows how racialized participants of this community were not simply treated as outsiders by white working-class persons: those who engaged in (what I am terming) norms of mutuality and solidarity were sometimes perceived as part of the collective, notwithstanding their race. Therefore, echoing earlier findings by Edwards (2000), Tyler observed that the Leicestershire community she studied recognized newer arrivals who adapted and engaged in the local sharing and assistive practices, potentially entwining them in the collective body. Tyler and Edwards show that although a newcomer might not attain the status of being 'born and bred', with time and through their contributions, they can increasingly be seen to belong—belonging being a matter of degree.

Combined, these anthropological insights highlight the complexities of what on the surface might appear to be racism or xenophobia simpliciter. By developing a thicker account and an emic perspective, we can understand how migration is experienced in conditions of precarity and make better sense of some exclusionary tendencies. In so doing, this chapter is somewhat reflective of classic accounts of working-class collective struggles during former periods of migration (e.g. Thompson, 1963: ch 12; Williams, 1983: Part IV; Young and Willmott, 1957). This book's larger explanation of prima facie racist or xenophobic incidents, however, will need to extend beyond this chapter. I noted in the Introduction that while Paul and his friends are predominantly motivated by norms of the mutuality framework, nonetheless the modern human condition (as Taylor discusses it) finds us strongly oriented towards more than one good. Accordingly, I will argue, to make sense of certain interactions, we must also interpret them by reflecting on the influence of the framework of autonomy, tasks I take up in the following chapters and especially Chapter 8 when assessing moral motivation.

I open the present chapter with reflections on the UK vote to leave the European Union, for which a majority of Corby also voted. I suggest one way of understanding this leaning within Paul's community is as a collective instinct to limit changes perhaps experienced as harming support networks. In the next section, I deepen the analysis by incorporating Smith's (2012) insights on notions of fairness and belonging. Extending this to Paul's community opens the door to seeing an internal perspective: that the nature of contributions people make to a collective way of life may matter more than the individual characteristics of those making them. Tyler's work here helps illuminate how newer arrivals to Corby can become part of the collective body, when they are seen to contribute to and become part of the

160 Foreigners

collective way of life. In the fourth section, I reflect on a claim frequently made by Paul's friends that when someone is part of the collective body, racial differences dissolve. Holes in this assertion become apparent in the final section when we examine a tendency for unknown racialized persons to be treated as threats against whom the collective must defend. By the end of the chapter, we will have a better understanding of the internal anxieties of Paul's peers and how these bear on issues of racial inclusion.

Resisting Difference and Change

During my fieldwork, I observed notable tension between longer term Corby residents who lived through an earlier wave of migration predominantly, though not exclusively, from Scotland, and newer residents who migrated under EU policy. A report commissioned by the European Parliament in 2018 listed the UK as the main country of residence for EU migrants, and together with Germany as hosting almost half of EU movers of working age, especially from Poland.[1] Five years earlier, The Economist (2013) published a report finding Corby to have the highest rates of Polish migration in the country. These migration figures stem from national government policy, the UK being one of only three EU member states to permit unrestricted migration from the European Accession-8 countries, instead of implementing a gradual approach as adopted by other countries (Okólski and Salt, 2014). Notably, an Eastern European diaspora lived in Corby prior to this period; several hundred individuals and families in displaced person camps from Latvia, Poland, and (former) Yugoslavia settled in Corby following the Second World War, some of whom joined the steelworks (cf. Shilliam, 2018: 86). Therefore, recent migration from Poland to Corby can be seen as a continuation of earlier patterns.

A couple of years after my main fieldwork finished, in June 2016, the British public voted on whether to stay in the EU or leave. Most of the voting nation, 52 percent, voted in favour of leaving the EU, while 48 percent voted to remain. Contrary to a media stereotype, it was predominantly the most advantaged sectors of English society who supported the leave vote (Dorling, 2016; Dorling and Tomlinson, 2019: 28). Still, out of 74 percent

---

[1] A report commissioned by the European Parliament in 2018 states: 'Most of the EU citizens residing in the UK are Polish (1,021,000), Romanian (411,000), Irish (350,000) or Italian (297,000)' (Grütters et al., 2018: 24).

of the population eligible to vote in Corby, 36 percent voted to remain and 64 percent voted to leave. Although reasons for the Brexit vote in Corby were multifaceted (cf. Koch, 2017c; Mckenzie, 2017), plausibly tensions related to migration rates were one factor (cf. Dorling and Tomlinson, 2019; Gest, 2016; Winlow et al., 2017).

State-led migration to Britain has been a recurring feature of the capitalist political economy, which includes migration of labourers from Ireland, alongside Jewish migration, in the nineteenth century; commonwealth migration in the twenty-first century; and EU migration in recent years (see Thompson, 1963; Virdee, 2014; Shilliam, 2018; Wemyss, 2016). The form of free movement facilitated by the EU, like periods of migration before it, treated workers as though they were unencumbered and free-floating individuals who could easily move from one social space and settle in another, as and when economic requirements demand. Such a form of migration accords with the 'reflexive worker' thesis developed by Ulrich Beck (1992), Anthony Giddens (1991), Zygmunt Bauman (2000), and Margaret Archer (2007), who theorize that in conditions of late modernity, collective class structures have dissolved, and workers have become reflexive individuals, no longer tied to traditional communities, instead acting in pursuit of self-fulfilment, individuality, and lifestyle choice (for a critical exposition see Atkinson, 2010). In accordance with the reflexive worker thesis, mass migration will not severely disrupt existing relational ties, since, it presumes, atomization has reached an advanced stage. Indeed, it seems that the model of free movement supported by the EU operated as though a state of atomization existed. In the words of Will Atkinson (2010: 24), people were treated as 'autonomous, responsible individuals *de jure,* even if, in reality, they remain far from autonomous individuals *de facto*'.

Contrary to the atomized view, I maintain that the most socio-economically disadvantaged sectors of British society do not receive sufficient state support to realize their autonomy. Consequently, precariat communities such as Paul's have developed alternative means of subsistence in times of hardship, which involve nurturing relationships of trust, fostering social norms of mutuality, and engaging in diverse sharing practices. Such underlying social realities mean that places like Corby are not empty spaces; therefore, they may not easily absorb migrant labour as and when the economy requires in the way suggested by the reflexive worker thesis. Indeed, these locations contain dense interconnected relational webs which hold significance and meaning (following Degnen, 2005; Edwards, 2000; Koch, 2018b; K Tyler, 2015; Walkerdine and Jimenez,

162 Foreigners

2012). Without being able to formalize this social support structure within the state apparatus, ensuring its subsistence depends on locally derived knowledge—about people, places, anecdotes, standards of behaviour, and the morals of mutuality—carried within and between community participants. Preserving the social order, then, may require as a general commitment that the collective protects against those who lack knowledge of the local way of life and those perceived as potentially undermining it.

It is against this backdrop that we can begin to understand concerns over EU Accession-8 migration. Several long-term Corby residents with whom I spoke during the research period expressed anxiety about the rate of migration, which they described in the vocabulary of losing or being out of control. On different occasions it was suggested to me, with a heavy heart, that the town had become more like 'Little Poland', playing on the town's previous identity of 'Little Scotland'—or, with extra emphasis, as one of Paul's friends had posted, 'little fucking Poland'. The steelworks days and connections to Scotland form an important part of the town's collective memory, and residents who remained in Corby following the closure of the works lived through a harsh period of economic decline, structural neglect, stigma, and loss. By emotively sharing memories of the steelworks, and invoking relationships of the past as well as present, community participants kept the imagined community body alive (cf. Walkerdine and Jimenez, 2012), albeit in a faded form (cf. Fraser and Clark, 2021). From this view, the concerns of some about migration may have been rooted in anxieties about what they feared losing.

Continuing this thought, tensions towards those deemed to be 'foreigners' concerned behaviours that diverged from local norms. This sometimes surfaced in comments about not liking the smell of Polish food. At other times, concern was expressed over rumoured behaviours thought to be vastly different to the local way of life, as is apparent in the next conversation among Paul's neighbours.

ANDY: There's 2 trampy looking foreigners in the woods with a fire, eating pigeons, feathers all around them
EVE: Eww dirty twats
TONY: This is just the beginning trust me, it's getting worse these days, and its gunna get weirder, these people are nuts.

Our first response might be to classify this discussion as simple prejudice. But a closer look reveals more going on. Tony's comment draws our

Resisting Difference and Change   **163**

attention to one source of tension, which is that the alleged behaviour is experienced as 'weird' and 'nuts'. Moreover, Tony believes that this is the beginning of further negative changes to come. If such concerns were raised only in relation to the behaviour of 'foreigners', then this might indicate that the outsider, or even racialized, characteristics were the source of anxiety. However, my sense is that difference and change more generally is liable to be met with negative reactions.

Numerous examples illustrate resistance to change in Corby. The local press reported an apt case which shows how such reactions manifest (see Wilson, 2021). A young man in Corby opted to ride a 'pay as you go' electronic scooter home, which were newly introduced in the town, following his late shift at a fast-food chain restaurant. But on his way home, on two separate occasions and within the space of ten minutes, different drivers attempted to run him off the road. As the young man relayed: 'The first car decided to throw a drink at my back, and the passenger in the second car shoved me to the floor in the middle of the road'. Notwithstanding the wrongfulness of these actions, and the limited knowledge we have about the culprits, to me it seems likely that this was prompted at least partially by a local instinct to react, sometimes quite violently, against new forms of behaviour. Extending Walkerdine and Jimenez (2012), we could see this as an attempt for residents to feel secure in the context of intergenerational precarity and an expression of fear that the next wave of changes might be even worse than the ones that came before it. This is not to suggest that these responses are conscious expressions of anxiety, but to note that reactions to prevent change may be prompted by a deeper affect.

Notably, anecdotes about 'weird' behaviour of foreigners need not be true to serve a purpose. Smith (2012: 187–95) recites a research participant in her Manchester study informing her about a local church that allegedly excluded entry to white persons, which on investigation transpired to be false. She suggests that sharing (what were in her study) lies serves several functions, including marking out the boundaries of inclusion, as well as opening a gateway for others to express their frustrations about shared beliefs and anxieties, which anecdotes, even if falsified, in a sense make valid. Similarly, in reference to a US context, Roger Hewitt (2005: ch 4) explains how stories such as these can act as counter-narratives that compete with dominant discourses. So, while the governing discourse might, say, favour migration, one way for disadvantaged groups to challenge it is by sharing fictitious stories that undermine pro-migrant sentiment. Hewitt suggests that these counter narratives gain power by being spread through dense

164 Foreigners

networks, which operate outside of the remit of official communicative channels.

The circulation of counter narratives must also be seen as part of a historical process, in which elite institutions have become highly capable at conjuring up past mythologies about the immoral poor and disseminating these through policy and media discourse to create fear and division in society. Stuart Hall et al. (2013) capture this process in their seminal discussion on folk devils and the generation of moral panic in *Policing the Crisis*. The circulation of counter narratives by marginalized groups is an intricate part of the process Hall et al. describe, since it ensures myths are reproduced and feelings of panic and anxiety are invoked, which ultimately benefit elite actors. Smith (2012: 187–95) is also mindful of the effects that the circulation of racialized mistruths can have on less powerful groups, since these stories are liable to arouse anger and spark violence. Therefore, while the circulation of counter narratives might provide a means for those precariously positioned to voice their concerns, the larger effects of this process require scrutiny.

The telling of jokes is another strategy Paul's peers used to express concern about migration. For example, when one of Paul's friends asked why it was so hard to become employed, one man joked 'cus you're not Polish'; when a man announced that he had managed to secure a job, another joked that he'd 'taken it from the foreigners'; and following an increase in migration from Eastern Europe, a man joked: 'It's going to be hard for the Polish soon, all the Bulgarians and Romanians coming over here, stealing their jobs.' Participants in Paul's community also expressed anxiety about broader social changes through humour. 'I'm not replying to anyone who texts me in a Scottish accent', one young man joked: 'We live in England, the least we can do is speak Polish.' Jokes such as these invert the claim that jobs belong to locals and assertions that people ought to speak English. In so doing, perhaps the jokes communicate sentiments and fears of loss, with a built-in deflection against simple charges of xenophobia (since the remarks are delivered with humour). Smith (2012: 85) sees the pre-emptive expression 'I'm not racist but' as serving a similar purpose, in which precariously situated persons attempt to carve out a space where anxieties can be shared without being dismissed for being racist.

At times, concern about hearing a non-English language was expressed without the cloak of humour. Several national news outlooks which reported on recent migration to Corby emphasized ongoing linguistic changes occurring in the town.[2] A young man in Paul's community described these apparent changes in terms of a mosaic of accents created by different layers of migration: 'Polish/English with that fucked up version of Scottish accent Corby people have, fuck me, there's gonna be some fucked up kids with some fucked up accents pretty soon!'

Others expressed frustration over hearing another language. For example, a boy in his late teens asked, 'how many times do I have to say "I only understand English" before I stop being spoken to in Polish?', to which a woman replied, 'only like a thousand more times'. Another young man in Paul's community set up a Facebook group that demanded 'getting people speaking English' because 'we in England'. Although this group was unpopular and only attracted three members, I saw recurrent references to the requirement that people 'speak English in England'.

Sometimes complaints about the inability to speak English were couched in further suspicion: perhaps it evidenced intent to abuse local resources, by claiming benefits or requiring a publicly funded translator. For instance, a woman commented in a town-wide group: 'If they can't speak English, how will they work? We'll be giving them benefits!' Such anxieties are predicated on the belief that state resources are in short supply and there is not enough to go around. In the context of understanding how Paul's peers grapple with the topics of state resources, perceived scarcity, and distribution, Smith's discussion of fairness and belonging is particularly useful.

Fairness and Belonging

Fairness for participants in Smith's study intricately relates to local understandings of belonging, where those perceived to have the strongest claim to belong to the area were considered to be the most deserving of state resources, whereas those with weaker claims to belonging were considered to be less deserving. Participants in Paul's community regularly made comments indicative of a similar 'common sense', bound together also with a sense of national (and not just local) belonging. For example,

---

[2] For example, the Economist (2013) began their piece on Polish migration to Corby by noting that half the books in the foreign-language section of the public library were Polish. Likewise, on a visit to Corby in 2016, shortly after the Brexit vote, the BBC reporter Elinor Cross observed: 'The number of Eastern Europeans in the town was noticeable and a third of the people I approached said they couldn't speak English and were not originally from Corby' (see Woodger, 2016).

166 Foreigners

two of Paul's friends claimed that there were 'loads of people' in the job centre who 'can't even speak or understand English', arguing that 'the government should be putting natives first' (cf. Rhodes, 2010). Moreover, at other times Paul's friends expressed the view that Polish nationals were prioritized for jobs over longer term residents (cf. Gest, 2016: 137). In these discussions the (often unspoken) implication was that longer term residents were more deserving of access to work than newer migrant arrivals.

Entitlement to welfare benefits was a particular point of contention in Paul's community, and in such discussions, beliefs about fairness and belonging were pronounced. Two groups considered to be especially deserving of state support from the perspective of Paul's friends were soldiers and old-age pensioners: it seems that the legitimacy of elderly members derives from the *duration* of contributions made, and soldiers from the *nature* of their contributions. When Paul's peers emphasize the importance of such categories of person, they articulate or imply the value of contributing to the social good.

War efforts have great significance in Corby, as they do for other precariat communities in England, with regular displays of remembrance to sacrifices made during times of war. This included sharing memories of and pride in local veterans. A prominent example is James Ashworth, a young man from Corby who was killed while serving in Afghanistan in 2012. Ashworth was posthumously awarded the Victoria Cross, which is the highest national award for bravery in the face of enemy attack. In recognition of this achievement, the main square in Corby town centre was named 'James Ashworth VC Square', and Ashworth is recognized as a local hero; collectively, locals remember his achievements and the anniversary of his death.

Paul's peers see state failure to support returning soldiers as a grave injustice. One of Paul's older male friends commented in response to news about the suicide of a young soldier who fought in Afghanistan:

> Very sad indeed the way these young men and women are treated by the political class. None of the politicians' sons and daughters are likely to have fought in this war that's gone on for 12 years, longer than the 1st and 2nd world wars combined. No-one wins in war, only the ones producing the arms. Old men sending young men to die and be maimed physically and mentally. Tragic.

Fairness and Belonging **167**

This comment draws attention to the ultimate sacrifices of war as not made by those with the most power or its beneficiaries (in relation to the Second World War, see Todd, 2014: ch 6). Perhaps the significance of remembering war contributions stems partly from a normative ideal that self-sacrifice for the greater good of the collective ought to be recognized and compensated.

Alongside blaming the state for alleged failure to provide sufficient provisions for worthy recipients, Paul's peers also blamed 'foreigners'. They frequently suspected that foreigners were unjustly consuming scarce resources, leaving not enough for others in need (see also Rhodes, 2011: 108–11). This suspicion surfaced, for example, by sharing emotive images (we might say versions of a 'meme') which juxtapose figures such as a soldier, an elderly person, or a coal miner (always depicted as of white ethnicity), in a state of poverty, against an image of a racialized family (often non-white, and including a woman in a hijab), alongside the claim or depiction that they live in luxury at the taxpayer's expense (cf. Gest, 2016: 153). Such contrastive imagery need not be truthful to effectively serve the purpose of arousing collective grievance (see Hewitt, 2005; Smith, 2012 as discussed above).

Complementing the view that foreign nationals within the UK are undeserving, community participants sometimes saw foreigners overseas as undeserving of aid. Consider the comment of a middle-aged woman in a town-wide group: 'When I see people who have fought for our safety and our freedom living rough my blood boils. People who have paid into the system are told nothing can be done for them but then we insist on giving money away?!' Indeed, some community participants connected in different ways the idea that substantial amounts of public funds were assigned to help people abroad with a lack of more local funding. For example, at times they voiced frustration about governmental failure to offer adequate flood relief for local victims, alongside conjecture that had the injured families lived abroad then they would have received support from the British government. On other occasions, they made arguments against the accepting of Syrian refugees displaced by war on grounds that the needs of those already in Britain could not be met. As one of Paul's friends lamented, 'we have to become more concerned about our own problems before helping others'. Here we see anxieties about scarcity coming to the fore. Rather than calling for greater investment in public services or directing concern at the disproportionate consumption of resources by wealthy actors, those in need are seen as the root of the problem.

168 Foreigners

The anxieties so far outlined are anchored in age-old distinctions between the so-called deserving and undeserving poor, which right-wing media and policy discourse had historically conjured to deflect attention from structural causes (see Golding and Middleton, 1982; Hall et al., 2013). Yet, for these ideas to be effective, they must land in a social space which affords them significance. It seems to me that such anxieties latch onto the sensibilities of Paul's community which I have located in a framework of mutuality—i.e. as motivated by an ethics of sustainability, and guided by principles of fairness and belonging.

Perhaps we can get a firmer grasp on the notion of fairness at play here in the distribution of resources by considering the anthropological work of Susana Narotzky (2016), Don Kalb (2009), Insa Koch (2018b), and Smith (2012), among others. From the perspective of Paul's peers, fairness is not about accommodating individual difference, based on personal characteristics, but is instead about recognizing the different contributions an individual makes to the collective way of life and assigning access to privileges accordingly (following Kalb, 2009: 216–7; Narotzky, 2016: 83; Smith, 2012: ch 3). On this view, a newly arrived migrant worker, or a person living with drug addiction, is not deemed to have made sufficient contributions to the collective good and is seen as less worthy of support than a longer-term community participant who makes recognizable social contributions (cf. Flynn, 2018).

Becoming an Insider

Paul's precariat community is a 'heterogeneous, multi-ethnic formation', which, Satnam Virdee (2014: 162) reminds us, the English working class has been 'from the moment of inception' (see also Bottero, 2009; Rhodes, 2011). Accordingly, rather than remaining separate and divided, at different periods, newly arrived workers and longer term residents have been absorbed together, co-creating new forms of culture and tastes, and transforming what it means to belong. Several notable studies have exemplified ethnic diversity and assimilation among the English working classes (Gopal, 2019; Howard, 2012; Koch, 2016; McKenzie, 2015; Thompson, 1963; Tyler, 2012; Virdee, 2014; Watt, 2006). The ability of working-class communities to transcend racial divisions is striking, especially when compared with the levels of racial division maintained among the more advantaged sectors of society (see Tyler, 2012).

Therefore, while racial tensions might initially surface during periods of new migration, history indicates that newer arrivals and settled communities often become integrated and the standards for being 'born and bred' alter to reflect this (see McKenzie, 2015: 115–16). Anthropologists have captured how this process occurs, which includes moments when newer arrivals to a place actively engage in the local way of life and gradually become part of the collective. Edwards (2000: 133), for example, observes how English migrants to the former mill town of Bacup increasingly became seen as belonging by developing relationships through friendly greetings and engaging in sharing practices. Similarly, Tyler (2015) focuses on moments of connection between white working-class families and British Asian working-class families in England, countering the over-focus on moments of division in other literature. Tyler shows white working-class participants in her study, while expressing concerns in some respects, feeling solidarity with neighbours of Pakistani heritage who acted in ways deemed to be kind and caring. This leads Tyler (2015: 1178) to comment, 'what matters ultimately … is not the ethnic and racial identity of incomers, but whether they have and display the characteristics of reciprocity, neighbourliness and decency towards the estate and its community'.

Mirroring Tyler's observations, it seems that more recent migrants from Poland were already assimilating into the community alongside longer-term residents in Corby. Some such Corby residents went to great efforts to present the town as an inclusive place, especially in relation to families from Poland following the Brexit vote. Positive sentiments materialized on a town-wide group such as anecdotes being relayed when a person of Polish origin did something generous, like helping someone's relative who had fallen over in the town centre, or praise offered to the 'nice and kind' Polish family who shared homecooked food with their neighbours. These positive statements tended to contain adjectives such as 'hospitable', 'generous', 'lovely', and 'neighbourly', which imply acceptance, especially since generosity is a core value of the framework of mutuality, as discussed in Chapter 2. Newer arrivals, then, can be seen as becoming metaphorically interwoven within the web of mutuality, which forms the substance of informal spheres of support (following Degnen, 2005, 2013).

I observed additional discussion where Polish businesses were commended for offering cheaper and better quality products than the mainstream supermarkets, and in such cases these contributions were acknowledged (following Tyler, 2012). For example, a woman in a town-wide group commented that she 'love[s] the Polish supermarket' because she can purchase

170 Foreigners

loose vegetables without any plastic waste, and hence the Polish shop was contributing in important ways to the locality. Other commentators in such a group also referred to the much-needed affordability of the Polish supermarket. This praise notably contrasts with a handful of comments made by participants in Paul's community about supposedly overpriced and so-called 'paki prices' found in a smaller shop run by a family of South Asian heritage (an issue I soon return to). Whereas high prices were associated with personal profit and individual advancement, affordable services were viewed as a form of contributing to the local way of life rather than taking out.

We discussed above commendations of war efforts; it is notable that these were also extended to foreign nationals who fought alongside Britain in the wars. On several occasions, Polish contributions during the Second World War were brought up in defence of Polish migration to the town. Various individuals in a town-wide discussion group commented on the historic settlement of Polish families in Corby following the Second World War, adding that, in their view, Polish families were a 'welcome addition' to the town. Moreover, some longer-term residents described having 'great respect' for Polish people, who 'gave their all' during the Second World War, and referred to the 'sacrifices they made for this country'. In this context, words such as 'pride' and 'admiration' were used to refer to people of Polish heritage. Inclusive comments such as these legitimize Polish belonging by linking the history of migration to Corby's past, and hence bringing Polish families into the town's tapestry of memories and significance. Those holding these views considered Polish individuals to have earned their place in the community.

In the context of community recognition of racialized groups, it is worth reflecting on the use of stereotypes about, and criticisms directed towards, working-class brown persons. The aforementioned claim of unfair and exploitative pricing practices (invoked with the term 'paki prices'), in addition to failing to account for the higher running costs of small businesses and out-of-hours services offered, is rooted in colonial tropes. In the wake of the Indian Rebellion of 1857 (also referred to as the 'Indian Mutiny' or 'Sepoy Mutiny'), which was a major uprising against British colonialism, hostile attitudes towards Indian persons notably rose in Britain (see Hall, 2007). In the shadow of this, Stephen Heathorn (2000: 133) explains how Indian persons were depicted in school textbooks in the late nineteenth and early twentieth century: 'as a curious mixture of docility, timidity, and passivity on the surface, with a latent "treacherous," "untrustworthy," "fanatical," "ferocious," "cunning," and "cruel" persona lurking just below this surface'.

Studies about South Asians in contemporary British society show forms of this racism continuing into the present (e.g. Alexander, 2000; Parmar, 2011, 2015; Virdee, 2014; Wemyss, 2016). Consequently, even though a South Asian family might be second or even third generation in the area, continued usage of the racist term 'paki' indicates they can still be judged as outsiders. Centuries of contributions made by persons of South Asian heritage towards economic, cultural, social, and political developments in Britain, which were fundamental to establishing the welfare state, fail to be recognized in a way that translates into belonging (see Bhambra, 2022).

Indeed, despite concerted efforts by some longer term residents to present Corby as an inclusive and welcoming place, tensions and power imbalances remained. The expectation is that those deemed to be outsiders adapt to the local norms, in which assimilation is imagined as a one-way process—instead of the more accurate view of heritages merging into new collective forms (for examples of this see Gilroy, 1993; Gopal, 2019; Virdee, 2014). Moreover, power imbalances and histories of racial and economic injustices are unarticulated in calls that require migrants to conform to local ways, captured by Michel-Rolph Trouillot's (1995) seminal work on the silencing of aspects of the past: not all contributions are treated as worth remembering, and those of the least powerful—in the present as well as past—are too often forgotten.

'We're All the Same'

Up to this point, I have been suggesting that Paul's peers predominantly conceive difference not in terms of individualistic characteristics, such as race, but through (often perceived) contributions made to the collective way of life. According to such a practice, when a person is deemed to enhance the relational and material resources upon which other community participants depend, and in so doing better the social good, they are treated as part of the collective body. On this outlook, difference is marked when a person is perceived to insufficiently contribute to the collective or acts in ways which threaten it. While a feature of this practice is, thus, exclusion, I have also encouraged us to recognize other channels for inclusion. Yet this brings us to another concern raised by feminist critiques of community, which is the potential for underrepresented and less powerful voices to be drowned out by a collective which refuses to adequately recognize difference. I examine this worry in the context of an instinct in Paul's community

172 Foreigners

to reject claims of difference. I explain this position from the internal perspective, before returning to critiques to which this position opens itself.

In my observations, when Paul's friends vocally regarded a racialized person or newer arrival as properly part of the community, they tended to do so by referring to a sort of colour blindness—dismissing the idea that race is relevant (cf. Back, 1996: ch 5; Rhodes, 2010: 87–8). A widely expressed belief in Paul's community, repeated on multiple occasions, was that if an individual is nice to others, no matter the colour of their skin, they are part of the community. A young man in Paul's community expressed an example of such a view: 'Personally, I don't give a fuck what colour or religion you are, if you work hard, don't lie, cheat, steal, piss people off, pay your taxes and pay your way then you're alright with me.'

According to this perspective, abiding by the relevant local moral standards is the only prerequisite for acceptance. Another slightly older friend of Paul's summed up this position inversely: 'My philosophy is a cunt is a cunt and always will be a cunt regardless of skin colour.' Perhaps we can understand part of the insistence to disregard any racial significance as an aspect of the wider appeal for conformity within the collective, where norms of inclusion and belonging convey the importance of *not* standing out as a distinct individual. A similar logic is surely at work in town-wide online discussions when attempts to raise issues of race were dismissed, frequently, by a statement such as, 'Why does race have to come into it? We're all the same.'

Indeed, in a similar vein, Paul's community commonly resisted claims of racism. One method of rejecting accusations of racism was by appeal to analogous experiences, given that some people in Corby have faced persistent discrimination because of their links to Scotland. For example, in a town-wide discussion, a man refused to accept claims that there was discrimination towards Polish residents because he has also been 'told to fuck off back to [his] own country' when working outside of Corby and he just had to accept it. In a similar way, another man refused to acknowledge discrimination by claiming, 'I get called a jock, so what?' ('jock' being a British slang word to refer to a person from Scotland). Taking this a step further, a man suggested that he himself had 'been the victim of racial abuse by foreigners' when his work colleagues joked about him and other workers in Polish.

Perhaps there is something to the claim of similarities between experiences of Eastern European migrants in the present and those of Scottish migrants of the past. External associations of people from Corby with criminality were prominent in the decades of decline, which exposed Corby residents to different forms of prejudice. A friend of mine who once lived

'We're All the Same' 173

on the Lincoln estate recalled how during his trial for armed robbery (which involved a group of young men stealing electrical goods from the container of a heavy goods vehicle), he was told by a Crown Court Judge that a large fence ought to be erected around the whole of Corby, because, in the judge's view, the entire town was full of criminals. In line with the stigmatized assumptions of this judge, I experienced similar claims made about my criminal potential during the fieldwork when I disclosed that I was from Corby: a countrywide criminal justice professional asked me and my Corby colleague if we had brought our passports to travel outside of the town; and, on a separate occasion, the same person joked that he should advise everyone to lock their offices and hide the sugar now that there were two 'Corby people' in the building, implying that we would steal even the communal goods. The man took further pleasure in informing me that my estate was where 'all the troubled families come from'. I collected many examples of casual prejudice towards persons from Corby during the fieldwork. Resistance to claims of racism in Paul's community, then, occur against a background of multifaceted differences, which complicate the struggles taking place.

We might treat claims not to see race as strategies adopted by a majority to deny minority concerns the opportunity to be heard, in the process maintaining racial advantage. Indeed, such strategies are likely prevalent among different class sectors in Britain; claims of colour blindness and denial of racial significance are key methods of silencing the experiences of persons who are racialized and keeping racial power structures in place. However, I urge us not to instantly dismiss these appeals as such strategies, and instead to reflect on their meaning from the precariat position Paul's peers occupy. As noted in the Introduction, and a point I return to in Chapter 8, the most disadvantaged 10 percent in British society have faced exclusion from whiteness and have been exposed to forms of racial othering and exploitation, albeit not to the same degree as persons of colour and persons in former colonized nations (cf. Shilliam, 2018). Moreover, appealing to sameness and rejecting distinction on grounds of characteristics such as race is in keeping with a wider form of life. We have seen Paul and his peers act in accordance with a framework of mutuality, which is a normative landscape that valorizes solidarity over and above assertions of power. Therefore, rather than literally not seeing racial differences, appeals to sameness might sometimes be calls for comradeship. Still, other motivations for these claims are possible, which is a challenge I return to in Chapter 8.

174 Foreigners

At times, Paul's friends attempt to counter accusations of racism by asserting patriotism. For instance, a woman posted, 'we ain't racist we're patriotic', and in a similar vein, a middle-aged man warned his friends to 'be careful waving those patriotic flags, someone will accuse you of being racist and you'll be ordered to take them down'. Here, we can see a blurry line between what Paul's peers deem to be patriotic, demonstrating love for their nation, and what might ebb into a form of nationalism, which is to attach a sense of superior status to the nation. And of course, as Virdee (2014) has discussed, the line between nationalism and racism is itself a blurry one, these discourses having grown in tandem and being intricately entwined (see also Gilroy, 2002; Kundnani, 2007; Rhodes, 2010).

Indeed, arguments occasionally surfaced in Paul's community over the form of national pride that ought to be shown in Corby, and sometimes expressions of Scottish or Irish pride were challenged by claims of English superiority. For example, a man in Paul's community wrote in frustration about people in Corby refusing to support the English football team, displaying Rangers or Celtic flags instead (Scottish football teams): 'sour bitter mutant jocks, England pay our benefits and jobs but our footie team ain't good enough for yas.' In response, a woman contested this claim, 'Great Britain, not just England, pay the benefits. The Scots want independence from Great Britain and have done for hundreds of years.' In a similar vein, another man expressed annoyance at widespread celebrations of St Patrick's Day, asserting, 'it should all be about St George's Day, after all this is England'. Here, we see how claims of recognition involve relationships of differential power, where the dominance of Englishness may be asserted against expressions by those of former colonized nations or groups.

When Paul's peers, in the face of racial and national differences, nonetheless insist on sameness, they sometimes meet contrary claims made by persons who suffer differential treatment. However, instead of engaging with concerns raised by less dominant community participants, the majority tended to deny difference, which functioned to silence the voices of others. For example, in response to the efforts of some longer term residents to present Corby as a hospitable and pro-migrant place, especially following the Brexit vote, some individuals noted issues that needed addressing. Consider the comments of a woman in her late twenties in a town-wide group who notes, 'Corby HAS a problem with racism', citing for support a national televised programme about Corby on BBC's *Newsnight*, which documented several racist attacks against Eastern European persons in

'Stranger Danger'   175

Corby.[3] The woman further explained that 'it's frustrating when people try to downplay bigotry. Do you know how it feels to be told you don't belong somewhere you consider home?'

As I see it, the gap here between claims of sameness and credible accounts of racial discrimination may relate to the growth and reliance on imagined community forms in contemporary times, which connect strangers through a sense of togetherness. Within a relational community, such as specific networks of people from a housing estate, something like colour blindness might easily manifest: when a person becomes known, what largely determines belonging is the nature and degree of their contributions to the collective way of life—far more so than individual characteristics such as race. However, in an imagined community, such as Corby and the nation state, people must feel a sense of connection with those whom they do not know. Hence, how community participants read appearance now plays a stronger role in determining whether someone belongs. When these imagined communities are founded on a presumption of whiteness or Englishness, then the belonging of a person who is 'born and bred' might be unduly challenged because of their racialized features. In this respect, race matters (as well as other forms of difference) because some bodies are marked in a way that exposes them to greater exclusion than others. This is acutely apparent in how Paul's neighbours respond to 'strangers'.

'Stranger Danger'

Warnings shared about suspicious people and behaviours in the local area often manifested anxieties about safety and fears about foreboding harm. For example, on several occasions Paul's neighbours warned that 'foreigners' had been driving around trying to kidnap children, and on a handful of occasions they circulated warnings about 'foreigners going

---

[3] I recorded various data to support the claim that there are genuine issues of racism in Corby, which includes multiple racially motivated offices handled by local criminal justice programmes. Further to this, a retired police inspector informed me about a spate of racially motivated attacks towards persons who appeared Eastern European, on account of how people carried their backpacks. On a different occasion, I met a relative of one of the first black families in Corby, who experienced a significant amount of racial hostility. Similarly, I observed an archival article released by Stewart and Lloyds, which sought to encourage kindness among the workforce towards Eastern European migrants who had recently settled in Corby because of the events of the Second World War, which was seemingly written in response to some tensions that arose. In short, then, there is credibility to the claim that 'Corby HAS a problem with racism', which I return to in the final chapter.

176 Foreigners

round trying people's doors'. Walkerdine and Jimenez (2012: 64–6) note similar warnings shared in a deindustrialized community in Wales, which leads them to suggest that in a historical context of insecurity, concerns about the dangers posed by strangers indicate a state of collective anxiety and a heightened sense that the imagined collective body must be protected from further corrosion and harm.

As we can see, Paul's peers tended to specify if a 'foreigner' was involved in a crime or conflict, which contributed to an association of racialized persons with danger. For example, when someone was attacked in the woods, and when another person was violently assaulted on their way home from a public house, the crimes were attributed to 'a group of foreigners' and to 'two foreign blokes' respectively. Notably, ethnicity here going without mention, the term 'foreigner' is sufficient to invoke outsider status. Sara Ahmed (2000) has noted a linguistic usage which captures a multitude of ethnicities under a single rubric—which in Ahmed's analysis is the 'stranger' and, here, the 'foreigner'. Such a usage marks the subject as different from the majority group, while at the same time dissolving all other forms of difference between those who are cast as foreign (cf. Ahmed, 2000: 5–6; Back, 1996; Wemyss, 2016).

The exclusionary tendency of community is pronounced in the following Facebook discussion between two teenagers in Paul's community.

EVAN: who's party is it?
HARRISON: the foreign birds
EVAN: what's her name …
HARRISON: fuck knows just that foreign bird haha
EVAN: we should keep her name like that!

Instead of recognizing the girl's individuality and membership of the community, she is reduced to the status of 'foreign bird' (in British slang, 'bird' denotes, usually, a younger woman). In contrast to this 'other', the teenage boys demonstrate themselves as legitimately belonging. As Ahmed (2000: 26) reflects, the very act of identifying an outsider—the 'them'—affirms the legitimate subject who belongs: '[t]he enforcement of the good "we" operates through the recognition of others as strangers'. Not only are the boys positioned to identify the stranger, but they also assert a claim to be able to classify and fix in place who constitutes the foreign.

In a more explicitly racialized incident, a teenage boy updated his status to ask, 'who knows these three pakis walking round our end?' There was

'Stranger Danger'   177

no suggestion of wrongdoing, yet the very presence of three racialized men on the estate was enough to alert concern. On the one hand, being unknown is sufficient to invoke suspicion, regardless of race. On the other hand, even though a racialized person might be a long-term member of the imagined community, skin pigmentation operates as a shorthand for outsider status of those unknown regardless of contributions to the wider group. When persons of South Asian heritage are othered in this racialized way, the meanings read into brown bodies present in the UK must be understood in the context of several centuries of historical stereotypes and hostility employed towards persons from one of Britain's most exploited former colonies, as noted above (cf. Lamont, 2009 in relation to the treatment of Algerian persons in France). However, an awareness of this history and the colonial relationships is not articulated in Paul's community, and so from the local perspective, the unknown brown body is simply believed to be dangerous, without acknowledgment that this intricately relates to how race is coded in Britain (cf. Ahmed, 2000; Hall, 2017).

In the following discussion, a mother in Paul's community claims that a group of foreign men took pictures of her teenage daughter as they drove past:

GINA: dirty foreign bastards taking pictures of my kid!!
CHRIS: the bastards, was this in Corby?
GINA: yeah bud, down the old village, 4 black men and 2 white in a people carrier, but police say no crime has been committed
CHRIS: its bad mate, this country has gone to the dogs now. You can't go anywhere without some foreign scumbags hanging about
SEAN: it was only a few weeks ago foreigners were busted for human trafficking in Corby
DONNA: if we were to go to their country and start taking pictures of their kids we'd have our fucking hands cut off. Bet if someone gave them a good beating the police would soon change their tune.

The language used here diverges starkly from the claims of racial inclusion noted above. When a person is treated as an outsider, they are marked as immeasurably different and are completely excluded from the norms of the group, including those of friendship and care. As we saw in the last chapter, the need to protect children—a vulnerable category—is always of pressing concern. And, once again, community participants express frustration that the police apparently fail to act in these cases, which

178 Foreigners

leads Donna to suggest the vigilante strategy of giving the perpetrators 'a good beating' to make the police respond (see Koch, 2018b on personalizing the state). The move to vigilantism here reflects the etymology of the word 'community' traced by George Pavlich (2001: 58), deriving not just from 'common' but also 'to defend'. Although Paul's peers do not reserve collective retaliation only for racialized outsiders, when a suspected sex offender was identified as a 'foreigner', their outsider status is what came to the forefront of explanations about why the wrong was committed; they treated such an instance as indicative of risks posed by all racialized groups against which the collective ought to defend.

However, the assumption that the source of harm predominantly lay outside of the collective was all too often wrong. Indeed, I observed several instances of Paul's friends erroneously assuming that the perpetrator of a crime was a 'foreigner'. When someone posted about a criminal incident on Facebook, at least one person tended to ask if it involved 'foreigners', to which the poster often replied that it had not. This is evident in the following neighbourhood grievance:

HELEN: Found a rotten bag of food in our front garden, my neighbours are disgusting. Thank you very much Corby council for putting a troubled family next door
JAQUELINE: The council are shit. Are they foreigners?
HELEN: Not foreign, English.

Alongside foreigners, persons from Gypsy, Roma, and Traveller backgrounds were also presumed suspects in crimes, the most prevalent and open form of racism in the UK being towards Gypsy, Roma, and Traveller persons (see Bhopal, 2011; Phillips, 2019; I Tyler, 2015). In an online discussion group, open to the wider Corby town, there were often 'warnings' shared about the arrival of Gypsy, Roma, and Traveller communities, and there were intermittent updates about the behaviour of the visiting group. These associations with criminality are apparent in the following discussion among Paul's friends.

LEE: Young girl getting stabbed in broad daylight. Anyone know if it was foreign scum or the pikeys that done it? It's not on, the towns going fucked again
CALLUM: Another innocent person attacked but this time a young girl stabbed in broad fucking daylight. Let's get everyone together and show

'Stranger Danger' **179**

them THIS IS ENGLAND. That's what happens when you let all the bastards in

JORDAN: Was it a foreigner then?

MAX: Nah, an Englishman and his 3 Scots.

From the earliest days of the steelworks, violence has been prevalent in the town (see Ortenberg, 2008). Despite this, the conversation presumes that the perpetrators are outsiders. Perhaps they assume so because they deem the manner of violence to be illegitimate: they portray the victim as innocent and the perpetrator(s) as having used a weapon (not a 'fair fight'). Plausibly, however, it is simply more frightening to accept the source of the danger comes from within the community, and hence from those who know better the norms of the community. Evi Girling, Ian Loader, and Richard Sparks (2000: ch 3) note a perhaps related tendency among locals in an affluent English town who expressed the view that crime was primarily committed by outsiders. Girling et al. (2000: 79) suggest that this belief represents a 're-assuring threat' by reinforcing categories and expectations about where the source of danger lies, namely in the 'other' against which the internal character of the collective, as a distinctive place of relative safety, is reflected.

In the above conversation, degrees of belonging are pronounced. When Jordan asks whether the alleged perpetrator was a foreigner, Max's reply indicates that the people of Scottish heritage do not easily fall in this outsider category. Similarly, Lee asks if the crime was committed by 'foreign scum' or the 'pikeys'. Reading beyond the racist terminology used here, Lee is drawing a distinction between those who are 'foreign' and hence have limited claim to belonging and persons of Gypsy, Roma, and Traveller backgrounds, who are part of Corby, albeit in ways that continue to be racialized. Notably, when Max describes the offending culprits as English and Scottish, the ultimate power of the 'Englishman' over others is brought to the fore. Within this short snippet, we can see the complexity of belonging and racialization in the context of the heterogeneous and multi-ethnic working classes in Britain (cf. Virdee, 2014).

Just as ethnicity is complicated by earlier periods of Scottish migration, a good number of Paul's friends were from Gypsy, Roma, and Traveller backgrounds. The complexity of these mixings is evident in the following extract, where community participants discuss an alleged fight that occurred between local girls and girls from a visiting community (as distinct from settled Traveller communities in Corby). The first three comments are by teenagers, and the final two comments by older women.

180 Foreigners

REID: Apparently some girl got smashed by 5 gyppos.

ZOE: These young gypsy girls came to the park and started on everybody, kicked 2 of my friends, punched me in the stomach and pulled my hair, one wanted my necklace, I said no, got hit again. I didn't hit back 'cus they were younger. It was so disgusting, I walked away angry and pissed off.

RUBY: yesterday they threw juice over Carrie and hit us, and today they chased us in a van full of them.

EVELINE: The gypsy boys are stealing scooters and bikes off people, it's sick and twisted, so much shit's gunna kick off at the fair this year.

HEATHER: Not all gypsies are the same. I've never stole anything in my life and I'm a gypsy.

Like Heather, on several occasions Paul's friends challenged racism towards persons of Gypsy, Roma, and Traveller ethnicity by revealing their shared heritage. For example, in response to the above conflict, a teenage boy posted the following message:

> All this stuff on news feeds about 'gyppos' and 'pikeys', they are travellers and I have some traveller mates on here. Just 'cus someone started something that doesn't mean they're all like that. Calling them gyppos and pikeys won't help the situation... someone obviously annoyed them to make them do that.

In reply to this message, a woman commented, 'good on you, I come from Roma and it does my head in when I hear all of that. As if people in brick houses never had the police called on them. There's good and bad in all walks of life.' On another occasion, a woman in her twenties made a similar challenge, 'all these people slating gypsies and moaning about them making a living by collecting metal wind me up. Wind your fucking necks in fools, that's my culture you're slagging off.'

A man from a Gypsy and Traveller background offered the following explanation for why violence surfaced on a different occasion between a visiting community and settled locals:

> There's a reason it's all built up, with people calling us pikies and telling them to get back to their caravans and go home! A gypsy will not start for no reason, so there should be no issue unless someone provokes something. My friends are not the sort to go around looking for fights but if

Conclusion **181**

they feel they are getting a bad response, then they will defend themselves. There's loads of gypsies and travellers you probably don't even realise you're talking to. We have a better way of life so just leave it.

This young man explains the norms of fighting among Gypsy, Roma, and Traveller communities, which resonates, incidentally, with the justified uses of violence among Paul's community to resist abuses of power and protect the collective (see Chapter 3 for discussion). Challenging the claim that persons from Gypsy, Roma, and Traveller backgrounds seek out violence, the young man brings to the fore the defensive motive behind uses of force. Finally, he concludes his account by affirming the value of this way of life and advises that others should not comment from a place of ignorance. In these last examples, then, rather than submitting to the exclusionary attempts of some, community participants from Gypsy, Roma, and Traveller backgrounds challenge and assert claims of belonging.

Conclusion

In this chapter, I have sought to make intelligible different tensions towards foreigners as they surfaced in Paul's community. To do so, I draw on Smith's analysis of fairness and belonging among those who are precariously positioned in the social order. On this view, those who are 'born and bred' in an area are seen as having contributed to the local way of life, which makes them legitimate recipients of local resources and support, in contrast to newer arrivals who are viewed as having made fewer contributions and are therefore treated as less deserving recipients. However, when community participants recognize new arrivals as contributing to the local way of life through sharing practices and other means, they may include them as belonging. It is perhaps this inclusionary mechanism that explains the tendency for Paul's peers to insist that any individual characteristic differences among the collective (such as skin tone) are irrelevant; that the community instead insists upon relative equality among members of the collective.

It is in this context that I raised some common critiques of community, including the charge that collectives tend to suppress minority experiences and to exclude. Plausibly, it is the insistence on sameness which, while creating a sense of inclusion, also made it difficult for community participants to raise concerns about racism. These concerns, indeed, appeared to be valid, especially for those who might by virtue of racialization be treated as

182 Foreigners

though a stranger. In this respect, I discussed the multifaceted differences at play in respect of nationality and race. What is more, when community participants actively resisted the idea of difference among the collective, and so called for a kind of conformity, they were apt to require that less powerful groups adapt to a relative majority way of life. By doing so, they failed to recognize that historically and presently groups assimilate in a process of two-way exchange, through which new communities form. Despite that historical oversight, the forms of exclusion that we observed in Paul's community appear to be themselves guided by history: the racialized body is more likely to be marked as 'stranger' and a source of 'danger' than others.

Notwithstanding these tensions, important moments of inclusion warrant our attention. Far from being entirely hostile and closed spaces, newer arrivals can, and often do, become part of the collective. This is evident in how heterogeneous Paul's community is, consisting of persons from England, Scotland, and Ireland; of Gypsy, Roma, and Traveller heritage; or from Eastern Europe, the Commonwealth, and beyond. In this way, the local form of life is continually changing because of an assortment of diverse contributions. Since there is scope for newer arrivals to become interwoven within the webs of support upon which many in Paul's community rely, there is a case for widening the memory of the imagined community. Just as Paul's peers recognize the contributions of Polish soldiers in the Second World War, overcoming historical amnesia about other parts of British history (see Gopal, 2019; Trouillot, 1995; Wemyss, 2016) might pave the way for far greater inclusion.

By developing an emic account of how certain forms of racialization play out in Paul's community, this chapter has sought to disrupt a simplistic stereotype that racism in British society is prevalent within and sourced from the least well-off—there might be internal reasons for the invocation of hostility and fear towards persons unknown, which are not simply motivated by deeply bigoted discrimination. However, stopping the analysis here would be incomplete because Paul and his multigenerational peers do not only live within a framework oriented to the values of mutuality. In their daily activities, they must also, at times, be guided by the goods strongly valued by a framework of autonomy. Accordingly, I propose we must assess the moral motivation behind instances of exclusion or exclusionary tendencies, especially when cases involve a person who is racialized.

Before moving onto questions of moral motivation, we first require a deeper understanding of how the framework of autonomy guides moral action in Paul's community. For this task, I return to our discussion on violence, but this time we focus on the type of violence that is best made sense of by reference to the framework of autonomy, and hence the kind of violence that the state permits individuals to use in asserting their will over others.

The Boating Lake

Corby Boating Lake was constructed in the 1970s, close to the town centre. Like other parts of the town, before de-industrialization, the Boating Lake was a thriving hub of social activity, hosting widely attended fishing competitions and rowboat activities. But as decline set in, the lake turned grey, and the neighbouring ancient woodlands became places to avoid.

Regeneration gradually revived the lake. The old diner at the entrance reopened, sprouting into an affordable, well-used greasy spoon café. Unlike the rowing boats, which now exist in memories past, fishing returned. It was much quieter than before, yet it made socializing possible again.

My father loved visiting the Boating Lake; it was a regular haunt of ours for a quick cup of tea and a cooked breakfast. The smell of freshly grilled toast and the workings of a deep-fat fryer drew us in through a short, gated alleyway, into an outdoor seating area, part of which hovered over the lake's bank. A hollowed-out space in the middle of the quad, which once housed an outdoor pool for children, now offered floor-painted games and tunnels for youngsters to crawl through. On warmer days, an older group of folks squeezed around the table next to the outdoor brick toilets, drinking mugs of coffee and sharing cigarettes. We'd pop over to say hello and learn about some local happenings, before heading into the café.

My favourite part of the ritual came after eating. No matter the weather, we'd walk around the lake, first passing the entrance to the woods, then the children's playground, and onwards past a hilly patch of grass where a gaggle of geese loitered. There was usually a single herring to be spotted, standing sharp on one leg in a shallower part of the lake, patiently waiting for an ideal moment to pierce its beak into the murky water for a catch.

It takes around ten minutes or so to walk around the entirety of the lake, but with my father it could take three or four times that, depending on the day. Like most places in Corby, we tended to bump into people my father knew, sometimes an old friend he'd not seen in years, at other

A Precarious Life. Roxana Willis, Oxford University Press. © Roxana Willis 2023.
DOI: 10.1093/oso/9780198855149.003.0012

The Boating Lake 185

times someone from the daily van route. My father was a keen fisher, back when time off work was viable, almost beyond my recollection—a hobby he hoped to return to in retirement. The site of a familiar face at the lake, perched next to a bucket of wriggling maggots, brought him immense joy, his pastime vicariously rekindled. A friend might share an anecdote about the habits of the fish—'They can't get enough smoky bacon flavoured snacks these days.'

On one walk, halfway around the lake, we saw a young man set up for the weekend on an assigned fishing deck. The lad, a few years younger than me, was sitting in a camping chair, fishing gear laid out around him, with a reeled-out rod by his side, bobbing in the water. Behind him, a two-person tent was pitched on a small patch of grass. As we got closer, I noticed a girl inside the tent, cocooned in a sleeping bag, with her head poking out of the entrance, looking distantly over the lake. A few feet closer, and my father started smiling. When the lad noticed he jumped up to offer a warm greeting, 'Paul, I didn't expect to see you here!'

The young man, 'Scott', was from a well-known family on the estate. My father was good friends with Scott's mum, and he attended Scott's cage fighting events when he got off from work early enough—Scott was a gifted, up-and-coming athlete. Scott's elder brother had been imprisoned some time before for a notorious homicide on the estate, where recurrent bursts of violence inside kept him since. Steroids, which some young men take to aid muscle growth, have a bad habit of messing with heads—paranoia a lethal emotion to add to the mix of anger, grief, and frustration. I liked Scott, and when we passed by on the estate, he would always ask how I was getting on. But on a day, later in time, tragedy reoccurred. Scott lost his temper in a flash of road rage, and inadvertently found himself walking in his brother's footsteps. Another talented life on the Lincoln derailed, as though it were fated.

During a different walk, my father spotted an older friend at the end point of the lake, where it circles back round to the car park. The man was a decade or so younger than my father, a fact concealed by the cruelty of advanced cancer. Over the past few years, the man had progressively lost body parts and organs to related diseases—two legs amputated, an arm removed, a liver lost, a lung down. However, that day, luck was on his side. He'd already made some well-sized catches; a perch and carp gently floated back and forth in a tubed net at the side of the water, awaiting their release into the wider lake. When the man smiled sharing his good fortune, he revealed teeth had departed him too.

6
A Violence Continuum

We have examined violence and conflict resolution in Paul's community from an emic perspective. Rather than treating violence as disordered and unintelligible, a survey of the history reveals (as we saw in Chapter 3) the use of force as a once legitimate form of communication among all sectors of English society (see Wiener, 2004; Wood, 2004). This changed, particularly from the seventeenth century onwards, when Enlightenment thinkers began to associate violence with the 'savage' and 'barbarian' tendencies of uncivilized peoples and promulgated the virtues of self-control and rationality. As the bourgeois classes grew in power and influence over the centuries, the normative fabric of society increasingly discouraged conflict resolution through interpersonal violence in favour of using emergent modern state institutions, such as the police. However, up to the present we have noted that the most socio-economically disadvantaged in English society cannot use the services of the police to address wrongdoing in quite as simple a fashion as their more advantaged counterparts can. This relates partly to the criminal law's outlook on wrongdoing, which does not value harm to relationships and vulnerable persons to the same extent as precariat communities seem to, and partly to the general unresponsiveness of the police towards precariously situated groups. Consequently, communities such as Paul's find alternative ways to redress harm or else prompt the state to respond.

Given this disjuncture between the police and the precariat, I have argued that the failure of the British state to fully incorporate all persons within its remit has contributed to the continuing use of interpersonal violence among the least advantaged. However, although recorded rates of interpersonal violence might be higher for those at the tail end of the class system, this need not make precariat spaces the primary locations of violence. On the contrary, I suspect that the most extensive uses of violence are found among the advantaged, much of which is now inflicted in

A Precarious Life. Roxana Willis, Oxford University Press. © Roxana Willis 2023.
DOI: 10.1093/oso/9780198855149.003.0013

A Violence Continuum   187

legally permissible and less overt forms. For us to recognize this violence, it will help to trace how physical displays of force by English elites to attain advantage and mark their authority in the past—the chains of slavery and a whole host of extreme physical punishments inflicted on the lower orders—have transmuted into veiled forms facilitated by the modern state apparatus. Accordingly, I am taking W. E. B. Du Bois's (1917) argument that world powers did not simply abolish slavery but gradually transformed it into less overt forms of coerced labour, and extending it to the phenomenon of violence more broadly (see also Lowe, 2015; Winant, 2001). What I am proposing, then, is that elite violence remains widespread and injurious, yet it now operates in masked ways. To look under that mask, we require a thicker account of violence.

A valuable theoretical device for this task is the 'continuum of violence' which Nancy Scheper-Hughes and Philippe Bourgois (2004) develop: at one end of the continuum are overt and spectacular acts, such as the violence inflicted by colonists during transatlantic slavery and colonial rule, genocidal violence, torture, and extra-judicial killing; towards the other end of the continuum are concealed, less direct, and interpersonal forms of violence—'the "little" violences produced in the structures, habituses, and *mentalités* of everyday life' (Scheper-Hughes and Bourgois, 2004: 19). Importantly, the device of a continuum allows us to see and draw connections between uses of violence. And so what has become obvious violence— the physical and voyeuristic kinds—may not exist in isolation, instead being connected to an assortment of other forms of violence, which may feed into its spectacular displays.

In this chapter, I address two concealed and interrelated forms of violence common in Paul's community: namely, structural violence and symbolic violence. Following Johan Galtung (1969), Bourgois (2004: 426) defines structural violence as: 'Chronic, historically entrenched political-economic oppression and social inequality, ranging from exploitative international terms of trade to abusive local working conditions and high infant mortality rates.' Paul Farmer (2001, 2004) provides a sustained account of structural violence and its effects on the most socio-economically disadvantaged, with a particular focus on the experiences of persons in Haiti. According to Farmer, low mortality rates and extensive human suffering in Haiti are intricately connected with historical and economic processes, which disproportionately expose disadvantaged communities to lifelong illnesses without access to adequate treatment. Thus, structural inequality may have a snowball effect, exposing socio-economically disadvantaged

188 A Violence Continuum

persons to a range of harms which build up and worsen until relieved only in death.

In the UK context, historical and economic processes which shape structural violence in the present are manifold. From the continuation of a class system, and other forms of inequality in relation to race, gender, sexuality, and disability; to punitive state policies and the establishment of penal institutions; to lopsided employment regulation and an economic system that facilitates the limitless accumulation of resources by some to the detriment of less powerful actors. While several of these structural features become apparent in this chapter, I focus on the effects of unhealthy work and living environments, the violence of housing policy, and the injuries of poverty. Relatedly, I touch on how structural inequality impacts the health outcomes of the most precariously positioned.

Contrasting with structural violence, I incorporate the notion of symbolic violence as developed by Pierre Bourdieu (1984, 1989, 1998b). This form of violence only grows, I think, in the soil fertilized by a certain course of history. In the Introduction, I sketched the 'inward turn' in European thinking which helps the modern concept of the individualized self to emerge (following Taylor, 1989). We saw that, coinciding with the inward turn, poverty had transformed from an innocent into a blameworthy status, so that the pauper and the vagrant become increasingly culpable for their impoverishment (Golding and Middleton, 1982). It is historical factors such as this inward turn and the growth of the modern state which make possible symbolic violence: individuals born into poverty by chance may now internalize fault and individuals born into privilege (also by chance) may now internalize success and subsequent reward.

Symbolic violence happens when individuals misrecognize the difficulties they endure as a product of their own personal limitations and failures, instead of recognizing the difficulties as importantly related to the disadvantaged position they occupy in the social order. For example, when one of Paul's companions supposes that they are now consigned to insecure and coercive forms of employment because of their shortcomings at school, symbolic violence may be at play. That is, instead of explaining the outcome as a collective experience produced by educational inequality and the embedded class system, the principal explanatory factor becomes the individual.

A crucial feature of symbolic violence, then, is that individuals are in effect complicit in their own subordination, because the violence happens when social agents actively compare themselves to standards that

A Violence Continuum **189**

they cannot meet (Bourdieu and Wacquant, 1992: 167–8). As Bourdieu (1998b: 34) explains:

> [d]omination is not the direct and simple action exercised by a set of agents ('the dominant class') invested with powers of coercion. Rather, it is the indirect effect of a complex set of actions engendered within the network of intersecting constraints which each of the dominants, thus dominated by the structure of the field through which domination is exerted, endures on behalf of all the others.

Nonetheless, Bourdieu and Loïc Wacquant (1992) are keen to eschew thinking of dominated agents as simply responsible for their own domination. Rather, their point is that domination occurs mostly because what essentially determines domination are basic axiomatic structures of thought which agents are compelled to buy into, simply by virtue of being 'born in a social world' (1992: 168). In this way, the dominated also dominate, reproducing thereby the conditions for their own domination as well as the continued domination of the collective.

The standards individuals compare themselves to in the UK as part of the process of symbolic violence are, I suggest, rooted in the framework of autonomy, standards which I argue are not attainable by all. To recap, the autonomous moral ideal is something like a Lockean conception of (what Taylor calls) the punctual self: a rational agent who exercises self-control and is responsible for their actions. However, when I speak of autonomy as a moral framework the ideal is 'thicker' still; it represents a particular kind of 'self-made' character. Here we can think back to Enlightenment ideas about civility, and moral standards advanced through the bourgeois civilization discourse. Charles Taylor (1989) refers to this modern variation as the 'affirmation of ordinary life': a moral framework in which people place special value on (or in Taylor's language, strongly evaluate) work, family, and reproduction. Therefore, within the framework, it is not sufficient simply for an individual to make their own choices in life—to be deemed virtuous, the autonomous individual is expected to make the right kinds of choices and be held responsible if they fail to do so. Accordingly, as per the autonomy framework, those who do not meet the moral standards required of them are subjected to blame and condemnation, by themselves as well as others, and hence they become responsible for the effects of structural inequality.

During this chapter, how Paul and his multigenerational peers experience both structural and symbolic violence become apparent. Beginning

190 A Violence Continuum

with structural violence, we see the tendency for structural injuries to be blamed on the individuals who fall victim to them. The first example stems from the harmful conditions of the town steelworks, the effects of which Paul's community are still living through. The second example is the violence of housing demolition, through two waves of which the Lincoln estate suffered. Next, I investigate the interplay of structural violence with symbolic violence more closely by examining how persons exposed to unemployment and extreme forms of poverty are treated as immoral and personally responsible for experiencing their precarious condition. Nonetheless, in the final part of the chapter, we will see that Paul's peers remain aware of the structural reality which stifles their full agency and choice.

Enduring Loss of Life and Limb

The closure of the Corby steelworks caused immense injury. By 1982, over 30 percent of the town's population had lost their jobs, which gave Corby the second highest rates of unemployment in the country (Corby District Council, 1989). Just as those who protested the closure of the steelworks had feared, extensive unemployment led to a whole host of deprivations and hardships—increased interpersonal violence and other forms of crime, the spread of addiction, various forms of ill health, and more. Rates of employment have since returned to the national average, especially following a government regeneration drive and substantial investment in the town in more recent decades. However, many of Paul's peers remain in precarious employment and, as we saw in Chapter 1, are subject to excessive employer surveillance. Deepening levels of poverty accompany this labour insecurity in Corby (Northamptonshire Telegraph, 2019c; Ward, 2020), as well as increased debt (Corby was labelled the 'debt capital of Britain' in 2017 (Allen, 2017)), and life expectancies far below the national average (Corby was labelled the 'suicide capital of England' in 2018 (Davis, 2018)).

These features of poverty tend to be individualized in local authority and news reports, which habitually blame individuals for the effects of prolonged and ongoing structural violence. Let us look at lung cancer, for example. The prevalence of lung cancer in Corby is significantly higher than other parts of Northamptonshire County and the national average. In a local authority report on lung cancer rates between 1993 and 2010, the average rates in Corby were approximately 50 percent higher than the national average (Northamptonshire Country Council, 2013).[1] The same local health report cited smoking, diet, and alcohol consumption as causal factors for the high rates of cancers in Corby. Although socio-economic disadvantage is also noted as a risk factor, this is explicitly linked with issues such as high rates of smoking. Accordingly, the report's main recommendations to address lung cancer in Corby include encouraging reduction in smoking, addressing obesity, and urging residents to attend earlier screening—all of which bring individual agency to the fore of solutions.

Subsequently, in 2019, a mobile screening service was set up in Corby to improve lung cancer survival rates, targeting persons between the ages of fifty-five and seventy-four years with a history of smoking (Northamptonshire Health and Care Partnership, 2019). A local news report which encouraged people to use the screening service emphasized smoking as a risk factor. The report interviews a seventy-five-year-old resident as having smoked since school, even quantifying his earlier smoking habits, this being the factor the report author deemed to be of most significance to the news story. The journalist also quotes a local GP: 'We know that many people in our town have been smokers and that this increases the risk of breathing problems and lung disease as well as cancer' (Bagley, 2021). The elderly interviewee, however, mentions an additional factor: he suggests the screening service is important for those like him who had worked at the steelworks. The journalist herself touches on this factor only in passing, when citing the screening questions residents must answer to access the service, which includes whether they were exposed to 'occupational hazards such as heavy industry or working near asbestos'. Thus, despite these fleeting references to industrial work as a contributory factor of lung cancer, the emphasis in the news article remains on smoking as the chief cause. Certainly, tobacco smoke contains well-known potent carcinogens and is the main cause of lung cancer at present (Ferlay et al., 2010), and rates of smoking in Corby are recorded as the highest in England (Bagley, 2020).

Plausibly, the prominence here given to smoking as an explanation of the lung cancer rates in Corby invokes ideas of individual responsibility. However, bringing to mind the background factors contributing to the prevalence of smoking among particular groups should disabuse us of this

---

[1] The national standardized average was approximately 50,000 incidents of lung cancer; in Corby, the average during this period was around 75,000 incidents.

192 A Violence Continuum

relatively simplistic take. After all, we know that tobacco companies have been permitted to pursue aggressive marketing strategies which encourage smoking; that they add chemicals to enhance the addictive properties of tobacco; and that tobacco lobbyists had sought to conceal the known health risks from the public for almost half a century (cf. Buckley, 2010; Hilts, 1996; Sullum, 1999).

A deeper view also reveals even less direct causes for the prevalence of smoking. For example, it is plausible that some workers, subject to heavy employer surveillance and control over their bodies, as illustrated in Chapter 1, find smoking provides them a momentary break—a flash of autonomy in otherwise relentlessly coercive conditions. Moreover, smoking can be a form of sociability, entwined with the sharing practices as discussed in Chapter 2, infusing the practice with greater meaning (Edwards, 2000; Koch, 2018b). These examples (many more of which could be provided) remind us that smoking habits do not form in a vacuum and multiple factors influence them. It might be that after pointing out external factors as causes, they then strike us as obvious. But the thrust of individualized explanations is often to obscure this obviousness: we find ourselves encouraged to relegate to the background external causal factors, even when they might be much more significant than individual ones.

Beyond the wider structural factors which contribute to high rates of smoking, there are also risk factors posed by work itself, as the elderly interviewee above noted. Of relevance then is a class action lawsuit underway in Corby, pursued on behalf of former steelworkers, against the insurers for British Steel due to the company's failure to provide steelworkers with adequate protective equipment, which exposed the workforce to substances known to seriously harm their health (Irwin Mitchell, 2012; Northamptonshire Telegraph, 2018). In a slightly earlier case pursued by coke oven workers at the Phurnacite plant in South Wales, the insurers of British Steel accepted liability for corporate negligence, which has been extended to workers in Corby. These hazardous working conditions appear to have contributed to the development of severe lifelong lung conditions and fatal cancers, especially for former steelworkers in Corby who were based in the coke ovens like Paul.

The harmful effects of industrial and low-paid work on employees' health have been documented in a range of social and medical science research papers (e.g. Chandola and Zhang, 2018; Shildrick et al., 2012; Tombs, 2004, 2015). Perhaps such research challenges the place of work in the framework of autonomy as a value that is, in and of itself, an ultimate good (cf.

Wacquant, 2002). Indeed, as Steve Tombs (2004: 156) directly states it, '[w]ork kills'.

Steelworks-related injuries do not stop here. Faced with mass unemployment and ensuing social deprivation following the closure of the steelworks, the local authority, Corby Council, sought to entice new industries to the town. As part of the re-industrialization drive, the Council purchased land from British Steel and began clearing it. However, it seems the local authority was unprepared for the complex task of reclaiming such a highly toxic site, which included 'toxic ponds' (containing cadmium, chromium, zinc, dioxins, and polycyclic aromatic hydrocarbons), 'tar lagoons', and an asbestos pit.

The chief aim of the local authority was economically pragmatic: to clear the land as quickly as possible to make way for new industries and so to address unemployment. However, acting with such haste seemed to cause many problems. As residents reported—later affirmed in a legal ruling (cited below)—lorryloads of (toxic) waste were transported through public areas, in uncovered open-top trucks, which leaked onto roads, creating mud trails in the winter months and sandstorms of red dust that entered homes in dry periods, reportedly coating cars, clothing, and infants' prams. Accompanying the toxic dust, residents recalled a sulphurous smell in the air; one compared it to the stench of rotten eggs.

Pregnant women exposed to the highly toxic waste during the reclamation gave birth to children with severe birth defects. In press interviews, some of the mothers described feeling personally responsible for their children's disabilities, wondering what they might have done wrong during the pregnancy. Following the emergence of a pattern, eighteen families jointly pursued group litigation against the local state authority, led by Collins Solicitors, which resulted in a substantive 220-page High Court judgment: *Corby Group Litigation v Corby Borough Council [2009] EWHC 1944*. After reviewing the actions of Corby District Council between 1986 and 1999, Justice Akenhead ruled in the favour of sixteen claimants, finding 'negligence, breach of statutory duty and public nuisance on the part of Corby Borough Council and its statutory predecessor Corby District Council'.[2] The judgment details an abundance of reckless activity, including the haphazard handling and transportation of waste throughout the stages of the reclamation process; inadequate measures to prevent the public

---

[2] The two youngest claimants were excluded due to a time limit on those covered by the ruling.

194　A Violence Continuum

from entering the toxic site (there were reports of children swimming in the 'toxic ponds'); and the side-lining and dismissal of whistleblowers who sought to raise safety concerns during the reclamation.

Based on expert evidence, the judge ruled: (1) that the number of birth defects in Corby was statistically significant, up to three times higher than would otherwise be expected; and (2) that the levels of toxic air exposure were sufficiently high enough for the relevant birth defects to form. It is possible that exposure to airborne toxic waste—which has affected a significant proportion of the Corby population resident during the excavation of the works—could be a contributory factor in the development of cancers and other serious illness in the decades that followed.

Given this post-industrial landscape, losing loved ones has become a common experience even for young people in Paul's community—grief which is understandably accompanied by anger and pain (cf. Rosaldo, 2004). Several young people I worked with during the fieldwork period were experiencing the terminal illness or recent loss of parents. This was especially pronounced among the young people who were in contact with the criminal justice system. A boy on my estate had lost a brother and several friends before leaving his teenage years; large tattoos have since transformed his body into a site of remembrance. A woman in her thirties shared the difficulty her two-year-old was experiencing with the loss of his father: 'Think my little boy needs counselling, he says to me is daddy asleep? I miss daddy. How can I reply to that? That's the third day in a row he's asked for his daddy.' Another woman in her twenties struggled with the loss of her mother, explaining that she finds 'it so hard to face the reality she's not coming back'. A younger woman whose mother had also passed described feeling jealous when seeing other people with theirs. Common phrases circulated among the community, presumably informed by frequent experiences of loss; a teenage boy commented how 'the good die young'; others asked rhetorical questions such as, 'why do bad things happen to good people?'; or shared words of wisdom, such as 'don't regret growing old, it's a privilege denied to many' and 'live life to the full, you never know when it'll be taken from you'.

While community participants still live with collective trauma and loss caused by corporate and state negligence, state bodies now plan to transform parts of Corby into a major site of waste disposal. Up to four new separate waste plants are planned for Corby, in addition to the sewage works and waste disposal industries already operating in the town, which will see Corby become the recipient of waste from London, Birmingham, and beyond (see Willis, 2019). Many residents are concerned about the health effects of the proposed industries, particularly on children, and in town meetings some have raised questions about why they should trust new corporations and the state to not harm them again. Community resistance to the plans has involved petitions, protests, and notably the protest actions of a long-term local, Lee Forester, who pitched up a tent and camped outside one proposed site to communicate his opposition, drawing national attention to the plight (BBC News, 2015).

Nonetheless, local and county councils have consistently dismissed residents' voiced concerns. When the regional authority eventually granted planning permission for a particularly large waste disposal unit, without duly engaging with the fears of Corby residents, some of the local activists expressed frustration and hurt. In an online discussion, one man questioned why so much had been invested in the regeneration of the town if all the council planned to do was fill it with waste; a woman lamented, 'in their eyes we're just common people who don't matter'; and another declared that 'the Government gets away with murder!' Several people raised suspicions that corruption had been involved, the local authority having been investigated for this behaviour in the past.[3] And one man suggested (perhaps hyperbolically) that if the plans go ahead, the town should rally together and 'burn it down when they build it'.

Demolished but Not Forgotten

We have seen how structural violence shortens lives and takes loved ones prematurely. I wish to note a further aspect of structural injury that Paul and his neighbours suffer, which relates to the limited power socioeconomically disadvantaged persons have over their built environment. In Chapter 2, I provided a brief history of the Lincoln estate, its socioeconomic deprivation, and the accompanying stigma for its residents. We saw how, despite material hardship, Paul and his neighbours carve out alternative ways to survive harsh conditions and invest time in others. It is

---

[3] In 2010, Corby Borough Council sold a piece of land to Greatline for £82,000, which now hosts a Tesco supermarket. One year later, in 2011, the land was valued at £8 million (BBC News, 2012). In 2013, the local press reported that the land was sold onwards for £43m to Renduki, an offshore firm based in the Isle of Man (Northamptonshire Telegraph, 2016). The local police force undertook a criminal investigation; however, no criminal proceedings have been brought against the Council.

196 A Violence Continuum

within this context that a further form of structural violence took place: the state's destruction of the estate.

After decades of neglect, like many underprivileged council estates in England, parts of Paul's estate were assigned for demolition (see also McKenzie, 2015; Hyatt, 2003; Boughton, 2018; Crump, 2002; Lund, 2006; Rogaly and Taylor, 2016). In 2007, the local council announced that the Kingswood area had 'priority development' status due to its 'state of under-investment and urban decay' (Corby Borough Council, 2007). Phase one of the regeneration strategy involved the complete demolition of the Lincoln spine, stopping just next to Paul's house. Phase two, which took place mid-way through the research period in 2014, included demolishing Canada Square, another central meeting point on the estate next to the playing field and community centre. Consequently, by the end of the fieldwork period, both of the originally designed social areas in the estate had been turned to dust, and in their place a mix of local authority and (mostly) private housing erected.

In the week of Canada Square's demolition, the local newspaper published a news story about its history. The reporter, Kate Cronin (2014b), opened the piece sounding a nostalgic tone that reminisced about the estate in its award-winning days, sharing beautiful black-and-white archival photographs of the estate and recounting the memories of an older resident who worked a paper round there as a child. In contrast to these idyllic beginnings, Cronin asserts that after the closure of the steelworks, 'drugs, anti-social behaviour and violent crime became a real problem' on the estate; 'drug dealers ... moved in, driving away the respectable families who had once lived there'. The remainder of the article then outlines select crimes from the past: two violent homicides; 'the notorious Canada Square Girls gang'; repeat instances of the fire services being 'pelted with missiles'; alongside other forms of anti-social behaviour. As a result, Cronin claims 'Corby Council then took decisive action ... to demolish the worst areas and rebuild'. According to Cronin, 'residents were shipped out ... and new families moved in'. To complete the narrative, the piece cites a positive statement from a local counsellor, who talks about 'new beginnings' and the council's providing residents with a regenerated area that 'they can be proud of'.

The news article about the second phase of demolition generated much discussion in Paul's community. Some of Paul's friends supported the narrative presented by Cronin and explained the social issues on the estate in individualistic terms, as one man summed up: 'just goes to show, cunts ruin everything'. When people explained the dilapidation of the estate in individualized terms, they chiefly blamed 'the junkies'.

TERRY: Its good it's getting knocked down. It's a shit hole, full of loads of little shit heads, the place is a mess
KEN: They needed to knock it down 20 years ago. They shouldn't home the junkies
BRANDON: Running it down sort of worked to get rid of the junkies, but now they're all on the other side of Corby. Give it 10 years, they will be up the lakes injecting.

Brandon points out that state policy to relocate does not solve problems but rather shifts the social hardships to other places, which hints at deeper structural factors. In fact, many of Paul's friends who had lived through the harsh reality of the estate's decline strongly disagreed with the depiction of the Lincoln estate in the local press and drew attention to wider structural factors. The next conversation between a group of Paul's friends from the estate raises some of them. The first comment received a high number of 'likes', indicating it is well supported.

JADE: Biggest load of rubbish I've ever read. There was trouble on every estate not just the square and there were no gangs! This makes me mad, council let it go that way. Every other estate had shops. We had nothing and still don't now! They will build houses and still do nothing for our kids, the next generation. Even tried closing our community centre.
KEELY: Well said, we have nothing on our estate, so they knock down shops to build more houses. We don't need more houses, we need facilities for kids and families.
GEORGE: The council let it go downhill. All you hear from the council and see in the paper is how bad it is, but these people have never lived here or even been on the estate. Now they decide to build more houses, no shops or facilities for kids. Does anyone in the council live in the real world?

This conversation reveals a marked discrepancy between how those with the relative power to dictate a narrative about the estate and how some residents experience it. Instead of deploying individualistic explanations, those with lived knowledge can offer accounts that bring the structural causes of decline into sight. Residents' comments here accord with Ben Rogaly and

198 A Violence Continuum

Becky Taylor's analysis (2016: 10) which points to the classed nature of demolition. Indeed, it becomes glaringly obvious when we look at who is deciding to demolish council housing and who is being cleared from their homes: the state offloads the phenomenon of poverty onto the most disadvantaged and justifies clearing land for new forms of private housing in the process (Crump, 2002; Lund, 2006).

As well as contesting ascriptions of blame for the hardship on the estate, those within Paul's community discussing the pending demolition also shared memories about the estate (cf. Degnen, 2005; Koch, 2018b; Fraser and Clark, 2021). In response to Cronin's news article, a group of women in Paul's community point to the absences in the news report:

GINA: Makes it sound the worst place ever, what about all the good stuff?
BECKY: Have some great memories of hanging round the square
STEPHANIE: Yeah, many good memories of the Lincoln and Canada Sq
YVONNE: Years of memories, good and bad times up there, used to be a good place.

Men on the estate shared similar feelings (cf. Fraser and Clark, 2021). One young man had been struggling with the slow death of a parent alongside the demolition; he regularly demonstrated his sense of loss at different stages of the demolition. For example, prior to the demolition, he commented, 'Within a year my whole childhood will be gone. Just walked past the mighty bush and it's all chopped down and shit, within a year the square's gonna be gone? Total fucking raging.' In the week of the demolition, the young man shared a picture someone had taken of him standing outside his former flat, scheduled to be demolished. In response, one of his older friends commented 'RIP the square'. Another older friend joked, 'you'll be on the balcony like, "you have to take me down with it"'. And a third friend commented, 'it's ruthless man, used to be able to walk around and everyone would be sitting there waiting for their 10 fags and their frosty jacks (cheap cider)'. During the demolition, estate residents shared more pictures; surveying some, one man reminisced, 'This is certainly a chapter in our lives. Whoever lived in or around Canada Sq will remember this, for one reason or another, good or bad, it's what makes memories, and I'll miss it.'

These comments reveal the estate as more than just a place: relationships were formed here and memories made; the estate was laced with meaning (cf. Degnen, 2005; Desmond, 2016; Edwards, 2000; Koch 2018b; Wacquant, 2007: 101). The demolished buildings had been homes housing families, where friends had grown up together, and where important life events took place. In contrast to socio-economically advantaged individuals who might pass on material wealth to their next generations, the legacies of estate residents are instead in the anecdotes remembered: kind acts, brave moments, and good jokes of those who passed live on (cf. Edwards, 2000: 139). What the council classified as instances of unruly behaviour on the Lincoln comprised, for some, fond moments of togetherness, the locations to which they were tethered now evaporated. And what certain residents on the estate felt love towards and attachment to had now been marked as worthless by outsiders with the power to destroy it. Failure to appreciate local value is partly what makes possible the state's bulldozing the community away: and yet it is us, the estate's residents, not them, the employees of the state, who are labelled antisocial (see Koch, 2018b: Introduction).

The Immorality of Poverty

Up to this point, I have shown that what compounds structural violence, such as poverty, ill-health, toxic living and working conditions, is a tendency to blame those who must endure it. In this way, the victims of structural violence not only internalize it in the sense of suffering its injuries internally; they also may internalize the harm further by experiencing shame for their hardships—i.e. by coming to believe that their prior bad choices primarily explain the injuries they carry. The concept of symbolic violence captures specifically this second form of violence: in short, it is when a person experiences a sense of moral failure for their inability to meet the legitimate standards of their social order. And even when an individual tries resisting the shame of their apparent failure to make the right choices, British society has developed in such a way that others similarly positioned in the social order will bring symbolic violence into effect. Shaming an individual who does not meet the legitimate standards and permitting structural features to remain in the background simply reinforces the moral standards of autonomy and individual responsibility. Thus, the tendency to praise or blame individuals for the social position they fill has an especially violent effect when we place responsibility wholly on the backs of the most unfortunate—not only must they live through material hardship, but they must also be condemned for it.

A person's apparent blameworthiness for their poverty is most pronounced when they are also unemployed. The moralization of work itself is

200 A Violence Continuum

rooted in the historic bourgeois drive to make the lower orders labour in the capitalist order (cf. Beier, 1985). At first, masters used overt forms of punishment to force enslaved persons and servants to labour for their benefit (cf. Hay, 2004), but as the political economy became more established, uses of violence became subtler, and the propertied have since effected their will primarily by moralizing work and socially shaming those who fail to labour. Although political thought in Britain has long accommodated the view that certain people are unemployed through no fault of their own, a prevailing belief is nonetheless that most who are unemployed choose not to work and therefore must be forced into productivity (see Welshman, 2014; Wiener, 1994). In this context, the very fact of unemployment is sufficient cause to suspect a moral defect of character.

The Conservative-led coalition government had especially revived Victorian notions of the immoral poor in the form of austerity policies, implemented from 2010 onwards. As a flavour of the reforms, the Jobseeker's Allowance (Employment, Skills and Enterprise) Regulations, implemented in 2011, required long-term unemployed persons to participate in unpaid work activity for up to six months—which the Supreme Court in 2013 subsequently ruled unlawful.[4] And in 2013, the government introduced the Personal Independence Payment (PIP), requiring millions of persons living with disability in the UK in receipt of welfare support to undergo retesting. The policy was implemented alongside Universal Credit, which reduced net benefit payments and imposed longer sanctions when conditions were not met. Injurious effects of these policies, particularly on persons living with disability in Britain, have been documented in several harrowing accounts (see Barr et al., 2016; CRPD, 2017; Ryan, 2019: ch 2).

What compounded the violence of austerity is the suspicion and blame directed towards unemployed persons, circulated through media and policy discourse, and reproduced through ordinary channels of communication—a process which is now well-documented (Hall et al., 2013; Golding and Middleton, 1982; Hancock, 2004; Jensen, 2018; Morrison, 2019; Skeggs, 2004; I. Tyler, 2015). In Paul's community, those most vulnerable to accusations of 'playing the system' were long-term unemployed individuals due to disability. Less visible disabilities and illnesses especially tended to be viewed in a suspicious light. In particular, back problems were susceptible to the charge of being 'made up' in order to claim benefits, which is

---

[4] *R (Reilly and Wilson) v Secretary of State for Work and Pensions* [2013] UKSC 68.

The Immorality of Poverty **201**

a recurrent finding in studies among the least advantaged (Howe, 1990; Koch, 2018b: 72). Repetitive assembly line work and industries that require regular lifting are liable to cause bodily injury, as the autobiographical writings of Didier Eribon (2018) and Édouard Louis (2017, 2019) vividly bring to light.[5] It therefore seems especially cruel for back injuries, which must be endured by many precariat workers, to have become a signifier of dishonesty and immorality.

I also observed a tendency for some of Paul's peers to be suspicious of mental health problems, much as they are of certain invisible bodily injuries. For example, one of Paul's friends alleged that a participant on a widely watched *Channel 5* televised debate about benefits 'misused' bipolar disorder to justify being out of work. This was met with outrage on Paul's newsfeed and one woman sarcastically suggested that 'bad backs have been misdiagnosed all these years, it was bipolar all along'. Another woman expressed anger at the suggestion that those with bipolar cannot work and asserted, 'I have bipolar but I pay my way.'

The next extract illustrates the struggle experienced by Mikey, who lived with chronic depression, amid the frustrations of his working friend Cheryl.

MIKEY: Every time things start being bearable, something comes along and fucks it up. Why can't I be happy and be done with it. I've either gotta keep going or just give up

CHERYL: You depressed fanny, I'll give you a slap if you don't shut it

MIKEY: And if I did shut it who would listen to your shit when you needed it?

CHERYL: No shit for me these days Mikey. I'm in control of my life again and I'm staying on top

MIKEY: Well maybe you can be there for me now

NICK: Shit Mikey, you're sounding so miserable, you'd make my mum's plants wilt!

---

[5] Didier Eribon (2018: 80–1) captures the violence of coercive labour in his working-class memoire about growing up in France: 'As I look at my mother today, her body stiffened and painful as a result of the harsh tasks she performed for nearly fifteen years, standing on an assembly line attaching tops to glass jars, with only one ten-minute bathroom break each morning and another in the afternoon, I can't help but be struck by what social inequality means concretely, physically. Even the word 'inequality' seems to me to be a euphemism that papers over the reality of the situation, the naked violence of exploitation. A worker's body, as it ages, reveals to anyone who looks at it the truth about the existence of classes.'

202 A Violence Continuum

MIKEY: Aw, sorry about that man, if I still had ma money coming in I'd gladly buy her some new ones

NICK: They've stopped your benefits pal? Unbelievable. Fart, and the bastards will sanction you. What happened?

MIKEY: Fucking Joke Centre mate. One wee error and now I've been sanctioned 13 fucking weeks!

NICK: They're unreal. Ma mate has an irreversible condition corroding his back, on high doses of pain killers and that, but the wankers say 'fit to work'. He's a sound man ma mate. He's gonna find work even though it'll leave him totally disabled. I hope he sues the cunts. This government is disgusting, gimme a gun and I'd shoot the lot of 'em

CHERYL: They should scrap JSA [job seekers allowance] and only give benefits to mothers and the disabled, lower taxes for the working people, and free healthcare for the working class who actually pay into society, instead of giving it to people who are draining society

MIKEY: But how are we draining society if we can't get a job. No company in their right mind would employ me, criminal record going back to when I was a youngster

CHERYL: You can beg for money. There you go sorted! Most agencies don't even check up on that shit. I'm fed up working my arse off to give £500 to people who choose not to work! That's like a holiday a month I'm giving away. Just get a job Mikey, you've been on benefits for like forever. Stop feeling sorry for yaself and sort your shit out. No one else is gonna to do it for you.

Mikey shares the difficulties of accessing welfare support and the hardship of being sanctioned. In other posts, Mikey spoke of suicidal feelings and detailed his complex metal health problems. Notably, the biggest cause of death of men under thirty-five years of age in the UK is suicide, and rates of suicide in Corby are among the highest in the country (ONS, 2019; Davis, 2018). According to Frances Ryan (2019), in an account of the impact of austerity politics on persons living with disability, multiple deaths, including those by suicide, have followed the withdrawal of welfare support. Consequently, Ryan contends that the government's introducing fines under Universal Credit was tantamount to punishing disability. Ryan's findings reflect what Pierre Bourdieu refers to as the '*law of the conservation of violence*', which suggests that structural violence is 'matched sooner or later in the form of suicides, crime and delinquency, drug addiction, alcoholism, a whole host of minor and major everyday acts of violences' (Bourdieu, 1998a: 40; see also Fraser and Clark, 2021).

The Immorality of Poverty   **203**

As we see above, Mikey's friends respond in starkly different ways to his struggles. Nick is compassionate and understanding, which accords with the moral orientation I have described as the framework of mutuality. First, Nick acknowledges the punitive tendency of the state by referring to the ease with which sanctions are given. He employs again the language of being punished for farting; this time signifying the arbitrary levels of control to which the precariat is exposed when out of work, not just when in work (see Chapter 1). Second, Nick offers a comparable anecdote of a friend denied support, who consequently now must return to work and bear the risk of permanent disability (cf. Louis, 2019). Nick's thoughts bring into view structural factors that create hardship for the collective, also thereby showing that Mikey's struggles are shared by others. Indeed, Ryan (2019: 27) reports that by December 2017, nearly half of persons living with disability in Britain who were assessed under PIP had their welfare support reduced or altogether stopped. However, by 2018, 70 percent of those who appealed the 'fit to work' decision had it overturned (Ryan, 2019: 50).

In contrast to Nick's empathetic response, Cheryl's replies are heavily infused with sentiments of individual responsibility and blame. I suggest such normative standpoints align well with the legitimate framework of autonomy. Notwithstanding her suggestion that persons living with disability should receive state support (nor her calling Mikey a 'depressed fanny'), Cheryl implies that Mikey's mental illness is outside of this legitimate category—that Mikey is fully responsible for his situation. In contrast to Mikey, Cheryl presents herself as having attained an autonomous status, which she attributes to personal determination and having gained control over her life (cf. Silva, 2013). It is plausible that Cheryl, who is not so far removed from Mikey's circumstances, believes that individual choice and fortitude is sufficient to ward off structural violence in order to have peace of mind in the present. By blaming Mikey for his predicament, Cheryl distances herself from the destitution, stigma, and shame that sits so close (indeed, with her 'no shit for me these days', she perhaps hints at recent hardship). Yet, by accepting the narrative of choice to explain Mikey's circumstances, Cheryl inadvertently fosters on him a form of violence which awaits her too, should she ever find herself in Mikey's shoes.

At the time of the fieldwork, the effects of austerity politics and welfare cuts were beginning to surface, with a rise in the use of food banks and increased reliance on discarded food in commercial bins (Cooper and Whyte, 2017; Garthwaite, 2016; Lansley and Mack, 2015). Many of Paul's friends responded to news reports of supermarkets pouring bleach on waste food (to prevent

204 A Violence Continuum

people searching in the bins for it as food poverty spread) as 'so wrong' and 'so bad', since the supermarkets 'were chucking it out anyway and people were starving'. However, on two occasions, when people were seen rummaging in local bins for food, I observed participants in Paul's community express disgust rather than sympathy, directing moral condemnation at the impoverished persons rather than supermarkets. For instance, a middle-aged woman claimed, 'I always see them behind [the supermarket] with their torch and black bags –rank'. A young woman witnessing a similar event in the daytime informed her friends: 'Oh my days, there's a lady in her 50s raiding the bins at the back of [named supermarket]. Haha, and she just asked one of the workers having a fag for a carrier bag to take it home with her!' In response, the woman's friend remarked 'yuck'. The terms 'rank', to indicate a foul smell, and 'yuck', to communicate strong distaste, express disgust.

In his reflections on disgust, William Miller (1997) describes it as an emotion which signifies a hierarchical relationship between the person who feels disgust and the inferior object that disgusts. In keeping with Miller, Sara Ahmed (2014) portrays disgust as creating a symbolic sense of distance between an object that revolts one but is close enough to be seen. It might be that when we witness other human beings in such severe states of destitution—searching for food in bins, where dirt, waste, contamination, and disease could fester—our own mortality and co-dependency is brought into view (cf. Nussbaum, 2004). It is conceivable that witnessing such base human vulnerabilities is especially disturbing for observers so situated that a similar fate could befall them too; one bit of bad luck might be all that separates a person's present place and the uncomfortable state of destitution that they bear witness to. Under such circumstances, the social distancing is as much an expression of what 'I am not' (Lawler, 2005: 438) as it is of what 'I am scared to become'.

Paul's community were also divided on the issue of homelessness. Many community participants cared about people experiencing homelessness, joined local initiatives to supply those sleeping rough with food and blankets in the winter, and donated money to support shelters and volunteering initiatives. During a snowy winter, one of Paul's friends asked the town-wide community to help cover the costs of accommodation for homeless people affected by a deficit in community services, and within days, sufficient donations were received to meet the needs of the season.

Yet, in stark contrast to these acts of support, on occasion I observed hostility towards homelessness and the assignment of blame to anyone so situated.

The Immorality of Poverty   205

SARAH: My heart is aching, I just watched an old man who appeared to be homeless get dragged out of the train station. I asked why he'd been taken out, he wasn't hurting anyone, just warming up, the man said 'just doing my job'

MICHELLE: I can't stand jobsworths. Poor man

JOHN: The dirty tramp should get a job, too much junkie scum in Corby. People like that fuck it up for the rest of us

DAN: Some people are dealt a shit hand – we should look out for those with less

FRANK: Anyone can make money if they want it bad enough, on or off the books

JOHN: Aye Frank, those dog breath tramps chose the life they live.

In this example, three of five community participants are sympathetic towards an apparently impoverished person who was removed from a place of warmth in winter. They perhaps subscribe to a maxim noted by Dan, rooted in the ethos of mutuality, 'to look out for those with less'. According to Sarah's recounting of the event, she attempted to challenge the decision to evict the homeless person, which aligns with the tendency in Paul's community to protect those in more vulnerable positions and to challenge power imbalances. And by calling the employee a 'jobsworth' for evicting the homeless person, in effect Michelle challenges the prioritization of the legitimate norm which strongly values work—to do one's job—over the mutuality norm—to care for each other, especially in moments of need.

Frank and John, however, are notably less sympathetic to the homeless person's plight. Both associate the condition of homelessness with choice and accordingly appoint blame to the individual, rather than focusing on the structural aspect of poverty. John makes the unsubstantiated claim that the homeless person has chosen a life of addiction, hence employing a logic of 'prior fault' which is core to the criminal law in England and Wales. By offering alternatives to homelessness, and explaining it as a series of bad choices, John and Frank create distance between the precarity they have likely experienced in their lifetime and utter destitution which sits so close. Though their reactions might be explainable, offloading this fear onto an identifiable scapegoat in turn burdens the individual with the full weight of structural and symbolic violence.

Some of Paul's peers disdained begging as much as homelessness. A young woman explained the extent of her hatred for people in the town centre asking her for money; they should 'get a job or at least save some of

206 A Violence Continuum

your dole money to feed yaself!' Again, assumptions are made about the kinds of choices people make. The woman describes the person requesting money as unable to feed themselves, and hence as failing to attain a basic feature of independence. An even greater emphasis on blame is evident in the following frustrations expressed by a man in his thirties: 'Two junkie bums come up to me while I'm eating ma sausage roll, asking ME for money. I told em tae get te fuck, I aint funding their skag habit. Fucking yaself up is no one's fault but ya own – get a job!'

Rachel Sherman (2017: 63–4) found comparable disdain towards begging in her study of the American elite,[6] most of whom had incomes in excess of half a million dollars per annum, in addition to other forms of financial assets. The presence of similar moral evaluations among the most well-to-do and the most disadvantaged in liberal societies perhaps indicates the spread and influence of autonomy-related ideals, which can create the illusion of common ground between persons from incomparable walks of life.

When one views poverty while morally oriented to the framework of autonomy, one emphasizes the role of agency and choice for those in impoverished circumstances. However, in a society where precarious employment exists, where affordable housing is in short supply, where the cost of living has risen at higher rates than wages, where people have become increasingly reliant on debt, and so on, inevitably, a subset of the population is destined to occupy the most gruelling of positions. Instead of critiquing the systemic factors which create this circumstance, and channelling discontent towards elites that create poverty, citizens direct blame and moral condemnation towards the least fortunate—including towards themselves in acts of symbolic violence.

The Reality of Unemployment

Symbolic violence works by individualizing poverty and structural inequality. Rather than recognizing that markers of poverty are inevitably

---

[6] One of Sherman's (2017) male research participants, an earner of $500,000 per annum, justified not giving money to people he passed on the streets because, in his view, they 'don't do shit'. Another participant in Sherman's study, a stay-at-home mother married to an executive who earned $500,000 annually, similarly commented that 'there's certainly people that work really, really hard, and just can't get ahead, or even buy a house. But then there's also a lot of fucking lazy people that are on the dole, that want to stay there.'

The Reality of Unemployment **207**

worn by those least well-off in a class society—those recurrently exposed to structural violence—we instead place blame chiefly on them, as the foremost causes for the circumstances in which they find themselves. Not only does the tendency towards individualization reduce a multitude of factors into a single explanation, but the foundation of symbolic violence is often rooted in fictional beliefs rather than empirical reality. Time and again, research has found that policy claims by the UK government about the immoral poor fail to be supported by evidence (Dean and Taylor-Gooby, 1992; MacDonald et al., 2014; Morrison, 2019; Shildrick, 2018; Welshman, 2014). We have long known that in conditions of full employment, the so-called 'unemployable' cannot be found (see Jones, 2013).

First-hand experience of precarity exposes these poverty myths, since those who experience a period of unemployment, without having chosen or wanted this situation, suddenly find themselves cast as immoral and underserving of support. Several participants in Paul's community expressed the view that, having paid into the system for a lifetime, they were entitled to receive state support when the time came. However, when community participants eventually did require the support they believed they had earned and deserved, they suddenly found themselves having to fight against being represented as the immoral poor (see also Howe, 1990: 147; Louis, 2019: 70; Ryan, 2019: 7). Consider this conversation between mothers of young children.

KELLY: I can't believe the Conservatives are claiming stay-at-home mums are a waste of space. Who's going to look after our children if we're at work all day? Have they seen the cost of childcare? We'd be working all day for fuck all and our children will be calling some child-minder 'mummy'!

AMBER: I've worked since I was 14, and I gave up last year to be around for my kids. After paying into the system for nearly 20 years, it's my turn to get something back

KELLY: I can't wait to go back to work when my children are older. But for now, I'm going to be the best mum I can be. No good mum is a waste of space.

Rather than representing themselves as permanently unemployed, mothers in the extract draw attention to their history of employment, adolescence being a common period in which those in the precariat begin their working lives: they worked before performing the mothering role and they intend

208   A Violence Continuum

to return to work in the future. Accordingly, the mothers use their work histories, and their aspirations to return to work, to mark themselves as deserving claimants. What the women seek here is an exception from the norm of work for them to perform what they deem the necessary duties of motherhood. However, the national scapegoating and demonization of disadvantaged mothers, especially when lone parents, exposes precariously situated women during periods of motherhood to symbolic violence which they must attempt to deflect (cf. Gillies, 2007; Jensen, 2018; Koch, 2018b; Skeggs, 1997).

Likewise, when Paul's friends spoke about weathering unemployment, rather than wishing to remain without work, they expressed despair at losing a job and others shared in a collective dread about the prospect of needing state assistance. For example, even though the next extract largely consists of criticism of the immoral poor, it nonetheless makes plain some of the misgivings and fears about accessing state welfare.

LELAH: It's an absolute joke trying to get my own place whilst working. It is so expensive and hard to do on my own but if you don't have a job you get it all paid. I work so much and still can't afford it

MOLLY: Yet they give smack heads brand new flats

STUART: Cunts man, if a cardboard box was big enough they'd probably still charge rent. It's actually beneficial to sign on, its so wrong

LELAH: I've never had to sign on and hopefully never would, touch wood, but I have friends that do and it seems like a lot of effort to get not very much money. I've seen loads of people in there when I've searched for jobs that can't even speak or understand English and they get money. It's pretty much logical for people to get pregnant and not have jobs cus it's easier that way

STUART: The government should be putting natives first, it's like their main priority is foreign imports, focusing on their well-being before our own. It'll only get worse. We can't change shit, we can only whinge and it gets you nowhere. And yes, I've signed on before, fuck it man, they want to know who ur fucking and ya life story for fifty quid a week! We're better than this shit.

Despite claiming that not working is 'beneficial' and 'easier', Lelah and Stuart are close enough to the reality to know that this is untrue. Lelah has seen friends attempt to access welfare support, which she acknowledges involves a lot of toil for limited gain. Moreover, Stuart recalls accessing

The Reality of Unemployment   **209**

benefits in the past and its significant intrusions into his privacy, such as being made to reveal details about sexual partners. In Stuart's view, such an invasion of autonomy is not worth the £50 weekly sum of support which he reportedly received in return. Comparably, a research participant in Koch's study made the following comment about Job Centre officers: 'They want to know everything, down to what toilet paper you are using' (2018b: 99). Another woman in Paul's community bemoaned the insensitivity of job centre staff who were apparently looking at takeaway menus while she waited to be seen with barely enough money in her pocket to feed her children. These personal experiences indicate that accessing state support in moments of necessity is far from an easy or chosen option. On the contrary, it is described as a humiliating experience which entails substantial loss of what limited personal autonomy people have managed to attain.

Indeed, Paul's peers exchanged gestures of solidarity when a friend lost a job and faced the prospect of the job centre, the inverse of their response to someone's finding a job (see Chapter 1).

GREGG: Shitty day today, been laid off. Job centre here I come
SIMON: Shit mate, good luck
DEAN: Good luck mate, you'll need it. They'll treat you like a foreigner
KELLY: Good luck. You'll need it as the job centre is hard work, they're not going to make it easy to claim any money even though you paid your stamp and taxes.

Dean suggests that using the Job Centre is akin to losing status as a citizen in the eyes of the state—to be treated 'like a foreigner'—regardless of a worker's contributions up to that point. Once again, luck comes to the forefront, which points to the psychological dependence on belief in forces outside of the person's control; it does not matter how good one is, the fact of precarious employment removes individual autonomy, and one must hope for good fortune. Perhaps recurrent appeal to luck in these situations exposes autonomy as an illusion; for if the political economy fails to ensure that workers from all class backgrounds have access to work, then there is only so much that any given individual situated precariously can do to alter their fate.

Rather than seeing it as a support system, Paul's community often portrayed the job centre as ineffectual and undesirable. Consider their re-branding of the institution as the 'joke centre' and similar variations. One man in Paul's community announced, 'joke centre done me over once again',

210 A Violence Continuum

and a woman in her thirties called the job centre 'a fucking joke', to which her friend replied, 'joke shop, glad I don't have to deal with them anymore, bunch of twats'. We might see this linguistic play as an attempt to challenge the authority of the intrusive state, so that the least advantaged may deflect the shame that a class system exposes them to in inevitable moments of hardship. That is, by rebranding the state institution as clown-like, perhaps they succeed in deflecting some of the symbolic injuries of the punitive state (for a reflective comparison of precariat resistance in the Cameroonian city of Douala, see Ndjio (2005)).

We have shown, I think, that there exists a gulf between how, in a mode of being oriented by the framework of autonomy, we may treat unemployment—by centring agency, choice, and responsibility—and how precariously positioned persons actually experience unemployment. Such a disjuncture indicates to me that the tendency to blame those out of work is misplaced, even when expressed (as we saw above) by those themselves inches away from the same fate. Those who are exposed to the reality of labour insecurity gain an awareness of the structural features which bear on work, health, and other such outcomes. As this chapter has shown, exposure to certain risks and injuries is part and parcel of precarity, phenomena outside the individual's control. That the modern state has developed to blame those it harms most quite literally adds insult to injury.

Conclusion

Violence is not only interpersonal but also structural and symbolic. These less obvious forms of violence effectively subordinate a segment of society, ripe for exploitation, whose lives must accordingly be lived, at least in part, to serve as means to another's ends—whether it be the shame-laden fear of unemployment which moves less powerful individuals to accept coercive and exploitative forms of employment, or actual unemployment which is described through frames that distort a person who is out of luck into an immoral figure against which the moral ideal is reflected. Instead of recognizing how structural disadvantage reduces health and life expectancy, impacts on the places where people live, and leaves some unable to work, symbolic violence individualizes the effects of structural inequality. When observed through the lens of autonomy, the meanings attached to markers of poverty and overt dependency on others—which are inevitable features

Conclusion **211**

of the present economic structure—are ones of individual fault, shame, and blame.

When we are normatively guided by the framework of autonomy, we relegate structural factors to the background of significance, something that happens too in the process of symbolic violence, and we place a hyper-emphasis on the individual. This is emblematic of how the criminal law operates: structural factors and conditions which contribute to bringing about an offence are deemed irrelevant and pushed out of sight, and great weight and social meaning is placed on what an individual is deemed to have done and thought at the time of an offence. For those who are found guilty, the most severe form of symbolic violence is inflicted, for they become labelled as 'criminal' and bear the social branding of being responsible for society's greatest wrongs.

Equipped with a deeper understanding of violence, it seems to me that the claim by notable criminal lawyers (e.g. Gardner, 2003; Hart, 1968)— that to treat people as autonomous and responsible is to treat people with dignity and respect—is deeply misguided. Treating as autonomous a person who is not structurally situated to attain the moral ideal of autonomy, and so holding them fully responsible for an end-of-the-line act, without due recognition of other significant contributory factors that came before, fails to understand the person being judged. From the position of precarity, dignity involves taking a holistic view of the person, comprehending them relationally within the world in which they are embedded, and building a fuller account of their lives and the conditions in which they act. I thus contend that a dignified approach is to acknowledge that autonomy requires certain preconditions for individuals, and therefore those who are prevented from attaining this ideal have a diminished form of responsibility at best. Considering these factors during the sentencing stage of the trial is too late, for the symbolic violence of being convicted of theft, criminal damage, murder, and so on has already been inflicted. Hence, I am suggesting that a wider array of factors is relevant in the determination of what ought to be a crime and who ought to be criminalized.

The effects of structural and symbolic violences are less direct, and at times less immediate than their interpersonal cousins, yet the injury of these violences is significant and arguably fuels the more spectacular kinds that surface. Whether it be anger that builds up over the untimely loss of loved ones, the weight of bearing hardship after hardship, or pent-up shame, these small violences are liable to escalate into more direct kinds.

212   A Violence Continuum

Violence may then be worn on the bodies of others, when anger is released in an act of interpersonal violence, or anger may be turned inward in an act of suicide. Structural and symbolic violence are no less serious than those the criminal law presently concerns itself with—these violences are more complex but we can address them with greater sustained intellectual attention and thought.

The harm of internalizing shame and accepting responsibility for conditions out of one's control necessitates an alternative moral framework, that oriented towards mutuality, within which socio-economically disadvantaged individuals can appraise themselves and others. In this chapter, we have seen fragments which suggest that making sense of difficult circumstances with an ethic of mutuality at hand offers a far more compassionate appraisal of the plight of others. I flesh out this possibility in Chapter 7 by examining how Paul's neighbours understand their own struggles in the context of competing frameworks which significantly alter how to judge an action. I offer this as a taster for how lawyers could better accommodate wider factors and moral deliberations in the process of determining criminal wrongdoing.

An Ending Looms

The ending of our relationship is etched into memory.

I drove home from Oxford to see you for our usual weekend visit. The house was notable for your absence. Mum was standing in the kitchen with one brother and sister. They fell silently when I entered. I asked where you were—on the van.

You were standing under a dim artificial light at the very back of the van. You said you went for an x-ray; they discovered a shadow on your lung. I moved home that same day.

When you spoke to a local doctor on the phone, he examined your x-ray. He suggested the cancer was contained in one lung—you had a chance. And then we didn't hear anything for a couple of weeks, so we thought it must be okay, or surely, they would have informed us otherwise.

You read about treatment options and decided to have your hair cut in case you needed chemotherapy. You thought it would be easier for us if you did this while you had strength.

We drove to a local barbers run by a close friend of yours. I sat behind and watched your hair fall in wet lumps to the ground; you'd never worn it this short before. The worry reflected in your face in the mirror. Your jovial self, who could connect an entire room of strangers with laughter, was no longer with us. The little boy next to me told his mother a story from a comic book while he waited for his trim. Your friend refused payment. You insisted he accept.

You were eventually called in for an appointment at the local hospital, in a town nine miles away. The entire hospital was dated, yet the area you were summoned to was especially run down. In the first waiting area, there were several people, bone thin, close to the end of life. One man, pale and shrunken, appeared to be without company. I wasn't sure if his moans expressed pain in his joints against the stiff plastic chair or the agony of going through this alone.

As we moved closer to our assigned waiting zone, people looked like they had more time left in them. It was like a conveyer belt of mortality, revealing

A Precarious Life. Roxana Willis, Oxford University Press. © Roxana Willis 2023.
DOI: 10.1093/oso/9780198855149.003.0014

214　An Ending Looms

a glimpse of what was to come. I was struck by how industrial death has been made for some.

The consultation took place in an office, which looked like any other doctor's office, but smaller. Half of our family squeezed into the room, shrinking it further. I can't remember many pleasantries before the doctor put your x-ray on a screen in front of us and revealed you had cancer in both lungs, which was spreading through your body. He asked to feel your glands, and not waiting for an answer, began to prod you. He nodded; it was in your lymph nodes too. You were terminally ill.

Before the information sunk in, the doctor had already moved on to other matters. 'Did you ever smoke?' he asked. You answered a simple 'yes'. The doctor nodded again, 'well then,' he said, 'smoking causes cancer'.

Within a few sentences, the doctor had announced your looming death and inferred it was your fault. I wanted to challenge him and point to other relevant questions: did you stop smoking and when—*you quit almost 30 years ago*; were you ever exposed to workplace toxicity—*you worked in the coke ovens of the steelworks, you used to leave coughing up spots of blood*; did anyone in your family die from cancer—*your father died from lung cancer*, and so on. But the shock made it difficult to speak. You were left to carry the shame of the doctor's words.

You subsequently refused the lung biopsy the doctor insisted you must have. If the cancer's spread from your lung, you reasoned, then relevant information could be attained from another cancerous bump in your body, without piercing your internal organs. The first doctor said you were wrong. A second doctor listened and agreed—a biopsy in your neck would more than suffice. You accepted the less invasive procedure.

Then came the consultation with the oncologist in a cheerier part of the hospital. They offered you palliative chemotherapy to extend your life. You thanked the doctor but declined the treatment. The oncologist's sharp response indicated she didn't understand your decision—instead of spending your last months travelling to a town you hated, and being surrounded by strangers, you opted to spend your remaining time at home with those who loved you; those for whom your life was irreplaceable and who experienced your death as an immeasurable loss. You spent your life avoiding contact with the state and you hoped to ward it off a little while longer.

As your health deteriorated, you booked one last visit to the local doctor. He skimmed your medical notes and confirmed you were moving into the end stages of life. An NHS nurse and a nurse from the Macmillan cancer

An Ending Looms   **215**

charity would visit you at home and prescribe medicine to ease your suffering.

You asked the doctor a final question—should you stop working now?

The question invoked a seemingly well-used cynical tone in the doctor. He turned to his computer, showing you his back as he answered, 'Oh right, of course. I'll provide you with a sick note.'

'I think you may have misunderstood,' I spoke up, 'my dad is self-employed. He's worked his whole life and he's asking you if it's okay to stop.'

The doctor cleared his throat with a light cough and agreed you should.

It's remarkable you worked for as long as you did.

7
Moral Dilemmas

I have argued that the moral figure of the autonomous person is not a given feature of reality but rather an aspiration, which the modern state helps certain individuals to realize, while the least advantaged endure working and living conditions that restrict their autonomy in various ways. In the context of these restrictions (structural barriers which impede the realization of the moral standards of autonomy), I have suggested that the precariously positioned research community lives by a normative framework of mutuality. The mutuality framework as I have discussed it normatively orients people towards a bundle of goods, such as kinship, solidarity, care, and substantive forms of equality. This, I suggest, aligns well with our ontological condition of co-dependency, and so the mutuality framework is in a sense prior to the framework of autonomy: communities suffering precarity must fall back onto, or into, mutuality. However, as the last chapter indicates, Paul's peers do not only draw on this framework—the competing framework of autonomy is still dominant, as it is reflected in institutions of power; autonomy-centric values still exert an aspirational pull. I found this to be evident, e.g. in cases of moral condemnation directed towards those deemed to be illegitimately unemployed. In this chapter, we examine in greater depth how those within Paul's community orient themselves at times towards the goods of autonomy, and how consequently their moral orientations may clash with those of the mutuality framework. We home in specifically on the phenomenon of symbolic violence and how this plays out during moments when community participants struggle for social recognition.

In his seminal article on the politics of recognition, Charles Taylor (1997: 26) notes how each human *qua* human needs the recognition of others: 'Due recognition is not just a courtesy we owe people. It is a vital human need'. Whereas, Taylor notes, persons in previous societies derived recognition from the social position each held in society, from the eighteenth century onwards, recognition became increasingly individualized, and the source of morality turned inwards; for example, instead of

A Precarious Life. Roxana Willis, Oxford University Press. © Roxana Willis 2023.
DOI: 10.1093/oso/9780198855149.003.0015

being born into the position of a blacksmith and holding this social status for life, in the present, a person is seen as responsible for what is treated as their chosen path in life. Taylor (1997: 34–5) explains that in contrast to the socially derived identity, which as it were builds recognition into the social position that a person had occupied from birth, and is thus taken for granted, the inwardly derived identity 'doesn't enjoy this recognition *a priori*. It has to win it through exchange, and the attempt can fail' (see also Honneth, 1995).

I suggest that acquiring recognition in accordance with the ideals of autonomy is markedly different to attaining recognition on the terms of mutuality. The moral person within the framework of mutuality is the person who actively supports others especially in times of need and who recognizes the common humanity among those within the collective. Conversely, achieving moral standing on the terms of autonomy requires that individuals demonstrate self-reliance, good taste, rational judgement, prudent decision-making, and so on. However, rather than being defined as moral on account of these traits alone, liberal society has developed in such a way that the autonomous moral figure comes into being by marking out the dependent 'other'. As Beverly Skeggs (2004: 56) remarks, 'the individualized essence is only available to the privileged few and is premised upon the exclusion of others' (see also Mehta, 1990). And so it is against the figure of immorality that the autonomous individual is reflected (Bhabha, 2004; Fanon, 1968; McClintock, 1995; Said, 2003).

Pierre Bourdieu (1984) aptly terms the classed practice of differentiating oneself from others, 'distinction'. Scholars have documented distinction in the UK, US, France, and elsewhere (Bennett et al., 2009; Evans, 2006; Finch, 1993; Gillies, 2007; Hoggart, 1957; Koch, 2018b; Lamont, 2009; Lawler, 2005; Nayak, 2006; Reay and Lucey, 2000; Rowe, 1995; Sayer, 2005; Skeggs, 1997; Wacquant, 2007), finding it among the most elite (Sherman, 2017) and the most impoverished (Bourdieu, 1999). Skeggs (1997) discusses white English working-class women employing the moral markers 'respectable' and 'rough' to navigate their way through the social order, and Anoop Nayak writes of white working-class men in the north of England self-defining as 'Real Geordies', clinging to notions of respectability while distancing themselves from the more disadvantaged 'ruff' (2006: 825).

Criminological literature sometimes works with comparable binary distinctions. One of the most prominent examples is Elijah Anderson's ethnography, *Code of the Street* (1999), which examined the experiences of black residents in a disadvantaged neighbourhood in Philadelphia, USA.

218   Moral Dilemmas

Anderson found that neighbourhood participants in his study drew distinctions between 'decent' and 'street' families. While Anderson ascribed to decent families a commitment to mainstream norms, he ascribed to street families an alternative value system involving the regular use of interpersonal violence, governed by a so-called code of the street. Subsequently, Anderson's 'street' distinction influenced a large body of work in criminology (e.g. Berg and Stewart, 2013; Mitchell et al., 2017; Rosenfeld et al., 2003; Stewart et al., 2006; Stewart and Simons, 2006), and has been extended to European contexts (e.g. Sandberg, 2008; Sandberg and Pedersen, 2011; Fraser, 2013; Holligan, 2015).

In my view, distinctions like that between 'decent' (respectable) and 'street' (rough) involve judgements about autonomy, among other things. The 'decent' figure instantiates a version of the autonomous moral ideal; the 'street' figure is the immoral antithesis who is deemed to make bad choices and is marked by dependency. The risk for criminological accounts which work with decent-street type distinctions, then, is that they may miss important emic perspectives which are in a sense prior to and more foundational than that binary. To capture such perspectives requires thinking outside of the legitimate framework of autonomy, instead reflecting on how different moral frameworks condition behaviours, make them intelligible, and offer internal justifications. And so we might better understand some community or group not as motivated by the logic of individualism and self-advancement but instead as acting in ways that benefit the wider group as per some framework of mutuality. In such a case, what is judged on the terms of autonomy as immoral behaviour would have a deeper moral meaning at the local level, which we will not recognize until filling out in more detail the alternative moral orientation which makes it intelligible.

In this respect, recall the distinction Insa Koch (2018b: ch 2) makes between being a 'good citizen' and being a 'good person': whereas the good citizen is defined by the dominant norms of the state, the good person is determined by standards valued and upheld by the community. Michèle Lamont (2009: 46–51) similarly describes black working-class men in her US sample as prioritizing the 'caring self' over the 'disciplined self'. There is not exact overlap, but, in my terms, we can reframe being a good citizen (or the disciplined self) as acting in accordance with the standards of autonomy, while being a good person (or the caring self) involves acting in accordance with the moral framework of mutuality. In this chapter, I show how the community sits within and is guided by both the frameworks of autonomy and mutuality, which is, I argue, why there is an abundance of moral conflict. We will examine *when* people explain their behaviour in terms of mutuality rather than autonomy, and vice versa (cf. Lamont, 2009). What is more, in keeping with Taylor's (1989) thought that the modern-day condition requires humans to make sense of their lives in a terrain of competing, overarching values, we will see how the moral conflicts of Paul's friends often lack straightforward resolutions. Therefore, unlike Anderson (1999), we are not looking at how an individual might behave in accordance with a normative order on the estate (i.e. adopting the code of the street) and then adapt to another normative order in school (i.e. the legitimate, decent code), which Anderson refers to as 'code-switching'. Instead, we are examining how people within a precariat space appeal to the norms of one framework over another differentially. Hence, we are interested principally in moral conflict and moral dilemma, rather than code-switching.

By virtue of being born into contemporary conditions, most, if not all, people in Britain are oriented towards autonomy to some degree. As I noted in the Introduction, nineteenth-century bourgeois efforts to disseminate the moral standards of autonomy throughout English society were markedly successful (see Hall, 2007; Jones, 2013; Skeggs, 1997; Virdee, 2014; Wiener, 1994). New channels of communication, such as newspapers, popular literature, and other forms of entertainment, alongside the development of modern state institutions, such as schools and welfare services, expanded the avenues for this dissemination among all class sectors. Importantly, these ideas were extremely popular, and even the least advantaged actively participated in the spread and instillation of the respectability discourse. Consequently, given the widescale valorizing of hard work and respectable behaviour, the framework of autonomy has become the legitimate (i.e. hegemonic) moral order.

While I argue here that Paul and his peers are committed to autonomy and strive to demonstrate themselves as moral on these terms, material conditions of precarity often prevent their acting in accordance with this legitimate framework. It is worth distinguishing here between a 'thick' and 'thin' sense of autonomy. Paul and his peers are autonomous in a relatively thin sense in that they can make choices within certain domains of life and can aim to meet respectability standards—they have agency. But they fail to manifest autonomy in a thicker sense in that they do not have the resources and freedom to make their own destinies however they might choose, not being free of dependencies on others and free of much debilitating social

220   Moral Dilemmas

stigma. Because, perhaps, of limited opportunities to manifest thick autonomy, some participants in Paul's community strove to present themselves as autonomous (in what amounts to a thinner sense) whenever the chance arose. It seemed to me that one of the most accessible means of doing so was to highlight the behaviours of others who failed to meet the ideal of the autonomous individual. Hence, I find the moral framework of autonomy as the most pronounced orientation when community participants critiqued the purported failings of others as products of free (and bad) choices.

Conversely, when a community participant had first-hand experience of barriers to autonomy—i.e. limits on their ability to present as autonomous in the public space—they would often make intelligible their behaviour by invoking values situated within the framework of mutuality. Accordingly, there was a notable contrast between the moral language of autonomy used to explain the deficiencies of others and the language of mutuality used to explain personal struggles. To me, this seems a critical feature of symbolic violence (as we discussed in Chapter 6): those exposed to barriers to their autonomy become aware of them as structural features, and yet, due to these barriers, they also lack the power to substantively challenge the judgements imposed by others—in the process often internalizing structural injuries and 'owning' the harm. In such circumstances, effectively situating themselves within the framework of mutuality and so making claims to moral personhood becomes a vital means to securing recognition.

The first part of this chapter will articulate the immoral figure in Paul's community on the terms of autonomy, which community participants denote by 'tramp'. Here, we can observe how Paul's peers explain the morality of other people's behaviour by appealing to the values within different frameworks. We then examine Paul's neighbours actively engaging in daily moral deliberations. Since the standards of autonomy are normally unattainable for those exposed to precarity, Paul and his friends find themselves amid many moral dilemmas—struggling to meet the standards of autonomy, feeling morally responsive to those standards anyway, and articulating alternative moral values as justificatory pleas. And so I suggest it is in fact a condition of this precarity that Paul's peers are enmeshed in so much twisting moral deliberation. By illuminating the reasoning and resolving of daily moral dilemmas in Paul's community, I hope to prompt reflections on how the criminal law could likewise be more attuned to the plurality of frameworks in contemporary Britain.

The Markers of a Tramp

The main epithet Paul's peers use to describe rough forms of behaviour is 'tramp', a term documented in other studies in England (Evans, 2006; Hanley, 2017: 179; McKenzie, 2015: 111). The figure of the tramp is embedded in the framework of autonomy in being the moral antithesis of that central value. It thus has historical significance in Britain; vagrancy legislation is one of the earliest developments of the modern law, also widely implemented in the colonies aboard (Beier, 1985; Hay and Craven, 2004; Lowe, 2015). According to John Welshman (2014), in the nineteenth century the figure of the tramp was transformed into a dangerous, pathological, and criminal character. For example, researchers in the US investigated the family histories and characteristics of 'vagrants' to predict who was most at risk of falling into vagrancy. In accordance with these studies, it was believed that individuals defined as tramps carried diseases, were genetically unsound, and that their failure to socially progress was linked to internal biological factors rather than wider structural causes (see also Jones, 2013; Gray, 1931; Cresswell, 2001). Although alleged biological deficiencies of socio-economically disadvantaged persons have failed to be evidenced, remnants of these ideas linger, as soon becomes apparent.

The most significant marker of a tramp in Paul's community is dirt. Recall the internal case of theft detailed in Chapter 4; the conversation about the incident included descriptions of the children of two alleged addicts accused of stealing a purse: 'I've never seen kids like it, they need disinfecting, teeth cleaned, and hair brushed. It's a real shame.' The apparent victim in the example similarly described the parents as 'junkies' and 'dirty thieving tramps'. The most disadvantaged in English society have long been characterized in terms of dirt (see McKenzie, 2015; Orwell, 2021; Skeggs, 1997; I Tyler, 2015). Cleanliness was a core aspect of the bourgeois drive towards respectability, with new standards of hygiene and manners actively disseminated throughout the social order (McClintock, 1995; Skeggs, 1997). As with other markers of morality, the hygiene of ladies and gentlemen was brought into view by drawing attention to the dirty bodies of workers and colonized subjects, and the insanitary conditions of slum dwellings (Darwin, 2015; Orwell, 2021; cf. McClintock, 1995). Associations of the poor with dirt continue to traumatize disadvantaged communities; Lisa McKenzie (2015) speaks of her embarrassment and pain when reading George Orwell's *Road to Wigan Pier* as a teenager, and realizing that her

222 Moral Dilemmas

family was judged in similar fashion. Paul and his neighbours appear to be haunted by these same anxieties.

Bad teeth are also a mark of roughness, which indicates a lack of brushing and general hygiene. Paul's friends frequently pointed out the bad teeth of guests appearing on the reality television talk show, *The Jeremy Kyle Show*,[1] which was a stereotype applied also to non-respectable people seen in the town centre, or the type of people expected to appear in a particular nightclub in the town. For example, Katie, a woman in her late twenties, highlights poor teeth, among other factors, to exemplify the roughness of a group of men she encountered earlier that day: 'There were four blokes in McDonalds today with manky teeth, wearing joggers and matching hoodies, all bragging about their 'mad' nights out and how pissed they got, and one was like "we're the definition of Corby lads". That's nothing to be proud of sunshine!' In addition to 'manky teeth', Katie reprimands the men for their style of dress and their behaviour. She does not contest that they might meet the 'definition of Corby lads', but, in her view, those rough marks fitting them is something rather to be ashamed of. Although the men perhaps meet the thinnest requirement of autonomy by apparently choosing this lifestyle, and maybe even professing to enjoy it, Katie's critique of their behaviour is based on a thicker notion of autonomy, for the men here fail to exercise the right *kind* of choice. By sharing this critique with her friends, Katie signals her own orientation towards norms of respectability.

Another discussion between two of Paul's friends in their thirties likewise refers explicitly to bad teeth, among other appearance traits, in their description of 'trampy people'.

JESS: I can't stand going up the town centre, too many trampy people with too many kids. Even though I've had a fucked up life, I don't go round looking like that.

GARY: I know what you mean. They wear the same clothes day in and day out with their prams and rotten teeth, covered in misspelt homemade tattoos.

In this discussion, repeatedly wearing the same clothing, having rotten teeth, and bearing misspelt homemade tattoos are 'trampy' markers.

---

[1] *The Jeremy Kyle Show* was a daytime British tabloid talk show, presented by Jeremy Kyle, and produced by ITV Studios. It is comparable to the Jerry Springer show in the US in format and delivery.

The Markers of a Tramp **223**

Although such markers are also those of poverty, we can see how the meaning attached to signs of poverty here is infused with immorality—the individual has failed. By pointing out that even having had a 'fucked up life', she never behaved in the manner reprimanded, Jess distinguishes herself by implying her own personal achievement, dismissing the significance of structural factors. Here then, in order to present herself as meeting the ideal of independence, Jess marks out the trampy 'other' who fails to meet these legitimate moral standards; hence, the character of the autonomous individual is invoked to devalue the moral worth of a more impoverished group (Savage, 2000: 106–7).

Also of note in the last extract is the excess indicated in '*too* many trampy people with *too* many kids' (emphasis added), perhaps echoing nineteenth-century concerns about the 'hyper breeding of the poor' (Weeks, 1991: 19–20), which fuelled the fear of a so-called residuum taking over good society (Jones, 2013: ch 18). Discussions about socio-economically disadvantaged mothers were especially common sites for ideas about the biological inferiority of certain immoral groups (see Jensen, 2018; Hancock, 2004). The next extract provides a fitting example.

CHRISTINE: To get given over two grand a month for kids you don't look after, incredible

PETE: I hate people that are on benefits, that's more than I get a month on my wage

SARAH: I just hate people that have kids so they know they don't need to look for a job, then spend all that money on drink and drugs

PETE: Castrate them

ELLI: This frustrates me, that's more than most working parents like me get and we have to pay for childcare as well. It's disgusting

SARAH: I know there are parents out there that genuinely can't work because their babies are too small or need extra care or they aren't in a fit state of mind themselves. But then there's type 2, the slaggy lazy dirty scroungers

DAVE: What, if I have kids, I get my drugs for free? Just need to find a breeder

SARAH: Plenty of breeders in Corby hen.

Although the gender-neutral term 'parent' is used here, as Tracy Jensen (2018) points out, this is often shorthand for 'mother', perhaps carrying the underlying presumption that socio-economically disadvantaged fathers are absent. The conversation above employs stereotypes which imply that

224 Moral Dilemmas

the parents under observation have made bad choices: immoral characters do not look after their children; they have children with the sole intention of avoiding work; and they spend welfare support on illegitimate personal habits, such as alcohol and drugs. Accordingly, the above group locates socio-economically disadvantaged mothers within a framework of autonomy: the critique emphasizes mothers choosing to have children for the wrong reasons.

Notably, the discussion did not cast aspersions equally on all parents receiving welfare support; a distinction between an allegedly deserving and underserving poor comes to the fore (see Golding and Middleton, 1982; Howe, 1990). Sarah distinguishes between parents who 'genuinely' require support and another kind of parent whom she refers to as the 'type 2' benefit claimant. This comment uncomfortably echoes older typologies and sub-classes of degenerate beings (cf. Jones, 2013: 289; McClintock, 1995: 46; Skeggs, 1997: 43). In keeping with these mythologies, Dave and Sarah refer to immoral mothers as 'breeders', resurrecting old tropes of disadvantaged women being sexually unrestrained, and presenting a threat to society through over-reproduction of supposedly degenerate humans (cf. Skeggs, 1997: 43; Weeks, 1991: 19). Indeed, in response to the imagined threat, Pete puts forward a eugenicist solution: 'castrate them'. Although proposals for sterilization of underprivileged women did not realize in the UK to the same extent as elsewhere, early pregnancy was widely discouraged and birth control usage encouraged (cf. Gould, 1996: 365–6; Platt, 2018: 164–74; Saini, 2019: 84; Shilliam, 2018: 74–5).

The language of 'types' also surfaced in discussions about immigration. For example, a discussion in a town-wide group raised concerns about perceived mass migration to the town, and a woman suggested that there are 'two types of Romanians': 'The dirty bastards who live 14 in a 3-bed house and cause rat infestations and the nice and clean ones'. Thus, in an almost identical way to Sarah's distinguishing between 'types' of benefit-claiming parents, sometimes typologies were deployed to explain the behaviours and characters of migrants; the good are associated with cleanliness and congeniality, and the bad are associated with dirt and infestation. By such deployments of 'type' analyses, issues of choice and responsibility, which are central to the moral framework of autonomy, merge with debunked beliefs about biological superiority.

Children in Paul's community were also acutely aware of classed distinctions. For example, another friend of Paul's conveyed anxiety about walking

The Markers of a Tramp   225

her filthy child home from school, who had been playing with clay and according to the mother looked like a 'right tramp'. The mother commented that even her son was calling himself a 'tramp'. Similarly, during my offline observations, I became close to a group of young people, ranging from the ages of two to fourteen, who congregated in a square of grass while waiting for Paul's mobile shop to arrive. Some of the children described others in the square as 'trampy' for wearing second-hand or dirty clothes and advised me to maintain a distance from them. These examples demonstrate how finer distinctions between levels of respectability are drawn at a young age (Reay, 2000: 157–8; Reay and Lucey, 2000: 415).

Paul's friends further distinguish between respectable and rough characters in discussions about neighbours, mapping roughly onto differences between homeowners and council tenants. According to John Boughton (2018), in a history of council housing in England, the state introduced various housing policies which both encouraged home ownership and the stigmatization of those still in council housing (see also Koch, 2018a), corroding council tenancy respectability over the past half-century. Some homeowners in Paul's community expressed frustration at not being able to move to a new house, and the council having 'dumped' a 'troubled family' next door. The word 'dump' connotes dirt, rubbish, and waste, and implies the worthlessness of certain families. And the reference to 'troubled families' mirrors the terminology of Cameron's Conservative government's *Troubled Families Programme*, which has its roots in the nineteenth-century construction of the so-called problem family (Crossley, 2018; Welshman, 2014: ch 4).

Government policy discourse on troubled families has also been reproduced through reality television, a phenomenon noted as compounding individualized explanations of behaviour (Hall et al., 2013; Skeggs, 2004; I Tyler, 2015). A widely watched reality television show in Paul's community at the time of my fieldwork was *Benefits Street*, which is a documentary series filmed on James Turner Street in Birmingham, UK, where a high number of residents were unemployed and reliant on state support. While *The Jeremy Kyle Show* was filmed in a television studio, and hence derogatory comments were directed at personal appearance and the behaviour of people on the show, *Benefits Street* probed a little further into lives by filming inside homes. This intimacy opened the door for some in Paul's community to insult the participants even more. Widespread comments on the show described one family as living in a 'shithole'. A few of Paul's friends asserted that even if the residents on the programme are poor,

226 Moral Dilemmas

'soap is cheap', and at the very least people can 'clean their house and wash their children'. One man posted that 'being poor doesn't mean your house should be a shit tip, or that you should mishandle your children, drink on the streets, or smoke weed in front of them. These families give the dole a bad name' (cf. Evans, 2006: 32).[2] As I read them, the moral framework of autonomy is central to these criticisms, which dismiss economic disadvantage as a valid explanation for dirt and assign blame to the individual for making bad choices. Of course, it is perhaps even easier than normal to dismiss the explanatory role of structural factors given the surface-level portrayals of poverty which reality television often presents (see Skeggs and Wood, 2012).

Tensions between neighbours in Paul's community often relate to the appearance of houses and behaviours around them. Allowing gardens to become overgrown or having old furniture or rubbish in the garden is cause for critique, as are behaviours which create disturbances, such as hosting many visitors. Young adults are sometimes pinpointed as a cause for concern, especially when their meeting spot is close to someone's home. For example, a woman complained about a group of youths that congregated outside her neighbours' house, claiming that 'people's property is getting broken, our kids are getting hurt, their language is absolutely disgusting, the whole while their parents watch and say nothing'. Other comments referenced the way neighbours lived, castigating parents, for example, who 'dragged their kids up', constantly shouting at them, leading some to comment that 'they shouldn't have had so many if they can't handle the ones they've got!'—another implication that the rough figure has children in excess (cf. Skeggs, 2004: 99–105).

Neighbours' illicit lifestyles are another source of criticism. A woman reported finding her alcoholic neighbour asleep on the shared doorsteps to a block of flats when she left for work in the morning, and still passed out when she returned; she desired that they 'clean up and get a job'. Similarly, neighbours described as 'junkies' were accused of stealing Christmas presents, and a 'trampy' neighbour was accused of leaving rubbish in someone's garden. One woman ironically summarized her neighbourhood: 'Ace neighbours round this end. On one side we've got a

---

[2] These observations echo George Orwell's memorable description of the London poor (2021: 60): 'The squalor of these people's houses is sometimes their own fault ... there is no need to have unemptied chamber-pots standing about in your living room.'

The Markers of a Tramp   **227**

scrawny eejit [idiot] who thinks he's hard booting a dog and nutting his missus. On the other side we've got the crack-heads proper fighting over a bottle of Frosty's [cheap cider]'.

In contrast to distinctions between rough and respectable, and the marker of the 'tramp', some of Paul's neighbours offer counter-arguments to those critiques located within the moral framework of autonomy by appealing to moral sentiments rooted in mutuality: whereas distinction concerns itself with marking one's individuality and uniqueness from others, mutuality concerns itself with acknowledging the shared humanity and struggles of others. For example, Paul's friends sometimes challenge the heavily individualized assessments of poverty by appeal to a mutuality ethos of empathy. One young man, in response to a tirade of abusive comments about a particular family on *Benefits Street*, said he feels 'sorry for the people' on the programme: 'Don't be so quick to judge, you never know when you'll find yourself in that situation'. An older woman posted a similar sentiment: 'It's sad to think people actually live like that, but you never know when you might just find yourself walking in another person's shoes.' Comments such as these are more attuned to an ethics that eschews individualism by tacitly recognizing universal vulnerability and co-dependency.

Paul's peers also sought to counter moralized criticisms of poverty not with the sentiment 'it could have been you' but with 'it is you': i.e. that the criticized behaviours actually reflected those within the community. One of Paul's male friends, for instance, compared *Benefits Street* to the Lincoln Estate: 'Benefits Street is the Lincoln! It's mental seeing people who have grown up in Corby slating people like that. You're probably related to far worse!' A young woman identified a similar hypocrisy in comments being made about participants on the programme: 'the girl with no job claims to be "shocked", the woman who puts her kids to bed late is riotous about bad parents, and the bloke with binge drinking problems is calling them morons'.

Supposing these are accurate charges of hypocrisy, it is plausible that what explains them is that the televised depictions of poverty are so uncomfortably close to the conditions that Paul's community find themselves in, some of them feel a heightened need to demonstrate their own personal commitment to a respectable autonomy by contrast (Skeggs and Loveday, 2012). By engaging in public critique of those who become the demonized 'other', one momentarily deflects judgements that might be directed one's way (Koch, 2018b).

228 Moral Dilemmas

Ethical Deliberations

In conditions of framework pluralism, moral conflicts and dilemmas are rife. Here, 'moral conflict' refers to a clash of two or more norms, which might be satisfactorily resolved, while a moral dilemma involves an element of moral failure whatever the outcome (see McConnell, 2018). Moral dilemmas that Paul's community grapple with often involve an inability to meet the legitimate standards of autonomy, due to material hardship, alongside an underlying need to maintain the mutuality norms which secure the subsistence of the self. Therefore, overcoming a moral dilemma might require setting aside one moral framework to meet the requirements of another. However, building on Rosalind Hursthouse (1999: 44), in these instances it is helpful to recognize that there can be a moral 'remainder', which refers to feelings of remorse, guilt, or regret that might (appropriately) result in moments of moral dilemma, since a particular good is achieved but only by violating another moral norm (cf. Taylor, 1989: 102; Williams, 1973).

In this section, I explore several interrelated moral dilemmas. As is apparent in these discussions, the weight of these moral struggles lies primarily, though not exclusively, with women. Indeed, the civilization discourse positioned women as the moral guardians of the emergent civil order, tasked with the responsibility of ensuring men were able to perform their assigned roles and of raising children in obedience to the dominant norms (Hall, 1992; Skeggs, 1997). As the deliberations here show, socio-economically disadvantaged women continue to carry responsibility for perceived moral failings and must work hard to deflect judgements when, inevitably, they do not meet legitimate standards.

The trampy mum dilemma

The need to protect children from accusations of being rough is a common source of moral dilemma in Paul's community. One of the few ways disadvantaged parents can shield children from the unfavourable classification of being a tramp is to direct their limited resources to the child. For disadvantaged mothers in Paul's community, who were raising children under punitive austerity policies, the sacrifices they needed to make included going hungry to ensure children have enough food, only heating the house at intervals when children are home from school, and prioritizing children's

Ethical Deliberations **229**

purchases (see also Cooper and Whyte, 2017; Garthwaite, 2016). However, making such sacrifices, mothers opened themselves up to being judged by others as 'trampy'—failed individuals. The next two contrasting snippets of conversation in Paul's community offer a window into the struggles that precariat mothers on the receiving end of judgement face.

JOSIE: I can't stand it when people claim to be skint all the time, and struggle to buy their kids stuff, but they're always out in new clothes. If parents can't afford to support their kids, they shouldn't be spending money on themselves. I walk about looking like a tramp so my daughter can look good instead of me

HELEN: Whereas others go out in designer clothes and their kids look like tramps!

JOSIE: Yeah, and when people say they have fuck all and then go out to pubs and clubs all the time. I stopped going out and completely changed my life to suit ma daughter. Pisses me off when I see poor kids looking a mess

HELEN: Kids are for life not just for benefits!

We can compare this with the struggles of Ava who feels exposed to such moral critique.

AVA: I haven't had my hair done in months, I feel like a tramp, and I need new jeans 'cus mine don't fit anymore. But if I buy them, I'll be called a bad mum

STACY: Income support is for you as well as the baby. And child benefit is for the child. If you need new jeans then buy them hun, fuck what any nosey twat thinks

AVA: I just feel constantly judged

STACY: Ignore what people say. If you want to treat yourself, do it. You need to look after yourself as well as the baby. People need to look at their own lives before sticking their nose in others.

As with the women in Beverly Skeggs's study (1997), motherhood presents a period in Josie's life where the requirement to uphold the norm of respectable appearance is transferred from the self and placed onto the child. Similarly, another mother in Paul's community remarked, 'I remember the days when I used to get up and decide what to wear, take time to paint my nails, do my hair, and get ready to go out. Oh how times have changed!' On

230   Moral Dilemmas

one view, the transference of the obligation to follow the autonomy norm of maintaining a decent appearance from mother to child can be seen as upholding the standard of respectability, for a mother who invests in the appearance of her child, even though thereby investing less in the self, nevertheless demonstrates a commitment to the norm and its reproduction in the next generation.

On the other hand, we might ask why the moral standard not to look like a tramp is prioritized for the child over the adult—is it simply because of the virtue of reproducing the autonomous standard of respectability, or is there something more to it? It seems to me that there is an even weightier standard operative in these discussions, which is to be a good parent on the terms of mutuality: in this case, to equip children with sufficient social resources to survive the tough conditions that lay ahead. When a child manages not to look like a tramp, they stand a good chance of forming friendships, which, as we saw in Chapter 6, is the basis of mutual support upon which they will come to rely. Moreover, not looking like a tramp allows the child to fit in and avoid being singled out as an easy target of violence. Therefore, I suspect that the harsh judgement directed towards parents who do not so prioritize their children (or seem to) reflects the seriousness of the wider and more enduring social harm the child might consequently experience.

In the above, Ava's struggle offers a perspective on the other side of the experience. As a new mother, Ava shares the difficulty of meeting the requirement of directing everything towards her child while feeling like a tramp. Ava's friend tries to reassure her that it is permissible to care for herself as well as her baby, and advises that Ava ignore the judgements she might incur. At this early stage of motherhood, it seems Ava still experiences the symbolic violence of looking 'trampy'. In time, Ava may acclimatize to the conditions of precariat motherhood, and gradually internalize the virtue of motherhood and its hierarchical placement above the virtue of respectable appearance, as Josie has seemingly managed to.

A contrast can be drawn between the experiences of precariat mothers in Paul's community and elite stay-at-home mothers interviewed by Lisa Sherman (2017). Sherman found that elite mothers also experienced a pressure not to spend money on themselves; however, they had the means to spend freely on their children and did not have to sacrifice the self to the degree Ava does. Hence, elite mothers may experience a similar kind of moral conflict, but not a moral dilemma which requires them to carry the burden of moral failure whatever they do. The particular tension that socioeconomically disadvantaged mothers experience is pronounced in the next

Ethical Deliberations   **231**

moral dilemma which concerns the judgements mothers incur by taking their children to school in inappropriate attire.

The pyjama dilemma

Pyjamas—comfortable attire worn for sleeping in—are a common form of dress in Paul's community; however, there are limits to the spaces where such clothing is deemed acceptable to wear. The word 'pyjama' (a Hindi addition to the English language and form of life) is often abbreviated to 'PJs', or occasionally 'jim-jams'. A type of pyjama commonly worn during the fieldwork period is called the 'onesie', which is an all-in-one pyjama suit that covers the legs, body, and arms, zipped up at the front. Participants in Paul's community frequently referred to being in their pyjamas, at any time of day, or the joy of getting home from work and changing into them. Pyjamas represent a starkly different form of dress to uniforms, which many community participants are required to wear at work or school—relaxation and freedom from pretence. Wearing pyjamas marks the home as a different social space which prioritizes family and comfort (Bourdieu, 1984). By permitting, or even encouraging, the wearing of pyjamas, parents signal to children that home is a place where they may be themselves, a place for which their habitus is well-suited, free from the formalities and judgements of the school (Evans, 2006; Gillies, 2007: 94–5).

Paul's community permit the wearing of pyjamas outside of the house but only in certain contexts; straying too far from the house in pyjamas risks becoming seen as 'trampy' (cf. Appleford, 2016). Several women made references to having 'popped out' to a shop in their onesie, sometimes aware of the judgement that this might invoke, but professing to be unfazed, since it was 'comfy'. It seems to me that pyjamas might be more acceptable in spaces where the norms of a mutuality framework are more obviously operative, but in normative social spheres where the framework of autonomy prevails, wearing pyjamas invites critique. Consequently, there is a notable (blurred) line between acceptable and non-acceptable places to wear house clothing. Numerous posts commented on 'states' who had ventured too far from the house, such as a woman wearing pyjamas and a dressing gown at a car boot sale, mothers wearing pyjamas to drop their children off at school, and a man seen at the shop and later at the pub in his onesie. Sentiments about wearing pyjamas in such contexts connected it with dirt, the assumption being that if someone is still in their pyjamas from the night before, then

232 Moral Dilemmas

they have not yet washed. On occasion, pictures were uploaded too, adding to the shaming process. Therefore, it seems that while the local estate shop is generally considered an acceptable place to venture to in nightwear, and even more so to Paul's van in the evenings (since it stopped right outside residents' houses), wandering much further in pyjamas is liable to incur negative judgement.

In response to a string of negative conversations about women dressed in pyjamas at school, which indicated a lack of respectability, a mother shared her own personal experience in a town-wide discussion group and asked the community to comment. The mother, Emily, explained that her son was involved in a school project to raise money for a soldiers' charity, and at the last minute, he told her that he needed to be in school early that day. Without a second thought, Emily said, she ran out of the house in her pyjamas and slippers to drive her son to school. On arrival, Emily discovered another mother in a broken-down car at the school entrance. Emily explained how she jumped out of her car to help the lady push the broken-down vehicle to the side of the road, and then gave the woman a lift to work, all the while in slippers and pyjamas. Emily explained that 'seeing a woman on her own panicked was more important than me being seen in my jim jams'. Emily ended the post by asking whether this behaviour made her a tramp.

In raising this moral dilemma, Emily is self-aware that she has not lived up to the standard of wearing respectable attire to her son's school. It is quite possible that Emily experienced symbolic violence while being seen in her pyjamas. Perhaps prompted by a need to dissolve these uncomfortable feelings, Emily seeks community affirmation that her contravening the norm was morally justified. She does not do so by actively rejecting the norm and adopting its antithesis (cf. Miller, 1964; Willis, 1977); instead, Emily offers exculpatory reasons rooted, on reflection, in an alternative moral framework of mutuality to explain why she was unable to meet the ideal standard of autonomy in that particular situation.

The values of a mutuality framework are here evident when Emily asserts and prioritizes motherhood over self-presentation. Indeed, caring for children comes before all else in the community; few norms may trump it (cf. McKenzie, 2015: 91). Moreover, Emily appeals to the importance of wider collective needs; she highlights her son's charitable activities as the reason he was required to be in school early that day, and notes the need of another mother, whose vehicle had broken down, to reach her workplace. Accordingly, Emily pitches the virtues of charity, generosity, and kinship as more important than an individualized notion of respectability—being a caring person takes precedence over self-cultivation (Lamont, 2009: 46–51; Skeggs, 1997: 56; Koch, 2018b: ch 2).

Most of the responses to Emily's dilemma affirmed her choices in this instance, meaning perhaps that Emily is granted the moral status of a 'good person' (following Koch, 2018b: ch 2). One young woman commented that the most important thing was getting children to school, and people should not be so quick to judge others. Several other women admitted to having dropped children off at school while in pyjamas themselves, such as a mother who shared the difficulty of trying to juggle work and mothering, so that getting herself dressed was often the last thing on her list of things to do. In these instances, first-hand experiences of structural barriers preventing autonomous choice (in a thin sense of autonomy) and independence (in a thicker sense) are made explicit. Motherhood inevitably presents a challenge to meeting the standards of autonomy, for the dominant motherhood ideal is to sacrifice individual desires and independence for the needs of the child. Even among the most advantaged, where *au pairs* can be employed to free up a mother's time, women struggle to fill the boots of the fictitious independent individual, and those who get close to this ideal invite further critique, for the ideal mothering role opposes such a disencumbered figure (Lawler, 2002; Sherman, 2017).

As we might expect in conditions where moral frameworks compete, even though Emily explained and justified her actions in the language of mutuality, she did not entirely reject the importance of autonomy. Even in raising the dilemma, Emily opens herself up as someone situated within and feeling the pull of the framework of autonomy. Moreover, Emily did not seek collective support to overthrow the norms of respectability—she is not requesting for a change in conditions whereby all parents are free to drop their children off at school in pyjamas if they so wish. Rather, Emily is seeking a moral exception to not meeting the norm on this occasion. The exception is justified by way of mutuality, a moral framework that subsists (sometimes uneasily) alongside autonomy, but it does not mean that values of mutuality trump autonomy as the ultimate suite of goods to which she and those supporting her aspire. Rather, the needle in the moral compass oscillates between moral orientations. This is captured by another comment on Emily's post by a middle-aged woman who agreed that Emily's behaviour was acceptable, but also noted that, in her view, mothers who arrive at school every day in their pyjamas exhibit unacceptable behaviour. Thus, while accepting Emily's warranted exception, she explicitly does not endorse this as a general practice; the legitimate norms of respectability must still be upheld.

234 Moral Dilemmas

The smoking dilemma

A more complex moral dilemma related to a mother's need to smoke while pregnant or while looking after children. Smoking and other forms of intoxication while pregnant are heavily stigmatized in the UK because of the harm this can have on the foetus and life of the child. Yet overcoming addiction under the stresses of precarity is immensely challenging, which mothers in Paul's community explain.

CRYSTAL: I'm trying to give up the fags, and I just can't. I know I'm gunna get a lot of jip for being pregnant and smoking. People don't understand how hard it is to stop!

GRACE: I quit the moment I found out both times. It's difficult but you are strong enough petal.

SARAH: I quit with the first four. This time has taken a little longer and I am on e-cigarettes at the moment.

ZOE: I quit but had the odd few if I was going to lose my temper with someone.

SARAH: I think it's up to the mother if they want to drink or smoke, people can have their opinion but it's up to them. I didn't find out I was pregnant till three months in, so was drinking up till then not knowing. Soon as I found out I stopped. I don't see a problem with it, if that's what someone wants to do, it's up to them. Saying that, I didn't smoke while pushing a pram 'cus I didn't feel comfortable, but I'd never judge someone who done it. Some of my good friends do and it don't bother me

ZOE: I was sixteen when I first got pregnant and I was drinking up until the day Kayla was born. So I wouldn't slag anyone for smoking or drinking, my best friend smoked through hers.

ANGIE: I smoke 'cus I ain't got the patience to stop! But drinking is a different ball game when you know you're up the duff. Drinking changes you, makes you less aware and stuff.

LAURA: I smoke. I know I shouldn't and I really wish it was that easy to stop but I can't. Literally can't. I'm unbelievably stressed when I'm pregnant, and I'd feel sorry for my friends and family if I didn't smoke! Although I smoked, I never touched a drug or alcohol, and my kids are fine. Even junkies have perfectly healthy babies.

The several women of this discussion share their struggles with smoking while pregnant and seem acutely aware of being judged for it. Sarah attempts to justify smoking during pregnancy by asserting that such a choice should simply be determined by the mother. While this satisfies a thin notion of autonomy, *I do what I choose*, it fails to meet a thicker moral ideal of autonomy, which invokes a respectable individual who ought to practise self-control and not succumb to certain base temptations like smoking, being dirty, not brushing teeth, and so on. Acting in accordance with the moral framework of autonomy, then, it is not sufficient simply to exercise choice—the *right* choice must be made. Sarah suggests that whether a woman smokes is simply a matter of personal choice, which may differ to the opinions of others, but rather than there being a right or wrong choice, the way she presents the issue here is that both smoking and not smoking while pregnant have the same moral weight. Perhaps this form of reasoning reveals postmodern influences in the moral deliberation, hinting at a culturally relative position—or perhaps even relative to the subject herself. However, Sarah also acknowledges that this position is unfeasible, for there is an evaluative backdrop and a wider moral framework whose pressure she has also felt, and was moved to act in accordance with, as when not smoking while pushing the pram.

Rather than a simple matter of choosing to stop smoking, several women in the discussion share the difficulty of giving up. Crystal, who starts the conversation, proclaims that she is trying to give up smoking, but 'just can't'. Similarly, Laura feels that she 'literally can't' stop, and even Sarah admits finding it hard this time compared to her past experiences, having now moved onto e-cigarettes as an alternative. Whereas Zoe was able to survive on 'the odd few' in times of stress while pregnant, the struggle for Laura was greater; she describes being 'unbelievably stressed' throughout her pregnancies, which prevented her from stopping. Significantly, both women justified smoking in these circumstances to maintain good relationships; they balance the vice of smoking when pregnant against the virtue of maintaining good relations and avoiding harming family or friends with explosive emotions. Moreover, the practice of smoking itself can be seen as a significant aspect of sociality, the sharing of a cigarette between friends being yet another opportunity to form and nourish caring relationships (following Degnen, 2005; Edwards, 2000; Koch, 2018b). Therefore, although Zoe and Laura experience structural conditions that limit their ability to make the right choices by autonomy's thick standards, they can find moral goodness by situating their actions within the framework of mutuality.

This example illustrates the difficult decisions disadvantaged mothers must overcome. Even if they strive for autonomy, it may be out of reach.

236 Moral Dilemmas

This does not leave women in a normatively empty space, but rather brings the framework of mutuality to the fore. Since mutuality accurately reflects our ontological conditions, it is a framework inevitably used to make sense of life by groups trying to subsist without the full structural support of the state. In circumstances such as these, women are not simply dismissing the risk of smoking when pregnant; they are not treating the dilemma as an easy one to solve, where one value smoothly trumps another. Instead, they express deep regret about being unable to meet the dominant moral standard but weigh this against upholding another value which also has great significance—cohesion and harmony (cf. Hursthouse, 1999).

Nevertheless, the women do not completely dismiss the demands of autonomy. By criticizing women who drank alcohol or took heroin, they were able to partially demonstrate their commitment to autonomy by distinction; the above mothers were able to make some of the 'right' choices, despite their inability to make them in certain other respects. In shifting the target of critique, symbolic violence was passed onto another more unfortunate group: women with alcohol or opioid addictions while pregnant became the marked 'other', forming an antagonism through which the fiction of the morally autonomous individual could momentarily be forged. This indicates that while mutuality is important, autonomy remains relevant and aspirational for Paul's peers even in moments when its standards are out of reach.

Although the moral burden of lone parenthood mostly fell on mothers, fathers were not completely exonerated. Fathers were also susceptible to criticism for failing to prioritize family life and for engaging in activities such as going to the pub with friends (see Didier, 2018: 92–3). A man in his thirties cast his judgement on fathers who persist with certain social activities: 'If you're a dad that goes out at weekends, selling drugs or taking drugs, then it's time to man up you useless bastard.' Consider the following conversation between Michael and Tom:

MICHAEL: Can't believe social services are investigating me for having a can of lager while I'm with the boy. I'm not a raging alcoholic. It was one bevy for fuck sake. I'm a better dad than I'm given credit for
TOM: You shouldn't be drinking at all if you're taking care of the kids mate
MICHAEL: I don't drink all the time. I had one last week that was all
TOM: You gotta prove them wrong.

Michael shares the struggle of trying to be a good father while meeting the requirement of not drinking, presumably while already being on the social services radar for other behaviours deemed problematic (cf. Rogaly and Taylor, 2016: 89). Like the absolute prohibition experienced by mothers, any amount of alcohol is viewed as irresponsible parenting.

There seemed to be a tendency for men in Paul's community who had initially resisted the fatherhood role to attempt to reclaim it at a later stage in life. Yet, by this point, it could be too late; the opportunity to be an active father may have already passed them by. This is evident in the pain shared by a man in his thirties:

> Despite what people say, I'm not a shit dad. Yeah, I fucked up when I was younger, I was a dick in the past, but I now bend over backwards for my ex so she lets me see the kids. I don't agree with it but I messed up in the past so now she calls the shots.

In this example, the father is aware of his past faults, and that to redeem a role for himself, he must accommodate the family's needs. Other men shared similar frustrations about feeling as though they were like a childminder but being resigned to this circumstance, given earlier failings. The following comment from a man in his thirties invokes karma to explain his predicament:

> Miss my boys lots, it really gets me when I can't see them on their birthday. Karma is a bitch and I shouldn't have been a knob in the past then things might have been different. I'm gonna get lost in a bottle of wine tonight.

Declarations such as these drip with yearning to be part of family life. Notably, while mutuality recognizes the moral good of the dedicated lone mother, there is less to redeem a father who fails to take on the traditional patriarchal role of the family provider, which is a restricted avenue in modern conditions of labour precarity (see McDowell, 2003; Maguire, 2020). The precariat father, who is expected to take on the role of provider, likely needs to support kin by providing physical protection and security, and perhaps by engaging in the informal economy, given a lack of formal opportunities, which in turn exposes him to the moral luck of being criminalized. In keeping with the framework of autonomy, in which people

238   Moral Dilemmas

principally hold themselves responsible, the men in these examples express the view that their current predicaments stem from their own personal failings and are deserved. Thus, not being part of moral discourse to the same extent as the women in Paul's community, and not finding alternative justificatory reasons for their behaviour in a framework of mutuality, the men are less faced with moral dilemmas than simply a predicament of symbolic violence—they internalize and own the harms, some of which are structural.

Conclusion

Paul's peers do not reject autonomy as the legitimate moral framework. On the contrary, even during moral deliberations, when the ideal of autonomy is unreachable and must be set aside, community participants continue to recognize its validity. When this community appraise and explain their behaviour by appeal to an alternative framework, they do not advocate for the complete rejection of autonomy in preference for other guiding moral principles. Rather, sometimes the alternative framework simply provides the moral justificatory context to an exception to a perceived wrongdoing by the standards of autonomy. Since living by these standards is so often prohibited when precariously situated, Paul's neighbours still strive to attain social recognition and hence explain the choices they make by reference to mutuality norms. When beset by moral dilemma, which may involve a norm of autonomy clashing with a norm of mutuality, Paul's peers have tended to prioritize mutuality because this framework is of fundamental importance in precariat lives. What is more, the framework of mutuality may function as a moral safety net which fills the gaps left by a class system that prohibits the attainment of autonomy for all.

Mutuality seems to play another important role in equipping Paul's peers with the means to counter symbolic violence. Precariat mothers appear especially skilled at countering symbolic violence by drawing on mutuality virtues and engaging in public ethical deliberations, which makes their choices comprehensible to others in the community and offers up moral guides and reminders for others to live by. By articulating the structural inequalities they experience, and by making explicit the impossibility of attaining autonomy in such conditions, women (at least partially) disrupt the moral space in which symbolic violence thrives. However, in contrast to mothers, unemployed men, and fathers in particular, seem less able to draw on the framework of mutuality in the same way, and are consequently required to carry the undiluted injuries of symbolic violence. For men when unemployed, perhaps living within mutuality as an alternative moral framework might mean pursuing alternative sources of income or taking on the role of a protector, as documented in Chapter 3. While these alternative routes to recognition might redeem precariat men suffering unemployment, it also carries the risk of criminalization, and hence becoming tarnished as immoral by the standards of autonomy.

Criminal lawyers could better reflect on the ethical terrain of what I am calling framework plurality, along which many who meet the reaches of the criminal law must traverse. Just as those in Paul's community must settle (at times difficult) moral deliberations, sometimes accepting uneasy outcomes, criminal lawyers could likewise be more attuned to these struggles. Complementing considerations about the choices people are presumed to have made, the criminal law could recognize the choices that people are deprived of, which may account for different decisions further down the line. Hence, mirroring the logic of prior fault, the criminal law could be receptive to a notion of prior necessity which results in a diminished form of responsibility. If we were to alter how we view our moral landscape, then we could open up possibilities and innovations—a thought I return to in the conclusion of the book.

We now proceed to the last chapter. In contemporary circumstances, characterized by a plurality of frameworks within which people may pursue different ideals, a challenge surfaces: it becomes a task in itself to make clear what a person's true incentives are for a given action. Hence, we must finally address questions of moral motivation.

'Only love can kill a demon'

My teenage love was a skinhead racist. For a time, my brown body did not know his ideology and his tattooed pink flesh failed to register the darkness of my skin. It could be a tan, he thought, a leftover from a long holiday abroad. When the 'tan' failed to fade, he resigned himself to the fact I may have Spanish or South American heritage—tolerable. A few months later, for the briefest of moments, Stevie met my mother. It was then he knew for certain, I was born from what he despised.

* * *

Stevie joined the National Front as a youngster, one of the most violent political hate groups founded in the UK. Satnam Virdee (2014: 130) describes a summer of violence in 1976 when the National Front experienced electoral success, which began with a series of racially motivated stabbings and culminated in the killing of Mohan Dev Gautam, a sixty-year-old woman who was dragged from her home and set alight.

* * *

Some years before I met Stevie, waiting alone in a bus stop, I noticed graffiti sprawled on the side of the shelter wall—'Burn a Paki to Death'. An image of my mother encased in flames entered my head. I looked away from the words, but the painful picture remained. I became acutely aware of my skin colour. A lingering sense of shame, anchored in my earliest memories, resurfaced.

I willed for no-one to walk by and bear witness to the moment.

* * *

It felt different when Stevie told me about his racist past. We were in his flat, above a shop in the town centre. Stevie stopped the music. I remained seated as he paced the room, rubbing the back of his neck with his hand, struggling to tell me something he said I needed to know.

A Precarious Life. Roxana Willis, Oxford University Press. © Roxana Willis 2023.
DOI: 10.1093/oso/9780198855149.003.0016

'Only love can kill a demon' **241**

'I dunno how to put it,' he tried, 'I was young and stupid... and... and... it doesn't mean shit... not anymore.' His cheeks turned crimson.

After a few more paces, Stevie sat beside me and tried again.

'I love you... I hope this doesn't fuck everything up,' he said, bowing his shaven head downwards, still coarsely rubbing the back of his neck. His hand tightened, wrinkling the skin beneath. When Stevie finally released his grip, a tattoo at the start of his spine was exposed for observation.

At first, the symbol was meaningless. Then Stevie filled me in on what each letter stood for.

For a time, neither of us spoke. I didn't want to be there, but my body remained fixed in place. I released an uncomfortable laugh. We made eye contact then looked away.

After a longer silence I told him I didn't understand why he'd do that.

He explained his uncle tattooed him when he was a kid, how it was just a phase, part of being young and immature. He said he had not accepted the situation when we first met, he felt a pull he couldn't make sense of. And then, by the time he met my mother, we were already close, no longer strangers.

Shielded by the naivety of youth, I couldn't grasp the significance of what Stevie revealed. I didn't appreciate the extent of the hatred, the levels of violence, and the freshness of the cause. My race was usually a silent feature I could forget until a racial slur was injected into a moment to make visible my born inferiority. This was the first time anyone had spoken so openly about their racist beliefs while I was in the room.

Unlike the graffiti and racial injuries that marked my earlier years—the kind of hurt that former Stevie might have himself inflicted—Stevie's admission was different. Now he shared the weight of shame and likewise willed for the moment to pass.

'So, what shall we do?' I asked.

'I want to be with you,' he said, 'leave all this shit behind me.'

8
Questions of Moral Motivation

The foregoing analysis of racial tensions in Paul's community began with a focus on some of the hostility directed towards those deemed to be 'foreigners'. In Chapter 5, I sought to develop an emic perspective of this hostility (i.e. an internal view), and to do so I located the attitudes towards foreigners within a framework of mutuality. I suggested that we can understand at least some hostility as stemming from collective instinct to protect the normative way of life on which many depend. Hence, the complaints Paul's peers raised about foreigners often concerned behaviours which they seemingly thought undermined local practices and what I have called the norms of mutuality. We have also seen that community participants are oriented towards autonomy, which is especially apparent in their criticisms of those with relatively less advantage and when they appraise behaviours which contravened the legitimate standards of autonomy (in particular, those of respectability). While I have suggested that participants in Paul's community are committed to autonomy, as the legitimate moral framework, nonetheless structural conditions of material disadvantage often make these standards unattainable. Therefore, to demonstrate autonomy (at least in a thin sense), some community participants point to the noticeable failings of comparably positioned others.

Since those within Paul's community are oriented towards autonomy as part and parcel of being born into contemporary English society, it is plausible that some of their interactions with 'foreigners' follow the social practice of distinction: marking oneself as moral by the standards of autonomy in pointing to the moral limitations of another. Indeed, the concept of race is central to the respectability discourse and the hierarchical social ordering of English society which advanced top-down from the nineteenth century onwards (Hall, 1992; McClintock, 1995; Shilliam, 2018; Skeggs, 2004; Virdee, 2014). Not only was the autonomous moral ideal the 'self-made' man in possession of property, but it was also conceived as white (Hall, 1992: 55; McClintock, 1995; Pieterse, 1989: 256; Shilliam, 2018). Therefore,

A Precarious Life. Roxana Willis, Oxford University Press. © Roxana Willis 2023.
DOI: 10.1093/oso/9780198855149.003.0017

just as one might signal commitment to autonomy by marking out the lower-class status of 'trampy' others, so too might one point to the inferiority of those marked by their race. However, under the law in England and Wales, when an individual differentiates another person on grounds of their race, they risk violating the law in ways that class distinction does not—a point to which I soon return.

Historically, racialized forms of distinction in Britain have followed a similar trajectory to class-based distinction. In the Introduction, I detailed how the respectability discourse transfused top-down into the English social order, and how a segment of the working class were co-opted to align themselves with bourgeois interests. Gareth Stedman Jones (2013: 303) describes this tendency as 'wooing the respectable working class' into protecting the newly established civil order against the threat of the least advantaged. Likewise, the working classes in England were wooed into embracing the bourgeois discourse on whiteness, which elevated the most down-and-out in Britain to a higher social status than that of colonized persons abroad.

Race, then, has been a crucial means for European elites to stoke division among the working classes in order to consolidate power and reduce the masses' potential to collectively rise against imperial masters (Allen, 2012; Baker, 1998; Du Bois, 2007; Haider, 2018; Lowe, 2015; Winant, 2001). Prior to the development of race, enslaved persons and indentured labourers, including emigrants from Ireland, Scotland, and England, were comparably (though differentially) subordinated—a plight in common which allowed solidarities to form among the exploited. The potential for the masses to join forces terrified European elites, who were significantly outnumbered, exemplified by Bacon's Rebellion in 1676 (see Haider, 2018: 55). And, as Catherine Hall explains (1992), in the wake of the French Revolution, the bourgeoisie became obsessively concerned about the risks posed by the lower orders. A colonial logic of divide and rule somewhat appeased bourgeois anxiety, affording certain groups advantages and social status over others in return for loyalty and cooperation (Lowe, 2015; Pieterse, 1989). Part of the divide and rule process is to incentivize subjugated factions to invest in the capitalist system of exploitation and to reward them (however slightly) for their commitment to protecting the civil order against the threat of those cast as morally inferior (Allen, 2012; Cope, 2015; Du Bois, 2007; Lowe, 2015; Roediger, 1999). Race, and its partial diffusion into the modern concept of nationality, has been a chief means of dividing the masses in England.

244 Questions of Moral Motivation

Ideas about racial difference were propagated by certain European bourgeois thinkers from the eighteenth century onwards, in a process that involved applying scientific (we might say, scientistic) modes of thought to understand human beings and the social world (see Bindman, 2002; Wheeler, 2000). European scholars advanced various claims about significant biological differences purportedly existing between human beings on account of small differences in features such as skin pigmentation. These ideas culminated in the notorious race pseudoscience, which accelerated in the late nineteenth and early twentieth century. A great number of influential bourgeois English gentlemen bought into these ideas—about the biological inferiority of subjugated groups—especially prior to the Second World War (see Hall, 1989, 2007: Prologue). However, in the shadow of genocides (including of the Nama and Herero peoples in Namibia, Jewish people and other targeted groups in Europe, and the Tutsi people in Rwanda), race science has been irrefutably debunked—and has, for the most part, fallen out of favour (for critical accounts see Gould, 1996; Saini, 2019). While such pseudoscientific ideas still circulate in English society, they are no longer treated as legitimate, and in certain (limited) contexts the law responds to their expression.

The concept of race as advanced in the colonies was imported into Britain (Allen, 2012; Pieterse, 1989; Stoler and Cooper, 1997). But a problem arose: the bourgeois were reluctant to include the most disadvantaged sections of English society in the white category—'most whites, at least within Britain, were unworthy of whiteness' (Bonnett, 2000: 22). Consequently, as Alastair Bonnett (2000: 32–5) discusses, the nineteenth-century British working class were white in colonial settings but racialized in the social hierarchy at home; the bourgeoisie often described the poorest members of society as a 'race apart' and referred to them by similarly racialized terms as used for the subjugated abroad (see McClintock, 1995; Morris, 2002; Shilliam, 2018; Virdee, 2014). When the English bourgeois classes reflected on eugenicist ideas in the context of the UK, the poorest 10 percent were among those targeted (Jones, 2013; see Morris, 2002; Welshman, 2014).

Contemporary studies among the British working class indicate that an ambiguous racial status continues into the present—the most socio-economically disadvantaged are still racialized or marked as the wrong kind of white (Haylett, 2001; Lawler, 2012; Reay et al., 2007; Skeggs, 2004). For example, Steph Lawler (2012) compares working-class whiteness, as hyper-visible and widely commented on, to middle-class whiteness, which remains concealed and muted. Consequently, the middle-class white body may be treated as normal and unquestioned, while the bodies of the 'white working-class' and/or non-white individuals stand out as deviations from the norm, open to scrutiny (cf. Ahmed, 2007). In this context, for precariously positioned individuals to access the benefits of racial privilege, they must assert their claim to whiteness in contrast to the more 'natural' kind of racial privilege embodied by the socio-economically advantaged, which can be invoked in unspoken and more discrete ways (Tyler, 2012; van Dijk, 1993; Young, 1994).

Whereas, within British society, the concept of race did not fully transcend class differences, the concepts of culture and nationality, into which race is fed, have been a powerful means to unify across classes (Gilroy, 2002; Hall, 1991; Hall et al., 2013; Virdee, 2014). Like race, the rise of national identity was an elite-driven process, which became increasingly popularized in the course of the nineteenth century (Newman, 1986; Valluvan, 2001). According to Satnam Virdee (2014) in his historical study of the English working class, from the late nineteenth century onwards a top-down, cultivated form of 'racist nationalism' generated a racialized British identity, embedding itself eventually in the English psyche (see also Anderson, 1991: 150; Hall et al., 2013). Virdee (2014: 64) suggests that as a result of this state-building project, racist nationalism transformed from an elite into a popular cultural form, reimagining English workers as white and hence as sat atop a racialized global order (see also Du Bois, 1999; Lake and Reynolds, 2008). Through the growth of a unified national identity, diverse class interests have been artificially unified in Britain, to which the ruling strata can appeal in moments of crisis (cf. Hall et al., 2013).

In contemporary conditions of what I have called framework plurality, hostility towards persons who are racialized may be motivated by sentiments located within a framework of mutuality or a framework of autonomy. The framework of mutuality strongly values empathy and makes a virtue of co-dependence. Accordingly, when one is motivated by mutuality, one seeks to mute differences in preference for a substantive form of equality among those within the collective. For those assimilated into the local way of life and actively engaging in the sharing practices, a 'colour-blind' relationship purportedly exists: rather than being defined by race, the racialized person becomes an insider, and the racialized features of their identity become insignificant, at least by the mutuality ideal. Of greater importance than race, then, would be the contributions a person makes to the collective. Therefore, when those seemingly living by the norms of mutuality exclude a racialized person or group, they may be motivated by (as

246 Questions of Moral Motivation

seen from the emic perspective) aiming to protect the collective way of life on which group survival depends, rather than by racial hostilities per se. The situation is different when persons act within the framework of autonomy. Oriented strongly to autonomy, a person may emphasize individual difference over and above unity and collective interests; an individual can demonstrate their personal commitment to the autonomous ideal by articulating the moral failings of others—for example, by drawing attention to 'trampy' and rough forms of behaviour which do not meet the standards of respectability. This process may silence the histories that shape inequalities in the present, simply placing responsibility fully on those exposed to material hardship. Notably, in contemporary British society, attempting to assert distinction publicly by pointing to racialized forms of difference falls short of expectations, for the morally autonomous individual ought no longer to assert their morality on grounds of racial differences alone. Yet, for those excluded from attaining autonomy due to structural barriers, it might only be possible to demonstrate a commitment to the moral ideal of autonomy in the thinner sense by pointing to the moral failings of comparably positioned others who exhibit markers of racial, as well as class, 'inferiority' (as shown in Chapter 7).

Further complicating matters, expressions of hostility may be motivated by prejudicial beliefs about the biological superiority of certain peoples, which are legally prohibited in certain situations. For example, in the context of equality law, when an employer or a public or private services provider discriminates against an individual because of a protected characteristic (which includes age, disability, gender reassignment, marriage and civil partnership, pregnancy and maternity, race, religion or belief, sex, and sexual orientation), they could be in breach of the Equality Act 2010. Of greater relevance to the precariat community, when an offender marks out a victim by their race, religion, sexual orientation, disability, or transgender identity during the commission of a criminal offence (including offences against the person, criminal damage, certain public order offences, and harassment offences), their behaviour could constitute a hate crime (see the Crime and Disorder Act 1998, ss 29 to 32, and the Public Order Act 1986, ss 18 to 23 and ss 29B to 29G). In accordance with hate crime jurisprudence, the usage of certain words is especially susceptible to evidencing hostility.[1] As the Law Commission (2021: 1) explains, 'if an offender assaults an

---

[1] See McFarlane [2002] EWHC 485 (Admin), [2002] All ER (D) 78 (Mar); Howard [2008] EWHC 608 (Admin), [2008] All ER (D) 88 (Feb).

Asian person while using the racial slur "p**i", this would become a race-based hate crime, namely racially-aggravated assault' (per the Crime and Disorder Act 1998, s 29).[2] Hence, usage of certain terms risks being treated as a demonstration of racist hostility that aggravates a criminal offence. The aim of this chapter is to reflect on moral motivations when hostile expressions are used in Paul's community, with a focus on race, ethnicity, and religion. As noted, in limited circumstances, the law interprets derogatory expressions about a person's race, religion, sexual orientation, disability, or transgender identity as a demonstration of hostility. However, an alternative moral motivation might be at play, which becomes apparent when we take into consideration the classed conditions in which usages of expressions surface. Extending the analysis of Chapter 7, Paul's peers might use certain hostile expressions as an attempt to demonstrate a personal commitment to the legitimate (i.e. dominant) moral framework of autonomy through the classed process of distinction. In these circumstances, the direct intention might be to portray oneself as moral; however, since such a portrayal (if successful) would be achieved by marking out the moral inferiority of another, a person making distinction that involves race can easily land themselves in the realms of racism. Alternatively, a person might be acting in pursuit of mutuality, attempting to level out difference, a possibility we began to explore in Chapter 5 and return to here. Or, finally, the motivation might rightly be treated as a demonstration of bigotry, as per the legal interpretation.

I suggest that sometimes the community's appearing to invoke hierarchical racial distinctions is really a strategy to neutralize distinction, in pursuit of mutuality. Whereas the framework of autonomy sanctions social hierarchy and the marking of one's individuality against the failings of a subordinated other, the framework of mutuality is averse to the imposition of power, orienting those within it to a group conformity. Therefore, being guided by such a framework, individuals may invoke racial differences to challenge assertions of class difference and vice versa, counteracting power imbalances and perhaps momentarily realizing a form of equality between parties. This is not to suggest that racial vocabulary and insults in Paul's community are never motivated by racist beliefs (i.e. a commitment to the racialized hierarchy and supremacy of whiteness). Rather, I seek to reveal how the moral motivation is not always clear-cut and might need to be read at a deeper level than, say, that of language usage or speech acts; I suggest

---

[2] See also Pal [2000] Criminal Law Review 756 at [16].

248   Questions of Moral Motivation

that lawyers should be attuned to these other layers when deliberating suitable applications of equality law and hate crime, for example.

Building on the work of Nicola Lacey (1988: ch 3, 2016), I tentatively suggest that one way forward for criminal lawyers grappling with such issues as these could be to adopt a character approach to responsibility. This approach entails examining the wider context in which racialized language is used in relation to the general character of the actor. Lacey (1988: 66) explains the character conception of responsibility: 'actions for which we hold a person fully responsible are those in which her usual character is centrally expressed'. For example, does the actor demonstrate a commitment to beliefs in racial superiority in the way they live their life, or is the remark uncharacteristic of them? Moreover, if a person appears drawn to hierarchical divisions on grounds of race (and other characteristics), how committed to these beliefs are they? Such an approach aligns with the much less used second limb of the legal test for assessing whether a crime is aggravated by hostility, which looks to the subjective motivation of the offender, considering wider patterns of behaviour (Crime and Disorder Act 1998, s 28(1)(b)). Importantly, however, Lacey's approach takes us beyond the subjective, and provides scope for wider considerations such as reputation. In relation to Paul's community, despite the prevalence of derogatory terms, the collective does not seem to act primarily to maintain a racialized social hierarchy, since many practices are oriented towards levelling out differences. If a commitment to such a hierarchy exists in England, as I see it, it is likely to be found among those who primarily benefit from the spoils of autonomy and the services of subordinates. Conversely, as we will see, participants in Paul's community are broadly critical of such tendencies.

I start the analysis by examining characteristics which Paul's peers mark as inferior, reflecting historical forms of distinction. This section alone might lead a reader to conclude that prejudice is endemic in the research community. However, I challenge this assumption in the following section by showing how, in practice, characteristics or markers of one form of inequality are often used to counter those on another ground. Therefore, I suggest that the practice of raising differences plausibly operates to diffuse them, as per a framework of mutuality which encourages a form of equality among comparatively situated persons. In this discussion, I engage with Katherine Smith's (2012) work on banter, and return to her work on fairness to assess how equality legislation is experienced as unfair from the perspective of Paul's precariously situated peers; this provides context for how and why participants in Paul's community seek to 'personalize the state' in this area (following Koch (2018b)).

In the last section, we reflect on community perceptions of those with greater privilege. In accordance with previous studies (Skeggs, 2004: 114–18; Walkerdine and Lucey, 1989; Savage et al., 2001; Sayer, 2005), rather than valorize the behaviours of more socio-economically advantaged individuals, the community critiques certain privileged ways of being for failing to accord with mutuality values. This leads me to conclude that considering the framework of mutuality offers the most comprehensive explanation for the normative orientation which guides those precariously positioned in the social order. Consequently, I contend that the criminal law ought to engage more with the framework of mutuality moving forward.

The Morally Inferior

Classed societies are hierarchical. In the Introduction, I noted that religious beliefs about people born into divinely ordained positions fed into conceptions of social hierarchy in older eras. But as the bourgeoisie grew in power, new social formations were justified on the terms of autonomy and the value assigned to work, vindicating social differences by conceiving individuals as having earned the right to control a greater distribution of the world's resources. Pseudoscientific beliefs about the inferiority of certain categories of persons, which grew in tandem with the normative significance of autonomy, provide alternative reasons for social disparities, which allegedly stem from innate deficiencies of disadvantaged persons and thus form the natural order. In this way, pseudoscientific ideas incorporate elements of older religious beliefs, since this pattern of belief validates the existing social order as natural and inevitable. Furthermore, such beliefs incorporate the tendency of the autonomy framework to explain social outcomes in individual terms, though notably on putative biological grounds rather than through claims of good and bad decision-making.

While the source of the justification for social hierarchy has changed, the immoral figure within hierarchies is remarkably consistent, reflecting historically subordinated groups. These categories overlap with the nineteenth-century 'dangerous classes' outlined by Anne McClintock (1995: 5): 'the working class, the Irish, Jews, prostitutes, feminists, gays and lesbians, criminals, the militant crowd and so on'. In Paul's community, differentiation often (though not exclusively) involved marking out

250 Questions of Moral Motivation

the characteristics of structurally disadvantaged groups according to class, race, gender, sexuality, disability, religion, and nationality. In this section, I provide an overview of the main markers of social difference that surfaced in Paul's community. I then move on to develop a thicker account of these practices in the context of precarity.

Paul's community applied racial distinctions relatively frequently, in different ways, sometimes as a form of exoticization and other times as a form of hateful expression: in all instances, the racialized person is othered and conceived in group terms, in contrast to the individual who is not racialized. Persons of East Asian heritage and black persons were especially exoticized. I commonly saw the word 'chinky' used to describe Chinese food. This middle-aged woman's announcement is representative of the ordinary usage of the term: 'had a nice bath, now going to have a chinky with the family and get settled in for the night'. Less frequently, the word 'chink' was used to describe people who appeared to be of Chinese heritage, such as a girl in her late teens who commented, 'had a right laugh in the Chinese shop with the chinks, lovely people'. On a handful of occasions, the racist term 'nigga' also appeared (with this spelling): once by a white girl to her mixed heritage black friend, and on several instances by white men in reference to other white friends.

Certain people in the community directed the most hostile forms of racial othering towards persons of Gypsy, Roma, and Traveller heritage and South Asian heritage. They frequently used the racist terms 'pikey' and 'gyppo' as insults to refer to Gypsy, Roma, and Traveller persons generally. Occasionally, I saw the insult 'paki' used, especially in reference to individuals with brown skin. In one instance, the term 'blackastani' was directed at a boy of visibly Sikh heritage. These usages were overtly derogatory, without allusion to positive features such as friendship.

I saw much hyper sexualization also (cf. Lowe, 2015; McClintock, 1995; Skeggs, 2004). On several occasions, I observed women of East Asian appearance exoticized sexually. Likewise with black males, at times from a young age. For example, on one occasion a teenage girl claimed, 'as if my 4 yr old brother just said he needs fanny, he's a ruthless kid', to which a teenage boy replied, 'he's black that's why'. Further, I came across frequent claims that racialized men pose a risk to women and tend towards sexual violence. This presumption is evident in the following joke a woman shared with her female friend, following a night out which ended with her friend spending the night in a police cell—'they should lock you up with a paki and throw away the key!'

Another source of marking out difference is religion, or religion as it intersects with race and ethnicity. On a handful of occasions, I noticed anti-Semitic insults, such as the use of 'Jew' in order to allege uncharitable or uncooperative behaviour of a person. Even more frequently, some in the community seemed to associate Muslim men with sexual deviance (cf. Lamont, 2009: 169–72; McKenzie, 2015: 179), and several stories from far-right websites circulated which accused Muslim men of kidnapping young women. Such claims featured in demands for Muslims to 'fuck off back to where they came from'. When a man in his twenties challenged a friend by asking where exactly Muslim people were supposed to go back to, the man replied 'muslimland'. At times, racism involving religious markers combined with hostility towards people of certain nationalities; this was especially evident when persons of Turkish heritage were portrayed as sexual predators.

Racial undertones also characterized some discussions about migrants from eastern Europe. As discussed in Chapter 5, Paul's friends tended to employ the term 'foreigner' in hostile discussions about migration. In recognition of this, a woman in her thirties started an online debate in a town-wide group by suggesting that the word 'foreigner' made her feel uncomfortable. This woman's perspective is reflected in the English and Welsh law—in Rogers [2007] UKHL 8, the House of Lords ruled that the term 'foreigner' might at times demonstrate racial hostility. However, the majority opinion in the community discussion was that 'foreigner' was not a problematic word and that the very suggestion was another instance of 'PC [political correctness] gone mad'. I also recorded two overtly derogatory uses of the term 'fozza' (short for 'foreigner').

Discussions about imagined national purity provided the most explicit nods to racist beliefs about biological superiority in Paul's community. Consider this young woman's frustrations: 'I'm absolutely fed up of people thinking I'm foreign (Latvian/Russian). It offends me so much. I'll just clear it up: I am full WHITE BRITISH and I was born in lovely England! Now stop trying to insult me!' In a similar vein, a middle-aged man announced, 'I'm 100% British and proud'. And a man in his late twenties opined, 'if ur lucky enough to have a beautiful girlfriend, i.e. 100% British beef, why the fuck would u cheat on her with some beat down dirty horse meat'—a sentiment presented in different formations at various points of the fieldwork. References to being 'full' and '100% British', as well as the explicit reference to whiteness, show that beliefs about biological purity circulate in the community, where the purity ideal conveys the highest moral worth and

252   Questions of Moral Motivation

affords superior status. Michèle Lamont (2009: 188), in talking of national superiority in the French context, discusses a 'caste-like relationship that the French have historically maintained with members of former colonies' (cf. Alexander, 2010 in the US context). Rather than hierarchy being tied to race per se, we can see how it may merge with the concept of nationality, which accounts for how racial tensions can surface in communities receiving what might otherwise appear to be 'white' migration. This phenomenon has been discussed by Paul Gilroy (2002) and Stuart Hall (1991, 2017), among others as a new form of cultural racism which has displaced the biological, essentialist variety.

A young man on Paul's estate, not content with what he perceived to be a high rate of Eastern European migration into the town, started a group focused on demanding that people speak English while in England. As part of this plight, the young man claimed, 'foreigners should clean my shoes, that's it'. This assertion is plausibly based on the belief that England is a superior nation, and on this view, English nationals ought to be served in some way by non-nationals (cf. Loader and Mulcahy, 2003: ch 5). For context, this is a young man without school qualifications and limited literacy, who is nationally situated among the most disadvantaged, and who is unlikely to advance from this position in his lifetime. Despite such structural disadvantage, it seems that this young man has inherited the national belief—previously explicit (cf. Heathorn, 2000), now implicit (cf. Hall et al., 2013)—that English nationality, and especially white English status, contains social value. Consequently, he expects that his 'superior' characteristics should afford him privileges which are not forthcoming (cf. Hochschild, 2016).

Despite the tendency to other people on account of racial characteristics, in Chapter 5 we saw that Paul's community and the wider community of Corby are ethnically heterogeneous in character. Many of the people who are racially othered in the above discussions are part of the Corby community, and in some instances part of Paul's community. Yet references to racial difference create the impression that persons who become racialized exist outside of the collective. Of significance, racial characteristics are not the only means by which people are othered—differences sitting along a range of axes, which contain historical significance, are singled out in similar ways.

Indeed, race, religion, and nationality are not the only markers of inferiority. Similar distinctions involved sexuality and gender. Derogatory terms related to homosexuality have a continuing presence in Paul's community; I frequently saw the term 'gay' used as an insult, especially to challenge a

The Morally Inferior   253

man's masculinity. The derogatory insult 'faggot' also appeared on several occasions, particularly in the build-up to a fight to suggest physical weakness. Édouard Louis (2017) reveals the violence contained in this word in a vivid account of growing up as gay in working-class France. Gendered insults directed at women included 'slut' and 'slag'. The term 'breeder' was occasionally used towards disadvantaged mothers (as we saw in Chapter 7). Additionally, a handful of men used the term 'mong' to describe an unattractive woman. For example, one of Paul's companions informed his friends that he 'just got smiled at by a woman who, to put it nicely, was in need of a lead, collar and muzzle... so not only do I attract the wrong women I get the mong ones too'. Historically, the word 'mong' has been derogatorily used towards persons living with Down's syndrome, itself used ('mongol') in medical contexts owing to racist associations made between physical symptoms of the condition with the facial features of people from East Asia. The above use of the term to describe socio-economically disadvantaged women is meant to invoke, I think, ideas of poor breeding and genetic inferiority, yet again reminiscent of the mistaken assertions of race science.

There were other forms of ableist language, including the use of the term 'spastic', or a shortened version, 'spaz', as an insult when someone lacked the ability to do something or said something unwise. Relatedly, when asked to explain what the insult 'dinlo' meant (to refer to someone as stupid), a woman explained that it meant 'a fucking spaz'. Likewise, I saw the word 'retard' occasionally used to connote a lack of intelligence.

Another characteristic susceptible to marking out a person as inferior included being overweight, especially when intersecting with perceived female gender. Moreover, being red-headed marks one out. For example, consider the following discussion between teenagers:

FELICITY: gingers shouldn't wear orange, reminds me of Chucky [an evil red-haired doll character of horror film fame]
SEAN: futures bright the futures orange
FELICITY: hope you get a ginger baby!
SEAN: fuck that, gingers should be getting disability
FELICITY: why for having no soul?

Here we see an echoing of past associations of red hair with immorality— historically, red hair has been associated with Christian sin, sexual deviance, and genetic inferiority (cf. Baum, 1922; Kalikoff, 1987; Nelson, 2017).

254   Questions of Moral Motivation

Some of Paul's peers also mocked the red-haired by insinuating or claiming that it undermined a man's masculinity and ability to fight, much as they sometimes portrayed male homosexuality.

The relative frequency and harshness of the language I have outlined in this section could lead us to conclude that Paul's peers are committed to these prejudices. Indeed, it seems that the law in England and Wales treats the usage of such derogatory language (in certain and limited circumstances) as indicators of hostile intent (see Law Commission, 2021). However, I propose we take a deeper look at the social practices in which these insults figure, in order to properly comprehend what role they play and how their usage or prevalence reflects on Paul's community.

Neutralizing Distinction

When Paul's community use derogatory terms, it might indicate prejudice. Alternatively, it might relate to the process of distinction we saw in Chapter 7, where a person attempts to demonstrate their moral worth by pointing to the failings of others, who are often comparably positioned. Indeed, the most prevalent insults I observed involved class-based distinctions: people often accused others of being a 'tramp' or 'junkie', of being 'lazy' or a 'bad mum', and so on. My argument in this section is that some uses of language to mark characteristics are not fuelled by prejudice or distinction and serve a deeper purpose: to militate against interpersonal superiority and to maintain equality among the group. Hence, what might seem like distinction in accordance with the social hierarchy of autonomy may in fact comprise an attempt to assert commonality, as per mutuality.

A local practice which we might misrecognize as distinction-based, but which I find is better understood as mutuality-oriented, is banter. In an ethnographic study in the north of England, Smith describes 'having a banter' as a form of everyday speech in working-class conversations, which entails 'taking the piss' (joking or mocking) in a witty and humorous way, delivered with such speed that it appears to be second nature for those who have mastered the practice (Smith, 2012: 117; cf. Charlesworth, 2000). Les Back (1996) refers to this practice as 'cussing' and 'wind-ups'. Smith (2012: 115) locates the practice within friendship groups, and hence here there is a sense of equality between the participants. Yet there are important limits; for instance, topics related to ill-health, loss of loved ones, and material hardship are out of bounds.

Neutralizing Distinction 255

The following text, from a post delivered in a humorous manner, is a good example of banter in Paul's community even though the language may be misinterpreted when taken out of the original context.

> Facebook's a fuckin joke nowadays. My newsfeed's full of tramps, weirdos, gimps, faggots acting hard, shitty dogs all dolled up, gayos postin selfies, and depressed messes beggin for some attention. Moral of the story get a grip ya fuckin aliens.

Lots of people 'liked' the post, and in response, other community participants joined in with the jesting nature by offering additional forms of insult. For example, one woman tagged her friend into the post and told her to 'shave ya indicator pubes ya fat ride'; to which her friend replied, 'away u and take ur face for a shite, ur breath smells like a homeless man's body'.

Smith explains that being teased through banter can indicate inclusion and belonging rather than insult or disrespect; those who banter show themselves to be down-to-earth and part of the group. Therefore, in contrast to distinction-making which singles out difference to assert oneself in a social hierarchy, banter involves mocking features of difference in a way that may create a sense of equivalence among community participants (cf. Skeggs, 2004: 114; Vicinus, 1974). Back (1996: 96) interprets the practice differently, suggesting that insults are used to deflect feeling hurt by another's insult. As I see it, Smith's analysis captures the spirit of the practice, which is why it principally occurs between friends, though there may be circumstances where banter indeed morphs into tit-for-tat power struggle and defensiveness, as Back observed. That said, the metaphor of balance may still be apt even here, for if the motivation of banter is to hurt someone as a form of defence, the act of returning an insult may restore the status of those insulted.

Another circumstance which involves the use of insults as a levelling force is a particular kind of trade. That is, Paul's community use insults which derive from one historical axis of structural disadvantage to counter insults from another. Race-based insults and sentiments provide particularly good examples, since they were often met with class-based replies. For example, on several occasions when a longer-term Corby resident made comments in a town-wide online group that Eastern European migrants ought to speak English, another resident would counter the claim by demanding that those criticizing migrants ought to first learn to speak 'proper English' before commenting on the linguistic abilities of others. Accordingly, by drawing

256 Questions of Moral Motivation

attention to the educational and linguistic struggles of the person making demands of migrants, the reply aims to defuse what seems to be racial distinction by pointing to class markers (cf. Bourdieu, 1991; Charlesworth, 2000; Lareau, 2011; Mehta, 1990). While highlighting class markers in these circumstances might itself become distinction—an assertion of power over a less advantaged other—we must at least recognize it as consistent with action guided by the framework of mutuality, since everyone is reminded of their equivalent moral standing. Thus, the moral motivation here is not clear cut.

The community gestured similarly towards class markers to counteract negative reactions towards the arrival of Gypsy, Roma, and Traveller communities. For example, a man said of complaints in the town-wide online group about mobile homes reaching a local playing field that it 'would be far worse to have a load of junkies camped up outside your house'. On another occasion, one of Paul's friends joked, 'I don't know why everyone's moaning about the pikeys down by Lidl, when they realise they have set up camp on the ecky estate they'll soon be gone'. These references to the 'rough' elements of the community—drug addicts and a notorious council estate—are used to counter hostility towards Gypsy, Roma, and Traveller communities. Again, these insults and slights could operate as distinction, or could serve to level out distinction itself, in responding to assertions of superiority. And so once more the moral motivation remains in question.

The levelling effect or intention is perhaps even harder to make out in some 'trades', such as when racial distinction is challenged with forms of class distinction that reproduce beliefs in biological inferiority. For example, in response to a friend of Paul's who was encouraging others to vote for the BNP (a far-right party) in an upcoming general election, another man responded by saying, 'you're an uneducated, uncultured retard'. Someone's being 'uneducated' here is anchored in the structural reality, with real barriers locally to educational attainment, and it is compounded by an additional ableist distinction. One of Paul's friends in his late thirties exhibited even more explicitly his beliefs about biological human differences: 'Watching this immigration debate. Sterilise and deport the home-grown lazy parasites and bring in more hard-working migrants, simple.' Such retorts against anti-migration sentiment were common. The reference to sterilization echoes eugenicist ideology. Moreover, the notion of deporting the 'home-grown lazy parasites' recalls past episodes of forced migration of impoverished groups during imperial growth. And calling on 'good' migrants to relocate to Britain is reminiscent of the state's previous encouragement of migration from Ireland, the commonwealth, and beyond to support British labour needs. We can thus see how historical ideas continue to circulate and be available for making sense of present circumstances. Still, in some cases, the motivation by drawing on these ideas might be directed towards other ends than asserting biological superiority.

I observed class-based insults used to counter other forms of prejudice too. For example, commenting on another televised debate, a friend of Paul's in his mid-twenties challenged homophobia:

GAVIN: This debate about whether gay people should be allowed to adopt, considering the mutants allowed to have children, gay adoption should be compulsory.
CLAIRE: The question should be, should we allow eejits to breed?

Gavin's comment was popular and received almost thirty likes. Gavin applies a classed insult about bad parents to argue for the right of gay partners to adopt, and accordingly marks the relative moral status of gay couples as against the immoral low-class figure. Claire's comment once again brings us back into the realm of eugenics; in questioning whether 'eejits', which refers to a person of low intelligence (an idiot), should be allowed to 'breed', she draws on mistaken ideas about intelligence being hereditary and past practices of social engineering.

As is apparent in the extracts so far, classed insults often involved or implied claims about a lack of intelligence, and overt forms of racism were often challenged with assertions that such beliefs were 'stupid'. This is illustrated in a statement by a boy in his late teens following a string of anti-migrant sentiments expressed in Paul's community:

Stop being stupid and make an educated decision. If you're one of those people who just don't like foreigners then you best stop watching your Korean tv, put down your Taiwanese mobile phone, throw away all your Indian made clothes, chuck out your German beer, and change the plans you had to go to the Chinese/Mexican/Indian/Italian restaurant tonight.

Here, the young man aims to highlight the hypocrisy of disliking 'foreigners' while being beneficiaries of a culture infused with diverse contributions. The comment, variations of which were made by others, challenges racial prejudice by illuminating the interconnection of different nations and co-dependences (cf. Hall, 1991; Lowe, 2015; Virdee, 2014). Yet perhaps

258 Questions of Moral Motivation

the statement also reveals an essentialist view of culture by glossing over the fluid interconnectedness of globally produced resources, cultures, and peoples, instead affording each nation its own artificially separate and isolated contribution (cf. Gilroy, 1993; Gopal, 2019; Said, 2003).

Community participants sometimes interpreted accusations of racism as assertions of power, and challenged the accusations of racism by alleging class privilege. An instance of this occurred in a town-wide online group when a woman expressed her discomfort with migration, saying also that she hated the thought of trying 'foreign foods'. In response, another woman called her racist. Several other residents then came to the defence of the woman accused of being racist and claimed that the accuser was herself 'being a bully'—bullying, which involves the illegitimate use of power against a weaker person, is strongly opposed in Paul's community (see Chapters 3). Similarly, several instances involved the community disparaging a person who accuses others of racism, arguing by return that they act 'better educated', are 'arrogant', or 'think they're better' than others. When Paul's precariously situated peers thus saw accusations of racism as assertions of power, they collectively resisted them in a way comparable to how they challenged other perceived inflictions of power (see Chapter 4).

In conditions where a plurality of frameworks exist, it is not always clear what the moral motivation is, and ways of behaviour typical to levelling practices, such as banter, can undoubtedly be misused. It seems to me that the task of working out the motivation behind a particular instance of banter requires assessing the wider context and the broader character of the person involved in the practice (following Lacey, 1988: ch 3, 2016). For instance, we might ask whether an individual only uses banter towards racialized persons within their friendship group or more broadly, and whether banter tends to be used among relatively positioned equals or against those in less advantaged positions. When banter is consistently used against persons with less power, this perhaps indicates it does not operate as a levelling force but is rather a smokescreen covering abuse or bullying. Alternatively, if banter is more commonly used among friends, drawing on a range of character axes, and is applied as a form of 'punching-up' and across, then a more apt description of the activity may be as a challenging of distinction itself. We could, moreover, examine how people live their lives, since those who live in accordance with the principles of mutuality as I have been spelling them out may have a greater claim of being motivated by a levelling-out ambition than those who prioritize ideals of self-advancement and self-gain.

Attempts to level out differences among Paul's friends through practices such as banter, and by countering claims of distinction, can help to explain tensions which are created when equality legislation is invoked. Sometimes, when an individual makes a rights-based claim, citing how equality legislation accepts claims of racism, sexism, and so on, Paul's community actively resists them. In fact, a too easy readiness to assert the rights afforded by equality legislation can be treated as behaviour which runs counter to the framework of mutuality and the collective norms. I explore this further by examining how Paul's peers interpreted legal equality in the sphere of religion.

Equality Rights in a Sea of Class Disadvantage

Race activism, punctuated by civil unrest and riots, pushed the UK government to widen equality legislation prohibiting unequal treatment on grounds of race, alongside other protected characteristics (now contained in the Equality Act 2010). Notably, however, this legislation does not include class, an omission which stems from the individualistic logic underpinning the legal system and the inherently collective nature of class (cf. Sayer, 2005: 52–3). The legal subject is the autonomous individual and legislative protection against discrimination is primarily provided at the level of the individual, rather than in the form of collective rights. And so, in response to civil rights movements in the UK, which were collective struggles, the legal system rechannelled collective demands through the lens of individualism, which transformed calls for structural change into the extension of certain individual rights (cf. Táíwò, 2022). Since class inequality is less susceptible to individualization, which requires structural changes, class has remained outside of the remit of equality legislation. Moreover, alongside the individualization of gender and race struggles, the collective rights of workers have also been severely dismantled (see Hall, 2021).

Notwithstanding the necessity of legislation to counter sex discrimination and racism, the development of individual rights for certain forms of disadvantage to the exclusion of class, and the accompanying curtailment of collective rights, has contributed to a sense of unfairness among precariat communities such as Paul's (cf. Rhodes, 2010; Smith, 2012: ch 5). Reflecting on similar experiences of a white working-class community in Poland, Don Kalb (2009: 216–17) points out that individual rights and equality legislation clashes with the rationality of socio-economically disadvantaged

260   Questions of Moral Motivation

groups who gain their strength from conformity and solidarity. Thus, collectives who live within a framework of mutuality might find appeals to individual rights, themselves well recognized within the framework of autonomy, as at odds with local conceptions of fairness (cf. Day, 2001; Smith, 2012).

An apt illustration of how equality rights may jar with precariat appeals for group conformity relates to the accommodation of certain religious beliefs by the state. Persons of Muslim faith have been heavily demonized within the advanced liberal state, particularly since the turn of the millennium and the global 'war on terrorism' (see Kundnani, 2014). In the shadow of this hostile turn, research has frequently found Islamophobia among working-class communities, as well as within liberal nation states more broadly (e.g. McKenzie, 2015: 115–17; Rogaly and Taylor, 2016: 205–11; Lamont, 2009: ch 5; Gest, 2016). And as the ensuing discussion reveals, a good number of Paul's friends expressed hostilities towards persons of Muslim faith.

Mirroring Smith's (2012: 86–96) findings, there appeared to be support for banning the burqa (or niqab) in Paul's community as well as the wider town: approximately two thirds of people who commented in town-wide discussions about the topic supported this position when the issue was periodically raised, whereas around a third actively resisted it, and many did not comment either way. A common reason put forward for banning the burqa was that *in England* individuals are not permitted to cover their face in certain situations with motorcycle helmets and balaclavas; therefore, Muslim women ought similarly to show their faces in public.

Arguments such as these, which appeal to a formal application of equality regardless of protected characteristics, are not limited to socio-economically disadvantaged groups, and can be seen as a way class interests artificially align in England. For example, a national news piece in 2019 reported on a doctor who had asked a woman to remove her niqab during a medical consultation on the premise that he needed to understand her better. In a press interview, the doctor explained: 'I asked a lady to remove her face veil for adequate communication, in the same way I'd ask a motorcyclist to remove a crash helmet' (Payne and Stubley, 2019). As Michael Sandel (2009: xiii) explains, in such instances, religious freedom is thinly conceived as a private right, something that an individual simply chooses to do, and the deeper good tied to religious practice goes unheeded. On a thin description, wearing a niqab is the same as covering part of the face any other way, since by any means the face is covered; however, there are thicker

Equality Rights in a Sea of Class Disadvantage   261

ways to describe the significance which makes intelligible the offence of asking a woman to remove her niqab.

Yet, compared to when a socio-economically privileged person appeals for formal equality as in the doctor example, when a precariously positioned person makes a similar appeal, there is a seemingly important difference. An advantaged individual in England, who is well supported by state infrastructure, might be fully oriented to autonomy as a moral framework. Such an orientation often includes a preference for a procedural form of equality and fairness, on whose grounds a person may brush aside differences of gender, sexuality, race, religion, disability, class, and so on. However, following Smith (2012), I have suggested that an alternative 'common-sense' view of fairness operates in Paul's community, where differential treatment *is* expected, but on account of a person's status and contributions to the local way of life, rather than due to religious difference. From this (emic) perspective, when religious practices are accommodated, it might feel doubly wrong because it involves prioritizing the rights of the individual as well as affording what seems to be preferential treatment for (what they regard as) a less deserving group than those whom they consider to belong (see Chapter 5), which conflicts with the norms of mutuality (see Rhodes, 2010). Hence, the outcome is topsy-turvy with respect to local notions of common sense.

Alongside critique of the burqa, Paul's community debated whether shops ought to accommodate the religious beliefs of minority groups. For example, consider the following conversation about an alleged supermarket policy allowing cashiers of Muslim faith to refuse to serve customers purchasing alcohol and pork.

DONNA: if they can't sell pork and alcohol due to religion then don't get a job in a supermarket, what is the world coming to!
PAULA: that's crazy, it's like saying Catholics shouldn't have to serve people buying condoms
JIMMY: if they can't do all the tasks of the job then they should be let go
ALAN: sack them all
BETH: but it's okay for them to sell it to us from THEIR corner shops
ALAN: money comes first before religion
LISA: it's the supermarket's policy that they can politely decline, it's up to the individual, it's about respecting their wishes due to religion.

The main argument in this extract is that Muslim people have a choice where to work and should therefore find a job that is suitable to their

262 Questions of Moral Motivation

religious beliefs, rather than expecting the employer to adapt to the needs of an individual. Adopting a position that prioritizes the employer over the worker might seem harsh, yet it also reflects the reality for many precariat workers who find themselves bearing the brunt of employer control and management on a daily and relentless basis (see Chapter 1). Paul's peers have learned that to survive precarity and maintain a wage, regardless of how loathsome the task, it must be done. From this lived internal perspective, it might seem unfair for the needs of certain individuals to be protected from the power of employers under equality law, when on the whole workers are denied autonomy and have limited collective protections under employment law.

Alan's call to 'sack them all' features in a socio-economic context where participants in Paul's community have themselves become dispensable to employers and could be laid off from work at any time; nonetheless, his comment ('all' meaning all Muslims) is ultimately objectifying. And when a person of Muslim faith relies on waged employment, they are likewise exposed to heavy employer surveillance and job insecurity; hence, we might question just how much autonomy or personal advantage is gained when (putative) minor adjustments for religious difference are accommodated. Notably, in these exchanges, the critics do not challenge this treatment as a collective and demand fairer working conditions for everyone; rather, the demand voiced here is for individuals to adapt to the requirements of capital. Hence, what are collective struggles are reimagined at the level of the individual, which Koch (2018a) identifies as the rise of individual lawfare over collective welfare.

Also apparent in the above conversation is suspicion about and mistrust of religious choices, with an assumption that persons of Muslim faith dishonestly invoke religion as a way to self-advance. For example, Beth contributes to the debate by pointing to the apparent hypocrisy of members of religious communities who are alleged to claim religious beliefs to secure advantages in one context and then profit from breaching these beliefs in another context. To make this claim, Beth implies that religion is a simple choice that people can opt in and out of, rather than it being constitutive of who they are. Moreover, Beth treats persons of Muslim faith as part of a single homogeneous group, without differentiating between diverse communities, racialized communities of other faiths, class differences, individual agency, and so on. In agreement with Beth, Alan offers the explanation that 'money comes first before religion'. Accordingly, the moral motivation of Muslim employees is put into question, and there is an assumption that they strategically manipulate equality rights for self-advancement.

At least one interlocutor would contribute counter-arguments into heated discussions on religion and race in Paul's community, and it was rare for a controversial claim to pass without challenge (cf. the insights of Tyler, 2012). In the last discussion, Lisa contests the views and explains the supermarket policy. Lisa suggests that this policy is fair, since it protects individual choice, as well as allowing for religious preferences; she thus locates her rationale within the moral framework of autonomy.

The moral motivation behind these discussions needs to be unpacked and remains somewhat unclear. While there are appeals to group conformity and resistance to equality legislation (cf. Kalb, 2009), the group articulates concerns primarily in individualistic terms, which indicates the sentiment behind these comments is located in a framework of autonomy (cf. Koch, 2018a): they suggest Muslim persons should simply choose to work elsewhere, or that the customer's choice of product is not a matter for the salesperson. However, a repeated complaint here is that religious minorities are afforded greater privileges over others, which feeds into a sense of unfairness that recalls how it is conceived in the framework of mutuality. Since race and religion are protected characteristics under the law, some of Paul's peers seem to interpret these rights as the state giving support to certain (minority) groups, who are similarly positioned in the class order, while the needs of longer-term locals are dismissed and ignored. Of course, the reality is that all precariat groups, regardless of skin tone, receive limited support from a classed state, and the tendency to foster blame on comparably positioned others is itself a feature of distinction and divide-and-rule politics.

Suspicions about the motivations of racialized persons, who in the examples above are alleged to invoke collective protections for personal ends, might stem from the fact that those in Paul's community must themselves strategically gain power in interactions with the state. We can explore this idea by returning to the process of 'personalising the state' (Koch, 2018b).

Personalizing Equality Rights

Let us return to the discussion of Chapter 4 which applies Koch's insights about socio-economically disadvantaged persons who are excluded from the full remit of state services finding ways to 'personalize the state'—i.e.

264   Questions of Moral Motivation

making the state respond to local needs in indirect ways. Since the classed state regularly fails to meet the needs of the least well-off and does not include sufficient provisions for or does not recognize the violation of mutuality norms, Paul's peers must creatively engage state services to tackle injustices and make the state intervene in wrongdoing. Likewise, I show in this section that Paul's neighbours personalize the state in attempts to overcome what they deem to be limits of equality legislation and the state's failing to recognize or respond to collective class interests.

Much like their view on religious minorities, some of Paul's friends asserted that the state gives 'foreigners' preferential treatment. Neighbourhood disputes and noise disturbances were prime sites for this claim. Studies in the English context regularly note tensions between neighbours who are required to live together on tightly packed council estates, issues which are compounded by the architectural inadequacies of hastily constructed housing provisions (Koch, 2018a; Reynolds, 1986; Rogaly and Taylor, 2016: 119). Complaints about neighbours by community participants tended to emphasize the foreign status of the apparent noise-maker in explaining disturbances and the apparent lack of state intervention (cf. Koch, 2018b: 68). These convictions are evident in the following discussion among two women in Paul's community.

PAM: My neighbours were at it again this morning! Foreigners make so much bloody noise all the time
MAGGIE: You poor thing, nothing worse than rowdy neighbours
PAM: Wish they'd piss off back to where they came from. Loads of 'em in one house, full of attitude and they and don't care about anyone living near them
MAGGIE: Sounds about right, 6+ to one bedroom then they wave the race card if you complain, argh boil my blood they do. Fran was having the same problem, so she went round and asked them to quiet down. The cheeky rat answered the door and told Fran to fuck off, then they called the police and said Fran called them a 'Polish cunt'. She never said anything of the kind!
PAM: Pisses me off, they've got more rights in our own country than we have.

Pam interprets household noise as a sign that her neighbours 'don't care about anyone living near them', behaviour which would thus fail to act in accordance with the mutuality norms about caring relationships and good neighbourliness. Further to this, Maggie shares an anecdote (which, as we saw in Chapter 5,

Personalizing Equality Rights **265**

need not be true) of a friend who had the same problem and attempted to address it by talking with her neighbours; however, the Polish neighbour allegedly acted counter to mutuality norms enjoining friendliness, and (again allegedly) strategically invoked the power of the police. I recorded several anecdotes of this nature (cf. Rogaly and Taylor, 2016: 177; Gest, 2016: 136).

Without recourse to similar protection on grounds of class, Maggie and Pam portray their situation as one of limited power. This is apparent in Pam's explicit claim to possess fewer rights in circumstances where they perceive the other party to have the tactical defence of a 'race card'—both parties are positioned in the precariat, and yet one party has a claim to a protected characteristic, whereas the other does not. Paul's friends frequently suggested that racialized persons were 'playing the diversity card', 'using the racist stick', or somehow deploying race as something 'profitable'. While all these phrases allude to power, the phrase 'racist stick' invokes the idea that equality rights are akin to a weapon, wielded against others without such protection.

Against this background, I observed Paul's neighbours adopt strategies to overcome perceived power imbalances; for example, to counter perceived racial advantage and rebalance power, they might invoke other protected characteristics:

BEN: what's up, noisy neighbours?
SHELLY: yeah mate, they act like they don't understand English when I ask them to keep it down, went on till 2am today
BEN: if they're gonna play dumb, call the police and let them deal with it
SHELLY: I did last night, they told me it aint a police matter, they put me onto the council and said someone will get back to me
JANICE: police won't do anything till something happens next door. I lived 4 years next door to someone like that and police only did something cus she lied and told them I had threatened her life
KIRSTIN: tell them you've got a disabled daughter and the council and police will have to do something
JANICE: you're also disabled, make up a horrible story that you fear for your life, you'll get put into a special category like my neighbour did, even though she lied the police believed everything she told them. Glad she finally fucked off and moved.

This example reiterates precariat experiences of the police and local council failing to listen and intervene in local problems that have a significant

266 Questions of Moral Motivation

impact on quality of life. As a suggestion to make the state respond, Janice shares a tactic purportedly once used against her, which transformed a council matter into a criminal matter. Here, we see an awareness that the state is disposed to react to crime—a marker of social disorder to which historically bourgeois anxiety instinctively responds—in contrast to issues of welfare which are susceptible to being sidelined and dismissed.

Kirstin's suggested strategy is for Shelly to inform the police that she has a disabled daughter, and hence to assert a legally protected characteristic out of concern for which the police must respond. It is unclear whether Shelly and her daughter live with disability and how this disability relates to the dispute. Nevertheless, we can see that from this perspective, for the state to recognize issues, they must be translated it into an individualized rights-based form (cf. Koch, 2018a; Merry, 1990).

On the one hand, then, I have noted that when Paul's peers tactically appeal to the services of the state, the underlying motivation may be the good of mutuality, including norms which concern protecting family and friends, enforcing the conditions of collective living, and protecting the social order on which the collective depends. The way participants in Paul's community live their lives reinforces this interpretation; we have seen in the prior chapters that, normatively, they do not prioritize self-advancement through legitimate channels, instead (and first and foremost) aiming to subsist and protect kin. On the other hand, although this process may prioritize mutuality, in keeping with Koch's observations (2018a), what are essentially collective struggles become individualized when pursued through legal mechanisms, instead of being fought as shared struggles for better housing, more responsive policing, better employment laws, and so on. That is, since class—an inherently collective condition—is not individualized under the law, the precariat might alternatively appeal to other characteristics. Therefore, while mutuality might often be the primary moral motivation, individualized strategies appear necessary to make the liberal state engage with the needs of precarity.

The Ignorant, Arrogant, and Out of Touch

Although participants in Paul's community engage in the practice of distinction, largely, they do not seem committed to the continued existence of a social hierarchy within which certain groups remain in a state of subordination and live a chunk of their lives to satisfy the will of individuals

The Ignorant, Arrogant, and Out of Touch   267

with greater power. Thus, while at times Paul's friends seek to distance themselves from behaviours deemed rough, this does not mean that they strive more generally to be seen as superior to others. There is, by contrast, a broad sense that no-one should perceive themselves to be 'better' than anyone else, and it is thought to be a great wrong for someone to assume otherwise (cf. Lamont, 2009: 47; Savage et al., 2001; Sayer, 2005: 171–6; Smith, 2012: 59). Numerous examples attest to this, such as a man expressing fury at his niece for ignoring him when she saw him in the town centre while with friends: 'does she think she's better than us, she better not deny that she saw me, I'm fuming with the cheeky fucker. I don't care who she thinks she is, I'll put her right in her place.' Being averse to pretention is a common theme in English working-class communities (Skeggs, 2004: 114–18; Vincent, 1974; Walkerdine and Lucey, 1989): '*Not* being middle class is certainly valued in many working-class social groups', as Beverly Skeggs puts it (1997: 11).

One way of critiquing individuals who act morally superior is by valorizing character traits that might otherwise be described as common (cf. Evans, 2006: 31). For example, a woman in Paul's community proudly described herself as brought up on 'council pop' (tap water) and another said she was 'born with a plastic spoon in [her] mouth', inverting the English saying about being 'born with a silver spoon in the mouth' to indicate wealth and privilege from birth. Here, virtue lies not in acquiring excess privileges, but fitting in with local standards. A woman in her late twenties emphasized the value of being good humoured and grounded to counter the negative reputation of her local public house:

> People who drink in the Star getting slated all the time, I'd rather have a drink there with people you can have a laugh with, down to earth people, I'm a Star girl and proud to go there when I go out, sick of people bad mouthing the place all the time.

The community also criticizes the morally superior by highlighting vices of pretence, arrogance, and ignorance. I recorded many comments along the lines of 'I can't stand ignorant, arrogant people'; a woman was described as 'being on her high horse', and a man as being 'stuck up his own arse'. Indeed, at various points in this work we have seen how first-hand experience of structural disadvantage reveals the reality of co-dependence and the limits to attaining autonomy. From a position of relative disadvantage, it might be easier to identify structural class privileges from which others have

268 Questions of Moral Motivation

benefited, whereas the experience of one's own privilege can be more readily taken for granted and translated through the lens of the autonomous ideal.

Paul's community likewise condemn politicians and other elites for their ignorance about the 'real world', and their frequent political cynicism is infused with talk about class (cf. McKenzie, 2015: 99; Koch, 2017b, 2018b). Discussions among Paul's peers refer to the 'political class', the 'ruling class', and 'the elite', which tends to indiscriminately include politicians on all sides of the political divide—'they're all the same'. Some did not just see politicians as ignorant, but wilfully so (cf. Mbembe, 2017 on 'wilful ignorance'). Discussing a politician who used a racist term in a televised public debate, a man in a town-wide group commented that 'it's not good enough for educated senior politicians to use casual racism', which he contrasted with an old-age pensioner who uses outdated terminology. Accordingly, some of Paul's friends recognize that differently situated groups have different abilities to self-censor, which relates to age as well as socio-economic status. Thus, they may expect those with greater advantage to meet the legitimate standards and speak in the appropriate ways—indeed, these are elite-made moral standards. It is highly unlikely that the socio-economically powerful are, as a class, committed to a normative framework of mutuality, and so when they use racial insults and vocabulary, it is plausible that the moral motivation is prejudice and requires redress.

There is a collective sense of unfairness in Paul's community about the moral failings of those in power. For example, a man in his thirties expressed a common sentiment about elite actors:

> All we hear on the news these days is about people ripping off the system for their own gain and greed and those from the top of the ladder are worse. Fucking pisses me right off! We're all struggling and they're lining their own pockets. It's about time someone pulled the ladder down... that time is coming soon.

The man invokes sentiments of mutuality—including fairness, empathy, and collectivity—in critiquing the self-serving actions of an elite who appear to exclusively operate within the framework of autonomy. Moreover, his reference to 'the ladder' portrays hierarchy, yet he is also aware that the ladder is held up by the masses and could be pulled away when the time comes—from this view, it is those on the ladder who are truly dependent on those holding it up. Such critique of elite behaviour, which was widespread among Paul's precariat community, reminds us that the moral motivations of the least advantaged can be markedly different from the motivations of elite professionals who may be judging them.

Conclusion

Being oriented within multiple frameworks inevitably bears on the moral motivation of a person in any given moment. Therefore, when someone marks out another on grounds of race, they may be acting in pursuit of the moral standards of autonomy by a process of distinction. Since autonomy in the thick sense is often unattainable for those positioned in the precariat, we have seen how Paul's peers attempt to demonstrate autonomy in a thinner sense by pointing to the moral limitations of others, and in so doing to position themselves as closer to the moral ideal of autonomy. This was particularly acute in the context of class distinctions in Chapter 7, in which we saw comparably situated others often described with the class marker of a 'tramp' and so on. As an extension, I have suggested here racial distinctions might serve a similar purpose, where a person may challenge the moral attainment of similarly positioned persons on grounds of racial differences, and in so doing momentarily display their commitment to the autonomy ideal in a thin sense. Moreover, in conditions of rife structural and symbolic violence (see Chapter 6), it is possible that some of Paul's peers lean on racial distinction to deflect the humiliation and injuries of being socially positioned at the bottom of the British class system.

Notwithstanding the potential for moral motivations to be rooted in the framework of autonomy, I argued that in general something deeper appears to be going on. This chapter, in the context of the fuller book, shows the value of developing a thicker account of language usage and the importance of capturing what people do beyond words. On a relatively surface-level analysis, the frequent use of classist, homophobic, ableist, racist, and sexist language indicates that community participants are committed to social hierarchy. However, by recognizing the framework of mutuality, we can gain a more nuanced account of how and why this language is employed. Contrary to the state's prioritization of individual rights and the nurturing of hierarchy, there is a deeper and more sustained commitment in Paul's community to prioritizing relational ends principally and resisting imbalances of power. Rather than striving for distinction and difference, Paul's peers regularly appeal for conformity, a social order that recognizes contributions made to the social good, and a fairer distribution of resources.

270 Questions of Moral Motivation

This is not to suggest that the derogatory language detailed in this book should be simply overlooked or neutralized. There will be times when racism, homophobia, sexism, ableism, classism, and so on are clear moral motivations, and in such cases, some form of intervention is warranted. However, lawyers could certainly be more attuned to the complexities of moral motivation in conditions of framework plurality as presented in this book, and more responsive to these contemporary challenges. I hope that the discussions initiated across these chapters offer a point of departure for fine-tuning our attention to such matters.

Hard Goodbye

My father lived a Corby life, and he died a Corby death. A bad cough in spring led to an X-ray and MRI scan by summer. My father was diagnosed with advanced lung cancer on 19 August 2015 at the age of sixty-eight; eleven years younger than the national life expectancy, but average for his area. The mobile shop ran its last round on 31 August 2015.

My father's body shut down with the van. He was never one for rules or conventions, and he characteristically opted for cannabis oil over palliative chemotherapy or radiotherapy. He purchased a small cannabis farm's worth of street (high-THC) cannabis and researched his preferred method of oil extraction. Funnels, beakers, and slow burners in place, my father set to the task of making oil. He was in his element: for the last time in his life, Paul was able to put his chemistry skills to use.

The cannabis oil was the first illegal drug my father tried. Mental illness is endemic in the family, and he frequently described himself as balancing on sanity's edge. When he started taking the cannabis oil, I learnt what he meant. The drug hit him hard, and for a time he was bedridden, floating away in his own incommunicable world. All I could do was sit at his bedside, and force back stinging tears.

My eyes absorbed the room that bound him. My father deserved more than this. It was a room under a state of redecoration for nearing two decades. The carpet had been ripped up, but never replaced, and woodchip paper had been pasted to the walls, but never painted. A patch of the grey wallpaper near the door had worn away, revealing original yellow paint from the council's 1950s decor. Cracks lined the ceiling's edge, and an unsettlingly large rectangular fracture crept across the entranceway. Above my head, part of the ceiling was patched up with plywood and Polyfilla from last winter's leak. The fixture swelled from the roof like a small island balanced on a dull white sea. *The cancer spread into his neck*.

A husky coughing grabbed me back into the room.

My father had woken from his confused haze, gasping for unreachable breath. He deserved more than this.

A Precarious Life. Roxana Willis, Oxford University Press. © Roxana Willis 2023.
DOI: 10.1093/oso/9780198855149.003.0018

Conclusion: Life after Loss

Now at the end of our enquiry into precariat life, let us return to the homicide that opened the book and reflect on a thicker account of what occurred. To recap, Adam owed Martin money, which via a chain of events led Martin to assault Adam fatally in an episode of prolonged violence on the Lincoln estate. At the time of the attack, Adam lived with drug addiction and the money he owed related to an unpaid drug debt. First, we might consider structural factors that contributed to the circumstances of the event. How did Adam and Martin's experiences at school and work impact on the event that occurred; how did government policy on education, de-industrialization, deregulation at work, housing privatization, and welfare provisions affect the choices they were able to make during their lifetimes; how much structural and symbolic violence were Adam and Martin exposed to by that point in time; and, relatedly, how much were they affected by the classed distinctions of 'junkie' and 'tramp'? Mindful of these structural factors, does the criminal law's focus on the unlawful act(s) and mindset of Martin at the time of the homicide fully capture the causal factors of the event and does the law succeed in preventing an event like this from reoccurring?

We can reach a further layer of analysis by situating the attack within the framework of mutuality, which reveals local meaning about what occurred. In this book, we have seen that sharing practices are the substance of an informal support system upon which Paul and his multigenerational peers depend, guided by the framework of mutuality. In accordance with mutuality, the harm of not repaying a £20 debt stretches beyond the monetary value of the amount owed, for it risks undermining relationships of trust, and in turn damages informal mechanisms of support. What is more, when someone fails to demonstrate themselves as trustworthy, they risk being classified as a 'bad person'. It is possible that Martin treated Adam as fitting this immoral classification—indeed, Martin was reported to have made Adam repeatedly say, 'I'm a bad person' during the attack. Compounding

A Precarious Life. Roxana Willis, Oxford University Press. © Roxana Willis 2023.
DOI: 10.1093/oso/9780198855149.003.0019

Conclusion: Life after Loss **273**

this, Adam's struggle with addiction risked his being categorized as an outsider, which may have reduced the channels of support he could draw on to escape the episode of violence on the estate.

From this perspective, we gain a fuller understanding of the nature of wrongdoing when someone fails to repay £20 as promised. However, the state cannot be relied on to redress this wrong for several reasons: the state only enforces particular moneylending arrangements; the money owed relates to an illicit drug economy; and the law of theft fails to capture relational harm, as examined in Chapter 4. Although Paul's neighbours have developed creative strategies to move the state to respond to issues of local concern—such as the use of vigilantism and making rights-based claims to address deeper relational problems—strategies to engage the state in the resolution of informal debts have not developed in the same way. At most, a person who owes money might employ the services of the state to protect them from immediate threats of violence, either by phoning the police (which was often done by female family members in Paul's community) or by running to places such as the local police station for safety until able to gather the support of others. But even when participants in Paul's community attempt to engage the police in moments of need, precariously positioned individuals might be dismissed and denied the help they seek due to being treated as 'rough' and undeserving of state resources. In this classed context, both Martin and Adam likely faced barriers to accessing state support which might have resolved the dispute in non-violent ways.

Without recourse to the state for assistance, Martin attempts to settle the debt using local methods of resolution. This includes public shaming, in Adam being paraded to different houses on the estate and made to repeatedly admit to being 'bad'. In addition to the shaming ritual, Martin used violence. At this point, Adam should have been able to contact the police. While limited force may have been an acceptable method to communicate the wrong of not repaying a debt in accordance with local norms, the amount of force Martin used was disproportionate and constituted an illegitimate display of violence. The length of the attack, the use of captivity, Adam's being outnumbered, the degree of force used, the repeat nature of the attacks, and the humiliation involved all indicate that this was not a 'fair fight' but a form of bullying, which Paul and his friends, living within a framework of mutuality, explicitly condemn. The use of excessive force in this case exemplifies the risks of using violent methods to resolve disputes, exposing the parties to the whims of moral luck in relation to the injury caused. When a person allows themselves to 'go mental' and releases the

274 Conclusion: Life after Loss

pains of precarity in a flash of violence, they risk going too far and being unable to stop.

We might question why no-one on the estate tried to intervene in the attack, since, as I have suggested, the collective instinct is to prevent abuses of power and bullying. I've noted that Adam's drug addiction, which was compounded by his not being 'born and bred', may have placed him in an outsider category. Moreover, the pool of persons who observed the bullying was limited in this instance—perhaps were an older arbitrator on the estate able to intervene, the attack would have been stopped. Here, I recall the times my father managed to defuse extreme violence on the estate, and I wonder if the attack had happened a few years earlier, when Paul was still running the mobile grocery shop into the late hours, whether Martin or Adam would have used the van for assistance. This points to a significant limitation with the informal support structure on which Paul and his peers depend—the webs of support are fragile and there are gaps through which people fall. When deaths and losses occur in the community, the fabric of support tears and opens larger gaps, which in some respects may never be repaired.

This case reveals that there is a great deal more to a criminal offence than what the individual actor does. Focusing only on the individual, while expedient, misrecognizes the event and leaves a great amount unaddressed. As I see it, individualizing a crime involves arbitrarily eliminating from view a whole host of contributory factors—what Achille Mbembe (2017: 17) describes in a different context as a 'relative closing of the mind' of a wilful sort. This relative closing of the mind has the consequence that a group of individuals, who are often among the least advantaged and most harmed by the British class system, carry the full weight and responsibility of poverty, inequality, and continued use of interpersonal violence. Conditions which nurture violence—in an assortment of forms that feed into one another on a continuum—are left untouched, and the shortfalls of society and the failings of the state continue. An account that stretches beyond the individual offers a more comprehensive explanation for the loss of Adam's life, as well as why Adam's untimely death was not the first distressing killing on my estate, nor the last. Without significant change, more avoidable losses are to come.

The framework of mutuality provides us with a thicker description of a given conflict; it shows the significance of relational harm and can account for why sectors of British society continue to use violence and other informal measures to resolve disputes. In this way, situating violence and conflict within the framework of mutuality helps explain why certain forms of harm reoccur and reveals other pressing harms yet to be addressed by the legal system. Importantly, positioning a conflict within the moral framework of mutuality need not exculpate individual actors. We may still recognize a person as having violated norms of both the framework of autonomy and mutuality, which arguably necessitates an individualized form of redress. Yet thinking about conflicts in the context of a mutuality framework, and reflecting on why such a framework subsists and makes these conflicts intelligible, also illuminates the fact that a focus on the individual actor alone is often an insufficient response. Hence, as well as holding Martin responsible for the crime, Adam's death presents an important opportunity to apportion some responsibility to the state, which likewise makes visible larger, structural factors that need redress.

One response to the concerns raised by this study might be to appeal for the state to support all persons in Britain, regardless of their socioeconomic status, to manifest their autonomy. According to that vision, all class sectors could, say, rely on the state to enact their will, regardless of their economic power, reducing the necessity for informal support mechanisms and leading to the elimination or substantial reduction of class-based hierarchies. On this (rather utopian) aspiration, the normative value of autonomy is recognized and valorized; the critical aim is simply to include more people within its reaches (see Nussbaum, 2009). However, subaltern groups and scholars have made compelling arguments for structural changes in this spirit for several centuries, but full inclusion, or anything close to it, is yet to come to fruition. While civil rights victories have allowed greater numbers to strive for autonomy—for example, in gaining more comprehensive individualized rights—many groups remain excluded, especially racialized non-citizens.

I am led, then, to question whether a liberal society could ever be fully or greatly inclusive, noting also its having been predicated on exclusion from the outset. Prior to the emergence of the autonomous ideal, it did not make sense for groups defined by gender, sexuality, race, class, disability, and so on to appeal for inclusion. The need for inclusion has only become comprehensible in conditions where certain groups are first excluded. Since the autonomous moral figure is held against those who are cast as immoral in its shadow, whether it be for exhibiting features of dependency or making what are deemed to be bad choices, we might wonder whether legislation and political structures situated within the framework of autonomy are inherently exclusionary and require substantive reform.

276 Conclusion: Life after Loss

Another response to the concerns raised in this book—the one I find most compelling—is to suggest the legal system better accommodate mutuality in its deliberations about wrongdoing and in the assignment of criminal responsibility, in a comparable way to how those in Paul's community manage moral deliberations, detailed in Chapter 7. There is a great deal to be said about how the criminal law could be re-made to make room for mutuality; a task I begin here by sketching some preliminary thoughts and hope to continue in future work and discussions. Firstly, lawyers could be more attuned to the different moral outlooks already encompassed by the modern criminal law, as revealed by the work of Nicola Lacey, Lindsay Farmer, and Arlie Loughnan, among others. Equipped with the knowledge contained in this emerging body of work, we could move beyond capacity conceptions of responsibility, which currently dominate mainstream criminal law scholarship, and engage more deeply with other forms, such as character responsibility, responsibility for harmful consequences (Lacey, 2016), and 'relations of responsibility' (Loughnan, 2019). And rather than simply arguing for law reform to eliminate these alternative constructions of responsibility, as some mainstream criminal lawyers might argue in pursuit of a pure subjective model of criminal law, normative plurality could be more widely embraced and indeed taught to trainee lawyers. When as lawyers we move beyond the individual offender as the primary concern, we allow for considerations of mutuality—about the significance of relationships, relational harms, and the wider context in which offences occur—to come into focus.

Further to our recognizing the ways the criminal law already does provide space for mutuality, we might reflect on reforming the criminal law to better accommodate mutuality within its conception of wrongdoing. For example, building on the discussion of theft in Chapter 4, we could suggest that lawyers recognize the existence and significance of a relationship, and a relevant breach of trust, as an aggravating factor in cases of theft—just as the co-occurrence of an assault elevates the offence of theft to that of robbery. This proposal echoes calls by Jonathan Herring (2019: ch 7) for the criminal law to acknowledge the importance of what he terms the 're-lational self', in contrast to the so-called individual self, and to accordingly widen the scope of relational abuse in the criminal law and related offences. Although this and similar suggestions might be tempting, I suspect the approach here creates further problems: such reforms, if implemented, would extend the reach of the criminal law, inevitably beckoning further state intrusion into the lives of communities already disempowered by the imbalanced application of the criminal law. In this punitive context, a good operating principle for scholars would be to accommodate mutuality in ways that aim to reduce rather than to extend the remit of the criminal law in the lives of socio-economically disadvantaged and racialized communities. For example, keeping a mutuality framework in mind allows criminal lawyers to contest the tendency to treat collective activity as exceptional and as an aggravating factor of a crime (such as in parasitic liability and public order offences), rather than its being the norm for many groups (cf. Herring, 2019: 185–94). Moreover, a contextual understanding of precarity and how mutuality ideals may guide action—as a matter of moral motivation, which we discussed in Chapter 8—might indicate that current legal interpretations of the use of hostile terms may be too simplistic.

Another way to counter the disproportionate reach of the criminal law in the lives of the least advantaged would be to expand our understanding of the crimes of state and corporate enterprises, crimes which are currently under addressed. As I argued in Chapter 6, it is partly the consequence of the criminal law's being so firmly grounded in a framework of autonomy, which centres the individual, that it fails to notice the wider factors that motivate interpersonal violence. By taking up the perspective of those guided by a framework of mutuality, we can more readily see the forms of violence that pre-exist and pre-empt so much of the violence that the criminal law does recognize. One course that we might take to open criminal law to these background factors is to broaden its conception of violence beyond the interpersonal to include symbolic and structural forms. This could involve proactive enforcement of health and safety laws in employment and housing, so that the police can be called on to respond to complainants at the point of a regulatory breach, hence relieving victims of the injuries they suffer and the burdens of civil redress they must pursue after the fact. Corporations which cause grievous bodily injury and mass homicide ought to be met with criminal sanctions: civil compensation in such cases is not enough. Symbolic violence is more challenging to address because it has become so deeply engrained in British society; however, since the criminal law has been instrumental in the moralization of poverty, which is core to the practice of distinction, there is arguably a case for the criminal law to proactively redress this problem. For instance, perhaps the criminal law should pursue a new figure of immorality: instead of disproportionately targeting the most socio-economically disadvantaged—the immoral poor—the focus of law reform could turn to those who have been the most active polluters and drivers of climate change, and hence those

278 Conclusion: Life after Loss

who are responsible for the social harms that are likely to plague the next generations.

The goods strongly valued in a framework of mutuality, and the norms derivative from them, present crucial sources of wisdom that could inspire an improved picture of the social good. Indeed, the law operates with, and legal theory has recommended for too long, a vision of the social good which centres autonomy to the exclusion of other values. Given the implicit wisdom contained within a framework of mutuality, it is likely that law and legal theory (and in turn, social outcomes) would benefit from re-orienting more towards mutuality. These values—fostered among diverse social groups to varying degrees and in various forms—include, among others, resourcefulness, being comfortable living without excess, demonstrating solidarity, engaging in a range of sharing practices, supporting relationships of trust and care, and countering power imbalances and abuses of power. We ignore the significance of these values, and the need to incorporate and account for them to some degree within legal institutions, at our peril.

There is, lastly, a deeper aspect to mutuality which makes embracing it worthwhile for the legal system. Mutuality aligns with our ontological nature of co-dependence and better captures the interconnections of human beings than the value of autonomy as presently understood does. By situating their concerns and priorities within the framework of autonomy, lawyers have been able to explain social phenomena primarily at the level of the individual and, although this level of explanation has made the system workable, have constructed partial accounts of the social reality in which judges and lawyers operate. Relatedly, legal thought has leant towards essentialist understandings of the social world in its perpetuating the reproduction of fixed categorizations of people—even when we grow increasingly aware that the lives and fates of human beings are intimately connected (see Gilroy, 1993; Gopal, 2019; Hall, 1991; Lowe, 2015). As I see it, then, it is vital for criminal lawyers to engage with the framework of mutuality, and with it, the complexities of social reality, so that the criminal law contributes to the shaping of a more just future, as it attempted to do in the nineteenth century (see Farmer, 2016; Wiener, 1994).

This is not to suggest that we should completely dispose of the value of autonomy. Important gains have been made by conceptualizing the self as autonomous, and there are goods contained under the framework of autonomy which we ought to retain. For instance, many in contemporary Britain (and further afield) would appreciate greater control over their life,

Conclusion: Life after Loss   **279**

a degree of privacy, more opportunity to pursue and shape their will, greater access to better qualitative choices, and so on. Promises such as these need not be incompatible with greater recognition of mutuality values.

As a closing thought, throughout this study Paul and his precariously situated peers remind us that self-interest and economic exploitation are not the only values British society recognizes—other possibilities exist and are ripe for cultivating. But crucially, we require a shift in how the precariat is perceived and treated. Rather than mere objects to be exploited, excluded, or demonized, those raised in conditions of material hardship possess a wealth of wisdom and knowledge, which collective survival would benefit from our heeding. However, if structural change is not forthcoming, the precariat class is not fully dependent on the social order as it presently stands. Even if progressive social change fails to materialize, precariat know-how about the real world will inevitably be put to its own uses: the precariat has what it takes to subsist and survive the difficult times that lie ahead, notwithstanding the injustice of their failing to be accounted for and understood.

References

Abbey R (2000) *Charles Taylor*. Teddington, UK: Acumen.

Abel R (1995) Contested communities. *Journal of Law and Society* 22(1): 113–26.

Addis I and Mercer R (2000) *Corby Remembers: A Century of Memories, 100 Years of Change*. Kettering: Diametric Publications.

Ahmed S (2000) *Strange Encounters*. London: Routledge.

Ahmed S (2007) A phenomenology of whiteness. *Feminist Theory* 8(2): 149–68.

Ahmed S (2014) *The Cultural Politics of Emotion*. 2nd edn. Edinburgh: Edinburgh University Press.

Alexander C (2000) *The Asian Gang: Ethnicity, Identity, Masculinity*. Oxford: Berg 3PL.

Alexander M (2010) *The New Jim Crow*. New York: The New Press.

Aliverti A (2012) Making people criminal: The role of the criminal law in immigration enforcement. *Theoretical Criminology* 16(4): 417–34.

Allen K (2017) 'I wonder if it's worth getting up': life in Corby, the debt capital of Britain. *The Guardian*, 29 July. Available at: https://www.theguardian.com/money/2017/jul/29/corby-debt-capital-britain-wonder-if-worth-getting-up-borrowing (accessed 18 September 2021).

Allen T (2012) *The Invention of the White Race, Volume 1*. London: Verso Books.

Alvarez A and Bachman R (2008) *Violence: The Enduring Problem*. Los Angeles: Sage.

Amussen S (1995) Punishment, discipline, and power: The social meanings of violence in early modern England. *Journal of British Studies* 34(1): 1–34.

Anderson B (1991) *Imagined Communities Revisited*. London: Verso Books.

Anderson E (1999) *Code of the Street*. New York: Norton.

Appleford K (2016) Being seen in your pyjamas: The relationship between fashion, class, gender and space. *Gender, Place & Culture* 23(2): 162–80.

Archer M (2007) *Making Our Way through the World: Human Reflexivity and Social Mobility*. Cambridge: CUP.

Ashworth A (1986) Punishment and compensation: Victims, offenders and the state. *Oxford Journal of Legal Studies* 6(1): 86.

Ashworth A (1989) Towards a theory of criminal legislation. *Criminal Law Forum* 1(1): 41–63.

Ashworth A (1993) Some doubts about restorative justice. *Criminal Law Forum* 4(2): 277–99.

Ashworth A and Horder J (2013) *Principles of Criminal Law*. 7th edn. Oxford: OUP.

Ashworth A and Zedner L (2014) *Preventive Justice*. Oxford: OUP.

Atkinson W (2010) *Class, Individualization and Late Modernity: In Search of the Reflexive Worker*. Basingstoke: Palgrave Macmillan.

282 References

Auyero J, Bourgois P, and Scheper-Hughes N (eds) (2015) *Violence at the Urban Margins*. Oxford: OUP.

Back L (1996) *New Ethnicities and Urban Culture*. London: UCL Press.

Bagley A (2020) Corby smoking rates top national table again with Wellingborough not far behind. *Northamptonshire Telegraph*, 7 August. Available at: https://www.northantstelegraph.co.uk/news/people/corby-smoking-rates-top-national-table-again-wellingborough-not-far-behind-2934884 (accessed 18 September 2021).

Bagley A (2021) Corby NHS project to offer free lung 'MOT' in bid to catch cancer earlier. 28 April. Available at: https://www.northantstelegraph.co.uk/health/corby-nhs-project-to-offer-free-lung-mot-in-bid-to-catch-cancer-earlier-3215653 (accessed 18 September 2021).

Baker L (1998) *From Savage to Negro: Anthropology and the Construction of Race, 1896–1954*. University of California Press.

Balazs G (1999) Rehabilitation. In: Bourdieu P (ed) *The Weight of the World: Social Suffering in Contemporary Society* (tr. P Ferguson). UK: Alhoda, 95–105.

Balchin P (1985) *Housing Policy: An Introduction*. London: Croom Helm.

Ball SJ (2003) *Class Strategies and the Education Market: The Middle Classes and Social Advantage*. London: Routledge.

Barr B, Taylor-Robinson D, Loopstra R, et al. (2016) 'First, do no harm': Are disability assessments associated with adverse trends in mental health? A longitudinal ecological study. *Journal of Epidemiol Community Health* 70(4): 339–45.

Baum PF (1922) Judas's red hair. *The Journal of English and Germanic Philology* 21(3): 520–9.

Bauman Z (1991) *Modernity and the Holocaust*. Cambridge: Polity Press.

Bauman Z (2000) *Liquid Modernity*. Cambridge: Polity Press.

BBC (2013a) Class calculator: Can I have no job or money and still be middle class? Available at: http://www.bbc.co.uk/news/magazine-21953364 (accessed 14 January 2016).

BBC (2013b) Lab UK—The Great British Class Survey. Available at: https://www.bbc.co.uk/news/special/2013/newsspec_5093/index.stm (accessed 01 December 2022).

BBC News (2012) Corby council sold Tesco land 'too cheaply'. 11 June. Northampton. Available at: https://www.bbc.co.uk/news/uk-england-northamptonshire-18392363 (accessed 18 September 2021).

BBC News (2013) Prisoner Lee Foye loses jail murder conviction appeal. UK. Available at: https://www.bbc.co.uk/news/uk-england-beds-bucks-herts-22337439 (accessed 18 September 2021).

BBC News (2014) Corby's Solway Foods: Factory to shut with 900 jobs lost. 24 March. Available at: https://www.bbc.co.uk/news/uk-england-northamptonshire-26720011 (accessed 18 September 2021).

BBC News (2015) Camp Brookfield protesters leave site. 2 April. Northampton. Available at: https://www.bbc.co.uk/news/uk-england-northamptonshire-32162710 (accessed 18 September 2021).

References   283

BBC News (2018) Corby baseball bat attack victim Francis Gillespie died after 'decline'. 16 May. Northampton. Available at: https://www.bbc.com/news/uk-engl and-northamptonshire-44142953 (accessed 18 September 2021).

Beattie J (1986) *Crime and the Courts in Early Modern England, 1660–1800.* Princeton, NJ: Princeton University Press.

Beck U (1992) *Risk Society: Towards a New Modernity* (tr. M Ritter). Newbury Park, CA: Sage Publications.

Beck U and Camiller P (2000) *The Brave New World of Work.* Cambridge: CUP.

Beier AL (1985) *Masterless Men: The Vagrancy Problem in England 1560–1640.* London: Methuen & Co. Ltd.

Beier AL (2005) Identity, language, and resistance in the making of the Victorian 'criminal class': Mayhew's convict revisited. *Journal of British Studies* 44(3): 499–515.

Bell D (1993) *Communitarianism and Its Critics.* Cambridge: CUP.

Bell M (2016) Situational trust: How disadvantaged mothers reconceive legal cynicism. *Law and Society Review* 60(2): 314–47.

Bennett T, Savage M, Silva EB, et al. (2009) *Culture, Class, Distinction.* Abingdon: Routledge.

Berg MT and Stewart EA (2013) Street Culture and Crime. In: Cullen FT and Wilcox P (eds) *The Oxford Handbook of Criminological Theory.* Oxford: OUP 370–88.

Bhabha H (1984) Of Mimicry and man: The ambivalence of colonial discourse. October 28. *Discipleship: A Special Issue on Psychoanalysis* 28(Spring): 125–33.

Bhabha H (2004) *The Location of Culture.* London: Routledge Classics.

Bhambra GK (2022) Relations of extraction, relations of redistribution: Empire, nation, and the construction of the British welfare state. *The British Journal of Sociology* 73(1): 4–15.

Bhandar B (2018) *Colonial Lives of Property: Law, Land, and Racial Regimes of Ownership.* Durham: Duke University Press.

Bhopal K (2011) 'What about us?' Gypsies, travellers and 'white racism' in secondary schools in England. *International Studies in Sociology of Education* 21(4): 315–29.

Bindman D (2002) *Ape to Apollo: Aesthetics and the Idea of Race in the 18th Century.* Ithaca, NY: Cornell University Press.

Blackledge A (2001) The wrong sort of capital? Bangladeshi women and their children's schooling in Birmingham, U.K. *International Journal of Bilingualism* 5(3): 345–69.

Bloodworth J (2016) *The Myth of Meritocracy: Why Working-Class Kids Still Get Working-Class Jobs.* London: Biteback Publishing.

Bonnett A (2000) *White Identities: Historical and International Perspectives.* Harlow: Prentice Hall.

Booth W (1890) *In Darkest England: And the Way Out.* London: Salvation Army.

Bottero W (2009) Class in the 21st Century. In: Sveinsson K (ed) *Who Cares About the White Working Class?* London: Runnymede Trust 7–15.

Boughton J (2018) *Municipal Dreams: The Rise and Fall of Council Housing.* London: Verso Books.

284 References

Bourdieu P (1977) *Outline of a Theory of Practice*. Cambridge: CUP.

Bourdieu P (1984) *Distinction: A Social Critique of the Judgement of Taste* (tr. R Nice). Oxford: Routledge & Kegan Paul Ltd.

Bourdieu P (1986) The Forms of Capital. In: Szeman I and Kaposy T (eds) *Cultural Theory: An Anthology*. [2011] Chichester: Wiley-Blackwell 81–93.

Bourdieu P (1989) Social space and symbolic power. *Sociological theory* 7(1): 14–25.

Bourdieu P (1990) *The Logic of Practice*. Cambridge: Policy Press.

Bourdieu P (1991) *Language and Symbolic Power* (trs. G Raymond and M Adamson). Cambridge: Policy Press.

Bourdieu P (1996) *The State Nobility*. Cambridge: Policy Press.

Bourdieu P (1998a) *Acts of Resistance: Against the Tyranny of the Market*. New York: The New Press.

Bourdieu P (1998b) *Practical Reason*. Cambridge: Polity.

Bourdieu P (1999) *The Weight of the World: Social Suffering in Contemporary Society* (tr. P Ferguson). Cambridge: Polity Press.

Bourdieu P (2000) *Pascalian Meditations* (tr. R Nice). California: Stanford University Press.

Bourdieu P and Wacquant LJD (1992) *An Invitation to Reflexive Sociology*. Cambridge: Polity Press.

Bourgois P (1995) *In Search of Respect: Selling Crack in El Barrio*. Cambridge: CUP.

Bourgois P (2004) The Continuum of Violence in War and Peace: Post-Cold War Lessons from El Salvador. In: Scheper-Hughes N and Bourgois P (eds) *Violence in War and Peace: An Anthology*. Malden, MA: Blackwell Publishing 425–34.

Box S (1983) *Power, Crime and Mystification*. London: Tavistock.

Box S (1987) *Recession, Crime and Punishment*. London: Macmillan.

Braithwaite J (1989) *Crime, Shame and Reintegration*. Cambridge: Cambridge Paperback Library.

Bregman R (2020) *Humankind: A Hopeful History*. London: Bloomsbury Publishing.

Broodryk J (2002) *Ubuntu: Life Lessons from Africa*. Pretoria: Ubuntu School of Philosophy.

Brown W (2019) *In the Ruins of Neoliberalism: The Rise of Antidemocratic Politics in the West*. New York: Columbia University Press.

Buckley C (2010) *Thank You for Smoking: A Novel*. New York: Random House.

Campbell C (2015) Popular punitivism: Finding a balance between the politics, presentation, and fear of crime. *Sociology Compass* 9(3): 180–95.

Carlen P (1992) *Truancy: The Politics of Compulsory Schooling*. Buckingham: Open University Press.

Chabal P and Daloz J-P (1999) *Africa Works: Disorder Ad Political Instrument*. Indiana: James Currey & Indiana University Press.

Chandola T and Zhang N (2018) Re-employment, job quality, health and allostatic load biomarkers: prospective evidence from the UK Household Longitudinal Study. *International Journal of Epidemiology* 47(1): 47–57.

Charlesworth SJ (2000) *A Phenomenology of Working-Class Experience*. Cambridge: CUP.

References 285

Christin R (1999) A Silent Witness. In: Bourdieu P (ed) *The Weight of the World: Social Suffering in Contemporary Society* (tr. P Ferguson). Cambridge: Polity Press 354–60.

Christman, J. (2009). *The Politics of Persons: Individual Autonomy and Sociohistorical Selves*. Cambridge: CUP.

Cohen AK (1955) *Delinquent Boys; the Culture of the Gang*. New York: Free Press.

Cohen G (2009) *Why Not Socialism?* Oxford: Princeton University Press.

Cohen GA (2017) Capitalism, Freedom, and the Proletariat. In: Miller D (ed) *Liberty Reader*. Abingdon: Routledge 163–82.

Cole I and Furbey R (1994) *The Eclipse of Council Housing*. London: Routledge.

Coleman JS (1988) Social Capital in the Creation of Human Capital. *American Journal of Sociology* 94: S95–S120.

Coleman JS (1990) *Foundations of Social Theory*. Cambridge, MA: Harvard University Press.

Comaroff J and Comaroff JL (eds) (2006a) *Law and Disorder in the Postcolony*. Chicago: University of Chicago Press.

Comaroff JL and Comaroff J (2006b) Law and Disorder in the Postcolony: An Introduction In: Comaroff J and Comaroff JL (eds) *Law and Disorder in the Postcolony*. Chicago: University of Chicago Press 1–56.

Conley D, Domingue B, Cesarini D, et al. (2015) Is the effect of parental education on offspring biased or moderated by genotype? *Sociological Science* 2(82).

Conley J and O'Barr W (1990) *Rules versus Relationships: The Ethnography of Legal Discourse*. Chicago: University of Chicago Press.

Cooper V and Whyte D (eds) (2017) *The Violence of Austerity*. London: Pluto Press.

Cope Z (2015) *Divided World Divided Class: Global Political Economy and the Stratification of Labour under Capitalism*. 2nd edn. Canada: Kersplebedeb.

Corby Borough Council (2007) Local Development Framework for North Northamptonshire: Corby Borough Kingswood Area Action Plan. Preferred Options. Atkins.

Corby Development and Corby District Council (1977) Report on Kingswood Neighbourhood Corby. Available from Corby Library.

Corby Development Corporation (1965) Corby New Town Extension: Master Plan Report. CDC: Corby.

Corby Development Corporation (1976) Items raised by Kingswood Tenants' and Residents' Association. Inter Departmental Notice from Housing Manager to Deputy Housing Manager.

Corby District Council (1989) Corby: A Strategy for the Nineties. Available from Corby Library.

CPS (2019) Theft Act Offences. Available at: https://www.cps.gov.uk/legal-guidance/theft-act-offences (accessed 18 September 2021).

Crawford A (2002) The State, Community and Restorative Justice: Heresy, Nostalgia and Butterfly Collecting. In: Walgrave L (ed) *Restorative Justice and the Law*. Cullompton: Willan 101–29.

Crawford A and Clear TR (2001) Community justice: transforming communities through restorative justice? In: Bazemore G and Schiff M (eds) *Restorative*

286 References

Community Justice: Repairing Harm and Transforming Communities. London: Anderson Publishing Co. 127–49.

Crenshaw K (1989) Demarginalizing the intersection of race and sex: A black feminist critique of antidiscrimination doctrine, feminist theory and antiracist politics. *University of Chicago Legal Forum*: 139–67.

Cresswell T (2001) *The Tramp in America*. London: Reaktion Books.

Cronin K (2014a) Notorious Corby murderer Lee Foye killed prison inmate. Available at: http://web.archive.org/web/20170214102401/http://www.northan tstelegraph.co.uk/news/notorious-corby-murderer-lee-foye-killed-prison-inm ate-1-6019025 (accessed 09 December 2022).

Cronin K (2014b) Turbulent history of Corby's Canada Square. *Northamptonshire Telegraph—'Retro'* (Thursday, April 17): 30.

Crossley S (2018) *Troublemakers: The Construction of 'Troubled Families' as a Social Problem*. Bristol: Policy Press.

CRPD (2017) *Concluding observations on the initial report of the United Kingdom of Great Britain and Northern Ireland*. 3 October. United Nations Committee on the Rights of Persons with Disabilities. Available at: http://docstore.ohchr.org/ SelfServices/FilesHandler.ashx?enc=6QkG1d%2fPPRiCAqhKb7yhspCUnZh K1jU66fLQJyHIkqMIT3RDaLiqzhH8tVNxhro6S657eVNwuqlzu0xvsQUeh REyYEQD%2bldQaLP31QDpRcmG35KYFtgGyAN%2baB7cyky7 (accessed 18 September 2021).

Crump J (2002) Deconcentration by demolition: public housing, poverty, and urban policy. *Environment and Planning D: Society and Space* 20(5): 581–96.

Cunneen C (2005) Thinking Critically about Restorative Justice. In: McLaughlin E, Fergusson R, Hughes G, et al. (eds) *Restorative Justice: Critical Issues*. London: Sage Publications 194.

Dalmiya V (2016) *Caring to Know: Comparative Care Ethics, Feminist Epistemology, and the Mahābhārata*. Oxford: OUP.

Darwin C (2015) *The Expression of the Emotions in Man and Animals*. Chicago: University of Chicago Press.

Davidoff L and Hall C (2013) *Family Fortunes: Men and Women of the English Middle Class 1780–1850*. London: Routledge.

Davies R (2016) How the town of Corby dusted off the ashes of post-industrial decay. *The Guardian*, 27 May. Available at: https://www.theguardian.com/uk-news/2016/may/27/corby-northamptonshire-twin-shijiazhuang-china-fastest-growing (accessed 12 September 2016).

Davis M (2018) Shock figures reveal Corby is the suicide capital of England. *The Daily Mail*, 2 March. Available at: https://www.dailymail.co.uk/health/arti cle-5454815/Shock-figures-reveal-suicide-capital-England.html (accessed 18 September 2021).

Day G (2001) *Class*. London: Routledge.

de Sousa Santos B (2015) *Epistemologies of the South: Justice against Epistemicide*. Abingdon: Routledge.

de Sousa Santos B (2018) *The End of the Cognitive Empire: The Coming of Age of Epistemologies of the South*. Durham: Duke University Press.

References 287

Dean H and Taylor-Gooby P (1992) *Dependency Culture: The Explosion of a Myth.* London: Routledge.

DeFilippis J (2001) The myth of social capital in community development. *Housing Policy Debate* 12(4): 781–806.

Degnen C (2005) Relationality, place, and absence: a three-dimensional perspective on social memory. *The Sociological Review* 53(4): 729–44.

Degnen C (2013) 'Knowing', absence, and presence: the spatial and temporal depth of relations. *Environment and Planning D: Society and Space* 31(3): 554–70.

Delgado R (2000) Prosecuting violence: A colloquy on race, community, and justice. *Stanford Law Review* 52: 751–74.

Dennis N, Henriques F, and Slaughter C (1956) *Coal Is Our Life: An Analysis of a Yorkshire Mining Community.* London: Eyre & Spottiswoode.

Desmond M (2016) *Evicted: Poverty and Profit in the American City.* London: Allen Lane.

Dickens C (2003) The Noble Savage. In: Harlow B and Carter M (eds) *Archives of Empire: Volume 2. The Scramble for Africa.* New York: Duke University Press 134–40.

Didier E (2018) *Returning to Reims.* London: Penguin.

Dorling D (2016) Brexit: The decision of a divided country. *BMJ* 354: i3697.

Dorling D and Tomlinson S (2019) *Rule Britannia: Brexit and the End of Empire.* London: Biteback Publishing.

Du Bois WEB (1917) The Negro's Fatherland. *The Survey* 39(Oct 1917–Mar 1918): 141.

Du Bois WEB (1999) *The Souls of Black Folks* (ed H Gates). NY: Norton.

Du Bois WEB (2007) *Black Reconstruction in America.* Oxford: OUP.

Dubber M (2005) *The Police Power: Patriarchy and the Foundations of American Government.* New York: Columbia University Press.

Duff A and Von Hirsch A (1997) Responsibility, retribution and the 'voluntary': A response to Williams. *The Cambridge Law Journal* 56(1): 103–13.

Duff RA (2007) *Answering for Crime: Responsibility and Liability in the Criminal Law.* London: Hart Publishing.

Dunne M and Gazeley L (2008) Teachers, social class and underachievement. *British Journal of Sociology of Education* 29(5): 451–63.

Durkheim E (2012) *Moral Education.* New York: Courier Corporation.

Dworkin R (2013) *Taking Rights Seriously.* London: Bloomsbury.

Edwards J (2000) *Born and Bred: Idioms of Kinship and New Reproductive Technologies in England.* Oxford: OUP.

Elshtain JB (2004) Toleration, Proselytizing, and the Politics of Recognition: The Self Contested. In: Abbey R (ed) *Charles Taylor.* Cambridge: CUP 127–39.

Ericson R (2007) *Crime in an Insecure World.* Cambridge: Polity.

Etzioni A (1993) *The Spirit of Community: The Reinvention of American Society.* New York: Simon & Schuster.

Etzioni A (1996) The responsive community: A communitarian perspective. *American Sociological Review* 61(1): 1–11.

Evans G (2006) *Educational Failure and Working Class White Children in Britain.* Basingstoke: Palgrave Macmillan.

288 References

Fanon F (1968) *The Wretched of the Earth* (tr. C Farrington). NY: Grove.

Farmer L (2010) Criminal Wrongs in Historical Perspective. In: Duff RA, Farmer L, Marshall SE, Renzo M, and Tadros V (eds) *The Boundaries of the Criminal Law*. Oxford: OUP 214–37.

Farmer L (2016) *Making the Modern Criminal Law: Criminalization and Civil Order*. Series: Criminalization. Oxford: OUP.

Farmer P (2001) *Infections and Inequalities: The Modern Plagues*. Los Angeles, CA: University of California Press.

Farmer P (2004) On Suffering and Structural Violence: A View from Below. In: Scheper-Hughes N and Bourgois P (eds) *Violence in War and Peace: An Anthology*. Malden, MA: Blackwell Publishing 281–9.

Fassin D (2011) A contribution to the critique of moral reason. *Anthropological Theory* 11(4): 481–91.

Fassin D (2013) *Enforcing Order: An Ethnography of Urban Policing*. Cambridge: Polity.

Ferlay J, Shin HR, and Bray F (2010) Estimates of worldwide burden of cancer in 2008. *International Journal of Cancer* 127(12): 2893–917.

Finch L (1993) *The Classing Gaze: Sexuality, Class and Surveillance*. North Sydney: Allen & Unwin.

Finn D, Grant N, and Johnson R (1978) Social democracy, education and the crisis. *On Ideology* 10: 144.

Flynn A (2018) Aesthetic gestures, moral frameworks: Performing landlessness in Brazil. *Critique of Anthropology* 38(2): 172–87.

Forrest R and Murie A (1991) *Selling the Welfare State: The Privatisation of Public Housing*. London: Routledge.

Fraser A (2013) Street habitus: Gangs, territorialism and social change in Glasgow. *Journal of Youth Studies* 16(8): 970–85.

Fraser A and Clark A (2021) Damaged hardmen: Organised crime and the half-life of deindustrialisation. *British Journal of Sociology* 72(4): 1062–76.

Frazer E and Lacey N (1993) *The Politics of Community: A Feminist Critique of the Liberal-Communitarian Debate*. London: Harvester Wheatsheaf.

Friedman M (1989) Feminism and modern friendship: Dislocating the community. *Ethics* 99(2): 275–90.

Fyfe N and Milligan C (2003) Out of the shadows: Exploring contemporary geographies of voluntarism. *Progress in Human Geography* 27(4): 397–413.

Galtung J (1969) Violence, peace, and peace research. *Journal of Peace Research* (6): 167–91.

Gardner J (2003) The mark of responsibility. *Oxford Journal of Legal Studies* 23(2): 157–71.

Garland D (1985) *Punishment and Welfare: A History of Penal Strategies*. Aldershot: Gower.

Garland D (2001) *The Culture of Control: Crime and Social Order in Contemporary Society*. Oxford: OUP.

Garthwaite K (2016) *Hunger Pains: Life Inside Foodbank Britain*. Bristol: Policy Press.

References 289

Gazeley L (2012) The impact of social class on parent–professional interaction in school exclusion processes: Deficit or disadvantage? *International Journal of Inclusive Education* 16(3): 297–311.

Geertz C (1973) Thick Description: Toward an Interpretive Theory of Culture. In: Geertz C *The Interpretation of Cultures: Selected Essays*. New York: Basic Books 3–30.

Gest J (2016) *The New Minority*. Oxford: OUP.

Giddens A (1991) *Modernity and Self-Identity: Self and Society in the Late Modern Age*. Cambridge: Polity.

Gillies V (2005) Raising the 'meritocracy': Parenting and the individualization of social class. *Sociology* 39(5): 835–53.

Gillies V (2006) Working class mothers and school life: Exploring the role of emotional capital. *Gender and Education* 18(3): 281–93.

Gillies V (2007) *Marginalised Mothers: Exploring Working-Class Experiences of Parenting*. London: Routledge.

Gillies V and Edwards R (2006) A qualitative analysis of parenting and social capital: Comparing the work of Coleman and Bourdieu. *Qualitative Sociology Review* 2(2). Available at: http://search.proquest.com/openview/b67759f399c30 771786eeed1f5576661/1?pq-origsite=gscholar (accessed 12 September 2016).

Gilroy P (1993) *The Black Atlantic: Modernity and Double Consciousness*. London: Verso Books.

Gilroy P (2002) *There Ain't No Black in the Union Jack*. London: Routledge.

Girling E, Loader I, and Sparks R (2000) *Crime and Social Change in Middle England: Questions of Order in an English Town*. London: Routledge.

Glyn A (2006) *Capitalism Unleashed*. Oxford: OUP.

Goffman A (2015) *On the Run: Fugitive Life in an American City*. New York: Picador.

Golding P and Middleton S (1982) *Images of Welfare: Press and Public Attitudes to Poverty*. Oxford: Martin Robertson.

Goldthorpe JH (1968) *The Affluent Worker: Industrial Attitudes and Behaviour*. Cambridge: CUP Archive.

Goldthorpe JH (1998) Rational Action Theory for Sociology. *The British Journal of Sociology* 49(2): 167–92.

Gopal P (2019) *Insurgent Empire: Anticolonial Resistance and British Dissent*. London: Verso Books.

Gorard S and Siddiqui N (2018) Grammar schools in England: A new analysis of social segregation and academic outcomes. *British Journal of Sociology of Education* 39(7): 909–24.

Gould S (1996) *The Mismeasure of Man*. New York, London: WW Norton & Company.

Graeber D (2011) *Debt: The First 5000 Years*. New York and London: Melville House Publishing.

Graeber D and Wengrow D (2021) *The Dawn of Everything: A New History of Humanity*. London: Penguin.

Granovetter MS (1973) The strength of weak ties. *American Journal of Sociology* 78(6): 1360–80.

290 References

Granovetter MS (1974) *Getting a Job: A Study of Contacts and Careers*. Cambridge, MA: Harvard University Press.

Gray F (1931) *The Tramp: His Meaning and Being*. London: J. M. Dent and Sons.

Grigg-Spall I and Ireland P (1992) *The Critical Lawyers' Handbook*. London: Pluto Press.

Grundy RFB (1966) Lincoln and Brookside Spine. Corby Development Corporation (available from the Northamptonshire Record Office).

Grütters C, Guild E, Paul Minderhoud, et al. (2018) *Brexit and Migration: Civil Liberties, Justice and Home Affairs*. PE 608.835, European Parliament's Policy Department for Citizens' Rights and Constitutional Affairs, October. Policy Department for Citizens' Rights and Constitutional Affairs Directorate General for Internal Policies of the Union.

Guyer J and Belinga SE (1995) Wealth in people as wealth in knowledge: Accumulation and composition in Equatorial Africa. *The Journal of African History* 36(1): 91–120.

Hagan J (1993) The Social Embeddedness of Crime and Unemployment. *Criminology* 31: 465–92.

Haider A (2018) *Mistaken Identity: Race and Class in the Age of Trump*. London: Verso Books.

Hall C (1989) The economy of intellectual prestige: Thomas Carlyle, John Stuart Mill, and the case of Governor Eyre. *Cultural Critique* 12: 167–96.

Hall C (1992) *White, Male and Middle Class: Explorations in Feminism and History*. Cambridge: Polity Press.

Hall C (2007) *Civilising Subjects: Metropole and Colony in the English Imagination 1830–1867*. Cambridge: Polity Press.

Hall S (1991) Old and New Identities, Old and New Ethnicities. In: Morley D (ed) *Essential Essays: Identity and Diaspora*. Durham: Duke University Press 63–82.

Hall S (1996) Introduction: Who needs identity? In: Hall S and du Gay P (eds) *Questions of Cultural Identity*. London: Sage 1–17.

Hall S (2017) *The Fateful Triangle: Race, Ethnicity, Nation*. Cambridge, MA: Harvard University Press.

Hall S (2021) *The Hard Road to Renewal: Thatcherism and the Crisis of the Left*. London: Verso Books.

Hall S, Critcher C, Jefferson T, et al. (2013) *Policing the Crisis: Mugging, the State and Law and Order*. 2nd edn. London: Macmillan International Higher Education.

Hamilton HGW (1976) Kingswood Sociological Survey. Corby Development Corporation (available from the Northamptonshire Record Office).

Hancock A-M (2004) *The Politics of Disgust: The Public Identity of the Welfare Queen*. New York: New York University Press.

Hanley L (2017) *Estates: An Intimate History*. Granta Books.

Harrison F (2008) *Outsider Within: Reworking Anthropology in the Global Age*. Champaign: University of Illinois Press.

Hart HLA (1968) *Punishment and Responsibility: Essays in the Philosophy of Law*. Oxford: OUP.

Harvey D (2007) *A Brief History of Neoliberalism*. Oxford: OUP.

References 291

Hay D (1975) Property, Authority and the Criminal Law. In: Hay D, Linebaugh P, Rule JG, Thompson EP, and Winslow C *Albion's Fatal Tree: Crime and Society in Eighteenth-Century England*. New York: Pantheon 17–63.

Hay D (2004) England, 1562–1875: The Law and Its Uses. In: Hay D and Craven P (eds) *Masters, Servants, and Magistrates in Britain and the Empire, 1562–1955*. Chapel Hill, NC: The University of North Carolina Press 59–116.

Hay D and Craven P (2004) Introduction. In: Hay D and Craven P (eds) *Masters, Servants, and Magistrates in Britain and the Empire, 1562–1955*. Chapel Hill, NC: The University of North Carolina Press 1–58.

Hayes L (2017) *Stories of Care: A Labour of Law: Gender and Class at Work*. London: Springer.

Haylett C (2001) Illegitimate subjects?: Abject whites, neoliberal modernisation, and middle-class multiculturalism. *Environment and Planning D: Society and Space* 19(3): 351–70.

Heathorn S (2000) *For Home, Country, and Race: Constructing Gender, Class, and Englishness in the Elementary School, 1880–1914*. Toronto: University of Toronto Press.

Heitmeyer W and Hagan J (eds) (2003) *International Handbook of Violence Research*. Dordrecht, The Netherlands, and Boston: Kluwer.

Herring J (2019) *Law and the Relational Self*. Cambridge: CUP.

Herrnstein R and Murray C (1994) *The Bell Curve*. New York: The Free Press.

Hewitt R (2005) *White Backlash and the Politics of Multiculturalism*. Cambridge: CUP.

Hey V (2003) Joining the Club? Academia and working-class femininities. *Gender and Education* 15(3): 319–36.

Hillyard P, Pantazis C, Tombes S, et al. (eds) (2004) *Beyond Criminology: Taking Harm Seriously*. London: Pluto Press; Black Point, NS: Fernwood Publishing.

Hilts P (1996) *Smokescreen, the Truth behind the Tobacco Industry Cover-Up*. Reading, Mass: Addison Wesley.

Hobbes T (1968) *Leviathan*. Baltimore: Penguin Books.

Hobbs D, Hadfield P, Lister S, et al. (2003) *Bouncers: Violence and Governance in the Night-Time Economy*. Oxford: OUP.

Hobsbawm E (1969) *Bandits*. London: Weidenfeld & Nicolson.

Hochschild A (2016) *Strangers in Their Own Land: Anger and Mourning on the American Right*. New York: The New Press.

Hoggart R (1957) *The Uses of Literacy*. Harmondsworth: Transaction Publishers.

Holligan C (2015) Breaking the code of the street: Extending Elijah Anderson's encryption of violent street governance to retaliation in Scotland. *Journal of Youth Studies* 18(5): 634–48.

Honneth A (1995) *The Struggle for Recognition: The Moral Grammar of Social Conflicts*. Cambridge: Polity.

Hopkins E (1994) *Childhood Transformed: Working-Class Children in Nineteenth-Century England*. Manchester: Manchester University Press.

Hornberger J (2013) From general to commissioner to general—On the popular state of policing in South Africa. *Law & Social Inquiry* 38(3): 598–614.

292 References

Horvat EM, Weininger EB, and Lareau A (2003) From social ties to social capital: Class differences in the relations between schools and parent networks. *American Educational Research Journal* 40(2): 319–51.

Housing Committee (1976) 'Canada Square and Kingswood', Minutes of a Meeting of the Housing Committee, 24th September 1976, (354/76). Available from the Northamptonshire Record Office.

Housing Committee (1977) Kingswood Neighbourhood—Minutes of a Meeting of the Housing Committee. HCM 10/77 (available from the Northamptonshire Record Office).

Howard P (2012) Workplace cosmopolitanization and the power and pain of class relations at sea. *Focaal—Journal of Global and Historical Anthropology* 62: 55–69.

Howe L (1990) *Being Unemployed in Northern Ireland: An Ethnographic Study.* Cambridge: CUP.

Hudson B (1994) Punishing the Poor: A Critique of the Dominance of Legal Reasoning in Penal Policy and Practice. In: Duff A, Marshall S, Dobash RE, and Dobash RP (eds) *Penal Theory and Practice: Tradition and Innovation in Criminal Justice* Manchester: Manchester University Press 292–305.

Hursthouse R (1999) *On Virtue Ethics.* Oxford: OUP.

Hyatt S (2003) Poverty in a 'Post-Welfare' Landscape. In: Shore C and Wright S (eds) *Anthropology of Policy: Perspectives on Governance and Power.* London: Routledge 217–38.

Irwin Mitchell (2012) High Court Victory For Coke Oven Cancer Victims. Available at: https://www.irwinmitchell.com/news-and-insights/newsandmedia/2012/october/high-court-victory-for-coke-oven-cancer-victims-jq-879845.

Jaggar A (1985) *Feminist Politics and Human Nature.* Brighton: Harvester Press.

James CLR (2001) *The Black Jacobins: Toussaint L'Ouverture and the San Domingo Revolution.* London: Penguin.

Jensen T (2018) *Parenting the Crisis: The Cultural Politics of Parent-Blame.* Bristol: Policy Press.

Jones C and Murie A (2008) *The Right to Buy: Analysis and Evaluation of a Housing Policy.* New York: John Wiley & Sons.

Jones D (1970). Towards a native anthropology. *Human Organization* 29(4), 251–9.

Jones O (2012) *Chavs: The Demonization of the Working Class.* London: Verso Books.

Jones S (2013) *Outcast London: A Study in the Relationship Between Classes in Victorian Society.* London: Verso Books.

Journal of Corby Consumer Group (1969) The Consumer.

Kalb D (2009) Conversations with a Polish populist: Tracing hidden histories of globalization, class, and dispossession in postsocialism (and beyond). *American Ethnologist* 36(2): 207–23.

Kalikoff B (1987) The falling woman in three Victorian novels. *Studies in the Novel* 19(3): 357–67.

Karandinos G, Hart L, Castrillo F, et al. (2015) The Moral Economy of Violence in the US Inner City: Deadly Sociability in the Retail Narcotics Economy. In: Auvero J, Bourgois P, and Scheper-Hughes N (eds) *Violence at the Urban Margins.* Oxford: OUP 41–73.

King J (2012) *Judging Social Rights.* Cambridge: CUP.

References 293

Kingswood Working Party (1977) Main Findings, Consultations and Recommendations. Available from the Northamptonshire Record Office.

Koch I (2016) Bread-and-butter politics: Democratic disenchantment and everyday politics on an English council estate. *American Ethnologist* 42(2): 282–94.

Koch I (2017a) Moving Beyond Punitivism: Punishment, State Failure and Democracy at the Margins. *Punishment & Society* 19(2): 203–20.

Koch I (2017b) When politicians fail: Zombie democracy and the anthropology of actually existing politics. *The Sociological Review* 65(1_suppl): 105–20.

Koch I (2017c) What's in a vote? Brexit beyond culture wars. *American Ethnologist* 44(2): 225–30.

Koch I (2018a) From welfare to lawfare: environmental suffering, neighbour disputes and the law in UK social housing. *Critique of Anthropology* 38(2): 221–35.

Koch I (2018b) *Personalizing the State: An Anthropology of Law, Politics, and Welfare in Austerity Britain.* Oxford: OUP.

Kornhauser RR (1978) *Social Sources of Delinquency: An Appraisal of Analytic Models.* New edition. Chicago: University of Chicago Press.

Kubrin E and Weitzer R (2003) New directions in social disorganization theory. *Journal of Research in Crime and Delinquency* 40(4): 374–402.

Kundnani A (2007) *The End of Tolerance: Racism in 21st Century Britain.* London: Pluto.

Kundnani A (2014) *The Muslims Are Coming!: Islamophobia, Extremism, and the Domestic War on Terror.* London and New York: Verso Books.

Lacey N (1988) *State Punishment: Political Principles and Community Values.* London: Routledge.

Lacey N (2008) *Women, Crime, and Character: From Moll Flanders to Tess of the D'Urbervilles.* Oxford: OUP.

Lacey N (2009) Historicising criminalisation: Conceptual and empirical issues. *Modern Law Review* 72(6): 936–60.

Lacey N (2016) *In Search of Criminal Responsibility: Ideas, Interests, and Institutions.* Oxford: OUP.

Lacey N, Wells C, and Quick O (2003) *Reconstructing Criminal Law: Critical Perspectives on Crime and the Criminal Process.* Cambridge: CUP.

Lake M and Reynolds H (2008) *Drawing the Global Colour Line: White Men's Countries and the Question of Racial Equality.* Cambridge: CUP.

Lamont M (1992) *Money, Morals, and Manners: The Culture of the French and the American Upper-Middle Class.* Chicago: University of Chicago Press.

Lamont M (2009) *The Dignity of Working Men: Morality and the Boundaries of Race, Class, and Immigration.* Cambridge, MA: Harvard University Press.

Lansley S and Mack J (2015) *Breadline Britain: The Rise of Mass Poverty.* London: Oneworld Publications.

Lareau A (1987) Social class differences in family-school relationships: The importance of cultural capital. *Sociology of Education* 60(2): 73–85.

Lareau A (2007) Watching, Waiting, and Deciding when to Intervene. In: Weis L (ed) *The Way Class Works: Readings on School, Family, and the Economy* Abingdon: Routledge 117–33.

294 References

Lareau A (2011) *Unequal Childhoods: Class, Race, and Family Life*. 2nd edn. Berkeley: University of California Press.

Law Commission (2021) *Hate crime laws: Final report*. Law Com No 402, 6 December. Available at: https://s3-eu-west-2.amazonaws.com/lawcom-prod-storage-11jsxou24uy7q/uploads/2021/12/Hate-crime-report-accessible.pdf (accessed 10 December 2022).

Lawler S (2002) *Mothering the Self: Mothers, Daughters, Subjects*. New York: Routledge.

Lawler S (2005) Disgusted subjects: The making of middle-class identities. *The Sociological Review* 53(3): 429–46.

Lawler S (2012) White like them: Whiteness and anachronistic space in representations of the English white working class. *Ethnicities* 12(4): 409–26.

Lewis O (1963) The culture of poverty. *Society* 35(2). 1998: 7–9.

Linebaugh P and Rediker M (2012) *The Many-Headed Hydra: The Hidden History of the Revolutionary Atlantic*. London: Verso Books.

Loader I (1996) *Youth, Policing and Democracy*. London: Macmillan.

Loader I (1997) Private security and the demand for protection in contemporary Britain. *Policing and Society* 7(2): 143–62.

Loader I (2006) Fall of the 'platonic guardians': Liberalism, criminology and political responses to crime in England and Wales. *The British Journal of Criminology* 46(4): 561–86.

Loader I and Mulcahy A (2003) *Policing and the Condition of England: Memory, Politics and Culture*. Oxford: OUP.

Loughnan A (2012) *Manifest Madness: Mental Incapacity in Criminal Law*. Oxford: OUP.

Loughnan A (2019) *Self, Others and the State: Relations of Criminal Responsibility*. Cambridge: CUP.

Louis É (2017) *The End of Eddy*. London: Penguin Random House.

Louis É (2019) *Who Killed My Father*. London: Vintage.

Lowe L (2015) *The Intimacies of Four Continents*. Durham: Duke University Press.

Lund B (2006) *Understanding Housing Policy*. Bristol: Policy Press.

MacDonald R (1999) The Road to Nowhere: Youth, Insecurity and Marginal Transition. In: Vail J, Wheelock J, and Hill M (eds) *Insecure Times: Living with Insecurity in Contemporary Society*. London: Routledge 169–84.

MacDonald R, Shildrick T, and Furlong A (2014) In search of 'intergenerational cultures of worklessness': Hunting the Yeti and shooting zombies. *Critical Social Policy* 34(2): 119–220.

MacIntyre AC (1981) *After Virtue: A Study in Moral Theory*. London: Duckworth.

Maguire D (2020) *Male, Failed, Jailed: Masculinities and 'Revolving Door' Imprisonment in the UK*. Cham, Switzerland: Palgrave Macmillan (Springer Nature).

Marshall A (1890) *Principles of Economics*. London: Macmillan.

Marx K and Engels F (2004) *The Communist Manifesto*. London: Penguin.

Mauss M (2002) *The Gift: The Form and Reason for Exchange in Archaic Societies*. London: Routledge.

Mayhew H (1985) *London Labour and the London Poor*. Harmondsworth: Penguin.

References   295

Mayhew H and Binny J (2011) *The Criminal Prisons of London: And Scenes of Prison Life*. Cambridge: CUP.

Mbembe A (2001) *On the Postcolony*. Berkeley: University of California Press.

Mbembe A (2017) *Critique of Black Reason* (tr. L Dubois). Durham : Duke University Press.

McClintock A (1995) *Imperial Leather: Race, Gender and Sexuality in the Colonial Contest*. Abingdon: Routledge.

McConnell T (2018) Moral Dilemmas. *The Stanford Encyclopedia of Philosophy* (Fall 2018 Edition) Available at: https://plato.stanford.edu/archives/fall2018/entries/moral-dilemmas/ (accessed 18 September 2021).

McDowell L (2003) *Redundant Masculinities? Employment Change and White Working Class Youth Blackwell*. Malden, MA: Wiley-Blackwell.

McKenzie L (2015) *Getting By: Estates, Class and Culture in Austerity Britain*. Bristol: Policy Press.

McKenzie L (2017) The class politics of prejudice: Brexit and the land of no-hope and glory. *The British Journal of Sociology* 68: S265–S280.

Mehta U (1990) Liberal strategies of exclusion. *Politics & Society* 18(4): 427–54.

Merry S (1990) *Getting Justice and Getting Even: Legal Consciousness among Working-Class Americans*. Chicago: University of Chicago Press.

Miliband D (ed.) (1994) *Reinventing the Left*. Cambridge: Polity Press.

Miller SM (1964) The Outlook of Working-Class Youth. In: Shostak AB and Gemberg W (eds) *Blue Collar World: Studies of the American Worker*. Englewood Cliffs: Prentice Hall: 122–33.

Miller W (1997) *The Anatomy of Disgust*. Cambridge, MA: Harvard University Press.

Mills C (2014) *The Racial Contract*. Ithica, NY: Cornell University Press.

Mitchell M, Fahmy C, Pyrooz D, et al. (2017) Criminal crews, codes, and contexts: Differences and similarities across the code of the street, convict code, street gangs, and prison gangs. *Deviant Behavior* 38(10): 1197–222.

Mollona M (2009) *Made in Sheffield: An Ethnography of Industrial Work and Politics*. New York: Berghahn Books.

Moody K (2019) *Tramps and Trade Union Travelers: Internal Migration and Organized Labor in Gilded Age America*. Chicago: Haymarket Books.

Morenoff J, Sampson R, and Raudenbush S (2001) Neighborhood inequality, collective efficacy, and the spatial dynamics of urban violence. *Criminology & Criminal Justice* 39(3): 517–58.

Morgan J (2007) *Aspects of Housing Law*. Abingdon: Routledge.

Morison J (2000) Government-voluntary sector compacts: Governance, governmentality, and civil society. *Journal of Law and Society* 27(1): 98–132.

Morris L (2002) *Dangerous Classes: The Underclass and Social Citizenship*. London: Routledge.

Morrison J (2019) *Scroungers: Moral Panics and Media Myths*. London: Zed Books.

Moynihan DP (1965) *The Negro Family in America. The Case for National Action* (Washington: For Sale by the Superintendent of Documents. US Gov. Printing Office).

Mulhall S and Swift A (1996) *Liberals and Communitarians*. 2nd edn. Oxford: Blackwell.

296   References

Müller D, Ringer F, and Simon B (1989) *The Rise of the Modern Educational System: Structural Change and Social Reproduction 1870–1920*. Cambridge: CUP.

Mullins D and Murie A (2006) *Housing Policy in the UK*. New York: Palgrave Macmillan.

Murray CA (1984) *Losing Ground: American Social Policy, 1950–1980*. New York: Basic Books.

Narotzky S (2016) Between inequality and injustice: Dignity as a motive for mobilization during the crisis. *History and Anthropology* 27(1): 74–92.

Nayak A (2006) Displaced masculinities: Chavs, youth and class in the post-industrial city. *Sociology* 40(5): 813–31.

Nayak A and Kehily MJ (2001) 'Learning to Laugh': A Study of Schoolboy Humour in the English Secondary School. In: Martino W and Mayenn B (eds) *What About the Boys*. Buckingham, UK: Open University Press 110–23.

Ndeunyema N (2019) Reforming the purposes of sentencing to affirm African values in Namibia. *Journal of African Law* 63(3): 329–57.

Ndjio B (2005) Carrefour de la joie: Popular deconstruction of the African postcolonial public sphere. *Africa* 75(3): 265–94.

Nelken D (1987) Critical criminal law. *Journal of Law and Society* 14(1): 105–17.

Nelson F (2017) The return of eugenics. *The Chesterton Review* 43(1/2): 169–74.

Newman G (1986) *The Rise of English Nationalism: A Cultural History, 1740–1830*. New York: St. Martin's Press.

Newman KS and Massengill RP (2006) The texture of hardship: Qualitative sociology of poverty, 1995–2005. *Annual Review of Sociology* 32(1): 423–46.

Norrie A (1996) The limits of justice: Finding fault in the criminal law. *Modern Law Revue* 59(4): 540.

Norrie A (2000) *Punishment, Responsibility, and Justice: A Relational Critique*. Oxford: OUP.

Norrie A (2014) *Crime, Reason and History: A Critical Introduction to Criminal Law*. 3rd edn. Cambridge: CUP.

Northamptonshire Country Council (2013) *JSNA Report 2013: Cancer*. Corby. Available at: https://www.northamptonshire.gov.uk/councilservices/health/hea lth-and-wellbeing-board/northamptonshire-jsna/Documents/JSNA_Cancer_ Report.pdf (accessed 18 September 2021).

Northamptonshire Health and Care Partnership (2019) Lung health scanning trucks to hit Corby in drive to improve cancer survival rates. Available at: https://nort hamptonshirehcp.co.uk/2019/04/lung-health-scanning-trucks-to-hit-corby-in-drive-to-improve-cancer-survival-rates/ (accessed 18 September 2021).

Northamptonshire Telegraph (2016) Corby Council in the clear after a 'thorough' police investigation. 25 April. Northants. Available at: https://www.northantste legraph.co.uk/news/exclusive-corby-council-clear-after-thorough-police-invest igation-781159 (accessed 18 September 2021).

Northamptonshire Telegraph (2017) Happy ever after for the Corby girl who touched so many hearts in the 1990s. 15 November. Northants. Available at: https://www.northantstelegraph.co.uk/news/happy-ever-after-corby-girl-who-touched-so-many-hearts-1990s-721754 (accessed 09 December 2022).

Northamptonshire Telegraph (2018) Deadline looms for former Corby workers to join legal action against British Steel. 12 February. Northamtonshire.

Northamptonshire Telegraph (2019a) Brave Corby woman shields homeless man from shocking gang attack. 21 June. Available at: https://www.northantstelegr aph.co.uk/news/people/brave-corby-woman-shields-homeless-man-shocking-gang-attack-687591 (accessed 18 September 2021).

Northamptonshire Telegraph (2019b) 'If you ask for help in Corby, they give it'—landlord overwhelmed by town's generosity. 5 September. Northamptonshire. Available at: https://www.northantstelegraph.co.uk/news/people/if-you-ask-help-corby-they-give-it-landlord-overwhelmed-towns-generosity-680189.

Northamptonshire Telegraph (2019c) More than 22,000 children are living in poverty in Kettering, Wellingborough and Corby … 3 July. Northamptonshire. Available at: https://www.northantstelegraph.co.uk/news/shocking-figu res-show-around-22000-children-kettering-wellingborough-and-corby-are-living-poverty-campaigners-call-government-action-686396 (accessed 13 October 2019).

Nussbaum M (2000) *Women and Human Development: The Capabilities Approach.* Cambridge: CUP.

Nussbaum M (2004) *Hiding from Humanity: Disgust, Shame, and the Law.* Princeton, NJ: Princeton University Press.

Nussbaum M (2009) *Frontiers of Justice: Disability, Nationality, Species Membership.* Cambridge, MA: Harvard University Press.

Nussbaum M and Sen A (1993) *The Quality of Life.* Oxford: Clarendon Press.

Nyerere J (1967) *Freedom and Unity—Uhuru Na Umoja: A Selection from Writings and Speeches, 1952–65.* London: OUP.

Nyerere J (1968) *Freedom and Socialism—Uhuru Na Ujamaa: A Selection from Writings and Speeches, 1965–1967.* Dar es Salaam: OUP.

Office for National Statistics (2001) Key Figures for 2001 Census: Census Area Statistics. Available at: https://www.nomisweb.co.uk/home/census2001.asp (accessed 11 December 2022).

Office for National Statistics (2014) Local Area Analysis of Qualifications Across England and Wales. Available at: http://www.ons.gov.uk/ons/dcp171776_355 401.pdf (accessed 14 January 2016).

Okólski M and Salt J (2014) Polish emigration to the UK after 2004; Why did so many come? *Central and Eastern European Migration Review* 3(2): 11–37.

O'Neill H (2013) Northamptonshire's violent crime rate higher than Merseyside's. Northamptonshire Telegraph. Available at: http://web.archive.org/web/201 70725010851/http://www.northantstelegraph.co.uk/news/northamptonsh ire-s-violent-crime-rate-higher-than-merseyside-s-1-5618522 (accessed 12 September 2016).

ONS (2019) Suicides in England and Wales by local authority. Available at: https:// www.ons.gov.uk/peoplepopulationandcommunity/birthsdeathsandmarriages/ deaths/datasets/suicidesbylocalauthority (accessed 18 September 2021).

Orock R (2014) Crime, in/security and mob justice: The micropolitics of sovereignty in Cameroon. *Social Dynamics* 40(2): 408–28.

298 References

Ortenberg V (2008) *Corby Past & Present.* Northamptonshire: Northamptonshire Victoria County History Trust.

Orwell G (2021) *The Road to Wigan Pier.* Oxford: OUP.

Oshana M (2014). Is Social-Relational Autonomy A Plausible Ideal? In: Oshana M *Personal Autonomy and Social Oppression.* London: Routledge 1–24.

Oshana M (2016). *Personal Autonomy in Society.* London: Routledge.

Page D (2000) *Communities in the Balance: The Reality of Social Exclusion on Housing Estates.* York: Joseph Rowntree Foundation.

Panfil V (2014) Better left unsaid? The role of agency in queer criminological research. *Critical Criminology* 22: 99–111.

Parmar A (2011) Stop and Search in London: Counter-terrorist or counterproductive? *Policing and Society* 21(4): 369–82.

Parmar A (2015) *Policing British Asians.* London: Runnymede Trust.

Pattillo M (1998) Sweet mothers and gangbangers: Managing crime in a black middle-class neighborhood. *Social Forces* 76(3): 747–74.

Pavlich G (2001) The Force of Community. In: Strang H and Braithwaite J (eds) *Restorative Justice and Civil Society.* Cambridge: CUP 56–68.

Payne J and Stubley P (2019) More than 60,000 sign petition to stop doctor getting sacked for asking Muslim patient to remove veil. *Independent,* 26 May. UK. Available at: https://www.independent.co.uk/news/health/doctor-remove-veil-muslim-patient-niqab-petition-keith-wolverson-a8930176.html (accessed 13 October 2019).

Phillips C (2019) The trouble with culture: A speculative account of the role of gypsy/traveller cultures in 'doorstep fraud'. *Theoretical Criminology* 23(3): 333–54.

Phillips T (2010) Inquiry into recruitment and employment in the meat and poultry processing sector: Report of the findings and recommendations. Equality and Human Rights Commission. Available at: https://www.equalityhumanrights.com/sites/default/files/meat_and_poultry_processing_review_report_0.pdf (accessed 9 November 2020).

Pialoux M (1999) The Shop Steward's World in Disarray. In: Bourdieu P (ed) *The Weight of the World: Social Suffering in Contemporary Society* (tr. P Ferguson). Cambridge: Polity Press 321–37.

Pieterse J (1989) *Empire and Emancipation: Power and Liberation on a World Scale.* New York: Pluto Press.

Platt T (2018) *Beyond These Walls: Rethinking Crime and Punishment in the United States.* New York: St. Martin's Press.

Police, UK (2022) Data downloads—Data from 2014. Available at: https://data.police.uk/data/archive/ (accessed 12 December 2022).

Portes A (1998) Social capital: Its origins and applications in modern sociology. *Annual Revue of Sociology* 24: 1.

Potter H (2015) *Intersectionality and Criminology: Disrupting and Revolutionizing Studies of Crime.* Abingdon: Routledge.

Power A (1987) *Property Before People: The Management of Twentieth-Century Council Housing.* London: Allen & Unwin.

Putnam RD (2000) *Bowling Alone: The Collapse and Revival of American Community.* New York: Simon & Schuster Ltd.

References 299

Radnor H, Koshy V, and Taylor A (2007) Gifts, talents and meritocracy. *Journal of Education Policy* 22(3): 283–99.

Ramose M (2001) An African perspective on justice and race. *Polylog: Forum for Intercultural Philosophy* 2: 1–27.

Ravetz A (2001) *Council Housing and Culture: The History of a Social Experiment.* London: Routledge.

Rawls J (1971) *A Theory of Justice.* Cambridge, MA: Harvard University Press.

Raz J (1986) *The Morality of Freedom.* Oxford: OUP.

Read C (1982) Diversification at Corby. *Geography* 67(3): 253–5.

Reay D (1998) *Class Work: Mothers' Involvement in Their Children's Primary Schooling.* London: Taylor & Francis.

Reay D (2000) Children's Urban Landscapes: Configurations of Class and Place. In: Munt S (ed) *Cultural Studies and the Working Class: Subject to Change.* London: Cassell 151–64.

Reay D (2017) *Miseducation: Inequality, Education and the Working Classes.* Bristol: Policy Press.

Reay D and Lucey H (2000) 'I don't really like it here but I don't want to be anywhere else': Children and inner city council estates. *Antipode* 32(4): 410–28.

Reay D, Hollingworth S, Williams K, et al. (2007) A darker shade of pale?' Whiteness, the middle classes and multi-ethnic inner city schooling. *Sociology* 41(6): 1041–60.

Reiman J (1979) *The Rich Get Richer and the Poor Get Prison: Ideology, Class, and Criminal Justice.* New York: John Wiley & Sons.

Reynolds F (1986) *The Problem Housing Estate: An Account of Omega and Its People.* Aldershot: Gower Publishing Company.

Rhodes J (2010) White backlash, 'unfairness' and justifications of British National Party (BNP) support. *Ethnicities* 10(1): 77–99.

Rhodes J (2011) 'It's not just them, it's whites as well': Whiteness, class and BNP support. *Sociology* 45(1): 102–17.

Riedel M and Welsh W (2008) *Criminal Violence: Patterns, Causes, and Prevention.* 2nd edn. New York: OUP.

Roberts S (1979) *Order and Dispute: An Introduction to Legal Anthropology.* Harmondsworth, Middlesex, England: Penguin Books.

Rodgers D (2015) The Moral Economy of Murder: Violence, Death, and Social Order in Nicaragua. In: Auyero J, Bourgois P, and Scheper-Hughes N (eds) *Violence at the Urban Margins.* Oxford: OUP 21–41.

Roediger D (1999) *The Wages of Whiteness: Race and the Making of the American Working Class.* London: Verso Books.

Rogaly B and Taylor B (2016) *Moving Histories of Class and Community: Identity, Place and Belonging in Contemporary England.* London: Palgrave Macmillan.

Roitman J (2006) The Ethics of Illegality in the Chad Basin. In: Comaroff J and Comaroff JL (eds) *Law and Disorder in the Postcolony.* Chicago: University of Chicago Press 247–72.

Rollock N, David Gillborn, Vincent C, et al. (2014) *The Colour of Class: The Educational Strategies of the Black Middle Classes.* London: Routledge.

300 References

Rosaldo R (2004) Grief and a Headhunter's Rage. In: Scheper-Hughes N and Bourgois P (eds) *Violence in War and Peace: An Anthology*. Malden, MA: Blackwell Publishing 150–7.

Rose D and Clear T (1998) Incarceration, social capital and crime: Implications for social disorganization theory. *Criminology* 36(3): 441–80.

Rosenfeld R, Jacobs BA, and Wright R (2003) Snitching and the code of the street. *British Journal of Criminology* 43(2): 291–309.

Rowe K (1995) *The Unruly Women: Gender and the Genres of Laughter*. Austin: University of Texas Press.

Rusbridger A (1979) Forty years on: boom town to doom town. *The Guardian*. Available at: http://www.theguardian.com/business/1979/oct/09/2 (accessed 14 January 2016).

Ryan F (2019) *Crippled*. London: Verso Books.

Ryan W (1971) *Blaming the Victim*. New York: Pantheon Books.

Said E (2003) *Orientalism*. London: Penguin Classics.

Saini A (2019) *Superior: The Return of Race Science*. Boston: Beacon Press.

Sampson RJ, Raudenbush SW, and Earls F (1997) Neighbourhoods and violent crime: A multilevel study of collective efficacy. *Science* 277: 918.

Sandberg S (2008) Street capital: Ethnicity and violence on the streets of Oslo. *Theoretical Criminology* 12(2): 153–71.

Sandberg S and Fleetwood J (2017) Street talk and Bourdieusian criminology: Bringing narrative to field theory. *Criminology & Criminal Justice* 17(4): 365–81.

Sandberg S and Pedersen W (2011) *Street Capital: Black Cannabis Dealers in a White Welfare State*. Bristol: Policy Press.

Sandel MJ (1982) *Liberalism and the Limits of Justice*. Cambridge: CUP.

Sandel MJ (2009) *Justice: What's the Right Thing to Do?* London and New York: Allen Lane.

Sara A (2014) *The Cultural Politics of Emotion*. 2nd edn. Edinburgh: Edinburgh University Press.

Savage M (2000) *Class Analysis and Social Transformation*. Buckingham: Open University Press.

Savage M, Barlow J, Dickens P, et al. (1995) *Property, Bureaucracy and Culture: Middle-Class Formation in Contemporary Britain*. London: Routledge.

Savage M, Bagnall G, and Longhurst B (2001) Ordinary, ambivilent and defensive: Class differentiation in the Northwest of England. *Sociology* 35: 875–92.

Savage M, Devine F, Cunningham N, et al. (2013) A new model of social class: Findings from the BBC's Great British class. *Sociology* 47(2): 219–50.

Sayer A (2005) *The Moral Significance of Class*. Cambridge: CUP.

Scheper-Hughes N and Bourgois P (eds) (2004) *Violence in War and Peace: An Anthology*. Malden, MA: Blackwell Publishing.

Schneewind J (1998) *The Invention of Autonomy: A History of Modern Moral Philosophy*. Cambridge: CUP.

Scott J (1977) *The Moral Economy of the Peasant Rebellion and Subsistence in Southeast Asia*. New Haven: Yale University Press.

References   301

Scott J (1985) *Weapons of the Weak: Everyday Forms of Peasant Resistance*. New Haven: Yale University Press.

Sen A (1999) *Development as Freedom*. New York: Knopf.

Sennett R (2011) *The Corrosion of Character: The Personal Consequences of Work in the New Capitalism*. New York: WW Norton & Company.

Sennett R and Cobb J (1972) *The Hidden Injuries of Class*. Cambridge: CUP.

Shammas VL and Sandberg S (2016) Habitus, capital, and conflict: Bringing Bourdieusian field theory to criminology. *Criminology and Criminal Justice* 16(2): 195–213.

Shaw CR and McKay H (1942) *Juvenile Delinquency and Urban Areas*. Chicago: University of Chicago Press.

Sherman R (2017) *Uneasy Street: The Anxieties of Affluence*. Princeton, NJ: Princeton University Press.

Shildrick T (2018) *Poverty Propaganda: Exploring the Myths*. Bristol: Policy Press.

Shildrick T, MacDonald R, Webster C, et al. (2012) *Poverty and Insecurity: Life in Low-Pay, No-Pay Britain*. Bristol: Policy Press.

Shilliam R (2018) *Race and the Undeserving Poor: From Abolition to Brexit*. Newcastle upon Tyne: Agenda Publishing.

Silva J (2013) *Coming up Short: Working-Class Adulthood in an Age of Uncertainty*. Oxford: OUP.

Simon J (2007) *Governing Through Crime: How the War on Crime Transformed the American Penal System*. Oxford: OUP.

Simon J (2012) Mass Incarceration: From Social Policy to Social Problem. In: Petersilia J and Reitz KR (eds) *The Oxford Handbook of Sentencing and Corrections* Oxford: OUP 23–52.

Skeggs B (1997) *Formations of Class & Gender: Becoming Respectable*. London: Sage.

Skeggs B (2004) *Class, Self, Culture*. London: Routledge.

Skeggs B (2011) Imagining personhood differently: Person value and autonomist working-class value practices. *The Sociological Review* 3(59): 496–513.

Skeggs B and Loveday V (2012) Struggles for value: value practices, injustice, judgment, affect and the idea of class. *The British Journal of Sociology* 63(3): 472–90.

Skeggs B and Wood H (2012) *Reacting to Reality Television: Performance, Audience and Value*. New York: Routledge.

Smith A (1976) *An Inquiry into the Nature and Causes of the Wealth of Nations*. Chicago: University of Chicago Press.

Smith K (2012) *Fairness, Class and Belonging in Contemporary England*. Basingstoke, UK: Palgrave Macmillan.

Smith K (2017a) 'Don't call the police on me, I won't call them on you': Self-policing as Ethical Development in North Manchester. In: Lewis C and Symons J (eds) *Realising the City: Urban Ethnographies in Manchester*. Manchester: Manchester University Press 187–202.

Smith K (2017b) 'You don't own money, you're just the one who's holding it': Borrowing, lending and the fair person in North Manchester. *The Sociological Review* 65(1_suppl): 121–36.

302 References

Social Mobility Commission (2017) State of the Nation 2017: Social Mobility in Great Britain. Open Government Licence. Available at: www.gov.uk/governm ent/publications.

Stacey J (1990) *Brave New Families*. New York: Basic Books.

Stack C (1974) *All Our Kin: Strategies for Survival in a Black Community*. New York: Harper & Row.

Standing G (2011) *The Precariat: The New Dangerous Class*. London: Bloomsbury Academic.

Stewart E, Schreck C, and Simons R (2006) 'I ain't gonna let no one disrespect me': Does the code of the street reduce or increase violent victimization among African American adolescents? *Journal of Research in Crime and Delinquency* 43(4): 427–58.

Stewart EA and Simons RL (2006) Structure and culture in African American adolescent violence: A partial test of the 'code of the street' thesis. *Justice Quarterly* 23(1): 1–33.

Stewart G (2017) The 'hau'of research: Mauss meets Kaupapa Māori. *Journal of World Philosophies* 2(1). Available at: https://scholarworks.iu.edu/iupjournals/index.php/jwp/article/view/917 (accessed 08 December 2022).

Stoler AL (1995) *Race and the Education of Desire: Foucault's History of Sexuality and the Colonial Order of Things*. Durham: Duke University Press.

Stoler AL and Cooper F (1997) Between Metropole and Colony: Rethinking a Research Agenda. In: Cooper F and Stoler AL (eds) *Tensions of Empire: Colonial Cultures in a Bourgeois World*. Berkeley: University of California Press 1–58.

Strathern M (1981) *After Nature. English Kinship in the Late Twentieth Century*. Cambridge: CUP.

Sullum J (1999) *For Your Own Good: The Anti-Smoking Crusade and the Tyranny of Public Health*. New York: Simon and Schuster.

Sutherland E (1983) *White Collar Crime*. New Haven: Yale University Press.

Sykes GM and Matza D (1957) Techniques of neutralization: A theory of delinquency. *American Sociological Review* 22(6): 664–70.

Táíwò O (2022) *Elite Capture: How the Powerful Took Over Identity Politics (And Everything Else)* London: Pluto Press.

Tamanaha B (2001) *A General Jurisprudence of Law and Society*. Oxford: Clarendon Press.

Taylor C (1985a) *Philosophical Papers: Volume 1, Human Agency and Language*. Cambridge: CUP.

Taylor C (1985b) *Philosophy and the Human Sciences: Philosophical Papers 2*. Cambridge: CUP.

Taylor C (1985c) What's Wrong with Negative Liberty. In: Taylor C *Philosophical Papers: Volume 2*. Cambridge: CUP 211–29.

Taylor C (1989) *Sources of the Self: The Making of the Modern Identity*. Cambridge, MA: Harvard University Press.

Taylor C (1997) The politics of recognition. *New Contexts of Canadian Criticism* (98): 25–73.

Taylor I (1999) *Crime in Context: A Critical Criminology of Market Societies*. Cambridge: Polity Press.

References   303

Taylor S (2018) *The Fall: The Insanity of the Ego in Human History and the Dawning of a New Era*. Winchester, UK: Iff Books.

The Economist (2013) The Polish paradox. *The Economist*, 14 December. Available at: http://www.economist.com/news/britain/21591588-britons-loathe-immigrat ion-principle-quite-immigrants-practice-bulgarians (accessed 15 January 2016).

Thomas D (2011) *Exceptional Violence: Embodied Citizenship in Transnational Jamaica*. Durham: Duke University Press.

Thompson EP (1963) *The Making of the English Working Class*. London: Gollanz.

Thompson EP (1975) *Whigs and Hunters: The Origin of the Black Act*. London: Allen Lane, Penguin Books.

Thompson EP (1993a) *Customs in Common*. London: Penguin Books.

Thompson EP (1993b) Rough Music. In: Thomson EP *Customs in Common*. London: Penguin Books 467–539.

Thompson EP (1993c) The Moral Economy of the English Crowd in the Eighteenth Century. In: Thomson EP *Customs in Common*. London: Penguin Books 185–258.

Thompson EP (1993d) The Moral Economy Reviewed. In: Thomson EP *Customs in Common*. London: Penguin Books 259–351.

Thompson FML (1988) *The Rise of Respectable Society: A Social History of Victorian Britain*. London: William Collins.

Tierney B (1959) *Medieval Poor Law: A Sketch of Canonical Theory and Its Application in England*. Berkeley and Los Angeles: University of California Press.

Todd S (2014) *The People: The Rise and Fall of the Working Class, 1910–2010*. London: John Murray.

Tombs S (2004) Workplace Injury and Death: Social Harm and the Illusions of Law. In: Hillyard P (ed) *Beyond Criminology: Taking Harm Seriously*. London: Pluto Press 156–77.

Tombs S (2015) Harmful societies. *Criminal Justice Matters* 101(1): 36–37.

Tomlinson S (2019) *Education and Race from Empire to Brexit*. Bristol: Policy Press.

Trouillot M-R (1995) *Silencing the Past: Power and the Production of History*. Boston: Beacon Press.

Tyler I. (2015) *Revolting Subjects: Social Abjection and Resistance in Neoliberal Britain*. London: Zed Books.

Tyler K (2012) *Whiteness, Class and the Legacies of Empire: On Home Ground*. London: Palgrave Macmillan.

Tyler K (2015) Attachments and connections: a 'white working-class' English family's relationships with their BrAsian 'Pakistani' neighbours. *Ethnic and Racial Studies* 38(7): 1169–84.

UK Census Data (2011) Corby—UK Census Data (UK Census Data 2011)UK Census Data Corby—2011. Available at: http://www.ukcensusdata.com/corby-e07000150 (accessed 12 September 2016).

UK Crimestats (2016) Crime in Corby Town. Available at: http://www.ukcrimest ats.com/Neighbourhood/Northamptonshire_Police/Corby_Town (accessed 12 September 2016).

Valluvan S (2001) *The Clamour of Nationalism: Race and Nation in Twenty-First-Century Britain*. Manchester: Manchester University Press.

304 References

van Dijk T (1993) *Elite Discourse and Racism*. Sage Series on Race and Ethnic Relations. Newbury Park, California: SAGE Publications.

Vicinus M (1974) *The Industrial Muse: A Study of Nineteenth Century British Working-Class Literature*. London: Croom Helm.

Vincent D (1981) *Bread, Knowledge, and Freedom: A Study of Nineteenth-Century Working Class Autobiography*. Cambridge: CUP.

Vincent M (1974) *The Industrial Muse: A Study of Nineteenth-Century British Working-Class Literature*. London: Europa Publications.

Virdee S (2014) *Racism, Class and the Racialized Outsider*. London: Macmillan International Higher Education.

Voltaire (1763) Treatise on Tolerance. In: Harvey S (ed) *Treatise on Tolerance and Other Writings* (tr. B Masters, 2000). Cambridge: Cambridge University Press 1–106.

Von Hirsch A (1992) Proportionality in the philosophy of punishment. *Crime and Justice* 16: 55–98.

Wacquant L (2002) Scrutinizing the street: Poverty, morality, and the pitfalls of urban ethnography. *American Journal of Sociology* 107(6): 1468–532.

Wacquant L (2007) *Urban Outcasts: A Comparative Sociology of Advanced Marginality*. Cambridge: Polity Press.

Wacquant L (2009) *Punishing the Poor: The Neoliberal Government of Social Insecurity*. Durham: Duke University Press.

Walkerdine V and Jimenez L (2012) *Gender, Work and Community after de-Industrialisation: A Psychosocial Approach to Affect*. Basingstoke: Palgrave.

Walkerdine V and Lucey H (1989) *Democracy in the Kitchen: Regulating Mothers and Socialising Daughters*. London: Virago.

Walkerdine V, Lucey H, and Melody J (2001) *Growing up Girl: Psycho-Social Explorations of Gender and Class*. Basingstoke: Palgrave.

Walzer M (1983) *Spheres of Justice: A Defense of Pluralism and Equality*. New York: Basic Books.

Ward S (2020) Councillor wants action to improve lives of Corby residents living in deprivation hotspot. *Northamptonshire Telegraph*, 10 August. Available at: https://www.northantstelegraph.co.uk/health/councillor-wants-action-impr ove-lives-corby-residents-living-deprivation-hotspot-2938152 (accessed 18 September 2021).

Watt P (2006) Respectability, roughness and 'race': Neighbourhood place images and the making of working-class social distinctions in London. *International Journal of Urban and Regional Research* 30(4): 776–97.

Weeks J (1991) *Sex, Politics and Society: The Regulation of Sexuality Since 1800*. London: Longman.

Weisberg R (2003) Restorative Justice and the Danger of 'Community'. *Utah Law Review* 2003: 343–74.

Wells C (2001) *Corporations and Criminal Responsibility*. Oxford: OUP.

Welshman J (2014) *Underclass: A History of the Excluded since 1880*. 2nd edn. New York: Bloomsbury Academic.

Wemyss G (2016) *The Invisible Empire: White Discourse, Tolerance and Belonging*. New York: Routledge.

References **305**

Wheeler R (2000) *The Complexion of Race: Categories of Difference in Eighteenth-Century British Culture*. Philadelphia: University of Pennsylvania Press.

Whitlock T (2016) Forms of Crime: Crime and Retail Theft. In: Knepper P and Johansen A (eds) *The Oxford Handbook of the History of Crime and Criminal Justice*. Oxford: OUP 155–69.

Wiener M (1994) *Reconstructing the Criminal: Culture, Law, and Policy in England, 1830–1914*. Cambridge: CUP.

Wiener M (2004) *Men of Blood: Violence, Manliness and Criminal Justice in Victorian England*. Cambridge: CUP.

Williams B (1973) Ethical Consistency. In: Williams B *Problems of the Self: Philosophical Papers 1956–1972*. Cambridge: CUP 166–86.

Williams E (1994) *Capitalism and Slavery*. Chapel Hill, NC: The University of North Carolina Press.

Williams R (1983) *Towards 2000*. Harmondsworth: Penguin Books.

Willis PE (1977) *Learning to Labor: How Working Class Kids Get Working Class Jobs*. New York: Columbia University Press.

Willis R (2009) *Everyone needs a little space, but just how little is enough? Exploring the role of property rights in the dilapidation of a council estate in England, UK*. SOAS, London. Unpublished.

Willis R (2017) Class, crime, and observations online: Feeling the ethical boundaries of Facebook research. *Research Ethics* 15(1): 1–17.

Willis R (2018) 'Let's talk about it': Why social class matters to restorative justice. *Criminology & Criminal Justice* 20(2): 187–286.

Willis R (2019) Working-class towns are becoming dumping grounds for waste. Available at: https://theconversation.com/working-class-towns-are-becoming-dumping-grounds-for-waste-121153 (accessed 18 September 2021).

Wilson A (2021) Corby McDonald's worker attacked by yobs in cars on first e-scooter ride. *Northants Live*, 18 April. Available at: https://www.northantslive.news/news/northamptonshire-news/corby-mcdonalds-worker-voi-e-5313142 (accessed 18 September 2021).

Wilson WJ (1987) *The Truly Disadvantaged: The Inner City, the Underclass, and Public Policy*. Chicago: University of Chicago Press.

Wilson WJ (1996) *When Work Disappears: The World of the New Urban Poor*. New York: Vintage Books.

Winant H (2001) *The World Is a Ghetto: Race and Democracy Since World War II*. Oxford: Basic Books.

Winlow S and Hall S (2006) *Violent Night: Urban Leisure and Contemporary Culture*. Oxford: Berg.

Winlow S, Hall S, and Treadwell J (2017) *The Rise of the Right: English Nationalism and the Transformation of Working-Class Politics*. Bristol: Policy Press.

Wittgenstein L (1953) *Philosophical Investigations* (trs. GEM Anscombe, PMS Hacker, and J Schulte, 2009). London: Wiley-Blackwell.

Wolfgang ME and Ferracuti F (1967) *The Subculture of Violence: Toward an Integrated Theory in Criminology*. London: Tavistock Publications.

Wood J (2004) *Violence and Crime in Nineteenth-Century England: The Shadow of Our Refinement*. London: Routledge.

306 References

Woodger A (2016) EU referendum: Corby, England's 'Little Scotland', votes Leave. *BBC News*, 25 June. Corby. Available at: https://www.bbc.com/news/uk-england-northamptonshire-36623047 (accessed 18 September 2021).

Woods P (1976) Having a Laugh: An Antidote to Schooling. In: Hammersley M and Woods P (eds) *The Process of Schooling*. London: Routledge & Kegan Paul 178–87.

Wynne-Jones R (1996) Girls accused of funfair killing. *The Independent*, 2 May. Available at: http://www.independent.co.uk/news/girls-accused-of-funfair-killing-1345226.html (accessed 12 September 2016).

Wynne-Jones R (1997) 'Someone batters us, we batter them'. *The Independent*, 27 April. Available at: http://www.independent.co.uk/news/someone-batters-us-we-batter-them-1269549.html (accessed 12 September 2016).

Young I (1986) The ideal of community and the politics of difference. *Social Theory and Practice* 12: 1–26.

Young MD and Willmott P (1957) *Family and Kinship in East London*. Harmondsworth: Penguin.

Young R (1994) *Colonial Desire: Hybridity in Theory, Culture and Race*. 1st edn. London: Routledge.

Zedner L (1991) *Women, Crime, and Custody in Victorian England*. Oxford: Clarendon Press.

Zedner L (2004) *Criminal Justice*. Oxford: OUP.

Zedner L (2006) Policing before and after the police: The historical antecedents of contemporary crime control. *British Journal of Criminology* 46: 78–96.

Zedner L (2010) Security, the state, and the citizen: The changing architecture of crime control. *New Criminal Law Review* 13(2): 379–403.

Index

For the benefit of digital users, indexed terms that span two pages (e.g., 52–53) may, on occasion, appear on only one of those pages.

affect *see* 'emotions'
Ahmed, Sara 157, 176, 204
alcohol use 44, 87, 91–92, 117, 130, 132, 134–35, 222, 226–27, 229, 231–32, 234–38, 267
Amussen, Susan 97–98, 102, 116, 121–22
Anderson, Benedict 26–27, 90
Anderson, Elijah 22–23, 103, 106, 114–15
code of the street 217–19
antisocial behaviour 2, 72–73, 79, 139, 143–44, 196, 198–99, 226
apology 85–86, 109, 149, 150, 202
arbitrator 109–10, 274
Ashworth, Andrew 3–5, 35–36
assimilation 171–75
see also 'race / racialization'
austerity 17–18, 130, 199–210, 228–29
autonomy 4–5, 7–24, 28, 33–61, 64–68, 71–72, 74–75, 80, 98–100, 128–30, 137, 140, 148, 151–52, 155–56, 161–62, 186–212, 216–39, 242–70, 272–79
thick and thin 219–20, 222, 227, 233, 234–35, 242, 246, 260–61, 269

banter 58–59, 201–2, 248–49, 254–55
Beier, A L. 14, 16, 199–200, 221
belonging *see* 'born and bred'
Bhabha, Homi 12, 21, 217
Blair, Tony 17–18, 66
Bloody Code 131
born and bred 46–47, 78–79, 91, 138–39, 158–59, 168–69, 170, 171, 174–81, 182, 261, 274
Bourdieu, Pierre 23, 26, 36–37, 38–47, 50–51, 64–70, 81–84, 103, 104–6, 202, 231

distinction 12, 43, 155–56, 216–39, 242–59, 266–69, 272–73, *see also* 'Taylor, Charles': 'recognition'
doxa 19, 43, 64–65, 82, 189
legitimacy 9–10, 15, 22, 219, 233, 242, 244, 247
symbolic violence 41, 146–47, 187–90, 199–212, 216, 232, 236, 237–39, 269, 272, 277–78
see also 'bourgeois'
bourgeois 12, 13, 15, 16–17, 20–21, 23–24, 26, 39–41, 64–66, 67, 82–83, 97–98, 99–100, 102, 141–42, 146–47, 168, 173, 182, 186–87, 199–200, 217, 230–31, 233, 243–45, 248, 249, 260–61, 266–67
see also respectability
Bourgois, Philippe 103, 187–88
see also 'moral economy of violence'
Brexit 156, 159–65, 169, 174–75
bullying 1, 58–59, 107, 116–17, 119, 123–24, 130, 144, 230, 258, 273–74

Cameron, David 160–61, 225
capacity 36–37
see also autonomy
care *see* 'mutuality'; 'relational self'; 'emotions'
Christianity 9, 11–13, 21, 97–98, 249, 253–54
civility *see* respectability
code of honour 7–9, 21–22, 97–98, 133
code switching 218–19
code of the street *see* 'Anderson, Elijah'
Cohen, G. A. 69, 129–30
collective efficacy *see* 'webs of support'
communitarian thinking 4, 5, 20–21, 23–24, 27–28, 33–35, 36, 46, 66, 68–70, 161–62, 165–68, 260–61, 278

308   Index

community 1, 2, 26–28, 66, 69–70, 103, 114–15, 152, 155–83, 227
   constitutive community 27–28, 46, 68, 84–87, 104–5, 109, 156–57
   exclusionary tendencies of community 26–27, 152, 155–56, 159, 170, 171–72, 175–82, 252, 275
   imagined community 26–27, 90–92, 161–62, 168–75, 176–77, 182
   relational community 2, 3, 24–28, 37–38, 41, 67–68, 69–70, 76–90, 103, 107–12, 132, 133–34, 156–57, 158–60, 198–99, 230, 269
computer (il)literacy 81–82
conflict 2, 69–70, 100
   family 3, 107–9, 110–12, 116, 148–50
   neighbours 56, 72–73, 143–44, 178, 226–27, 263–66
   work 52–53, 58–59, 148–49, 172
   see also 'violence'
corporate crime 4
council estate 1, 2, 3, 4, 26–27, 50, 71–90, 135–41, 195–99, 225–27, 231–32, 264–65, 272–74
   demolition 26–27, 49–50, 68, 71–72, 100–1, 195–99
   stigma 75–77, 195–99
counter narratives 163–64, 167, 264–65
Crime and Disorder Act 1998 246–47, 248
criminal class 16, 20, 26, 141–42, 172–73, 178–79, 249–50
   see also 'Hall, Stuart': 'folk devils'; 'self: immoral other'
critical criminal law 5, 18–19, 35–36, 210–12, 239, 248, 249, 270, 272–79
cultural relativism 10, 228, 234–35

Degnen, Cathrine 21, 67–69, 76–90, 161–62, 169, 235
deindustrialisation 3, 24, 49–51, 74, 190–95
   see also 'steelworks'
dirt 38, 132, 143, 162, 177, 203–4, 205, 221–27, 231–32, 234–35, 251–52
   see also 'self': 'immoral other'
disability 5, 42, 188, 199–206, 221, 223–24, 246–47, 249–50, 253, 256–57, 265, 266, 269–70, 275
distinction *see* 'Bourdieu, Pierre'
Du Bois, W. E. B. 59, 186–87, 243, 245
Duff, Antony 3–5, 35–36

education 42–43, 256–57, 268

see also 'moral education'; 'school'
Edwards, Janette 23, 67–69, 78–79, 108, 129, 130, 137, 140–41, 156, 158–59, 169, 198–99, 235
Elizabethan Act 1576 14
emotions 4, 46, 52, 55–56, 77–78, 81, 85–87, 89, 93, 107, 108–9, 111, 114–15, 119, 124, 140, 156–57, 159–60, 162–63, 164, 166, 167, 175–76, 180–81, 194–95, 197, 198–99, 201–2, 203–4, 205–6, 208–9, 210–11, 223, 227, 235, 237–38, 269
employment / work 45–46, 48–61, 81–84, 99–100, 172, 232, 233
   agency 52–53, 56–57
   coerced labour 12–13, 36–38, 44–45, 53, 56–61, 64–65
   morality of work 15–18, 39–40, 47, 51, 52–54, 55, 57, 58
   poor working conditions 48, 52–53, 55, 57–58, 88–89, 190–95, 200–1, 261–62, 263, 277–78
   unemployment 3–4, 12–13, 38, 44, 49–50, 52, 53–54, 56–60, 148–49, 164, 165–66, 199–210, 221–27, 237–38
Enlightenment 9, 11–12, 33, 98, 128–29, 186, 189
   see also 'modernity'
equality 246–47, 259–66
   collective 168, 171–75, 181–82, 247–49, 254–66
   individual 168, 260–66
   see also 'banter'; 'power imbalance'; 'virtues': 'not acting better than others'
Equality Act 2010 246–47, 259
eugenics 223–24, 244, 253, 257
Evans, Gillian 41, 44–45

fair fight 103, 110–19, 144–45, 178–81, 274
   see also 'history': 'fighting norms'
fairness 21–22, 88–89, 138, 146, 157–58, 165–68, 259–60, 261–62, 263
Fanon, Franz 12, 21, 98–99, 217
Farmer, Lindsey 3, 5–6, 15, 18–19, 135–36, 276, 278
fatherhood 3–4, 84–85, 103, 112, 148–49, 194, 236–39
Fitzjames, James 5–6, 18–19
folk devil *see* 'Hall, Stuart'
Fraser, Alistair 23, 73, 140, 162, 198, 202, 217–18

Gardner, John 4–5, 35–36, 211

Index   309

gender 3, 5, 12–13, 54, 85, 97–99, 102, 111, 113, 121–22, 142–45, 149–50, 198, 228, 231–32, 237–39, 246–47, 249–50, 253–54, 255, 259, 269–70, 275
  see also 'fatherhood'; 'motherhood'
Gilroy, Paul 25–26, 171, 174, 245, 251–52, 257–58, 278
Goffman, Alice 87, 142, 144, 145, 148–51
Goldthorpe, John 9–10, 16–17, 46
good personhood 1, 88–90, 93, 104, 106–7, 121, 145, 218–19, 233, 272–74
  see also 'money lending'
Graeber, David 9–10, 68–70

Hall, Catherine 12–13, 14, 15, 39–40, 98–99, 128–29, 170, 219, 228, 242–43, 244
Hall, Stuart 16–17, 25–26, 74, 129, 131–32, 133–34, 138–39, 141–42, 176–77, 245, 251–52, 257–58, 259, 278
  folk devil 9, 15–18, 22–23, 55, 76, 86, 164, 165, 167–68, 200–10, 221–27, 228–31, 234, 236, 244, 245, 249–54, 260, 263
  see also 'self': 'immoral other'
handling stolen goods 135
harm
  environmental 48, 190–95, 277–78,
    see also 'employment': 'poor working conditions'
  relational 3, 129–30, 132–33, 134, 135, 138–39, 143, 148–51, 194, 198–99
    see also 'responsibility'
Hart, H L A. 3–5, 211
hate crime 174–75, 246–48, 254
Hayes, Lydia 54, 59–60, 65
health 1, 3–4, 38, 47, 48, 52, 54, 55–56, 57, 77–78, 81, 86, 90–91, 147, 188–89, 190–95, 198, 199–206, 254
hegemony *see* 'Bourdieu, Pierre': 'legitimacy'
history
  class inequality 11–19, 20–24, 97–102, 121–22, 168–69, 170, 181–82, 186–212, 220, 221, 223, 242–45, 249–50, *see also* 'Thompson E P'
  fighting norms 97–102, 110–11, 112–13
  legal history 5–6, 59, 128–29, 131, 221, 278
  see also 'Enlightenment'; 'modernity'
Hochschild, Arlie 157–58, 252
homicide 1, 136–37, 188, 272–75
housing 64–65, 99–100
  Right to Buy 74–75

  see also 'council estate'; 'property'; 'Thatcher, Margaret'
Housing Act 1985 65
Hudson, Barbara 5, 35
humour 44–45, 46, 48, 58–59, 164, 172, 267
  see also 'banter'
Hursthouse, Rosalind 228, 235–36

ignorance 6, 19, 20–21, 22, 23–24, 25–26, 28–29, 39, 41, 64–65–, 68–70, 80, 92–93, 99–100, 180–81, 186–87, 192, 197–98, 199, 206–10, 220, 246, 267–68, 274, 279
  see also 'Bourdieu': 'Doxa'; 'Membe': 'wilful ignorance'
immigration *see* 'race'
inequality (structural) 2, 3–4, 7, 11–19, 20–24, 26, 33–61, 64–66, 67, 71, 74, 75, 76, 82–83, 85, 90–91, 97, 100–1, 114–15, 117–19, 122, 131–32, 133–34, 141–42, 186–87, 228–39, 256–57, 259–66, 267–69, 272–79
intoxication *see* 'alcohol use'

James, C L R. 12, 14, 99
jokes *see* 'humour'
junkie *see* 'substance use'

Kalb, Don 155–56, 168, 259–60, 263
karma 121–23, 132, 237
  see also 'luck'
knowing, being known 78–79, 90, 104, 106–8, 109–10, 159–60, 176–77
  see also 'good personhood'
Koch, Insa 7, 18, 22, 23, 67–69, 77, 80, 84, 88, 129, 130, 140, 141–42, 148–51, 168, 198–99, 208–9, 218–19, 232–33, 235, 248–49, 262, 263–64, 266
  see also 'state': 'personalizing the state'

Lacey, Nicola 4, 5–6, 26–27, 33–35, 98–99, 111, 157, 248, 258, 276
Lamont, Michèle 23, 52–53, 106, 218–19, 232–33, 264–65
language 44–45, 57, 58, 103, 119–20, 138–39, 164–66, 203, 209–10, 246–48, 251, 252, 254, 255–56, 265, 269–70
Lareau, Annette 36–37, 40–41, 115, 120
Lawler, Stephanie 36–37, 204, 217, 233, 244–45
legal cynicism 142, 268
  see also 'state': 'personalising the state'

310 Index

legitimacy *see* 'Bourdieu'
liberalism 3–24, 27–28, 33–37, 39, 60–61,
   66, 68–70, 128–29, 148, 151, 161–62,
   206, 217, 260, 266, 275
   see also 'neoliberalism'
Loader, Ian 16–17, 18, 141–42, 179, 252
Loughnan, Arlie 3–6, 36–37, 276
Lowe, Lisa 59, 186–87, 221, 243, 250, 278
luck 20, 51–61, 122, 188–89, 204,
   209, 210–11
   see also 'moral luck'; 'karma'
lumpenproletariat see 'criminal class'

Mauss, Marcel 69–70, 104
McClintock, Anne 12–13, 15, 58, 98–99,
   217, 221–22, 224, 242–43, 244, 249–50
McKenzie, Lisa 52, 68–69, 78–79, 131–32,
   134–35, 141–42, 143–44, 169, 221–22
Membe, Achille 12, 21, 98–99, 268, 274
wilful ignorance 193–94, 268, 274
memory 26–27, 38, 67–68, 78, 90–91, 108,
   113–15, 156–57, 158, 162, 166–67, 171,
   176–77, 182, 196, 198–99
method 2, 7, 10, 20, 21–22, 24–30, 37, 70–
   71, 157–58
   thick description 1, 7, 25–26, 40, 83–84,
      92–93, 103, 104, 159, 182, 186–87, 189,
      219–20, 222, 233, 234–35, 249–50, 260–
      61, 269, 272–75
middle class *see* 'bourgeois'
migration *see* 'race'
mobile grocer 1, 2, 3–4, 25, 49, 74–75, 76–
   90, 99, 118
modernity 6, 9, 11–19, 59, 97–102, 112–13,
   135–36, 188, 189, 199–200, 216–17,
   219, 242–43, 244
   see also 'Enlightenment'; 'liberal'
Mollona, Massimiliano 81, 88–89
money lending 1, 77, 88–90, 103, 104, 109,
   145, 190, 272–74
moral conflicts 2, 8, 113–14, 116–17, 118–
   19, 128–52, 159, 162–63, 168, 182, 201–
   3, 204–6, 218–19, 228, 230–31, 238–39,
   242, 245–46, 247, 258, 259–70, 272–79
moral criminal 131–32, 133–35, 138–39
moral deliberation 21–22, 23, 36, 97–124,
   216–39, 242–70, 276
moral dilemmas 216–39
moral economy *see* 'Thompson E P'
moral economy of violence *see*
   'Thompson E P'
moral education 112, 113–19

moral frameworks *see* 'Taylor, Charles'
moral luck 23–24, 28, 54, 124, 152, 237–
   38, 273–74
moral motivation 242–70, 276–77
moral remainder 228, 233, 235–36
moral/immoral self *see* 'self'
motherhood 41–43, 56–57, 65–66, 84–85,
   91–92, 109, 115–17, 118–19, 120–21,
   134, 143–44, 148–50, 193–94, 202,
   207–8, 223–24, 226, 227, 228–33, 234–
   38, 253
mutuality 1, 9–10, 20–24, 28, 44–45, 56–57,
   58–59, 61, 64–93, 97–124, 129–30,
   131–41, 151–52, 155–83, 201–3, 204–6,
   209, 212, 217, 218–19, 220, 227, 231–
   33, 235–36, 237–39, 245–46, 247–49,
   254–59, 263–70, 272–79

name and shame 120–21, 128–29, 273–74
Nayak, Anoop 44, 102, 217
Ndjio, Basile 23, 57, 209–10
neighbourhood watch 139, 143–44
neighbours *see* 'conflict': 'neighbours'
neoliberalism 16–19, 35, 49, 53, 56–60
New Towns Act 1965 71–72
Norrie, Allan 3–4, 5
Nussbaum, Martha 4, 5, 33–34, 64–65, 137,
   204, 275

offences against the person 1

penal turn *see* 'punitivism'
police 20, 73, 79, 91–92, 100, 106, 108, 110–
   19, 128–52, 177–78, 180, 186–87, 250,
   264–66, 273–74, 277–78
snitching 142–43, 144–45
poor laws 14, 16, 168, 200
   see also 'welfare'
Poor Law Act 1601 14
Poor Law Amendment Act 1834 14
power imbalance 112–13, 115–17, 122,
   129–30, 133–34, 135–41, 142–43,
   146–47, 152, 155–56, 157, 171–72, 173,
   174–75, 177–78, 179, 180–82, 197–98,
   205, 247–48, 255, 258, 264, 265–69
   see also 'bullying'
precariat 1, 20, 21, 23–25, 26, 38–47, 49–56,
   65–66, 68, 69–70, 71, 74, 76, 77, 93,
   100–1, 108, 118, 119, 131–32, 168–69,
   170, 173, 182, 188, 197–98, 206–8, 209,
   211, 217, 220, 230–31, 243–45, 255–58,
   259–64, 265, 266, 268–69, 274, 275, 279

Index 311

see also 'Hall, Stuart': 'folk devil';
'morality': 'immoral other'
prior fault 205, 239
prison / time inside 1, 58, 79, 107, 108, 123,
124, 131–32, 136–37, 149–51, 188, 250
property 69, 129–30, 131, 141–42
see also 'housing'
pub (public house) see 'alcohol use'
Public Order Act 1986 246–47
punitivism 18, 35, 41–42, 56–59, 136–
37, 148–50, 201, 203, 206–10, 261,
262, 276–77

race / racialisation 3, 4, 12–13, 14, 16–17,
22–23, 24, 25–26, 39–40, 52–54, 58–59,
98–100, 106, 112, 131, 155–83, 186–88,
208, 209, 217–19, 221–22, 224, 231,
242–70, 275, 278
immigration 18, 20, 35, 131, 157–59,
160–65, 169, 170, 179, 224, 256–57
migration 24, 90, 155, 156, 160–65, 251–
52, 256–57, 258
race (pseudo)science 12–13, 244, 246–47,
248, 249, 251–52, 253, 256–57, 269, see
also 'eugenics'
nationalism 174–75, 245, 251–52, 256–
58, 260, 263–66
religion 249–50, 251, 260–63, 264
see also 'community': 'imagined
community'; 'wars'
Raz, Joseph 4, 33–34, 60
reality television 139, 174–75, 201, 222,
225–26, 227, 256–57, 268
Reay, Diane 26, 36–37, 38–39, 40–41, 42,
147, 217, 224–25, 244–45
reciprocity 69–70, 83–84, 104
see also 'mutuality'
recognition see 'Taylor, Charles'
reflexive worker 161–62
reputation see 'knowing'
resistance 2, 14–15, 42, 43, 44–45, 57,
58, 130, 163–64, 193–95, 209–10,
243, 268
respect 103, 114–15
respectability 12, 15–18, 39–40, 57, 58, 98–
99, 102, 112–13, 144, 216–39
see also 'self': 'moral self'
responsibility
character 5–6, 86, 110–11, 135, 199–200,
221–27, 248, 258, 276
corporate 3–4, 48, 59–60, 190–
95, 277–78

individual 1, 3–6, 15–16, 18–19, 35–36,
75–76, 89, 188–89, 190–95, 196–97,
199–212, 216–17, 219, 221–27, 228–39,
248, 249, 274
relational see 'harm': 'relational'
state 4, 59–60, 64–65, 75–76, 200, 203,
206–10, 274–75, 277–78
restorative justice 110–19
Rogaly, Ben and Taylor, Becky 42–43, 44–
46, 47, 77, 78–79, 88, 131, 147, 197–98,
237, 260, 264–65
Ryan, Francis 200, 202–3, 207

Said, Edward 12, 21, 98–99, 217, 257–58
Savage, Mike 12, 15, 26, 50–51, 64–65, 222–
23, 249, 266–67
Sayer, Andrew 23, 46, 147, 217, 249,
259, 266–67
school 36–37, 38–47, 48, 81–82, 110–19,
144, 146–47, 170, 231–33, 256–57
see also 'education'
self
immoral other 3–4, 12, 13, 16, 17–19,
20, 21, 22–23, 43, 74, 75–76, 98–99,
112–13, 132–33, 138, 141–42, 143, 162,
164, 165, 167–68, 169, 170–71, 172–73,
175–81, 182, 199–206, 207, 208, 217–
20, 221–27, 228–38, 242–48, 249–63,
272–73, 277–78, see also 'distinction';
'folk devil'
individualized self 7–8, 11–19, 33–36,
46–47, 54, 57, 58, 59–61, 64–67, 68–70,
74–75, 78, 90, 92–93, 103–4, 106, 140,
168, 169, 217, 233, 242–43, 261–63, see
also 'moral self'
moral self 13, 15, 16–17, 18–19, 46,
53, 89, 98, 128–29, 155–56, 172,
189, 219, 228–38, 242–43, 244–45,
268, 278–79, see also 'distinction';
'respectability'
relational self 9–10, 46, 56–57, 68–70,
74–75, 76–90, 103, 104–6, 107–12, 135,
168, 194, 211, 232–33, 234, 235, 266–
69, 276–77
sexuality 111–12, 157, 246–47, 249–50,
252–54, 255, 257, 269–70, 275
sexual offences 100, 136–37, 142–43, 149–
50, 175–76, 177–78, 250, 251
sharing practices 21, 67–68, 69–70, 76–93,
156–57, 158–59, 161–62, 181, 235
see also 'webs of support'
Sherman, Rachel 206, 217, 230–31, 233

312 Index

Shilliam, Robbie 160, 161, 173, 224, 242–43, 244
Skeggs, Beverly 12, 15, 21, 22, 23, 25–26, 36–37, 39–40, 41, 64, 65–66, 68–69, 75–90, 104–5, 217, 219, 221–22, 225–26, 227, 228, 229–30, 232–33, 242–43, 244–45, 249, 266–67
slavery 12, 59, 99–100, 186–87, 199–200, 243
Smith, Katharine 21, 23, 58–59, 68–69, 84, 88–89, 98, 104, 105–6, 131, 134–35, 138–39, 141–42, 146, 155–56, 158, 159–60, 163–64, 165–68, 181, 248–49, 254, 255, 260, 261
see also 'banter'; 'fairness'; 'good personhood'; 'money lending'
social capital 64–68, 81–84, 93, 98, 101–2
social contract theory 33–35, 68, 104–5, 189
state
civil order 6, 15, 39–40, 135–36, 141–42, 218–19
personalizing the state 42, 130, 135–51, 194–95, 248–49, 263–66, 273
strained relationships 2, 3–4, 41–42, 53, 57, 59–60, 64–66, 67, 71, 75–76, 78, 79, 88, 99–101, 102–24, 136, 142, 145–47, 166, 167, 178, 186–212, 260–61, 268–69
see also 'police'; 'welfare'
steelworks 2, 4, 24, 38, 48–50, 74–75, 156–57, 160, 162, 179, 190–95
Stoler, Ann 12, 98–99, 244
subculture 22–23, 217–19
substance offences *see* 'alcohol'; 'substance use'
substance use 1, 4, 47, 52, 76, 77–78, 103, 105–7, 132, 134–35, 143, 145, 196–97, 205, 208, 221–27, 234–38, 256, 272–74
junkie 109, 132, 134–35, 143, 196–97, 205–6, 221–22, 226–27, 234, 235, 254, 256, 272
see also 'alcohol use'
supportive relationships *see* 'webs of support'

Taylor, Charles 7–24, 33–35, 188, 189
best account 10, 104–5
moral framework 7–24, 28–29
recognition 90, 216–17, 218–19
see also 'Bourdieu': 'distinction'

Thatcher, Margaret 17–18, 35, 49, 74, 75–76
theft 117–18, 131–35, 136, 143, 175–76, 180, 226–27, 276–77
Theft Act 1968 131–32, 133
Thompson, E. P. 7, 9–10
moral economy 9–10, 21, 68, 101–2, 104–5, 138
moral economy of violence 101, 104–6
riding the stang 150
rough music 139
tramp *see* 'vagrancy'
troubled family 17–18, 86, 172–73, 178, 225–26
Tyler, Imogen 35, 75–76, 178, 200–1, 221–22, 225–26
Tyler, Katharine 21, 23, 74–75, 91, 155–56, 158–59, 161–62, 168, 169–70, 263

underclass *see* 'precariat'
undeserving poor *see* 'self': 'immoral other'

vagrancy 13, 59, 188, 221–27
tramp 103, 132, 138, 162, 205, 220, 221–27, 228–32, 254, 255, 272
Vehicle Drivers (Certificates of Professional Competence) Regulations 2007 53
vigilante justice 135–41, 142–43, 177–78, 195
see also 'state': 'personalizing the state'
violence
continuum of violence 186–212, 274
domestic violence 3, 113, 149–50
fighting back 115–19, 140–41
fist fights 97–98, 102–19, 139, 140–41, 144–45, 179–81, *see also* 'fair fight'
interpersonal violence 1, 2, 97–124, 134–42, 145, 163, 175–81, 186–87, 188, 196, 265–66, 272–75, 277–78
strategies to displace violence 119–23, 139–40
structural violence 2, 64–65, 145–47, 186–212, 228–38, 269, 272, 274, 277–78
symbolic violence *see* Bourdieu
Virdee, Satnam 15, 16–17, 39–40, 98, 161, 168, 171, 174, 179, 219, 242–43, 244, 245
virtues 64–93, 123–24, 172, 205
authenticity 85–86, 91

aversion to pretence 146–47, 175–81,
195, 229, 231–32, 249, 258, 266–69
generosity 1, 90–92, 105, 166, 169, 204,
218, 232–33, 268
honesty 88, 90, 104, 133–35, 143, 268
see also 'good personhood'; 'Hursthouse,
Rosalind'; 'mutuality'
Von Hirsch, Andrew 3–5

Wacquant, Loïc 7, 18, 22–23, 35, 55, 74, 75–
76, 106, 111, 141–42, 188–89, 192–93,
198–99, 217
Walkerdine, Valerie 36–37, 45–46, 49–50,
120, 140, 156–57, 161–62, 163, 175–76,
249, 266–67
wars 38, 44, 166–67, 169–70, 182, 232, 260
wealth in people 107–8, 109–10, 274
webs of support 1, 49–50, 65–66, 67–70,
76–93, 103, 121, 133–34, 135, 140–41,
156–57, 159–60, 161–62, 169, 182, 195–
99, 205, 232–33, 264, 274
see also 'sharing practices'

welfare 12–13, 15–18, 20–21, 22–24,
38, 53, 54, 65–66, 74, 148–49,
165–68, 174, 199–210, 221–27, 228–
31, 236–37
Wiener, Martin 4, 12–13, 14, 15–16, 97–99,
100, 111, 128–29, 141–42, 186, 199–
200, 219, 278
Winant, Howard 59, 99, 186–87, 243
Winlow, Simon and Hall, Steve 23, 47, 87,
102, 103, 104, 111, 160–61
Wood, Carter, J. 79, 97–100, 102, 104, 110–
11, 112–13, 116, 128–29, 141–42, 186
working class see 'precariat'

youth 1, 36–37, 41, 43, 47, 71–72, 81, 82,
84–85, 87, 101–3, 110–19, 120–21, 122,
134–35, 139, 140–41, 143–45, 176, 179–
80, 194, 198, 224–25, 226, 230
see also 'education'; 'school'

Zedner, Lucia 5–6, 18, 35–36, 98–99, 111,
128, 131